EVOKING SOUND

The Choral Rehearsal

VOLUME 2

INWARD BOUND

PHILOSOPHY AND SCORE PREPARATION

D1501119

Other Publications by James Jordan
available from GIA Publications, Inc.

The Anatomy of Conducting DVD
Architecture & Essentials: Choral and Instrumental
with Eugene Migliaro Corporon
(DVD)-745

Evoking Sound: The Choral Conductor's Aural Tutor
A Companion to The Choral Warm-Up
(G-6905)

Evoking Sound: The Choral Warm-Up
(G-6397)

*The Choral Warm-Up Accompanist Supplement (*with Accompaniment CD*)*
(G-6397A)

The Choral Warm-Up Index Card Pack
(G-6397I)

Ear Training Immersion Exercises for Choirs
(G-6429)

Choral Ensemble Intonation: Methods, Procedures, and Exercises
with Matthew Mehaffey
(G-5527T)

Choral Ensemble Intonation: Teaching Procedures Video
(VHS-500)

Evoking Sound
(G-4257)

Evoking Sound DVD: Body Mapping Principles and Basic Conducting Techniques
with Heather Buchanan
(DVD-530)

The Musician's Soul
(G-5095)

The Musician's Spirit
(G-5866)

The Musician's Walk
(G-6734)

EVOKING SOUND

The Choral Rehearsal

VOLUME 2

INWARD BOUND
PHILOSOPHY AND SCORE PREPARATION

James Jordan

With chapters by
Eugene Migliaro Corporon • Gerald Custer • Lynn Eustis
Matthew J. LaPine • Tony Thornton

Supplemental Resources

The Choral Rehearsal
Volume 1: Techniques and Procedures (G-7128)

The Choral Rehearsal DVD:
Influencing the Choral Ensemble through Gesture,
Rehearsal Technique, and Accompanying Technique (DVD-720)

 GIA Publications, Inc.
Chicago

To my graduate students at Westminster Choir College,
past, present, and future…

This was written so you will have
tools and ideas available to you that I never had.

Evoking Sound: The Choral Rehearsal
Volume 2
Inward Bound: Philosophy and Score Preparation
James Jordan

Cover Images: Mahler's Symphony No. 8 from Margaret Hillis Collection, Rosenthal Archives, Chicago Symphony Orchestra. Used with permission.

Score Photographs: Walton's *Belshazzar's Feast* from Margaret Hillis Collection, Rosenthal Archives, Chicago Symphony Orchestra. Used with permission.

Art Direction/Design: Martha Chlipala

G-7129
ISBN: 1-57999-674-4
Copyright © 2008 GIA Publications, Inc.
7404 S. Mason Avenue, Chicago, IL 60638

www.giamusic.com

All rights reserved.
Printed in the United States of America.

Table of Contents

PART ONE
THE INSIDES OF REHEARSING:
PHILOSOPHICAL BASIS OF THE CHORAL REHEARSAL

PART TWO: CHOOSING A REHEARSAL PATH

PART THREE: SPIRITUAL AND HUMAN QUALITIES OF THE REHEARSAL

PART FOUR: OTHER CONDUCTORS INFLUENCE ON THE REHEARSAL PROCESS

PART 5: THE ACCOMPANIST AND THE REHEARSAL

PART SIX: COMPLETING THE PROCESS

Preface to Volumes 1 and 2

Body, Mind, Spirit, Voice...It takes the *whole* person to sing and rejoice.

—Helen Kemp

(*Irmgard Bartienieff in speaking about how many connections are possible as an artist*)

Well, you see, there are many possibilities. (p. vii)

—Peggy Hackney
in *Making Connections*

As human beings, we want to be fully present, embodied as we live our lives. We want to communicate who we are and what we are and what we stand for in action, so that our message reaches out to others. As we move, whether in dance, theater, sports, or simply being with others, we want to connect. In order to do this, we need to find means to connect inwardly, both to what we say and how all parts of the body relate to each other to support our statement and purpose.

—Peggy Hackney
in *Making Connections*

If one understands the profound and far-reaching implications of Helen Kemp's mantra, then perhaps there is no need for a book such as this. But below the surface of this deceptively simple quote lies the essence of both a humane and pedagogically rich rehearsal technique. Understanding the implications of those four words—body, mind, spirit, voice—have occupied many a conductor's lifetime. The rehearsal process can be both magical and frustrating. Unlocking the spirit and the music contained within human beings is our charge as conductors. Ultimately, I hope that as you finish the study of this volume, you will agree that rehearsal technique can be reduced to the profound implications contained in the words body, mind, spirit, and voice.

Choosing a title for a book generally poses a challenge, and choosing the title for *this* book posed a very unique challenge. To find a word or group of words that summarizes succinctly the complex atmosphere of the choral rehearsal was a bit daunting. But to find a title that also succinctly encapsulates both paradigm and philosophy that this book will try to describe brings particular challenges.

During the process of writing this book, I attended the American Choral Directors Association (ACDA) Western Division Conference in Salt Lake City in 2006. That convention proved to be a seminal event for me in many ways. I watched, once again, Paul Salamunovich rehearsing and conducting the *Requiem* of Maurice Durufle, and observed a rehearsal process that was born out of a life of a conductor who has become one with a piece of music. His rehearsal process was one in which the choir was constantly taken on an inner journey. As part of the convention, I also attended a concert by The Mormon Tabernacle Choir in their spectacular convention center space and was profoundly moved by a setting of *Homeward Bound*, a contemporary folk song by Mack Wilberg. This recently composed folk tune embodied in spirit and sound the idea of a journey toward home, with "home" being symbolic of a return inward to the place where one's life has resonance and deep meaning. Those ideals seemed intimately bound in this miraculous tune.

The tune haunted me for the entire convention. As I listened to it on my iPod, I was trying to figure out what it was about that tune that resonated so. In thinking about the many feelings the tune brought to the surface for me to consider, it occurred to me that one of the journeys we take in life that defines our experiences and our pedagogical lives are our rehearsals. Our "homeward bound" in any piece is a process by which we chart a mystical journey inward through rehearsal experiences that cause our singers to always begin the journey with listening that must be deeply inward to reveal the music's hidden secrets.

Rehearsals must be inward journeys of the spirit if any of our rehearsal techniques are to have resonance. Score study before the first rehearsal begins charts our journey. That initial study makes clear elements of structure, harmonic progression, and paths for teaching tonal and rhythmic materials. And finally, the rehearsal techniques we choose carefully chart the pedagogical path inward. Many approaches to learning about rehearsal technique are "outward" processes, and it has been my experience that any technique arrived at in such a manner ultimately fails in its intended outcome. It has also occurred to me that those who are masters of rehearsal technique, like Paul Salamunovich, are able to make an alchemic mixture of pedagogical techniques and spirit that take a choir on a truly profound inner journey.

It is for that reason (and many more) that this book is themed *Inward Bound*. I believe those two words, if taken to heart, will not only inform our pedagogical sensitivities but also provide a lasting mantra around which to design rehearsals that teach, educate, inform, and, most importantly, deeply inspire and change the lives of those who are guided on this special inward journey each minute in our rehearsals.

Body, Mind, Spirit, Voice...
It takes the *whole* person to sing and rejoice.

That mantra is all about an inward bound journey that brings us to the gifts that music holds through our times of being with each other—the choral ensemble rehearsal.

Introduction

The process—from repertoire choice to final performance—involves *imagination*, *improvisation*, and *inspiration*. I am firmly convinced that what we do as conductors—how we shape rehearsals, what we stress in rehearsals, the pacing of our rehearsals, the specific tools we use to transform the ensemble from beginners to artists, and the gestural language we use to rapidly communicate this information— emanates from our score-based imagination. Our *dream* guides us through the intricacies of sound, vowel shape, rhythmic vitality, dynamic variation, and the myriad of other choices that come our way. (p. 83)

—Jerry Blackstone
in "The Conductor's Dream"
from *Teaching Music through Performance in Choir*

They can go (without you) because you have given them the way and the know-how.

—Paul Salamunovich
in *Chant and Beyond* (video)

Instead of instilling fear, if a company offered a way for everyone in the business to dive within—to start expanding energy and intelligence—people would work overtime for free. They would be far more creative. And the company would just leap forward. This is the way it can be. It's not the way it is, but it could be that way so easily. (pp. 73–74)

—David Lynch
in *Catching the Big Fish*

The choir director must not only be capable of and prepared to respond to any new stimuli and thoughts which come to him beyond his anticipated reactions in the course of his preparation, but he must be ready to cast aside instantly even his best plans and procedures in order to follow the unanticipated but superior approach to his rehearsal. Like any pedagogical activity, choir directing is a creative activity—a creative work. Even though the unprepared rehearsals may occasionally turn out to be better ones and even if the director must occasionally discard his carefully prepared plan, these unanticipated switches of events are exceptions. The director should, therefore, under all circumstances, prepare himself thoroughly for each rehearsal, including the minutest details—even if this does nothing more than give him the satisfaction and the secure feeling that he has done everything humanly possible to meet the requirements for a good rehearsal. (p. 145)

—Wilhelm Ehmann
in *Choral Directing*

Coming out of my experiences with Robert Shaw, who was without equal in the preparation and performance of the repertoire for chorus and orchestra, I learned that he believed there could be no successful performance without appropriate preparation and score study, thorough knowledge of the score, and effective training of the musicians. All of this occurred at a level few could comprehend without being in his presence. Shaw's charisma, personal commitment, passionate intensity, and dynamic leadership notwithstanding, the stature he achieved was the result of hard work and constant problem solving as he attempted to find ways to make the great works in the repertoire communicate. (p. 65)

—Ann Howard Jones
in "Preparing the Chorus for Performance
with Orchestral Accompaniment"
from *Teaching Music through Performance in Choir*

When I envisioned this project, I imagined a one-volume text that would survey all aspects of the choral rehearsal. But as the manuscript developed, it became clear to me that the choral rehearsal as a topic was much broader than I thought. When I had finished writing and was examining all of the chapters to be included in my *Inward Bound* project, the sheer size of the book seemed to pose many publications issues. After considerable thought, it made great sense to me to divide the book into two volumes: the first volume devoted to rehearsal techniques and the second volume devoted to the critical aspects of a conductor's preparation for rehearsal. I believe personal preparation is both psychological and mundane. The psychological has to do with the "human" elements of rehearsal, and the mundane has to do with how we as conductors elicit musical information from a score we are going to conduct and teach through various approaches to score analysis.

On first glance, it may seem strange that this volume contains materials pertaining to the spiritual atmosphere of a rehearsal. However, an understanding of not only ourselves as conductors but also the spiritual alchemy of a rehearsal has everything to do with preparation. Time must be taken for careful thought and study to truly understand the human spirit. To that end, this volume offers guidance to help us along our way to such an understanding.

For those who have read my books and heard me lecture, one of my favorite quotes is:

As civilization advances, the sense of wonder declines. Such decline is an alarming symptom of our state of mind. Mankind will not perish for want of information, but only for want of appreciation. The beginning of our happiness lies in the understanding that life without wonder is not worth living. What we lack is not a will to believe but a will to wonder. (p. 41)

—Abraham Joshua Heschel
in *Between God and Man*

Such wonder can be created within a rehearsal through an understanding and empathy not only for the human condition but also through an intimate understanding of what it means to "be" together in any choral group. Awe and wonder can only be experienced when human beings are brought into a community through the rehearsal process. Spirit and musicing are equal parts of that equation.

This volume is also devoted to the analytical techniques we as conductors should individually practice, hence the title *Inward Bound*. Score study is a highly personal and individual journey. It is that journey taken personally and alone that allows us the privilege of taking others on the same journey through the rehearsal process and, ultimately, the performance.

Score preparation takes time, but it is time well spent. Regardless of the score analysis methods you choose, each technique will peel a layer away from the piece you will be studying with your choir and move through a process of becoming clearer and clearer. That clarity will energize and invigorate the rehearsal room and the singers. It is ultimately a question of efficiency: If you choose rehearsal techniques that are informed by score analysis, then your rehearsals will become both meaningful and productive, and pieces will be birthed sooner.

While we all would most likely admit that score analysis is a necessary part of our art, we often do not devote the time we should to careful and personal score study that takes us on an inward journey to discover the many moments of "awe and wonder" buried within the notes of the score.

Score study is an art. This volume is an attempt to present in one resource what I consider to be the major approaches to score analysis and preparation. The techniques espoused by Julius Herford and Margaret Hillis should be part of our score study regimen. We should also consider an analysis approach that informs and illuminates our pedagogy, such as looking at music from Haasemann, Laban, Dalcroze, and Tabiteau. Approaches that further illuminate how to make our choirs hear better should also be part of that process.

Score study needs to be a highly organized and practiced skill, a journey that must be taken alone and with great care. It must inform our rehearsal technique because we can then begin to understand, at least in some ways, the journey of the piece we are preparing to rehearse. As Howard Swan has said: "We must spend time in thought and study so that we can teach people how to live."

In this volume, my thanks to Tony Thornton for his revisitation of the work of Julius Herford. Herford's work receives much attention in this volume because it seems choral conductors are becoming unaware of his work. I thank Gerald Custer for his valued contribution on not only analyzing Renaissance music but also approaching this music in rehearsal. And thank you to Matthew LaPine for his insights on the use of Schenkerian analysis as a tool for choral conductors. I also want to thank my friends and colleagues at The University of North Texas, Eugene Migliaro Corporon and Lynn Eustis, for the unique perspectives they offer in their chapters.

This volume is intended to help us as choral conductors prepare better rehearsals and perhaps lead us on a path to find a composer's intent so the composer's voice can be heard through our ensembles. For experienced conductors, it is my hope that this resource will fill in any gaps and either prompt us to revisit techniques for score analysis we thought we knew or offer new techniques to try. For new conductors, I hope this volume will empower you with powerful analysis techniques that can inform and invigorate your rehearsals. In either case, there is no substitute for time spent on score analysis as you prepare for rehearsal.

—James Jordan
Yardley, Pennsylvania

PART ONE

THE INSIDES OF REHEARSING:
PHILOSOPHICAL BASIS OF THE
CHORAL REHEARSAL

Chapter 1

The Spiritual/Human Alchemy of the Choral Rehearsal

I was somewhat taken back recently when a Westminster conducting student asked me when they would learn how to merge rehearsal technique and the psychology of a rehearsal.[1] But after some thought, I realized that his question deserves attention. Why? Because it is the most important thing we do as conductors...the tone or feeling of the rehearsal or performance space has everything to do with our music making. How we establish that "spirit" within a space has as much to do with ourselves as with all we know about music.

Since being asked that question, I have given careful thought to those things that have molded and shaped my rehearsal "philosophy" and my approach to musicing as a conductor. I came up with the following broad brushstrokes:

- Belief and trust
- Knowing our center and never moving off that center
- The act of giving
- The act of deeply caring
- Listening to our inner voice
- The act of loving others
- Belief in the message carried and the power of symbolically laden gesture
- Humility

Belief and Trust

When entering any rehearsal, we enter into an incredibly personal space for musicians; being aware of this is an essential aspect of rehearsal technique. To be

---

1 Thanks to Reid Masters, who asked me this question on several occasions and, in a way, caused me to think seriously about an answer.

able to enter into that "sacred" space with a belief that beautiful music will be created establishes a momentum of energies that are difficult to stop.

A type of blind trust is also central to the rehearsal process. No matter the depth of a conductor's pedagogical gifts, without belief in the singers who are making the sounds (i.e., trusting that the singers can do what is asked musically), the realization of profound music making will most likely never be realized. The words "trust" and "allow" are synonyms in the rehearsal world. Belief in the human spirit's ability to accomplish what is necessary should be central to all that we do as conductors. When this is present, choirs will sing "better than they have a right to," as my teacher Elaine Brown always said.

Belief and trust are also forms of affirmation, and it is perhaps the act of affirming singers through the rehearsal process that can be the spark for musical combustion. In the summer prior to his retirement from Luther College, I asked Weston Noble for a sentence to summarize what he had learned from his fifty-seven years of teaching. As I look back, it was quite a bold and somewhat foolish question. However, when I asked it, he immediately replied, "Affirmation…all people need to be affirmed. I believe what I do and have done for most of my career is to affirm people. We ALL need to be affirmed…I need to be affirmed, too!"

Perhaps we would make great advances in our own rehearsals if we transform those rehearsals into places of human affirmation—that is, belief and trust in each person's musical abilities.

We must learn to know ourselves better through art. We must rely more on the unconscious, inspirational side of man. We must not enslave ourselves to dogma. We must believe in the attainability of good. We must believe, without fear, in people. (p. 21)

—Leonard Bernstein
in *This I Believe*

Knowing Center and Never Moving Off Center

When I began my study with Elaine Brown, she first instructed us to read two books: *Zen and the Art of Archery* by Eugene Herrigel and *Centering* by Mary Catherine Richards. Those two books made a deep mark upon me because they carefully explained the power of one's "center" to the creative process. It has been my long-held belief that productive rehearsals cannot take place without a centered soul at its helm. Being able to both understand what center "is" and how to access that center has everything to do with musicing.

Elaine Brown continually spoke of conducting from "that deep place within you." She believed all gesture emanated from one's center because that "place" was the repository of spirit, will, rhythmic impulse, honesty, and meaning. She also believed and taught that singers could perceive when a conductor was acting through his or her center or when a conductor was "centerless." In rehearsal, our greatest charge is to enter the rehearsal room knowing our center and then remain "grounded and centered" throughout the entire rehearsal. Center is the awareness of our spiritual core, and we must strive to rehearse while staying "on" and "in" that core.

The Act of Giving

I often think that a great synonym for conducting would be the word "giving." The rehearsal should be a time for conductors to "give" in a very human way, both musical things and things human. This giving establishes a spirit of how people "are" when they are together. As conductors, we must give energy and spirit to our ensembles so that, in the words of St. John the Baptist, one gives of oneself so others can become more. The giving of oneself is, in itself, a deeply affirming act because it engenders giving in return in the form of sounds and rhythmic vitality. A giving "persona" establishes a powerful dynamic within a rehearsal space.

The Act of Deeply Caring

I suppose the act of deeply caring for the people who sit in front of you in any rehearsal should be an understood commodity. However, in defense of all of us, many things interfere with this basic condition of humanity. Yet if we keep caring in our state of awareness at all times, then that caring will be evident to each person in the ensemble. That caring within a rehearsal is symbiotically connected to our ability to make everything in the rehearsal meaningful. Every word, every action must be born out of meaningfulness. If we care deeply about each spirit in the room, then almost by default, every gesture and every rehearsal technique will transmit a spirit of caring and loving to everyone in that space.

Listening to One's Inner Voice

I am not sure whether any of us can become better musicians than the musicians we already are. We can certainly achieve more in terms of musical accomplishments, but I believe the raw material of musicing is deeply embedded within us—almost like it's in our genetic codes. Yet many of us do not spend enough time with ourselves (either through some type of meditation or jounaling) to hear our truest inner musical voice. Rehearsing, in a way, needs to quiet the clatter of everyone's random thoughts so every person in the room can hear their own inner musical voice—where profound instincts for phrasing, rhythm, musical line, and expression are found—and respond to it. Self-doubt and insecurity are the biggest barriers to hearing that deep inner voice.

Musical expression that is rooted and connected to our inner voice is both powerful and deeply profound. Our inner voice speaks directly and almost wordlessly to everyone who comes in contact with it; it is the "warm core," as Leonard Bernstein called it, which fuels the musicing process and experience.

I believe in man's unconscious mind, the deep spring from which comes his power to communicate and to love. For me, all art is a combination of these powers; for if love is the way we have of communicating personally in the deepest way, then what art can do is to extend this communication, magnify it, and carry it to vastly greater numbers of people. Therefore art is valid for the warmth and love it carries within it, even if it be the lightest entertainment, or the bitterest satire, or the most shattering tragedy. (p. 20)

—Leonard Bernstein
in *This I Believe*

The Act of Loving Others

For me, no single awareness has translated my actions in rehearsal from gesture to meaningful action. If we place (and keep) ourselves in a loving and caring place, then the rehearsal process transforms from mundane day-to-day work into a life-nourishing experience. Yet I have found this is difficult to achieve because we must *want* to do this literally every second of a rehearsal. The world in which we live and function does not always encourage us to love. Hurt, fear, anger often derail our best efforts at every turn. Simple words in a rehearsal or in life can, almost unknowingly, augur injury to a person's very soul and soulfulness. Words and actions can cause people to close themselves off to others, which hopelessly mires the rehearsal and musicing process. Affirmation of people involves love in the most unconditional of ways. An open, vulnerable persona at the front of the rehearsal room is the catalyst for this powerful synergism within the rehearsal.

Belief in the Message Carried

If we seriously consider what it is that we do as musicians, we would likely see that each of us carries a viewpoint or perhaps a life perspective about each piece that we rehearse and conduct. We might program a piece that reflects our desire to have the singers experience a work that teaches about life and living. If that is the case, then that message must be clearly in the foreground of everything we do in rehearsals of that piece. Rehearsals that are colored by an understanding of the composer's message carried within the piece is a profoundly different experience for singers. Gestures carry meaning that go beyond words, and rehearsal actions have a seemingly more meaningful impact on the souls of the singers. Belief in the message and the messenger will divert the course of any rehearsal from mundane to meaningful.

Humility

Finally, all of the above characteristics or "attitudes" of a rehearsal will only be present if we operate at all times from a point of humility. Humility allows our vulnerabilities to be exposed and, in a certain peculiar way, esteemed. If humility is present, a type of "allowing" spirit enters the rehearsal space, which calms the space and the people within it so music can be truly heard.

Again, we must make ourselves less so others (i.e., the singers) can become more. This will energize and propel every rehearsal to higher ground.

Chapter 2

The Tethered Rehearsal

All actual life is encounter. (p. 62)

—Martin Buber
in *I and Thou*

Only he who himself turns to the other human being and opens
himself to him receives the world in him. Only the being whose
otherness, accepted by my being, lives and faces me in the whole
compression of existence, brings the radiance of eternity to me.
Only when two say to one another with all that they are, "It is
Thou," is the indwelling of the Present Being between them. (p. 30)

—Martin Buber
in *Between Man and Man*

Unfortunately, community in our culture too often means a group of people who go crashing through the woods together, scaring the soul away. In spaces ranging from congregations to classrooms, we preach and teach, assert and argue, claim and proclaim, admonish and advise, and generally behave in ways that drive everything original and wild into hiding. Under these conditions, the intellect, emotions, will and ego may emerge, but not the soul: we scare off all soulful things, like respectful relationships, goodwill and hope. (p. 59)

—Parker Palmer
in *A Hidden Wholeness*

Of course, solitude is essential to personal integration: there are places in the landscapes of our lives where no one can accompany us. Because we are communal creatures who need each other's support—and because, left to our own devices, we have an endless capacity for self-absorption and self-deception—community is equally essential to rejoining soul and role. (p. 22)

—Parker Palmer
in *A Hidden Wholeness*

Ordinary musical experiences are gratifying largely because they organize an aspect of human existence that generally comes to us as chaos: time. These ordinary musical experiences may also evoke pleasing memories, suggest touching characters (hope, sadness, grandeur), or set into motion a complex network of thoughts.

There is also, however, an extraordinary experience available through music. The greatest Western art music, well performed, can lead to no less than a spiritual experience, an experience that transcends the physical parameters of time and space. It is the feeling of becoming lost—of losing oneself in the experience. It is losing the self and becoming the sounds. It is the rare and magical musical experience of the entire work filling a single moment. This is the ultimate, highest, experience of musical beauty. (p. xv)

—Markand Thakar
in *Counterpoint: Fundamentals of Music Making*

Community does not necessarily mean living face to face with others; rather it means never losing the awareness that we are connected to each other. It is not about the presence of other people—it is about being fully open to the reality of relationship, whether or not we are alone. (p. 55)

—Parker Palmer
in *A Hidden Wholeness*

I don't think any conductor or teacher would argue if I said one's mental state going into rehearsal sets the tone of the rehearsal. As conductors, the way we "are" as we enter into rehearsal has everything to do with the success of the rehearsal. Thus, time spent establishing a mental attitude that is conducive to good—or even great—rehearsing is an important part of the rehearsal preparation process.

Spiritual/Psychological Connection

One of the most valuable terms I learned regarding rehearsal technique was given to me by Elaine Brown; she was the first person I had ever heard use the word "connection" in relation to music. While I have heard this word used by many conductors since, I'm not always sure they understand just how powerful a concept connection is and just how important it is to both human and pedagogical conduct of any rehearsal.

Connection happens between a choir and a conductor on two levels: (1) the spiritual/psychological level and (2) the level that "cements" the spiritual/psychological connection through gesture. If you desire connection between yourself and your ensemble, then that connective link must be built starting from you and moving outward to the ensemble. Connection has everything to do with being. Understanding how to "be" in a rehearsal should be at the core of all rehearsal planning. Connection is started, built, and established through the mental attitude of the conductor.

Elaine Brown once asked me to describe how I perceived my choir as I rehearsed. I was initially confused by the question. So she rephrased it; she asked me what I would draw if I were asked to draw a picture of me and my choir in rehearsal. She then pushed a piece of paper in my direction and asked me to draw my picture. I drew something similar to this:

What I drew depicted the choir as a faceless mass of people—a mass of people I conducted "at." It was like a wall of people at which I directed my pedagogical and musical energies.

Elaine looked at the drawing and remarked that she had observed some rehearsals where she knew that's what I believed, at least in my own mind. She told me I needed a paradigm shift.

She described her mental image of a choral rehearsal. Based upon her understandings of the principles of Martin Buber, she told me that she imagined being connected to *each* singer in the choir with a tether, or an umbilical cord. If the choir consisted of sixty members, then there were sixty umbilical cords that connected her directly to each singer. While I paraphrase, I believe the words she told me are identical to what she told me that day. "I and thou," she said. "You must have a one-to-one relationship, at least spiritually and psychologically, with each singer in the choir. And that relationship must be one of honesty at all times and caring."

Elaine then asked me to draw the picture again depicting in some way this new "idea." I drew something like this:

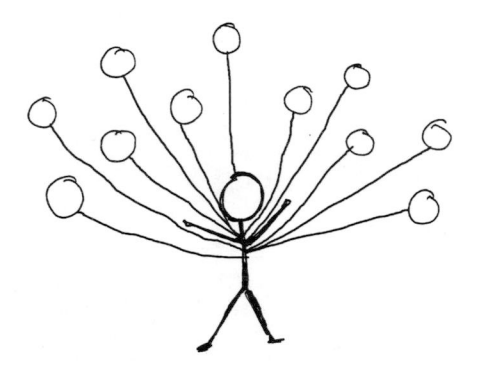

Powerful ideas are most often the simplest ones. There has been no stronger paradigm I have used in every rehearsal than this one of umbilical, intimate, human connection to each person in the ensemble. If you want to be connected to each singer, that want or desire will make it be. But for that connection to occur, you must not only *want* it, but *will* it to be. You must will and deeply desire the connection, or it simply will not be present in the room and certainly will not be sensed by the choir.

Before each rehearsal, make sure your mental perception of the rehearsal is in place. The tethering of you to your singers is perhaps the most important factor to ensure both the musical and human success of the rehearsal. You will quickly find that such a connection is not only powerful but empowering. Human spirits tethered together in a common cause can create great things both in life and in sound.

Before each rehearsal (even if only for a few seconds), take the time to "tether," and the course of your rehearsal will take a dramatically different turn.

Meaningful Rehearsing

Elaine Brown always used to speak of doing things in rehearsal that were "meaningful." At the time, that word did not connote much meaning in the mind of this young musician. But as time has passed, it has become clear that meaningful rehearsing is a standard by which all rehearsals should be judged. By meaningful, Elaine meant that rehearsals need to always be connected to larger life issues through the language of the conductor. It also seemed that all musical objectives would follow the "meaningful" language of the rehearsal. Bringing life's experiences into rehearsal and directly relating those experiences to the music at hand is the energy that drives any rehearsal toward a successful musical and human conclusion. Meaningfulness at times is truly elusive and generally takes a great deal of thought on the part of the conductor. But rehearsals that are meaningful are tremendously interior experiences that deepen the music making of any choir, regardless of age or experience.

Gestural Connection: The Power of Archetypical Image through Gesture

The term "archetype" began with Carl Jung. In Jung's terms, "archetype" is defined as the first original model of which all other similar persons, objects, or concepts are merely derivative, copied, patterned, or emulated. These patterns derive from a universal collective unconscious, which in metaphysics is called the Grids: Akashic Records or the Sea of Consciousness—that which creates our reality. In this context, archetypes are innate prototypes for ideas that may subsequently become involved in the interpretation of observed phenomena.

Archetypes are universal visual symbols that represent, in a physical sense, inherited memory. Archetypes are energetic visual imprints that exist in our psyches. Some are readily understood, while others bring subliminal messages to help you trigger your memory as to why you are here and see the real truth behind the illusion of reality. Archetypes can often convey messages that verbal and written information cannot.

Love, care, and compassion are all universal ideas that are represented through physical movement with the body and can be relayed devoid of facial influences. Physical gesture is a powerful expressive device, which is perceived immediately. Those who specialize in black light theater understand the power of archetypes to relay powerful and direct human emotions using just the image and movement of the body.

When examining rehearsal technique, consider the power of gesture to relay the depth and complexity of human expression devoid of the spoken language of a rehearsal. Conducting gesture is its own unique archetype. The manner in which we use our bodies in rehearsal has everything to do with not only the pedagogical effectiveness of the rehearsal, but also the spiritual and human "success" of the rehearsal. Gesture is a strong, deeply moving and powerful language that transmits human spirit and emotion to the choir in the most direct manner possible, which can (and does) transform the ordinary rehearsal into a profound experience.

Chapter 3

Encouraging the
Inner Journey

Choirs on the Edge

The circles of trust I experienced at Pendle Hill are a rare form of community—one that supports rather than supplants the individual quest for integrity—that is rooted in two basic beliefs. First, we all have an inner teacher whose guidance is more reliable than anything we can get from a doctrine, ideology, collective belief system, institution or leader. Second, we all need other people to invite, amplify, and help us discern the inner teacher's voice for at least three reasons:

• The journey toward inner truth is too taxing to be made solo: lacking support, the solitary traveler soon becomes weary or fearful and is likely to quit the road.

• The path is too deeply hidden to be traveled without company: finding our way involves clues that are subtle and sometimes misleading, requiring the kind of discernment that can happen only in dialogue.

• The destination is too daunting to be achieved alone: we need community to find courage to venture into the alien lands to which the inner teacher may call us. (pp. 25–26).

—Parker Palmer
in *A Hidden Wholeness*

Let the person who cannot be alone be aware of community. Let the person who is not in community beware of being alone. (p. 78)

—Dietrich Bonhoffer
in *Life Together*

Most choirs exist on a precarious emotional and human cliff overlooking what is, at least in their minds, a huge precipice. Understanding this precariousness has as much to do with good rehearsal technique as the "nuts and bolts" of rehearsal technique. The "human cliff" is an equal mix of pride, self-doubt, and insecurity, and too often conductors unknowingly make their rehearsals more difficult because they do not recognize these symptoms as they appear in the lives of their singers.

In great conductors I have observed, they either have thought about this issue or somehow intuitively knew how to handle it in such a fashion that the music truly flourished. How do you know a conductor has somehow mastered this? You can hear it in the sound of the choir. The sound has a warmth and depth that is unmistakable.

Choirs want to sound good. When people ask me what makes a good rehearsal, my response always includes some reference to the choir sounding better at the end of rehearsal than they did at the start. But that aspect of "sounding good" is intimately tied to the singers' own self-image, and that self-image is entwined with the singers' responses, both musical and human, within a rehearsal.

Choirs will respond to conductors when the "instruction" offered by the conductor deals directly with the musical issues at hand. However, choirs typically will not respond to conductors when the musical issues are buried beneath attacks to their individual personas. When the music isn't going well, sometimes we resort (out of frustration) to trying to move the choir to higher ground not by raising the singers' level of musicianship, but by inadvertently demeaning the singers. I don't think this is ever done intentionally, but when the music isn't beautiful, we sometimes default to some very negative approaches. Even the great Robert Shaw, a master of human motivation, confessed a bit of guilt to this rehearsal "sin."

It's a terribly shaming thing to get mad at rehearsals. Anyone with
an ounce of sense or honesty knows that music and anger don't
really mix. – For two very good reasons:

First, nothing technically sick, broken or out-of-sync is cured. On
some occasions (I can think of none), when skills and schooling are
perfect, everyone may rave to guard against indifference or lassitude, but for the most part conductors of choruses get mad when
they don't know how to fix the fool thing—so they kick its tires.

And, of course, in the second place, anger is completely
alien to the whole purpose of music—or of a chorus, for that matter. The purpose of these is communication (it does seem to me
that "communion" is a more suitable word except for its religious
connotations) and anger is a barrier, an isolation. (p. 26)

—Robert Shaw
in *The Robert Shaw Reader*

Once that line is crossed, music progress is stunted. And when musical progress
is stunted, the sound generally suffers. And when the sound suffers, the singers start
to get angry. In a mimetic sense, they stop loving the sound, and they begin to stop
loving themselves. This dangerous conundrum is the Achilles Heel of many a
rehearsal. Conductors fail to recognize when this cycle has begun. Instead of putting
the human issues in order first, they continue to hammer ahead on the musical
issues. And the musical health of the choir degenerates in direct proportion to the
choir's spiritual health.

When musicians work in groups, their musical power is multiplied—but so are
the human issues. Many conductors ignore these human issues. **The singers' feelings
are as important as the music**. Conductors who ignore the human issues do so
because the music, at least to their ears, is moving forward. They also believe that
by maintaining such a hard line with the choir and focusing on the music, they are

remaining faithful to their calling. They do not recognize that they are making the singers feel bad about themselves in the process. They do not realize that the choir needs encouragement along the way. They do not realize that a little trust, love, and care would go a long distance in rehearsal. It is crucial to understand that you can be demanding in rehearsal, but you should never be inhumane. So how can conductors strike a balance in rehearsal that is, in reality, a divided reality—the reality of the music and the very real realities of the persons in the ensemble? A simple strip of paper twisted into the geometric shape of a Mobius strip (as shown in **Figure 3-1**) might help to clarify the conductor's true role in rehearsal.[1]

Figure 3-1. Strip of paper twisted into the geometric shape of a Mobius strip.

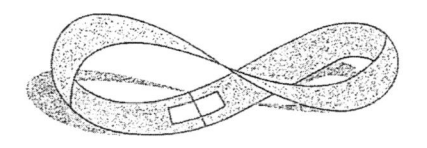

Striking the Balance: The Rehearsal as a Mobius Strip

Most conductors would agree that they must stay aware or in a state of awareness during an entire rehearsal. But what needs to be addressed is where that awareness is focused during rehearsal and whether a conductor is in any way erecting psychological barriers through body language or spoken language. Flexibility in awareness makes for a great rehearsal and keeps several important musical and human elements in play at all times during the rehearsal. Consider the following:

Figure 3-2. The rehearsal as a two-sided event.

---

1 Parker Palmer in his book, *A Hidden Wholeness*, uses a Mobius strip to discuss aspects of community. I found the idea of the Mobius strip intriguing and believe it has applications to the choral rehearsal. I want to acknowledge Palmer's insight for this incredible paradigm.

Some rehearsals can be depicted using a strip of paper (see **Figure 3-2**). The choir sees only the front side of the paper labeled "Musical Issues." Many conductors unknowingly hide behind these *musical* issues and use them to separate and, in a way, "protect" themselves from the other *human* issues in the rehearsal room. Because of the rehearsal techniques chosen, the choir is only exposed to musical issues and the singers only see or perceive the musical elements. The human elements and human interactions are kept to a minimum. Throughout the rehearsal, these conductors are behind the strip, obscured from the ensemble at all times. Each rehearsal is conducted in the same fashion; musical objectives are accomplished, but they pale because they are not nurtured with the important human factors that truly make the music come alive. Unfortunately, I have observed many conductors who operate under such a paradigm. Because of the strength of their musicianship, the musical product is always impressive but seldom compelling.

Figure 3-3. Single strip connected at ends to form a circle.

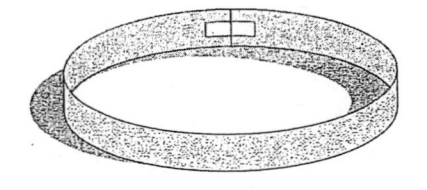

If you take the same strip and make it into a circle using a piece of tape (see **Figure 3-3** and **Figure 3-4**), the single strip now becomes a circular shape with two surfaces visible, in this case to the ensemble. The outside surface is more visible than the inside surface. And depending upon your perspective, the inside surface may not be visible at all. In this configuration, you could label both the inside and outside of the strip with the two most important issues in any rehearsal: (1) musical issues and (2) human issues involving care and love.

Figure 3-4. Single strip connected at ends to form a circle with labeling.

This connected circular strip implies that while human issues are in the mind of the conductor, the only thing visible or in the awareness of the choir is the outside of the strip. **It is the outside of the strip that gains the choir's attention.** The conductor's unawareness, as well as the rehearsal technique, makes it difficult, if not impossible, for the ensemble to be aware of the inside issues of the strip.

Figure 3-5. Single strip connected at ends to form a circle labeled with different rehearsal priorities.

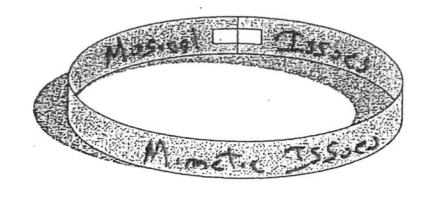

Similarly, you could construct a strip in the same fashion, but with different issues on the outside and inside of the strip (see **Figure 3-5**). For some conductors (like myself), we become so concerned and sensitive about the human issues in the room that at times we miss our musical marks. Those of us who at times experience this rehearsal situation are accused of "talking too much." I once heard a conductor who was sensitive in such a way accuse another conductor of constantly "messing with people's heads." I found that comment interesting, given the source. That particular conductor was a known master of negative psychological and spiritual manipulation, but never saw it himself. And what he did to choirs in rehearsal was cruel beyond a doubt.

The Ideal Rehearsal Paradigm

Life is about decisions and balance. And balance is achieved through a delicate interplay of many complex elements. The choral rehearsal is no less complex because it involves a community of human beings tethered to each other through sound.

The ideal rehearsal could be characterized as a type of Mobius strip. What began as strip of paper joined at the ends, when twisted inward and upon itself, becomes an ideal paradigm for rehearsal: the rehearsal should be a fluid give and take of both musical issues and human issues. The human issues inform the musical issues, and vice versa. In looking at the Mobius strip twisted into a figure eight (see

Figure 3-6), you can see both surfaces and be aware of both simultaneously. Moreover, both surfaces appear to be intertwined and infinitely connected, just as they should be in rehearsal. A good rehearsal is one in which the choir is kept aware of both aspects of music making at all times.

Figure 3-6. The Helix Mobius strip: a paradigm for rehearsal.

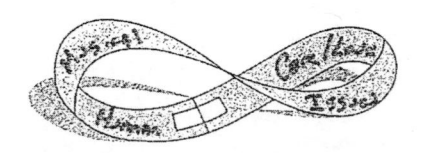

Using the Mobius strip as a model, the rehearsal becomes a fluid and constant interchange of both important elements. There is alchemy at all times between the musical elements in the rehearsal and the human/mimetic issues. As conductors, we must make sure singers are aware of both aspects at all times during rehearsal. Singers tend to become "on the edge" when the strip or helix paradigm (shown in Figure 3-6) is not used during rehearsal. The tendency of conductors is to instead use the paradigm shown in Figure 3-1 or Figure 3-2; that is, they become negative and self-mutilating because their musical objectives are not being achieved. And the choir is only aware of the one side of the paradigm that they can see—or rather, that they are aware of.

As my teacher, Elaine Brown always talked about rehearsals being meaningful. The ideal rehearsal is one that constantly demonstrates a delicate balance *and* equilibrium between the musical goals and the human conditions present in the room at the moment. Rehearsals that do not work like the Mobius strip tend to build a barrier between the conductor and the choir, the music and the musicians. The conductor unknowingly hides behind the barrier illustrated in Figure 3-1 or holds fort in the interior of the barrier illustrated in Figure 3-2. You can achieve a balance in rehearsal between the musical goals and the human conditions present through constant awareness. When this equilibrium is achieved, spontaneous, exciting, and productive rehearsals will result.

This inner and outer space of the Mobius strip has everything to do with the inward bound journey of any rehearsal. It is easy to lead a "divided" rehearsal (like the single strip or the oval strip); it is more difficult, but infinitely more rewarding, when both inward and outward aspects of the rehearsal are always present. So as conductors, we must not only explore the "outside" surfaces in rehearsal, but we must also be brave enough to venture into the interior spaces formed by the Helix

Mobius strip. And because the strip is flexible, we can move between the Mobius strip and the single continuous circle if we slip into rehearsal unawareness—that is, we fail to constantly "read the room."

The reverse could also be true. If our awareness is always upon mimetic or human issues, then the choir could lose awareness of the musical matters. This paradigm points out the importance of soul to the entire rehearsal process. Rehearsals are musical and human continuums. Rehearsals devoid of soul create silent and, at times, insurmountable walls between the conductor and the choir. It is the presence of soul in the rehearsal room that transforms mundane rehearsals into profoundly inspirational and life-changing events. The magic of any rehearsal is the ability to create and recreate the magic of being alone together in the same place with music as the "stuff" that binds all together.

The soul is generous: it takes in the needs of the world. The soul is wise: it suffers without shutting down. The soul is hopeful: it engages the world in ways that keep opening our hearts. The soul is creative: it finds a path between realities that might defeat us and fantasies that are mere escapes. All we need to do is to bring down the wall that separates us from our souls and deprives the world of the soul's regenerative powers. (p. 184)

—Parker Palmer
in *A Hidden Wholeness*

Chapter 4

Contextualizing the
Choral Experience

Gerald Custer

I will sing with the spirit, and with the understanding.

—St. Paul

Like the policeman in Gilbert and Sullivan's *Pirates of Penzance*, the choral conductor's lot is not always a happy one. The universe broadly described as "the choral experience"[1] is notoriously busy and densely populated: singers must be auditioned and placed in sections, repertoire chosen and sensibly arranged in program order, scores analyzed and prepared, rehearsals planned and conducted, questions of interpretation researched and resolved, risers moved, frayed nerves quieted, publicity managed, program notes written—the list is seemingly endless, and the pressure is unremitting.

Small wonder, then, that most choral musicians find themselves driven by what author Charles Hummel calls "the tyranny of the urgent."[2] Although we long to focus

---

1 Although I once helped prepare material ultimately released in a book bearing this phrase as its title, it is hardly unique to me (or to the book in question, for that matter).
2 Hummel, Charles. *The Tyranny of the Urgent*. Downers Grove, IL: Inter-Varsity Christian Press, 1967.

our energies on managing the critical few, we find ourselves confronted by the insistent clamor of the immediate many. We spend our days extinguishing fires, but cannot seem to find the time needed to discover how they're being set in the first place, or by whom.

One effective antidote to the madness of this perpetual motion sickness can be found by constructing a larger framework that organizes these disparate elements in a meaningful way, by creating a context for the overall choral experience. A robust context—that is, one that incorporates all major elements of a detailed process and structures them in logical sequence—offers the immediate benefit of perspective: the ability to know where you are, recognize where you've been, and determine where you should be going. If not a full solution, it is at least a guide for the perplexed.

Constructing a Context

The most effective way to construct a context is to group similar activities into larger phases. These tasks, and their successful completion, can serve as concrete points of reference (or measurements of progress toward the overall objective). In the business arena, where I spent ten years of my non-musical life,[3] these measurable items were known as "deliverables," and the process of periodically evaluating progress toward a goal was called "statusing the project." Although the language may differ, the principles transfer well to the challenge of preparing multiple scores and coordinating the efforts of multiple individuals to achieve a successful concert performance: the "end deliverable" or final product in project management terms.[4]

A second characteristic of the contextual approach is that it is, by nature, sequential: each phase of a context will typically contain discrete tasks that must be completed before proceeding to the next phase. Music educators familiar with the research and methodology of Edwin Gordon[5] will recognize that there is nothing inherently novel about this insight; what is perhaps new is the act of applying it explicitly to the activities of a group of musicians—specifically, a choral ensemble.

Implicit in the grouping of like traits into larger phases is the recognition that different phases will incorporate different activities and require different kinds of skills to successfully complete them. What works in one phase of the overall choral

---

3 I worked as a project and process management consultant at Ford Motor Company in Dearborn, Michigan, during the 1980s and 1990s.

4 A readable introduction to the principles and practices of the discipline of project management can be found in novelized form in *Critical Chain* by management consultant Elihu Goldratt (Croton-on-Hudson, NY: North River Press, 1997).

5 Gordon, Edwin. *Learning Sequences in Music*. Chicago, IL: GIA Publications, Inc., 1997.

experience may not necessarily succeed in the next phase. This is not a failure on anyone's part; it is merely a misalignment between tasking demands and skills required. Each new phase will likely pose unique challenges, both for the individual singer and for the collective entity called the "ensemble." And it is incumbent on the conductor—as convener, animator, facilitator, and leader of the ensemble—to accurately assess where in the overall context the ensemble is, what challenges the singers presently face, what skills are required to meet those challenges, and then transfer those skills to the ensemble as efficiently as possible.

In other words, frustration is directly proportional to expectation. If you are not obtaining the results you expect (or desire), you might be expecting the wrong things at this particular phase in the process, or you might not be teaching the skills needed to accomplish the task at hand. By successfully identifying where the ensemble happens to be in the contextual sequence of the choral experience, you can minimize your frustration as well as the frustration of the singers and progress toward the goal recovered and re-energized.

The Four-Phase Model

Ultimately, choral singing is a gift shared by an ensemble with an audience. But a gift cannot be bestowed unless the giver legitimately possesses it. The gift must be owned before it can be given away to another. Ownership is impossible without purchase. So acquisition, at a price or cost, is a necessary prerequisite for honest ownership.

At the same time, gifts are seldom given unless they are highly valued by the giver, and this high valuation normally proceeds from appreciation—coming to treasure the inherent worth of the object in question. Understanding what makes a gift valuable and worthy is an essential step in selecting a gift to give to another.

These human dynamics form the basis for a sequentially phased model that offers one useful context for understanding the choral experience. In its simplest form, the four phases of this context are as follows:

1. Acquisition
2. Comprehension
3. Ownership
4. *Communio*[6]

---

6 The vital aspect of the conductor's analysis and preparation of the score has been omitted from this sequence only because it takes place prior to the choral rehearsal process proper.

Each phase has specific tasks that must be completed before progressing to the next. Each requires particular skills that must be mastered and employed in accomplishing these tasks. But what are the goals, tasks, and skills associated with each phase of the choral experience?

Acquisition refers to the group of skills associated with encountering and mastering the fundamental materials of a piece of music—the raw data of a work: the series of pitches, intervals, durations, text, dynamics, phrasing, and articulation created by the composer. Skills required to successfully acquire musical material include:

- Audiation
- Intervallic discretion and recognition
- Pattern and tonal memory
- Fundamental vocal technique (respiration, phonation, diction)
- Basic notational awareness (identification of pitches, accidentals, scale and key, rhythmic durations, simple and compound meters, conventions of dotted and tied durations, etc.)

Demonstrating acquisition mastery is fairly straightforward: the gateway to the next phase of the process has been reached when individual singers and the ensemble can replicate the raw data given in the score with a high degree of accuracy on a consistent basis. (Individual conductors will establish cutoff points for accuracy and consistency differently given the age, experience, and skillfulness of their singers, as well as the number of rehearsals and overall time budget available before final performance, and the level of difficulty associated with the specific work.)

Comprehension comes from the Latin *cumprehendere*, a word formed by combining the preposition *cum* (with/together) and the verb *prehendere* (to grasp or seize). The comprehension phase tasks focus on the music's structure: understanding how the various elements of the raw data fit together to create a whole, grasping how one phrase of music relates to those preceding and following it, discerning how the various musical decisions made by the composer respond to cues contained in the text, sensing how the larger oratorical dimension (or narrative arc) of the music/ text marriage unfolds and develops over time, and so forth. Skills required to successfully negotiate the comprehension phase include:

- Ensemble awareness (the ability to listen to other lines while accurately performing one's own part)

- Some familiarity with basic compositional devices, such as motivic development, word painting, melodic and harmonic sequence, cadence types, agogic weight and syncope, augmentation and diminution
- Understanding basic textual elements (setting, character, story, conflict, resolution) and techniques (personification, metaphor/simile, alliteration, word order, onomatopoeia, etc.)
- Familiarity with structural forms and devices (strophic, binary, ternary, through-composed, canon, fugue, free imitation) and prevailing textures (homorhythmic, melody/accompaniment, contrapuntal)

This is a daunting list, and veteran conductors will realize that developing comprehension competency is a long-term objective for most choral ensembles. At the same time, it is one that can be approached by degrees. Informed programming decisions by the conductor over time can provide a series of pedagogical opportunities to teach and develop these vital skills.

Accurate assessment of an ensemble's comprehension status is more subtle than simply auditing the error rate at the end of the acquisition phase. Some key indicators include:

- The manner in which individual phrases are performed – Do they organically flow to the peak of the phrase? Do all of the individual moments "belong forward" in a sensible fashion?
- The way in which phrases are handed off from one section to the next
- The manner in which phrases are combined to create periods and larger structural sections
- The way in which internal and final cadences are approached and sung

Appropriate vocalism is another key indicator. Is the choral tone balanced in a way that is consistent with appropriate period performance practice and the style of the genre? Does the vocal color reflect the demands of the style and the requirements of the text? Are compositional devices that respond to the oratorical cues of the text—changes of texture, dynamic, articulation, weight—sung correctly and consistently?

Two practical strategies may be helpful in evaluating ensemble comprehension status. The first is **direct dialogue**—that is, occasionally stopping the rehearsal to ask, "Why did the composer write the passage this way? What effect is the composer trying to create here, and how does the composer go about it?" The second is to periodically put the music aside and **look at the text simply as text**. Seek to determine its structure and argument, and then return to the music in search of evidence that the composer has overtly interacted with the text.[7]

With older or more experienced ensembles, a third technique may also be profitably employed: **have small groups sing the work without a conductor while the rest of the ensemble listens**. Follow this with a discussion by both performers and audience about what worked well, what still needs improvement, and why.[8] Based on these and similar assessments, the gateway to the third phase—ownership— is reliably reached when the ensemble not only consistently sings just the basic musical data but also performs in a fashion that expresses an awareness of structure and interrelatedness. The comprehension phase has been reached when the music hangs together in a convincing, compelling way, indicating that the singers know both what the score contains and why it has been put there by the composer in the first place.

Journey Inward, Journey Outward

Ownership, although sometimes overlooked, is an indispensable ingredient for evocative final performance of choral repertoire. It signals a transfer of power from the conductor to the performers, both as individuals and as an ensemble. Ownership is the result of accomplishing two tasks: interiorization and personalization. If acquisition answers the question "What's here?" and comprehension answers the structural questions—"Why is it here?" and "How does it all fit together?"—then ownership takes up the increasingly challenging questions—"What does it mean?" and, more important still, "What does it mean to *me*, and to *us*?"

Enabling transfer of ownership is one of the more difficult tasks a conductor faces (in part because it requires an act of voluntary surrender and a willingness to trust), but it is one of the most important. Without it, true collaboration between the conductor and the singers is precluded; the development of authentic ensemble and ensemble artistry is impossible. For many of us, enabling ownership will first require a shift of paradigm from the conductor-as-performer/ensemble-as-instrument model to the teacher-learner/learner-teacher approach advocated by Brazilian educationalist Paulo Freire in *Pedagogy of the Oppressed* and *Teaching to Transgress: Education as the Practice of Freedom.*

---

7 I thank Dr. Jonathan Reed of Michigan State University (East Lansing, MI) for demonstrating this useful approach in an unforgettable rehearsal of John Corigliano's *Fern Hill*.

8 For a detailed explanation of this approach, see "Small Groups in the Volunteer Choir: Approaches, Challenges and Benefits," *Bella Voce*. Grand Rapids, MI: Michigan Choral Directors Association, Fall 2004.

Ownership builds on understanding but requires a different journey. The skills associated with comprehension are cognitive and intellectual—seeing interrelationships among musical data at the structural level and bringing them to life in an informed fashion. By contrast, ownership takes place in the emotional/psychological sphere. It requires singers to ask and answer questions such as, "What is the story of this music about?" "What emotion is it attempting to evoke?" "What is it attempting to say?" Allowing the music to read us, searching for connections in our own stories and life experiences that are consonant with the emotive content of the music, making a personal commitment to be present with emotional integrity to the music in the moment—these are the key tasks that take place in the ownership phase. When an ensemble sings not only the notes or the structure, but rather the truth of the music, it has reached the pinnacle of the rehearsal part of the choral experience: it has made the music its own.

Facilitating the ownership phase of the choral experience is challenging because, as conductor, you must mediate but not dictate; it involves a journey inward where there are "no wrong answers." Your task is one of Socratic facilitation rather than explicit direction, asking probing questions that aim ever deeper into the heart of the music and into the hearts and souls of the singers.

Asking the sort of open-ended questions presented above is an exercise in vulnerability on your part; answering them with honest sincerity requires no less vulnerability on the part of individual singers and the ensemble. Thus, mutual trust is essential for real success in the face of this vulnerability. To help create the atmosphere of trust and emotional security required, you must model the kind of introspection called for and frequently remind the singers that "you can't do it wrong."

One illustration of questions to consider can be found in the notes to my setting of W. B. Yeats's Innisfree.[9] Series editor James Jordan observes, "The choir should spend time in contemplation of the meaning and implications of the text for their own lives...," and the composer, commenting on the last line of the Yeats poem, asks

What is *your* deepest longing? What secret lives in *your* deep heart's core? Where is home for you? Are you there now, or still searching for it? Whatever your answers to these questions turn out to be, if you put them into how you sing *Innisfree*, the result will be true and honest music making....

Facilitating transfer of ownership is intense work, but it need not dominate the rehearsal process. It can be done in small segments, incorporated as part of the warm-up process, or it can even be assigned as "homework reflection" between

9 Octavo G-7005. Chicago, IL: GIA Publications, Inc., 2006.

rehearsals. But for conductors and ensembles desiring vibrant, meaning-full performances, it is an essential part of the choral experience. We can only give away what we authentically possess, and to that end, ownership is crucial.

Communio is the Latin word at the root of both "community" and "communication." Its use here is deliberate, because it underscores the vital living linkage between the two.[10] *Communio* can be translated as "common union"; it refers to the final phase of the choral experience, when an ensemble of individual singers who have acquired, understood, and personalized the music they sing have become a "community of interpretation" that shares the fruits of their work with the listening audience. This moment of human communion, which effectively completes the "circle of sound" favored by early music theorists,[11] is the capstone event of the choral experience—a sign that signifies the reality it embodies. Reaching this peak experience requires all involved to re-frame some familiar terms. The traditional dichotomy of active performers who display their talents in front of a passive audience will need to give way to a new paradigm: one in which those who give and those who receive are equally valued co-operators, each with a unique and irreplaceable part to play in an exchange of meaning. In a very real sense, the seeds of this exchange predate the first rehearsal if the conductor thought about the audience when initially selecting the repertoire that is finally shared with them.

Facilitating the moment of *communio* calls for great care and sensitivity. It requires training an ensemble most of all in the skills of empathy. Some of this can be accomplished in the small group performances suggested earlier by asking questions like, "What do you think is the emotional connection point between what you're singing and what the audience has been living?" Or to those who are listening to the small group as it sings, "What about this group's performance connected with you most powerfully, and why?" Then as the concert approaches, take time periodically to construct a portrait of the likely audience, their preferences, experiences, likes and dislikes, worries and needs; this will raise awareness of the listeners' expectations and increase empathetic sensitivity on the part of the ensemble.[12]

Thoughtfully crafted program notes and cogent, succinct comments by the conductor in the moment of the performance can also reinforce the empathetic connection necessary for true *communio*. By way of example, consider Leonard

---

10 "Our business is communication, and there is no communication without community." (Robert Shaw)

11 For more on this concept, see "Provoking Meaning: Thoughts About Choral Hermeneutics." *Choral Journal*. Lawton, OK: American Choral Directors Association, December 2001.

12 Promoting customer awareness is an established practice in many fields; at Ford Motor Company, it was common to encounter life-size cardboard figures of a range of men and women, each bearing the caption, "I'm looking for a new vehicle—are you designing this one with *me* in mind?"

Bernstein's brief preface to his unscheduled performance of Mahler's Second Symphony just after the tragic death of President Kennedy: "This shall be our response to violence: to make music more intensely, more beautifully, more devotedly than ever before." Who will forget that moment? Certainly no one who took part in that performance—or who was fortunate to have heard it that night.

One advantage of contextualizing the choral experience in phased fashion is that it opens up the holographic dimension of choral music making. It is not just the ensemble but also the originating composer and the receiving audience who pass through the stages of acquisition, comprehension, ownership, and *communio* as well. The composer encounters a text; acquires an understanding of its content, structure and meaning; reads it in the light of personal life experience; and responds by setting it musically. In a similar way, the audience encounters the composer's work, mediated by the agency of the choral ensemble, and through the power of *communio* has the opportunity to make it their own.

Authentic *communio* is the implicit entitlement of every audience. It is our vocation as artists to ensure that this expectation is consistently met. Mastery of content, structure, and meaning is one path toward that goal. In the end, we can only give away what we authentically possess. The transformative power of choral singing reveals a world of beauty that can be shared with others in a way that few other artistic disciplines can equal. By understanding the phases of the choral experience—acquisition, comprehension, ownership, and *communio*—our treasures can be more effectively communicated to a world sorely in need of the gifts we have to offer.

Sidebar

The table below summarizes the four phases of the choral experience contextual model, along with key mastery tasks, required skills, and criteria for assessing completion of each individual phase in the process.

Phase	Mastery Tasks	Skills Required	Assessment
Acquisition accuracy	—Raw data: pitches, rhythms, text, dynamics, phrasing, articulation	—Audiation —Intervallic discretion —Pattern/tonal memory —Basic vocal technique —Notation awareness	—Content (percentage correct over time)
Comprehension	—Structural understanding —Relation of music to textual cues and expectations	—Ensemble awareness —Familiarity with basic formal structures —Textual analysis —Textural awareness	—Presence of line —Appropriate vocalism —Appropriate color
Ownership	—Personalization of the performing impetus —Interiorization of the performing responsibility	—Surrender of conductor control —Internal reflection —Life experience application —Knowledge of story arc —Vulnerability —Mutual trust —Transparency	—Compelling small group performance —Performance "by heart"
Communio	—Understanding and valuation of audience needs, experiences, expectations	—Empathy —Presence in the moment —Lack of fear —Self-awareness —Desire to connect	—Audience response (admittedly subjective)

Chapter 5

Teaching Ensemble Silence

I have become fascinated with silence these past years, and I must admit that it is one of my most often-used rehearsal techniques. As an overriding philosophy, music is borne out of silence. Thus, it logically follows that without silence, music may have a problem being birthed in any meaningful way.

I have found that silence brings clarity to confused rehearsals. I have also found that silence calms my mind so I can listen. And silence is powerful in allowing me to hear others—in this case, the choir and the music they share.

Silence is a vanishing commodity in our world. When we were children, especially if we had no siblings, we often had playtimes when we were by ourselves. Out of our silence grew songs and singing. Out of our silence grew beautiful works of art. Crayons existed in a world of silence, where we could be alone with our quiet. Even today, children at points in their day seek out silence as a respite. Yet as children grow older and more "mature," they detach themselves from this childhood practice, usually at great detriment to their personal—and, in this case, musical—lives.

Since writing *The Musician's Soul* (GIA, 1999), I have experimented more with silence as a rehearsal technique than perhaps any other rehearsal technique, whether it is simply bringing rehearsal goings-on to an abrupt halt and allowing silence to work its magic, or forcing silence and calm upon an ensemble through QiGong exercises. I also recently found that the use of a pendulum in rehearsal produces magical musical results within an ensemble.

Let's explore various aspects of rehearsal "silence." Then consider bringing these soul-affirming moments into your rehearsals.

The Reality

Whether or not you admit it, many of the problems in a rehearsal are brought into the room by your singers and, at times, even you. But music cannot be made in the midst of this "noise." Singers unknowingly bring the noise of the world into the rehearsal room. The stereo system in our car, our iPod, our cell phone or other mobile communication device—and generally being in constant communication with others—have become an integral part of our lives. And slowly but surely we have been weaned away from knowing silence and its magic.

As conductors, if no part of our warm-up or rehearsal process addresses the "re-creation" of silence, then we will likely face a rehearsal with diminishing returns. Silences breed intimate understanding of both self and the music to be sounded. Without those silences, we may not be able to hear what music has to share with us. We live lives that are so noisy and so fraught with extraneous sound that it is becoming increasingly difficult to find even moments of silence to gain our spiritual composure. When I use the pendulum in rehearsal, there is both a centering and a calm that compels everyone in the space. And the music that follows is always truly remarkable. When I use QiGong exercises as part of my choral warm-up, the sung sounds that follow are stunningly beautiful. Overall, **silence has become my most effective rehearsal technique.**

Yet if you are to lead your ensemble to silence, you must first be able to quickly access such silent places yourself. Daily excursions into silence will deepen your musicianship and teach you how to listen because, I believe, we learn to listen by first listening to ourselves. Part of crafting a masterful rehearsal is being able to craft a space that encourages "silences." Silence must be both taught and practiced. Other than the music we sound in our ensembles, there is perhaps no greater gift we can give to our ensembles than the comfort of being able to access silence.

Quaker Meeting

I first became familiar with the power of silence in my first teaching position, at Plymouth Meeting Friends School in Plymouth Meeting, Pennsylvania. The lessons I learned there have formed and informed how I rehearse, and have formed the foundation of my whole respect for the power of such communal silences. Each Wednesday, the entire school met in the meetinghouse for a meeting.

It is interesting to note how a **Quaker Friends meetinghouse** is constructed. People sit in horizontal rows facing each other (see **Figure 5-1**), with only a grandfather clock at the end of the hall. (Did the Quakers know something about entrainment that the rest of the world didn't? The swinging pendulum and the ticking of the clock brought all present into a silent space....)

Approximately two hundred children were brought into the meetinghouse, where they sat quietly for an hour. Occasionally someone would speak to the "meeting" concerning a matter of importance. Sometimes the stories that were told by the children took me deep into my own life. After the hour had passed, the children would return to their classrooms. Not until years later did I realize that I had been taught how to access silence in those meetings. Silence can only be accessed through silence.

Figure 5-1. Quaker Friends meetinghouse.

The children at Plymouth Meeting Friends School had an uncanny ability to be with themselves when necessary. Needless to say, conducting an ensemble in that school still remains one of the more profound musical events of my life. And I am convinced that it is because of the silence and access to it that those meetings taught.

The secret formula: enforced communal silence. That communal silence was one of the most powerful and empowering things I have ever experienced, and it is that "empowered" silence that all conductors should make a part of their regular rehearsal routine.

Chapter 6

The Perceiving Choir

With respect to body movement and gesture, the choir will only
perceive what the conductor himself is aware of. If the conductor is
not aware of his legs, the choir will not perceive them, and this has
great impact upon sound.

—Barbara Conable
2000 Westminster Conducting Institute

A t some point in our development as conductors, we must acknowledge that
our gesture has a profound and lasting effect upon choral sound. Before
we become embroiled in the pedagogical intensity of any rehearsal, we should
seriously examine whether the genesis of problems within the ensemble is a product of our inattention to the power of our own perception and awareness of our
body. Why?

A choir will only perceive what you perceive. That statement has ramifications
for both the use of the body and the use of one's ear in the rehearsal process.
Perception can be either a powerful positive factor or a strong negative factor in any
rehearsal situation. The power of perception on the part of the singers should never
be underestimated in the rehearsal process.

In the simplest of terms, if you are aware of only your hands and the upper half
of your torso as you conduct, then that is all the choir will perceive. The choir will
see you at the front of the room and perceive you to be a headless, armless, legless
entity. That reduced perception is directly connected to the vocal health and vocal
resonance of the sound. If you call yourself into complete awareness of your entire

body as you conduct and rehearse, then the choir will likewise perceive you in the same manner, and the vibrancy of the sound of the ensemble will be in direct proportion to what the singers perceive.

From an aural viewpoint, the same holds true for pitch. If you are unaware of the actual pitches of a particular voice part, then the ensemble will not sing them in tune or with resonential clarity. If you *are* immediately aware of a specific voice part, then not only will that part be aurally present in the listeners' ears, but you will find that, if necessary, you can "will a part to be in tune" just by focusing your listening energy on that specific part.

As a conductor, awareness needs to be a part of your personal rehearsal decorum. As a part of your daily rehearsal process, the practice of perceiving your own body must become the rule rather than the exception. And the importance of this inclusive awareness of your own body at all times must occupy a high priority in the rehearsal process. If you are aware of your entire body at all times during rehearsal, then your choir will be the beneficiary of a vital and energized choral sound.

PART TWO

CHOOSING A REHEARSAL PATH

Chapter 7

Selecting Literature for Your Ensemble

What Music Is Worth Rehearsing?

This, of course, raises the question of "quality." It seems to me that we have to agree that in the worship of the Great Whoever or Whatever only our very best is "good enough"—only because it's our best. A God of Truth, Goodness and Mercy is not honored by laying Saturday Night's Disco Spin-offs on Sunday's altar. One does not gain strength from the stresses of virtue by gorging on fatty fraud. (p. 409)

—Robert Shaw
in *The Robert Shaw Reader*

The words, to put it mildly, should not stand in absolute contradiction to their bearer. Not every text is equally suited for mixed, treble, male, or children's voices, and if the composer should have made a wrong judgment in his choice of voice setting, the director always has the prerogative of looking elsewhere for another selection. (p. 146)

—Wilhelm Ehmann
in *Choral Directing*

Shall music making be for the purposes of entertainment, for public relations, as a means to win administrative support, or as one way to explore the unique and powerful realities in aesthetic education? …Make no mistake, either we opt for music which has popular appeal or we decide that music which has been considered great, because of compositional genius and the test of time, is the rightful heritage of our students. Where do you stand? Entertainment or greatness? (p. 78)

—Howard Swan
in *The Conscience of a Profession*

In musical performances, the disconnection I allude to above has manifested itself in performances in which technical virtuosity becomes the only goal, and the music student, both theoretical and historical, very often stops short of musical considerations. Meaning, which I believe can only be ascertained by allowing oneself to intuitively reflect upon the human/spiritual impulse of each musical gesture, allows a song to happen because the synthesis of cognition, intuition, craft and content, spirit and flesh, surface, and substance are in play. The full form of a musical work of art is allowed to communicate, not to dazzle, not to impress, but to communicate. Then the listeners' lives can be touched at the deepest level and be forever changed. (p. 9)

—Joseph Flummerfelt
in *Teaching Music through Performance
in Choir, Volume 1*

Before we address how to rehearse, it seems appropriate to at least begin with the thorny issue of *what* to rehearse. The decisions we make concerning the music we choose to teach, rehearse, and live with are some of the most important decisions we make for the vocal health, musical growth, and human growth of our ensembles. In short, I strongly feel that your rehearsals can only be as good as the music you choose to teach. Stated in another way, your rehearsals can only be as good as the music you choose to make educational bedfellows with.

For many young conductors, the selection of literature is a strange and somewhat mysterious process. They (and many others) often choose literature from CDs that arrive in their mailboxes. Or sometimes they choose literature they have sung in a choir. Familiarity is often the criterion by which those choices are made. Seldom is there a stringent list of criteria that are developed to measure potential selections for teaching and performance.

Many conductors choose music based upon an intuitive sense of what is beautiful, as filtered through their own musical tastes and criteria. This is certainly valuable. However, that alone should not form the basis on which music is chosen.

What follows is a description of the recommended criteria by which music for all choral ensembles should be selected. These criteria have been tried and tested, and have guided my literature selection for over twenty-five years. The criteria are listed in order of importance, with the most important criteria at the top of the list. While some of these criteria will be familiar to you, I caution you to keep an open mind about others that may be new.

Criterion 1 – Inherent Vocal Technique Requirements of the Piece

This is one of the most important criteria for selecting a piece for any ensemble, regardless of its programmatic function. Literature should be chosen based on what it can contribute to the building of vocal ensemble sound. Keeping in mind that the building of vocal technique is a sequential process, literature should be carefully chosen to teach specific vocal techniques (e.g., legato, staccato, marcato, leaps, crescendo/decrescendo, etc.).[1] The vocal technique required to sing a work directly affects its musical difficulty from a technical perspective, so we must consider this if we desire to set a firm pedagogical path for our choir.

---

1 This author believes that both the hierarchy of what should be taught and the vocal techniques to be taught must make sense from a vocal pedagogy point of view.

This criterion and the one that follows are the two strongest factors that determine the choice of repertoire. Thus, they should take precedence over all remaining criterion.

Criterion 2 – Aural Difficulty of the Piece: Considering the Mode

This criterion is perhaps as important as the criterion above. A choir can only learn a piece that it can hear. Conductors who try to teach a choir without knowing the singers' abilities may be choosing repertoire that is beyond their capability to learn—or maybe even below their capability to learn!

Without objective knowledge of how well an ensemble can hear, needless time will be wasted in rehearsal, leading to frustration for both you and your singers. *Ear Training Immersion Exercises for Choirs* (Jordan/Shenenberger, GIA) contains exercises arranged in order of aural difficulty, as determined from the work of and data compiled by Edwin Gordon as he developed both his standardized measures of music aptitude and his Music Learning Theory. My practical and musical experiences have taught me that the **list of difficulty levels** shown in **Figure 7-1**, in order from easiest to most difficult, is not only accurate, but it is a valuable tool for the selection of choral literature.

Figure 7-1. Literature difficulty levels by mode.

Major Ionian Mode
Harmonic Minor Mode
Mixolydian Mode
Dorian Mode
Lydian Mode
Phrygian Mode
Aeolian Mode
Melodic Minor Mode
Locrian Mode
Octatonic Mode

Choral music lacks an objective system for rating literature in terms of performance difficulty. Such rating systems exist in the instrumental world, and they are based upon the technical difficulty of the music. But in choral music, most systems are based on teacher opinion and lack objective criteria as to the reason for the rating. *Teaching Music through Performance in Choir, Volumes 1 and 2* (GIA), edited by Matthew Mehaffey and Heather Buchanan, attempts to develop such a system, and it is a significant first step to that end. The system used in those books separates vocal difficulty and aural difficulty; it also includes specific, objective criteria to engender an objective system that separates vocal technique from aural difficulty. I believe both must be considered independently to arrive at a valid difficulty level for any ensemble; this would, in turn, inform the rehearsal process and provide an even more effective pedagogical tool for conductors.

Another issue that contributes to the difficulty level of choral literature, which cannot be overlooked, is the language and diction requirements of a piece. Diction is perhaps a choral director's most insidious pedagogical enemy. After the notes and rhythms are taught for a particular piece, many of us have experienced the pedagogical backslide that occurs when the language is placed over the top of our musical teaching. Depending upon the experience of the choir, the language of a piece can increase its difficulty, sometimes exponentially. While not a major criterion for selection, we would do well as conductors to consider language as a factor that contributes not only to the difficulty level of a piece but also to its pedagogical rehearsal challenges.

Criterion 3 – Time Needed to Learn vs. Time Spent

This criterion is not always considered when choosing literature for performance, and it can be very difficult to judge. I have found that the aural difficulty levels presented in Figure 7-1 provide accurate insight. However, there have been times when I realized a piece would be difficult for my choir and yet I programmed it despite my informed instincts. While some of the difficult pieces I have taught have been valuable experiences for the choir, they did not in the end merit the amount of time devoted to the pieces. And because they posed such hurdles for the choir, it was difficult—if not impossible—for me to advance the singers to the level where they could begin to truly experience the pieces from a spiritual perspective.

You must weigh the pedagogical value of a more difficult piece against the rehearsal time expended to teach the piece. Experience has taught me to avoid such pieces lest I want to bog down the musical development of my ensemble.

While these choices are obviously important for choirs within educational settings, such choices are also important for church choirs. Church choirs have both a liturgical service "charge" and a musical "charge." Often, pieces with easier difficulty levels must be chosen simply because of the lack of rehearsal time. However, when choosing works for special occasions, you would do well to consider the pedagogical implications of your choices.

Criterion 4 – The Number of Musical Styles Presented on Any Program

I learned of this criterion many years ago from William Trego and Nancianne Parella, who at the time conducted the famed choral ensembles at Princeton High School in Princeton, New Jersey. This criterion is a fascinating one to consider. It was their view (a view I strongly share and support) that when working to build a healthy vocal sound within a choir, you should try to stay within one stylistic sound category, and only venture to a maximum of two styles within any particular program. For example, to choose a program of Mendelssohn, Mozart, English Madrigals, and Spirituals would demand that the choir sing in four distinctly different stylistic colors. It was their premise that this is simply too difficult for a young choir, and very difficult for any ensemble at the beginning of an academic year.

You would do better instead to delimit your stylistic choices in terms of sounds. For example, you might tackle a program of Mendelssohn and Schutz because the sounds and languages for both composers are similar. Then for flexibility of programming, you could venture outside those sound worlds to another style.

Over the years, I have found the approach of Trego and Parella to be highly successful when applied to the selection of literature for choirs I have conducted, regardless of the age level of the choir, and it is pedagogically sound to consider their approach.

Criterion 5 – Connection of Text to the Lives of the Singers: Honesty of Message

In Chapter 8, "The Rehearsal Atmosphere: Spiritual Obligations of the Conductor and Choir," I write of the importance of singers being able to connect themselves to music through their own experiences, perspectives, and life stories. It is for this reason that I will not program a piece of music unless it will improve the human lot of both the choir and me in some way! Of all the criteria presented here, perhaps no one criterion has played such an important role in my teaching. The inherent human message within a piece of music provides the direction for teaching a piece, from the first rehearsal to the last.

Never underestimate the power of the message to accelerate the music learning process. The human message in a piece is one of the strongest determinants in the profound quality of the final performance. For me to teach a piece, the music must speak to me first. When I feel a connection to a piece, then I step back and try to evaluate whether the piece will have the same effect upon my ensemble. I usually ask myself, "Will this piece take us on a journey?" If the answer is yes, then I will seriously consider programming the piece.

Criterion 6 – Staying Power

Criteria 5 and 6 are interrelated—and perhaps the same given your evaluative perspective. When we program music for our choirs, we generally have to live with that literature for a long period of time. The human message of a piece and its inherent compositional craft are the only criteria that can maintain and endure extended rehearsal and musical scrutiny over longer periods of time. Too often, I have programmed a musically "lightweight" piece only to find that the choir grew tired of the piece quickly. This idea of "staying power" is a criterion in literature selection that is important to consider, for it has everything to do with rehearsal technique.

Criterion 7 – Performing Acoustic

One of the mistakes I often see conductors make is to choose literature for performance without regard for the acoustic of the performance space. It makes little sense to me to choose literature without considering the ramifications of the acoustic of the concert space for which the music is being prepared. Primary in this consideration should be rate or speed of harmonic motion. Pieces that possess frequent chord changes should not be considered for highly reverberant spaces. Rather, pieces with slower harmonic changes work best in reverberant acoustics. Pieces with a great deal of harmonic motion and change work better in less reverberant acoustics.

While many conductors rely on rhythmic complexity to determine the best acoustic, I have found that the harmonic motion factor is most often overlooked when selecting literature.

Criterion 8 – Practicalities of the Rehearsal Situation

While most conductors likely take this into consideration, it bears mentioning at this point. When choosing literature, you should take into account the number of rehearsals and the ability of the choir, understanding that one directly influences the other. Choirs with higher "hearing" ability or music aptitude can learn pieces faster than choirs with lower aptitudes. Without knowledge of a choir's music aptitude, conductors are somewhat handicapped at being able to make accurate prognostications regarding how long it will take to learn a piece of music.

Language requirements must also be considered. Works in foreign languages always take longer to prepare because of the learning curve with a foreign language. Many conductors underestimate the amount of time actually required to teach the foreign language of a piece.

Criterion 9 – Program Balance and Building a Concert Program

Program "balance" has everything to do with musical style if choral pedagogy is a concern. While many models of programming encourage the use of "variety" and diverse musical styles within a single program, I have found that such programming confounds or even retards the vocal development of a choir. As a general rule of thumb when building a program for any choir, no more than two musical styles should be included in any single program. In other words, there should be no more than two ensemble "sounds" per program. In my experience with young or inexperienced choirs, I have found that the singers are incapable of successfully achieving more than two sounds per program. What usually happens when this rule is ignored is that all of the literature begins to sound the same: Palestrina sounds like Brahms, Haydn sounds either like Palestrina or Brahms, and so on.[2]

Criterion 10 – Inherent Singability of Works Selected for Rehearsal

For many of us, our tendency is to choose music we like; in fact, we choose most music we love. We believe at the time we select a piece we love that it is a perfect fit for our choir. We carefully consider every factor in our choice. Yet when we "read" the piece the first time in rehearsal, it doesn't sing. I don't mean the choir has problems with notes and rhythms; what I am referring to is the musical line. As the choir sings through the piece, it seems to slog along. The musical line seems thick and out of tune.

My experience has been that if a piece does not exhibit some degree of "singing" at the beginning of the rehearsal process, then it will probably never sing at any acceptable level. I have never been able to figure out why, except to reason that certain pieces of music and the "mixture" of voices and human beings simply do not share the appropriate chemistry. Yet many conductors, in a hard-headed fashion, continue with the piece because they believe their rehearsal technique can fix these factors. In most instances, they are proven wrong.

If a piece does not "sing" in the first rehearsal, then if possible, abandon ship and save the piece for a future choir and future program that may have better human and musical compatibilities.

Criterion 11 – Vocal Growth

Do not fully teach a piece of music for later performance when building vocal skills. Allow time for vocal growth! Many conductors do not consider this aspect of pedagogy. Yet I find it is one of the most important factors in charting the vocal and musical growth of a choir. If you are conducting a choir that is in the process of learning how to sing or is a relatively inexperienced choir, then you should seriously consider this.

---

2 In the beginning of this author's teaching career, this was one of the most valuable "pedagogical" tips I received that greatly assisted building the "sound" of an ensemble. William Trego and Nancianne Parella, who for many years conducted the Princeton High School Choirs, used this approach to programming and building the sound of their choirs. In my opinion, their choirs remain some of the finest high school choirs I have heard.

Vocal "maturity" and vocal "growth" take time—any voice teacher would agree. And most teachers would probably also refer to laryngeal or muscle memory. When a singer learns a piece, it is learned with a particular laryngeal memory. The larynx will *always* sing the piece as it was when it was learned—that is, the larynx will always sing the piece at the level of vocal development in which it was learned! So if a piece is fully taught to inexperienced singers in the early part of a choral season or school year, and then is put away for while, when the piece is "resurrected" later in the year, the choir will revert back to the vocal technique they possessed when they learned the piece! I learned this lesson the hard way; many pieces I had worked hard on in the beginning of the year had to be abandoned when I brought them back later in the year!

The larynx has long-term muscle memory, and the larynx never forgets. If you begin work on a piece early in the year that you have programmed in the spring, learn the notes and rhythms at a *piano* dynamic in the early part of the year, and then "add voice" when the choir gains more vocal technique and singing experience.

Sample Programs

Presented on the pages that follow are sample programs to provide insight into several approaches to programming. I have included some of my own as well as some that I admire to present a slightly different direction. All of the programs reflect the criteria discussed above. These programs are shared to study the criteria outlined in this chapter. Short narratives are included at the beginning of each example to show how the particular program fits the recommended criteria.

Remember that the first step to planning a rehearsal is understanding the big musical picture of the music programmed. Having an understanding of the big picture before the first rehearsal will enable you to make wise pedagogical and motivational decisions on what music should be presented first, and so on.

Sample Program #1

This program demonstrates one of the strongest principles I use when planning any program: to center the entire program around a single piece. I began building this program with the Brahms *Geistliches Leid*. That work embodied the musical message of an entire life journey in one work. Once I decided on the Brahms, the idea of "journey" became clear for the entire program. After that, it was relatively easy to select other pieces that would amplify this message.

JOURNEY

The Westminster Williamson Voices
The Inaugural Season
2004–2005

James Jordan
Conductor

Marilyn Shenenberger
Accompanist

Robert Ridgell
Organist

The Episcopal Cathedral of Philadelphia
November 14, 2004
8:00 p.m.

With a cooperative art exhibit by
Journey Home
Philadelphia

Diane Cornman-Levy
Executive Director

The necessary thing is after all but this: solitude, great inner solitude. Going-into-oneself and for hours meeting no one—this one must be able to obtain. To be solitary, the way one was solitary as a child, when the grownups went around involved with things that seemed important and big because they themselves looked so busy and because one comprehended nothing of their doings.

And when one day one perceives that their occupations are paltry, their professions petrified and no longer linked with the living, why not then continue to look like a child upon it all as upon something unfamiliar, from out of the depth of one's own world, out of the expanse of one's own solitude, which is itself work and status and vocation? Why want to exchange a child's wise incomprehension for defensiveness and disdain, since incomprehension is after all being alone, while defensiveness and disdain are a sharing in that from which one wants by these means to keep apart. (pp. 45–46)

—Rainer Maria Rilke
Letters to a Young Poet

Psychology has been unconcerned with myth and imagination, and has shown little care for history, beauty, sensuality, or eloquence—the Renaissance themes. Its pragmatism, whether in clinic or laboratory, kills fantasy or subverts it into the service of practical goals. Love becomes a sexual problem; religion an ethnic attitude; soul a political badge. No chapters are more barren and trivial in the textbooks of psychological thought than those on imagination, emotion, and the living of life or the dying of death. Psychology has hardly been touched by anima, until recently as the soul stirs and makes claims on it for relevance and depth. (p. 220)

—James Hillman
Re-Visioning Psychology

JOURNEY

The Westminster Williamson Voices

An Introduction to the Evening

It was a little over a year ago when I first visited *The Philadelphia Cathedral* at the invitation of its music director Robert Ridgell. It was clear to me upon entering the space that it presented a unique venue for *The Westminster Williamson Voices*. It has long been my belief that choirs need to explore new sonic possibilities both through the literature that they program, and their creative use of space and sight to enrich the listening experience.

This evening attempts to begin two journeys. The first journey is to use this space and sights within it in collaboration with sound to take listeners on a concert experience journey. The second journey was to choose music for this program that was reflective of life experiences, emphasizing music that employs primal elements of music that are reflective of the most deeply personal and profound elements of human expression. Someone once remarked that great music demands that one look back at one's life and to realize both the beauty and limited time we have to do our "work." I believe the music chosen for this evening's program looks at various aspects of one's life progression. The sustainment of sound both harmonically and temporally as symbolic of the progression of life is at the center of this evening.

The use of the glorious space of this place in various ways will, hopefully, enhance your experience of the music. And the art that hangs around us represents the individual Journeys of each individual artist. I wish to thank Journey Home and their visionary director, Diane Cornman-Levy for sharing their visual gifts in art this evening. We encourage you to view the show immediately after the concert when the art works will be appropriately illuminated for your viewing. *Feel free to speak with the artists who will be located near their works and to speak with staff from Journey Home if you wish further information on Journey Home or purchase.*

This program has at its center the *Geistliches Lied, Op. 30*, of Johannes Brahms. There is perhaps no more a succinct encapsulation of the total life experience than this piece. The Urmas Sisak, Oremus uses a compositional system that derives its structure from the rotation of the planets to present an intense sustainment of sound that is to reflect the journey that is taken during deeply personal inner prayer and personal moments in one's life.

World musics occupy a prominent place in the program this evening. Japanese influenced music frames the extremes of this program, and give it, I believe, an ancient rooting, respectful of centuries of life and culture. The opening premiere work, *Tears to Dust* by Robert Moran, is based upon a poem by the eighth century Japanese poet, Text: Chen Tzu-ang. The Urmas Sisak work is built around the basic mode of Japanese music called the *kumayoshi*, and the premiere work by Jackson Hill is a setting of the eighth century poem that uses several Japanese stylistic devices: a pentatonic scale, pentatonic harmonies, absence of harmonic motion and chord progressions, minimal rhythmic forward motion, a sense of suspended time, glissandos, and other ornamentation derived from Buddhist chant and ancient Japanese court music. *The Past Life Melodies* of Sarah Hopkins employs music from another part of the world, still ancient in its origins and reflective of the life lived by those that created the haunting textures. Finally, *Stimmen* by Robert Moran uses a poignant text by King Ludwig II as a vehicle for sustained choral sounds that provide the vehicle for a great inner journey on the part of both the ensemble and the audience. The intensely lonely and stark text by Ludwig paints a poignant side of the human experience and life journey. The intensely personal and inward part of each of our lives is reflected in this text, and is set by Robert Moran in a fashion that allows one to be taken on an inward journey.

One of the missions of *The Williamson Voices* is to not only perform the music of our time, but for the choir to become the voice for contemporary composers. My first commissioned work in 1984 was given to Jackson Hill. He is a long time friend whose music captivated me since the time I first heard it. I am indebted to his willingness to write this piece for us. The choir is deeply grateful for the honor of performing this work. Robert Moran is a recent acquaintance and a music kindred spirit. His music creates sound worlds that I believe should become staple in the choral repertoire not only for the sounds that they produce, but for the new frontiers of expression they explore with voices.

We ask that there be no applause until the end of the program so as to allow the audience to take an uninterrupted journey with us in both sound and sight. And please turn off cell phones and beepers so as not to destroy the atmosphere of the evening. At the end of the program, your applause will be received. We thank you for being part of this new performance chapter in the rich history of Westminster Choir College.

James Jordan

JOURNEY

The Westminster Williamson Voices

Program

I

Tears to Dust   Robert Moran

(1937–   )

World Premiere

Commissioned by the Jordan family for The Westminster Williamson Voices
in memory of Florence Mary Jordan.

Robert Ridgell, Organ

Gloria Patri: 24 Hymns for Mixed Choir (1988)   Urmas Sisak

XXIII: Oremus   (1960–   )

II

Geistliches Lied, Op. 30   Johannes Brahms

Lass dich nur nichts nicht dauren   (1833–1897)

The choir performs this evening from a new edition of the work
created for The Westminster Williamson Voices by the Conductor.

Robert Ridgell, Organ

III

Past Life Melodies   Sarah Hopkins

(1958–   )

Haru sareba hikoe moitsutsu   Jackson Hill

(When spring is born at last)   (1941–   )

Poem: Otomo no Sakune Yakamochi (8th Century)

Manyoshu XVIII: 4111–12, 4135–36

Translated by the composer

World Premiere

IV

Sleep   Eric Whitacre
Text: Charles Anthony Silvestri   (1970–   )

Stimmen des letzen Siegels (2001)   Robert Moran
(Voices of The Last Seal)

For chorus, four celli, organ, harp, and percussion.

Text: King Ludwig II of Bavaria

For choir, four celli, harp, percussion, and organ.

Sample Program #2

This program was constructed around the Eric Whitaker piece, *Leonardo Dreams of His Flying Machine*, and my want to use a gifted puppet company—The Spiral Q Puppet Company—to broaden the audience's experience. Again, once I had decided on the centerpiece for that program, it was relatively easy to decide on both the "theme" for the program and the other music that would compliment the Whitaker.

MUSIC OF THE HUMAN SPIRIT

A CANDLELIGHT CONCERT

The Westminster Williamson Voices

James Jordan
Conductor

Marilyn Shenenberger
Accompanist

with
Diane Crane, Actress
Jeremy Powell, Soprano Saxophone
Robert Ridgell, Organist

and

The Spiral Q Puppet Theater

Tracey Broyles
Director

The Philadelphia Cathedral
Friday, April 22, 2005
8:00 p.m.

MUSIC OF THE HUMAN SPIRIT

A CANDLELIGHT CONCERT

The Westminster Williamson Voices

Programme Notes

Transmitting the awe and wonder of the human spirit has been at the center of composers' fascination for centuries. The recent choral compositional history has been marked by several profound depictions of that spirit in sound. The works of John Tavener, Eric Whitacre and, most recently, Tarik O'Regan are performed this evening to guide the audience through several perspectives of the marvelous intricacies of the human spirit rooted in mysticism, spirituality and creativity.

As is the mission of *The Westminster Williamson Voices*, concerts are chosen in such a way as to use the spectacular performance space of *The Philadelphia Cathedral* as an equal partner in their music *Nunc Dimittis* making. The music chosen this evening was selected with this incredible space in mind.

The music of the evening is connected through the lineage of chant. It is the inherent simplicity of chant that seems to capture in sound the essences of the human spirit. The program opens with a piece of mystical proportions written by John Tavener, *Hymn to the Mother of God*. The choir will perform that piece utilizing unique spatial relationships with the cathedral space. The second set of the program groups three unlikely pieces together that bind themselves into a set because of their brevity of expression that concisely reflects the remarkable spirit of both text and composer. The third set consists of the Tarik O'Regan, *Nunc Dimittis*, scored for double choir and soprano saxophone. Also rooted in chant, this piece also utilizes the sonic and visual potential of the cathedral space. The glorious funeral anthem, *Hymn for Athene*, is performed in a unique acoustical circle that, hopefully, mirrors the glorious afterlife of the human spirit in enveloping sound. *Leonardo and His Flying Machine* performed with the *Spiral Q Puppet Theater* is a musical monument to creative spirit of man in the human form of one Leonardo DaVinci. The program closes with one of O'Regan's Dorchester Canticles, a vibrant setting of Psalm 67. Westminster Choir College and the Choir wishes to thank *The Philadelphia Cathedral*, Richard Giles, Dean, and Robert Ridgell, Director of Music, for the use of this magnificent performing space that creates such a miraculous blending of music and spirit through architecture and the space its creates.

MUSIC OF THE HUMAN SPIRIT

A CANDLELIGHT CONCERT

The Westminster Williamson Voices

Program

I
Hymn to the Mother of God   John Tavener
                                                               (1944–   )

II
Bogoroditse Djevo (1990)   Arvo Part
                                                               (1935–   )

Ave verum Corpus   Wolfgang Amadeus Mozart

Notre Pere   Maurice Durufle

III
Nunc Dimittis (2001)   Tarik O'Regan
                                                               (1978–   )

With solo soprano saxophone

For SATB Ripieno Choir and SATB Concertante Choir.

Song for Athene   John Tavener

IV
Leonardo Dreams of His Flying Machine: Eric Whitacre
Opera Breve   (1970–   )
Text: Charles Anthony Silvestri

With The Spiral Q Puppet Company

SSATB chorus and percussion.

Vs
Dorchester Canticles (2004)   Tarik O'Regan

II. Deus miseratur (God be merciful unto us)

SATB chorus and organ.

PART THREE

SPIRITUAL AND HUMAN QUALITIES
OF THE REHEARSAL

Chapter 8

The Rehearsal Atmosphere

Spiritual Obligations of the Conductor and Choir

It is clear that children should be instructed in some useful things...(but) to be always seeking after the useful does not become free and exalted souls. (p. 9)[1]

—Aristotle in Poetics
from *Touching Eternity*
by Tom Barone

---

1 In *Touching Eternity*, Tom Barone writes of an incredible arts program in Appalachia via a case study told through storying. This remarkable book, upon reading, will transform anyone's rehearsal. Its words provide the essence of the creative and artistic life. I enthusiastically encourage all to read it.

Our responsibility as choral musicians does not stop with the teaching of music. We must find time and energy for thought and study so that we can help teach people how to live. (p. 139)

When a mutual and sympathetic understanding of the human spirit is built, people finally become persons. (p. 149)

—Howard Swan
in *Conscience of a Profession*

It goes without saying that spiritual writing is not about God. It is about the human longing for all that God can mean. It may be possible to be an atheist, but it is probably impossible, once alive, not to respond to the presence of something—soul, spirit, life force, you name it—that the human core from which the cry of anguish and the whoop of joy emanate. The sheer instinct to record these experiences of extremity is, in itself, a spiritual act. (p. xxiii)

—Patricia Hampl
in *Spiritual Writing*
by Philip Zaleski

What is called for then is a means of discovering a wider human identity, not one that denies the polarities of nature and human feeling, but one that integrates them in a larger sense of purpose and connection. This shift would continue the process of spiritual transformation already taking place that is manifest now in the multitude of global initiatives that are striving to discover authentic international partnerships while respecting the uniqueness of ethno-national and cultural traditions. For individuals, this requires the discovery of a true core self of *I* through which we connect beyond ourselves to diverse others. This too is essentially a spiritual task. (p. 182)

—John E. Mack
in S*elves, People and Persons*

As civilization advances, the sense of wonder declines. Such decline is an alarming symptom of our state of mind. Mankind will not perish for want of information, but only for want of appreciation. The beginning of our happiness lies in the understanding that life without wonder is not worth living. What we lack is not a will to believe, but a will to wonder. (p. 41)

—Abraham Joshua Heschel
in *Between God and Man*

Spirituality is the most practical thing in the whole wide world. I challenge anyone to think of anything more practical than spirituality as I have defined it—not piety, not devotion, not religion, not worship, but spirituality—waking up—waking up! Look at the heartache everywhere, look at the loneliness, look at the fear, the confusion, the conflicts in the hearts of people, inner conflict, outer conflict. Suppose somebody gave you a way of getting rid of all of that? Suppose somebody gave you a way to stop the tremendous drainage of energy, of health, of emotion that comes from these conflicts and confusion. Would you want that?

Suppose someone showed us a way whereby we would truly love one another, and be at peace, be at love. Can you think of anything more practical than that? But that politics is more practical. What's the earthly use of putting a man on the moon when we cannot live on the earth? (p. 11)

—Anthony deMello
in *Awareness*

Then, Schwartz[2] makes this second query—"What are the psychological characteristics of a mature person?" He has great inner and outer awareness. He can work and plan and struggle and be creative. Hurts are easily overcome and hostility quickly done away with. There is empathy—the capacity to identify with others and to put oneself in the other person's position. "It is the opposite of an egocentric view; it is the allocentric, the feeling centering about how the other person feels…" The mature human being has the need, the wish and the freedom to be close to others emotionally and sometimes, physically. He recognizes leadership. He has the capacity to be free, not to have to agree and yet not to be "compulsively rebellious." There is the skill and the freedom to communicate. There is never the use of status as an index of human worth or the necessity always to be dependent upon others. (p. 124)

—Howard Swan
in *Conscience of a Profession*

---

2 Fairchild, Johnson E. *Personal Problems and Psychological Frontiers*. New York: Sheridan House, pp. 18–24.

Most people are unaware of what it is they believe. Discovering
self and our relationship to a power greater than ourselves
(represented metaphorically by the horse), contributes to the quality
of relationships we form with others in our lives. Learning to work
effectively and safely with unpredictable power (the horse) allows
an individual to internalize this skill and become comfortable
with—power. (p. 27)

—Barbara K. Rector
in *Adventures in Awareness:
Learning with the Help of Horses*

S ince writing *The Musician's Soul* (GIA, 1999), I have asked the students in each
of my classes who have read the book to identify at least three quotes that
resonate strongly with them and then write about those quotes to explain why.
Without exception, all students have chosen at least one or two of the quotes above.
I have found their selections fascinating and have pondered why these quotes have
a particular magnetism for them. By choosing these quotes, they are acknowledging
not only the importance of spirituality in their life but also that spirituality is indeed
important to each of them. Moreover, they seem to yearn for the comfort and
centeredness that spirituality provides—a safe haven for music making.

It is important to demand spiritual exploration within each singer, and it is also
important in rehearsal to offer moments for spiritual reflection coupled with times
for the singers to turn inward. In other words, rehearsals should provide the
opportunity for singers to become aware of their interior life. It is the singers'
interior space that makes for great ensemble singing. The moments for reflection
need to be both planned and improvised so the atmosphere of the rehearsal room
becomes a safe haven for such explorations.

The basis of this philosophy is that a choral ensemble's sound can be agitated or
can emanate from a calm core. Agitated sound will have characteristics such as
intonation problems, harshness, and overall inflexibility. Sounds that come from a
calm and spacious core will have a unique and particular resonance. They are rich,
vibrant, and colorful.

In many cases, spacious interiority is created through various contemplative means, from simple breathing exercises to structured QiGong exercises. A small amount of time devoted to such "calming" practices will do much to allow music to grow from a central core in each person. Here are some suggested "calming" activities:

- **Allowing quiet** – A period of quiet at the start of rehearsal is a powerful activity for allowing singers to become aware of themselves and their breathing. I often couple this with alignment reminders based upon Body Mapping principles.[3] The operative in this rehearsal suggestion is the word "allow."

- **Ensemble journaling** – Many conductors have found journaling to be extremely helpful at the start of rehearsal. Prior to the choral warm-up period, have the singers write in their journals for a few minutes. This activity can be structured with a specific journaling task or can be left unstructured. The point is that the activity allows structured time for singers to be with themselves in a calming and inward way.

- **Guided meditations** – There is an art to guided meditation. Guided meditation must be planned and should never be improvised. Conductors who employ this method should never use meditations they have not experienced first. There are many texts written on meditation; the best of those currently available are listed in the List of Supplemental Resources at the back of this book. An excellent example and model of such meditations can be heard on *The Musician's Soul: Meditations,* a recording by Fr. Bede Camera, designed to accompany *The Musician's Soul* (GIA).

- **Calming nature of sustained sound** – I have become increasingly fascinated by the power of sustained sounds to create both calm and internal spaciousness for musicians. The sounds of the quartz crystal bowls (either live or recorded) have a mesmerizing effect upon anyone who hears them. Sustained sounds have the power to open one's hearing awareness and calm the internal space of the body. Sounding a single crystal bowl (or playing a recording of the sound) at the start of warm-up or as singers enter the rehearsal room will establish a very different tone for rehearsal.[4]

---

3 Such alignment reminders can be found in two valuable resources for conductors. Verbal cues are listed in *The Structures and Movement of Breathing* (GIA) by Barbara Conable. A similar approach is summarized in the alignment section of *The Choral Warm-Up* (GIA) by this author.

4 Recordings of quartz crystal bowls made by Steven Halpern produce magical effects when used in this suggested context.

Recordings of didgeridoo music can also provide similar sonic respites for the ensemble.[5]

- **The magical power of QiGong** – While I realize I am suggesting many practices that are outside the mainstream of the choral rehearsal, there is nothing I have found as dramatically effective as the performance of a single cycle of QiGong exercises (which require four positions with twenty-six circular repetitions) before rehearsal begins. The effect these exercises have upon the singing tone of the choir is simply amazing, especially with older singers. More dramatically, these exercises provide the vehicle for achieving a remarkable sense of "in tune-ness" within the ensemble. Ancient Chinese medicine has long realized the value in these exercises because they balance the energy flow within the body. Consider experimenting with their use in your rehearsals and see the effect they have on your ensemble.

- **Centering activities** – Centering activities (e.g., meditation, yoga, journaling, among others) can have a profound impact upon the rehearsal process. When singers are able to access a center in themselves, sound within the ensemble gains resonential and pitch clarity that is unmistakable. Moreover, all gesture should emanate from your center, almost like a huge magnetic fulcrum around which you live and move. The time spent in centering activities is absolutely essential to the alchemy of a great—or even a good—rehearsal.

I said that experiences of centering, however they may come into a person's being—through the crafts, the arts, educated perception— may foster a healing of those inner divisions which set man at war with himself and therefore with others. A craftsman, for example, has the opportunity of acting out the daily wisdom of his organism, in its intuitive and other aspects. He has the opportunity to obey the poetic processes of fusing and unifying various elements in a single image. He knows that it can be done. He has experienced the mysterious powers of his material when he puts himself into a

---

5 The finest recordings of didgeridoo music I have discovered are by Astarius. His recordings can be found in many music stores or can be ordered online at www.Astarius.com.

certain fruitful relation to it. He knows what can happen of itself once certain rhythms are set in motion. He knows that hand and head, heart and will, serve in a process and a wisdom greater than his own. (p. 62)

To bring universe into personal wholeness, to breathe in, to drink deep, to receive, to understand, to yield, to *read* life. And to spend wholeness in act, to breathe out, to give, to mean, to say, to *write*, to *create* life. It is the rhythm of our metabolism and may not easily be put into words. (p. 65)

—Mary Catherine Richards
in *Centering*

- **Storying** – In the course of rehearsal, there is perhaps no more effective tool for encouraging and compelling human connection for musicians than storying. I am sure all of you would agree that some of the best rehearsals you have conducted have occurred when a compelling human story was told that caused you to go to a place in your life that was similar. These places of profound meaning are present in each of our lives, and it behooves rehearsal technique if we can use them as a vehicle to allow us to connect or reconnect with our center and spiritual core.

The acknowledgment of the power of spirit is crucial to the expressive clarity of any ensemble. Spiritual centering of some type provides the necessary calming of energies that are counterproductive to human musical expression. When the body is calmed and centered, then it follows that the breath process can be both deeper and more energized. And energized breath can only energize choral sound.

I suppose the point of this chapter is to encourage you to think "outside of the box" to structure rehearsal techniques that cause singers to become aware of their bodies and themselves. Consider this: If you spend time at the start of a rehearsal on various activities to correctly align the core of the body for singing, then it should naturally follow that you spend time on opening and aligning the internal core of the singers. This can only be accomplished through suggestive and meditative means.

So consider giving it a try, and you will find that one or more of these methods will have far-reaching effects on the conduct of your rehearsals.

The awareness of grandeur and the sublime is all but gone from the modern mind. Our systems of education stress the importance of enabling the student to exploit the power aspect of reality. To some degree, they try to develop his ability to appreciate beauty. But there is no education for the sublime. We teach the children how to measure, how to weigh. We fail to teach them how to revere, how to sense wonder and awe. The sense for the sublime, the sign of the inward greatness of the human soul and something which is potentially given to all men, is now a rare gift. Yet without it, the world becomes flat and the soul a vacuum. (p. 34)

—Abraham Joshua Heschel
in *God in Search of Man*

Chapter 9

The "It" of Rehearsal

Setting the Mimetic of the Room

A leader is someone with the power to project either shadow or light onto some part of the world and onto the lives of the people who dwell there. A leader shapes the ethos in which others must live, an ethos as light-filled as heaven or as shadowy as hell. A *good* leader is intensely aware of the interplay of inner shadow and light, lest the act of leadership do more harm than good. (p. 78)

Good leadership comes from people who have penetrated their own inner darkness and arrived at the place where we are at one with one another, people who can lead the rest of us to a place of "hidden wholeness" because they have been there and know the way. (pp. 80–81)

Everything in us cries out against it—which is why we externalize everything. It is so much easier to deal with the external world, to spend our lives manipulating material and institutions and other people instead of dealing with our own souls. We like to talk about the outer world as if it were infinitely complex and demanding, but it is a cakewalk compared to the labyrinth of our inner lives! (p. 82)

—Parker Palmer
in *Let Your Life Speak*

It's a terribly shaming thing to get mad at rehearsals. Anyone with an ounce of sense or honesty knows that music and anger don't really mix—for two very good reasons:

First, nothing technically sick, broken or out-of-sync is cured. On some occasions (I can think of none), when skills and schooling are perfect, everyone may rave to guard against indifference or lassitude, but for the most part conductors of choruses get mad when they don't know how to fix the fool thing—so they kick its tires.

And, of course, in the second place, anger is completely alien to the whole purpose of music—or of a chorus, for that matter. The purpose of these is communication (it does seem to me that "communion" is a more suitable word except for its religious connotations) and anger is a barrier, an isolation. (p. 26)

—Robert Shaw
in *The Robert Shaw Reader*

Mike Krzyzewski's interactive/feminine qualities of leadership are stereotypically feminine; the command and control ones, masculine. The books don't straight out tell male executives to be more like women, but that message is clear.

Mike Krzyzewski's interactive/feminine qualities of leadership may be partly innate, but to a large extent he learned them from his family.

"There's an empathetic part of leadership, and this is where my wife and my daughters have had a large impact on me," Krzyzewski says. "Guys don't share insights. If a guy does, we call him a blowhard or a know-it-all, so we don't do it. Every night at the dinner table, my wife and girls discussed their day. They remembered details. They remembered the feeling that the detail brought, and the feeling before that, whereas men, we remember only the final feeling. We're all about the end of the story, the punch line. (p. 100)

In Krzyzewski's office that day, a few minutes after he thrust his clawed hand toward my chest, I said to him that I noticed something about his approach to leadership: despite the unquestioned authority he commands, his style on balance is more feminine than masculine. At Duke games, after he gives his instructions during a timeout—the classic command-and-control moment—his players break away from him and form their own huddle to talk to one another. Duke players constantly consult with one another on the court without looking to the bench for direction or approval. Krzyzewski believes that even a practice should have a certain sound, by which he should hear his players communicating back and forth constantly.

When he recruits a player, Krzyzewski tells him, "We're developing a relationship here, and if you are not interested, tell me sooner rather than later." That word—relationship—is one he uses frequently. To players who may leave after a year or two for the National Basketball Association, he says: "If you come here, for however long, you're going to unpack your suitcase. We're going to form a bond, and your going to be part of this family." (p. 99)

—Mike Krzyzewski
Duke University Basketball Coach
in *"Follow Me"* by Michael Sokolove
The New York Times *Play Magazine*
February 2006

What did I discover I was doing to inhibit this miracle of wholeness in a rehearsal, or even in a performance? The first destructive factor present was negativism. It is impossible for a negative element to produce a positive one, and surprisingly, we are all prone to be negative. I remember seeing on the *Today Show* the results of a study regarding our normal thought patterns. The results were alarming! The average person thinks negatively **95 percent** of the time....

If this human computer is recording primarily negative thinking brought about by daily circumstances often (but not always) beyond our control, and if my unconscious constantly colors the way my conscious mind perceives daily experiences, the results are obvious. What a challenge to attack negative thinking not only in rehearsals but during the rest of the day as well! The second destructive factor is being judgmental, which is actually a source of negativism. Every time I was judgmental, I ran the risk of being negative. "How dare

he be tardy to my rehearsal!" "How dare she miss this performance!"
It is disheartening at times to listen to the general tone of the
conversation about students by faculty in the faculty lounges of our
schools. Then they walk out and teach that student! We are **never**
given the right to judge. "Judge not that ye be not judged!" That is
a statement with no qualifications. (pp. 25–26)

—Weston Noble
in *Creating the Special World*

But what grounds commitment to care, to respond positively, and
what puts limits on that response? An ethic of care—at least as I
have described it—is grounded in the human condition. Every
human being requires care initially in order to survive, and that
need—changing in form over time—continues as the organism
grows. A healthy teenager does not need the sort of care required
by an infant, and a mature adult does not require the care he or she
once needed as a teenager. But every human being, at every stage of
life, hopes for some positive response from other human beings. No
one wants to be harmed by others or live in fear of them. Everyone
hopes for a helping hand in time of danger or more trouble than
he or she can handle alone. Everyone wants enough respect to
maintain at least minimal dignity. (p. 148)

—Nel Noddings
in *Educating Moral People*

I frequently begin classes on rehearsal technique with the following admonition: Most choirs form an opinion about the conductor and what will be accomplished in the first minutes of a rehearsal. Most of that judgment is based upon nonverbal communication and body language that not only sets the rehearsal but, in a way, predetermines from the outset the course of future rehearsals and performances.

One of my most vivid memories that sparked my thought on this subject was an incident with my teacher, Elaine Brown. When she returned to Temple University for her "second career" in 1975, her first rehearsal with the Temple University Choirs wasat the annual choir retreat. While I was aware of her, I really knew little about her. She was given a brief introduction to the choir, and then she got on the podium. I expected a speech about goals or some sort of verbal discourse before the rehearsal began. Instead, she got on the podium, looked at the choir and stood with her arms outstretched in a conducting position that resembled an embrace, took a breath, and the rehearsal started. I will never forget what I felt at that moment. That moment, frozen in my mind, formed my opinion about this woman for whom I knew almost nothing.

My opinion? I immediately felt an incredible connection to Elaine Brown. I could feel her energy, her very spirit—all without any verbiage on her part! I must admit that her rehearsal technique was different from what I expected, but frankly, I didn't care. The rehearsal swept me away musically and personally. Those few minutes in her presence transformed my musical life forever.

Imagine that…No words. No speeches. No stage setting. Just a human presence that invited us all to sing. And somehow, without words, we knew she cared not only about the music, but all things human.

I have thought many times over the years about why those few fleeting seconds of rehearsal had such a galvanizing effect upon my very spirit. In the intervening years, it has become clear to me that a great rehearsal and great music making can only be birthed in such a manner. If we are to be successful in our rehearsals and teaching, then we must be masters of those few precious seconds that open every rehearsal.

I experienced the identical situation with Wilhelm Ehmann some years later in St. Moritz, Switzerland. I was in the choir that was to prepare a program of Bach, Mendelssohn, and Brahms motets. The program focused on three of the Bach motets.

Dr. Ehmann, one of the great choral conductors of the twentieth century, was not one of the warmest human beings I had ever met. And at times, his rehearsals were tedious and bordered on being boring. I remember being confined to the neutral syllable *duhn–duhn–duhn* for what seemed like an eternity. After approximately six rehearsals singing Bach on *duhn–duhn–duhn*, Dr. Ehmann came into the next rehearsal very different. He almost seemed like another person. I anticipated another boring rehearsal of *duhn–duhn–duhn*. But what I got instead was the musical ride of my life.

Dr. Ehmann looked at the choir. He outstretched his arms in the same way that Elaine Brown had done years earlier. He said to the choir "Text, bitte." I will never forget his eyes. It seemed as if they were the doors to an entire world. They were inviting and, I must say, loving and embracing. To this day, I have never experienced music making like that. It was set in motion nonverbally. Spirit and body language ignited the musical souls of all who were there. Rehearsal magic, to be sure.

The "It" of Rehearsal

I once heard a radio interview with Charles Barclay, the legendary basketball star. During the course of the interview, Barclay was asked about a chapter in his recent book that was written by Tiger Woods. The interviewer, Don Imus, asked Barclay why, despite the fact that he has no interest in golf, he has to watch the entire match every time Tiger Woods plays.

Barclay replied that Tiger Woods has "it." The "it" has nothing to do with golf; it has to do with the fact that you want to watch golf because of the spirit and energy that Tiger disperses. He is an honest, open human being who happened to play golf. His very presence compels people to watch, and even participate at some level. Barclay's observation resonated with me. I hate golf, but I must admit, I do watch Tiger.

Elaine Brown and Wilhelm Ehmann had "it"—all the great teachers and conductors have "it." And while this is often an instinctive quality, I believe it can (and must) be cultivated as a vital part of any conductor's rehearsal technique. "It" has everything to do with us and our mimetics.

Coach Like a Woman

In almost all cultures, women seem to develop the capacity to care more often and more deeply than men. Most care theorists do not believe that this happens because of something innate or essential in women. We believe that it happens because girls are expected to care for people, and boys are too often relieved of this expectation. (p. 19)

—Nel Noddings
in *Educating Moral People*

Mike Krzyzewski, the legendary basketball coach at Duke University, believes the secret to his coaching success is that he coaches "like a woman." In his many speeches and workshops on leadership, Krzyzewski speaks of his success in coaching based upon what he has learned from his wife and daughters. In short, women have the ability to discuss ideas openly in give-and-take forums, while men tend to be inward and consult outside "sources" rarely, if ever. He insists that his players talk with one another during both practices and games, and he believes deeply in the value and power of the communicative "community." The term "community" has several descriptors. Communities share ideas, share common beliefs and desires and, if they are to survive, cultivate an honest and open means of communication. Communities work at communication with each other, which can be initiated either externally or internally.

Robert Shaw wrote to his choirs regularly, which is documented beautifully in *The Robert Shaw Reader*. This was Shaw's way of creating open channels of communication. Without sounding sexist, letters and letter writing have traditionally been associated with women more than men. Through his eloquent language, the singers in Shaw's choirs were not only confronted to consider musical and human issues, but those letters served as a catalyst between and among the singers in his ensembles to talk about the musical issues at hand. It seems that no matter the communicative method, an ensemble that lies within a community of spirits who communicate will achieve the most. But this communication must be regular, almost daily. In looking back, my best rehearsals have occurred when I communicated with my choir through e-mail or through spoken word in rehearsals.

A well-known conductor once told me I talk too much in rehearsal. And I have had singers tell me the same thing. The conductor was a person who spoke little to his ensemble in human terms; he only used talking in rehearsal as a means of delivering rants and verbal abuse. So considering his standard, I am pleased to have his criticism leveled at me.

As for the singers, they communicate little with others because they believe they have all the answers about everything. Coach Krzyzewski divides his players into three categories: high maintenance, medium maintenance, and low maintenance.[1] Ensemble members who are in this critical category and who seemingly divorce themselves from the community of singers are *always* high-maintenance individuals. While they almost always contribute at high levels to the ensemble, they tend to neutralize their musical contributions somewhat when they engage in such behavior. (More on this later in this chapter.) The finest singers I have known are those who somehow understand how to be in a community and how to communicate with others.

My experience has shown that, in general, no matter how strongly women feel about an issue, they try hard to open the lines of communication and "talk it out." I have had a soprano in my choir the past two years who is a model of this "woman theory," as are most of the women in my ensemble. When this soprano has an issue, she talks to me in the most humane way possible, and we have a healthy exchange and always come to a resolution that is to the benefit of the ensemble. Also, on many occasions when this individual senses that communication is lacking within the group, she will e-mail the entire choir. Those e-mails are always positive in tone, stunning in their construction of ideas, and skillfully communicated through the written word. Without realizing it, this single soprano has been the spiritual leader of the choir.

On the other hand, I must make the somewhat uncomfortable observation that my most difficult singers throughout my career have been male. But that is not to say all men are like that. Some men who have had musical and personal issues with the ensemble have sought out patient dialogue and informed conversation between myself and other members of the ensemble.

However, there are others. Throughout the years, I have had many men who have become angry at the ensemble. While conversation took place, it was always one way, in a "winner take all" style of communication as I call it, because they believed they were right and the musical community was wrong. That being said, in almost every case the issues they brought forward were important. However, their

---

1 Sokolove, Michael. "Follow Me." *The New York Times Play Magazine*. February 2006, p. 101.

viewpoints were difficult to accept because they were relayed without an atmosphere of true communication and caring. So in applying Coach Krzyzewski's approach of "coaching like a woman," I carry their concerns anonymously to the ensemble through either spoken word or e-mail. And why do I do this? Because all of my major teachers have been women! Elaine Brown was the most amazing communicator I have ever experienced. Whether it was one on one or with a whole ensemble, her mantra was always open, free, and unbiased communication. She always spoke to her choirs unashamedly about the Martin Buber "I and Thou" philosophical perspective. And she almost demanded in a very caring way that we all communicate. Robert Shaw communicated through letters; Elaine Brown communicated through speaking and human connections; Leonard Bernstein always talked with the New York Philharmonic and, in fact, on many occasions wrote them letters. Great ensembles are in constant communication with each other. Whether the Emerson String Quartet, Chanticleer, or the Berlin Philharmonic, a community of open communication seems to be at the core of their "secret" to music making.

Pure and simple, great music is made by ensembles of people who communicate with *each other*. So one of the best rehearsal techniques conductors and teachers can develop is to become aware and foster communication with their ensembles and almost mandate that communication on musical matters occur within and outside of each rehearsal. In other words, do all in your power to foster a sense of community. I'm sure on our best days we do this naturally, and probably quite by accident. But we were never taught to do it—or at least I wasn't. Strive to become aware and act with great and deliberate effort to create "community ambiance" in every rehearsal. The following quotes summarize more elegantly than I the issues surrounding communal communication:

Only he who himself turns to the other human being and opens himself to him receives the world in him. Only the being whose otherness, accepted by my being, lives and faces me in the whole compression of existence, brings the radiance of eternity to me. Only when two say to one another with all that they are, "It is Thou," is the indwelling of the Present Being between them. (p. 30)

—Martin Buber
in *Between Man and Man*

Our equal and opposite needs for solitude and community constitute a great paradox. When it is torn apart, both of these life-giving states of being degenerate into deadly specters of themselves. Solitude split off from community is no longer a rich and fulfilling experience of inwardness; it now becomes loneliness, a terrible isolation. Community split off from solitude is no longer a nurturing network of relationships; it now becomes a crowd, an alienating buzz of too many people and too much noise. (p. 65)

—Parker J. Palmer
in *The Courage to Teach*

Learning to care is not a sequential process like, say, learning mathematics. It is probably true that one must learn how to be cared for and to care for oneself before learning to care for others, we must learn more about what it means to be cared for. As we learn how to care for ourselves, we become more discerning in assessing the efforts of others to care. (p. 32)

—Nel Noddings
in *Educating Moral People*

In the article on Coach Krzyzewski, Michael Sokolove points out that in *Built to Last,* authors Jim Collins and Jerry Porras suggest that companies that endure and prosper over time do not usually offer innovative products; rather, "The company itself is the ultimate creation." Perhaps a paradigm shift may be necessary when thinking about rehearsal technique. While many of us believe that the music is the creative product, maybe we would do better to focus our effort on the factors that create the human ensemble. The music, then, becomes the natural outgrowth of this powerful communal synergy.

Rehearsal Mimetics

I have found that a *constant* awareness of mimetics makes all the difference in any rehearsal or performance. Consider Elaine Brown, Wilhelm Ehmann, and Tiger Woods; they knew nothing about mimetics, yet their very beings were (and are) mimetical models for all of us.

The atmosphere of any rehearsal, I am sure we would all agree, is a strong indicator as to whether the rehearsal experience will be beneficial. And that atmosphere is created by the very spirit of the conductor in the front of the room. It is a part of the rehearsal that is felt, not observed. It is often wordless—a silent setting of the course of an entire rehearsal.

Envy and the Rehearsal

Envy unfortunately enters into the life of every person; artists are especially susceptible to the negative influences of envy. If not kept in perspective, envy can control and influence both the spirit and the music. In fact, envy has become so common to us that it often goes unchecked within us. It becomes second nature—a regular part of everything we do. We are constantly envious.

Envy in musicians can be categorized as follows:

- Envy of the perfect sound
- Envy of others' musical skills
- Envy of others' artistry
- Envy of others' creative spirit
- Envy of others' technical skills

The word "mimetic" comes from the Greek meaning *to imitate*. One is mimetic when one imitates the words or actions of others. "Mimesis" also means *to imitate,* but the definition also includes "...addicted to or having an aptitude for mimicry or imitation."

Mimetic theory was developed by René Girard for use in both literary and biblical criticism. His theories are very relevant to musicians and especially conductors who desire to establish a positive tone for their rehearsals. In fact, I believe mimetic desire in some form is at the root of many musical problems musicians face, especially conductors. Since mimetic theory was shared with me some ten years ago, the awareness it has brought to me has transformed my rehearsals and my ensembles to very different psychological and spiritual places.

We must understand that envy is pervasive throughout all aspects of our lives. In fact, it is omnipresent. The envy of things and possessions of others, of other persons and their abilities, causes huge firestorms in our lives that cast long shadows upon our rehearsals. While you might think envy is a psychological problem, in actuality it poses a spiritual dilemma of the greatest magnitude. Yet it goes unnoticed in us, especially when we think about the rehearsal room and the rehearsal process.

So how does mimetic theory translate into the rehearsal? Every musician desires to hear the perfect sound. That is both part of our love and part of our gift as conductors. At the moment sound is made, we face a dilemma of monumental proportions. If the sound the ensemble produces is beautiful, then we are fine. But more often than not, the sound is not perfect and we are then forced to deal with our immediate reactions to the sound. Left untended, our inner feelings can morph into one of the biggest factors that can profoundly change the direction of any rehearsal.

Mimetic theory tells us that at the moment a sound is made, we face a choice—and that choice is conscious. In other words, as conductors we should not focus upon the problems of the sound, but rather allow ourselves to focus upon the human characteristics of the room. At the moment a sound is made, you must tell yourself that you love and care for the people who are sitting in front of you. In essence, you must talk to yourself not only when the first sound is made, but also repeatedly throughout the rehearsal when you feel yourself "going to a bad place" because of the sounds the ensemble is producing. As a conductor, you need to exercise this privilege of conscious choice every time you are confronted with your own spiritual discomfort when the sound isn't right. Such mimetic "awareness" and mimetic "confrontation" may occur once during a rehearsal or hundreds of times during a rehearsal, depending upon the state of the conductor.

The Mimetic Triangle in Rehearsal

Mimetic energy is always generated within a conductor as the by-product of a three-sided relationship. The conductor is on one side of the triangle. On the highest point of the triangle are the things of which the conductor is envious; most conductors are envious of the sound that is "in their head." When the ensemble creates a sound, a conductor's mind unconsciously compares the sound that was sung to a model sound that is heard in his/her head. As a human being and an artist, the conductor desires and wants beauty. Consider the following paradigm:

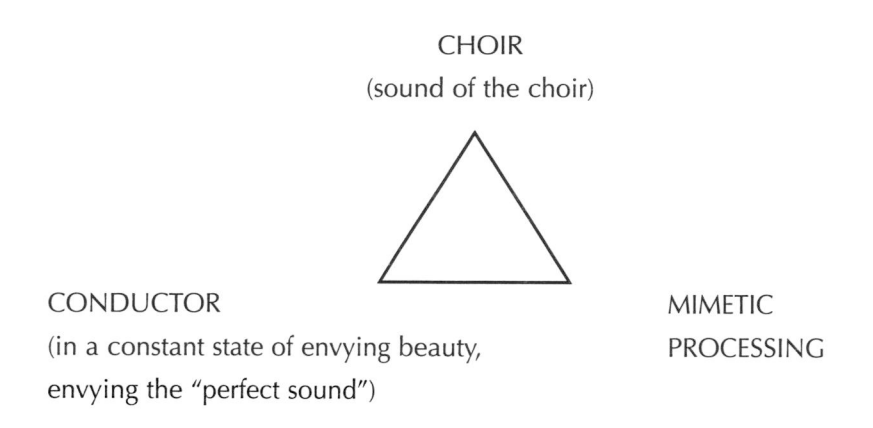

CHOIR
(sound of the choir)

CONDUCTOR
(in a constant state of envying beauty,
envying the "perfect sound")

MIMETIC
PROCESSING

At that moment, as conductors we have an instantaneous choice to make. A bad mimesis, or the beginnings of an unsettled rehearsal room, occurs when we do not make any choice. This happens because we either ignore our own feelings and reactions to the sound, or worse, we are simply so unaware of ourselves and our feelings that we exist in a world outside of ourselves. This detachment from the persons in the room is perhaps the most serious rehearsal technique error a conductor can make. When we hear the sound of the ensemble, we have the power to make the conscious decision, which will have a major impact on the sound in the room. In fact, the conscious choice I am advocating has profound and far-reaching effects upon the music making of the rehearsal.

Awareness of One's Reactions to Sound: The Moment of Conscious Choice

At the moment sound is created from the ensemble, as conductors we are, almost unknowingly, envious of the "perfect sound." When the ensemble does not create the perfect sound, the mimetic cycle is instantaneously set in motion. Left unattended through our willful and conscious thought, our negative feelings toward the sound will continue to snowball and gain momentum throughout the rehearsal. It is at that exact moment when we hear the first sounds that we must consciously choose the correct mimetic path. We must tell ourselves to go to the place that is loving, caring, selfless, self-emptying, helping, and trusting. If we do not consciously and willfully choose this path, human nature will thrust its spirit into a place of anger, mistrust of the ensemble, mistrust of self, inhumanness, varying degrees of violence both in gesture and words (especially gesture), and a general state of frustration. The ensemble will immediately perceive that spirit through a wordless transfer, which will be both immediate and profound.

In general, the most predominant characteristic of a bad mimesis in a conductor or musician is self-mutilation. This is usually characterized by "feeling bad" about a rehearsal. We feel bad that the rehearsal went poorly because the singers were not prepared or were not "being responsible." However, the resulting sound from the ensemble in a situation of bad mimesis is a phenomenon I like to call **mirrored mimesis**. That is, what we hear in the sound is, in essence, a reflection of our own mimesis. It is a reflection within the choir of our wrong mimetic choice, either consciously or unconsciously. The ensemble will always reflect the mimetic energy of the conductor regardless of each singer's individual mimetic situation in life. In other words, the mimesis of the conductor tends to override the individual mimeses each singer may bring into rehearsal or performance, and it is multiplied in intensity in direct proportion to the number of singers in the choir.

So how might we handle or attempt to deal with such a mimetic situation? Without conscious choice and of those qualities that provide for good mimesis, we instead select a scapegoat. We might focus our attention on one singer or a group of singers; one person or a small group within the larger group is "destroyed" to achieve cohesion. The larger the group, the larger the sacrifice will be.

As René Girard states, this situation is "unity minus one." Most conductors justify such destruction by rationalizing that it is "for the good of the music and the composer." In essence, a double scapegoat occurs. Not only are these conductors "taking out" their frustrations on the ensemble, but they also further complicate matters by using the music as an additional scapegoat for their actions. The next step, then, is rationalization of the sacrifice to avoid guilt. "They are bad, they deserve it," is one such approach. This type of "cover story" allows these conductors to keep hidden from themselves the reality, truth, and honesty in the choir. By engaging in such scapegoat activities, these conductors in essence conceal themselves from the choir. Their mimetic desire overcomes the music. Angular, almost violent gestures are the first manifestations of poor mimetic choice. Then they may engage in a type of self-laceration, where they are the scapegoat instead of the choir.

Left untended, such a "scapegoat dynamic" can destroy an ensemble and eventually the conductor, and can cripple music making. Ultimately, the music suffers the most. So at all costs, we must avoid magnifying the crowd mentality that can be set in motion by envy of "the perfect sound."

But why do we envy the perfect sound? Because as artists, we inherently love beauty in sound and in art. Beauty is a major reason for our existence. It is not difficult to understand, therefore, that striving for beauty in our lives and in the rehearsal room and concert hall can inadvertently fuel the mimetic furnace of the choir.

The Rehearsal Room as an Affirming Place

Over the past fifteen years, Weston Noble and I have become friends, and every time we get a chance to talk, we always seem to discuss music making. Several years ago, I asked him, somewhat naively, what he believed his fifty-seven years of teaching/conducting had taught him about both teaching and people. His answer was simple and very direct—and it moved me deeply. Weston replied that he believes everyone needs to be "affirmed." Notice he did not use the word "praised" or "reinforced," but "affirmed." And he said this act of affirmation must occur over and over again if one is to create an atmosphere that allows musicians to grow. In his eyes, affirmation is both empowering to the individual and enabling.

It struck me that in so affirming every individual spirit we teach or rehearse, we stay true to the essential principles of mimetics. We affirm another human being through loving and caring for them with each interaction, no matter how small. That affirmation may come in the form of spoken word. However, I believe (and I have witnessed this in Weston's teaching) that affirmation is truly a state of the spirit. To place oneself in an affirming place is a synonym for the mimetic principles I have described. We need to work hard each day of our lives to learn what it is to be an affirming/compassionate, caring, and loving conductor simply by standing in front of an ensemble and *being*.

The atmosphere of a rehearsal room is a volatile space, and as conductors we need to understand that. Our very beings can ignite the place into a pit of inhumane subtleties or, on the other hand, can create a space of warm affirmation—a safe haven for people and music. One of the most elegant statements of Weston's affirmation "theory" is contained in *Search for Excellence*. In that book, the author quotes a few paragraphs on the educational philosophy of Brookline (Massachusetts) High School. I have taken the liberty to adapt the subject of the quote and aim it directly at musicians.

The habit of reflection is the ideal trait of the educated mind, taking for its concern what others may be satisfied to take for granted. Education should foster this habit, should teach patience in the understanding and construction of ideas. But it should also teach us to consider feelings, to anticipate the probable effect of our actions and words on others, and to temper these when they augur injury. Education is this forethought rather than afterthought, abiding thought rather than sporadic thought.

—adapted and paraphrased from the philosophy of
the Brookline (Massachusetts) High School
In Search of Excellence

We also need to understand that while affirmation and a mimetic tone is set wordlessly in a rehearsal, mimetic damage can be set in motion by the words chosen to address musical issues. We need to realize that words are the carriers of our spirits, and if left unchecked, they can sabotage our best efforts. Many of us speak to our ensembles without first editing what we say by putting our words through a spiritual "spell check." Barry Green talks extensively about the profound effects of spoken word upon musicians in his book, *The Inner Game of Music* (Doubleday, 1986). Lynn Eustis, in her book, *The Singer's Ego* (GIA, 2005), presents a compelling argument for a singer's inability to separate the singing voice from his or her self. When singers are told (or know) that they are not singing well, they are unable to separate their technical difficulties from their spirits. This causes them to lapse into a hopeless spiritual abyss where their singing and their own spirit are inseparable. This spiritual confusion is often set in motion by the incendiary words of the conductor.

The rehearsal room is a place of both spirit and spoken word. We would do much to improve our own rehearsals by understanding the sacred nature of the dynamic of that place and do everything in our power through mimetics and affirmation to create what Weston Noble calls "a special world."

We need to recall the angel aspect of the word, recognizing words as independent carriers of soul between people. We need to recall that we do not just make up words or learn them in school, or fully ever have them under control. Words, like angels, are powers which have invisible powers over us. They are personal presences which have whole mythologies, genders, genealogies, histories and vogues; and their own guarding, blaspheming, creating and annihilating effects. For words are persons. This aspect of the word transcends their nominalistic definitions and contexts and evokes in our souls a universal resonance. Without the inherence of soul in words, speech would not move us, words would not provide forms for carrying our lives and giving sense to our deaths. (p. 9)

—James Hillman
in *Re-Visioning Psychology*

The Recipe for the Right Mimetic Choice

It appears on the surface that choosing a good mimetic path is an easy matter—but it is not. Choosing the proper mimetic path is not only a musical issue but also a profound life issue that will change the quality and interiority of one's life. The world around us does not reinforce correct mimetic choice; it more often than not reinforces the wrong mimetic path, and an awareness of that fact will already begin to redirect our thoughts. Moreover, our educational process does not reinforce, teach, or support proper mimetic choices. Mimetic choice must be self-generated, deeply internal, soulful, and conscious.

So how do you acquire—or better yet, access—a good mimetical place? **You will it to be**. You consciously choose it and push yourself to go there and stay there. You must stay in a loving and caring place during every minute of the rehearsal. You must stay there every minute of warm-up before a concert. You must be there throughout the entire concert. Acquiring the correct mimesis is a matter of choice, similar to the choices you make in life itself.

Perhaps another way to think about this is that throughout the rehearsal and performance process, you must work to become less. The choir must become more, and you must dwindle to the point that you reduce yourself to a real person. As a conductor, you publicly exhibit the unmaking of a bad mimetic personality in front of people so they become more.

We have many choices to make in life, and for the most part, we make them. But we also must realize that we are confronted with those same choices in every rehearsal and that our rehearsal room is a mirror of our life struggles. The struggle to be an affirming teacher and a human being is constant. When confronted with the sound from a choir, always remember that on a deep, profound, and subconscious level you will "envy" the beautiful. The beautiful sounds in life through music are what make us musicians; the human need for beauty in music drives our motivation to become better musicians and performers. In the struggle to acquire or experience perfection, we focus on all the technical aspects of our art: conducting technique, singing technique, and analysis seem to be at the core of all curricula. Often, too, we talk about the interpretation of the music. Unfortunately, seldom do we talk about or ponder the implication of that music on our lives. How does the piece of music we are performing impact our life experience and those who hear our choir? Does the performance speak to profound life issues that know no religious or ethnic boundaries?

To find the answers or to begin to understand any piece of music, we must bring our own humanity to bear on the music. A prerequisite to any interpretation is a person's ability to love others, care for others, and have the ability to be, at all times, humble and selfless (both during the rehearsal process and the performance). I know conductors who are gifted teachers and talented musicians. But every time I hear one of their choirs, there is a hardness to the tone that stems from their inability to love and care for the singers during the rehearsal process. For the most part, these conductors are also cynics because they constantly engage in bad mimetic processes by criticizing every other musical performance they hear. They are critical of colleagues and have a general inability to respect what others can offer. They are also unable to see themselves embroiled in this terrible mimetic predicament. They use the sheer force of their technical musicianship and control to bring about musical performances. Love, care, humbleness, and selflessness must be a constant during rehearsal; they should not be "turned on" just for the performance.

In summary, to place yourself in a good mimesis or good mimetic situation, you must tell yourself that you will love and care during the music rehearsal and performance process. First and foremost, you will love yourself and your gifts, also recognizing and accepting your musical weaknesses with love. You at all times will be humble and selfless, and place your own ego in a place that does not infect or interact with the music making process. You will consciously care more and love more. You will constantly self-empty, love, and care for others. (This self-emptying process is known as **kenosis**. One is said to be "kenotic" when in a state of constant self-emptying love.) You must strive for kenosis, without engaging in self-mutilation when you falter.

The constant struggle to keep yourself in a good mimetic place is a lifetime journey. That journey is, indeed, difficult. But to never begin to take the journey is a mistake. Ultimately, a bad mimesis will not only profoundly inhibit and damage the music but, in some cases, will also profoundly hurt people.

Solitude and Quiet: Gaining Access to Good Mimesis

Most persons reading this book will discover (as did I) that bad mimesis is unfortunately a vital part of everyday life. In fact, musicians will find to their dismay that it is a dominant factor in all rehearsal and performance situations. Being aware of bad mimesis is half the battle. Yet gaining access to the correct mimesis is difficult. Once you realize that bad mimetic choice is a part of your musical thumbprint, then you can move toward change. And as I have experienced, that change is dramatic and life changing.

Access can only be gained through quiet and stillness within oneself. Quiet solitude must be a daily occurrence. You must make a conscious choice to be still; the world will not give it to you. In fact, you will be continually challenged to choose it again and again in very difficult situations. Initially, accessing this stillness will bring great joy and freedom, but in time it will become more difficult. You will experience a very ordinary peacefulness, which provides a sobriety of context. You will discover that the newfound stillness unmakes personality so you can become a person, and who you are as a person can be subordinated to nothing. By being still, you are able to make yourself less so that others can become more—allowing the music to speak clearly through the ensemble.

There must be a time before rehearsal and performance when the conductor (and the choir) are quiet so as to explore one's center and to set proper mimetic acquisition in motion.

What would be the best way to describe that inner place? That place is spacious in feeling and calm. It is a place where the day-to-day issues of life are kept in perspective. It is the place where one's inner voice speaks and can be heard. That inner place is the place where trust in self resides. It is also the place where profound human loving and caring always reside. It becomes the place from which one creates all music.

Now, let us say a good word about depression. Sometimes it is good to be depressed, and we enjoy it, and I don't care what shrinks and therapists say, there are times when it is good to feel bad. For that moment, the only pleasure that we have is in the recalling of our woes, and the capacity to name our fears and to feel them indicates to us that at least we are not as far gone as we might appear to others. There is nothing worse than a friend or colleague who wants to help us out of our pit before we are ready to be helped, and in some perverse sense the frustration of their efforts adds little to our pleasure. It is said that Abraham Lincoln was at his best when in the midst of his frequent depressions, and the genius of Martin Luther is that he was both depressed and constipated. The black moods of genius have given much beauty, power, and purpose to the world. It is possible to think of depression, at least in its primary stage, as one of the few places of autonomy and self-preservation for one on whom the world appears to be closing in, and like pain it can from time to time be redemptive. (p. 160)

—Peter J. Gomes
in *Sermons*

Chapter 10

The Willful Choir

Have you ever considered the artificiality and phoniness of the usual musical rehearsal and performance? The conductor stands constantly in front of the chorus or the audience; he or she is always in the spotlight. The very nature of a rehearsal causes us to think and to speak in negative terms to our choirs. It is: "No, no—you missed that pitch." "Your blend is terrible." "Sopranos, you are flat." "Precision in attack is quite ragged." "You don't sing with proper quality." "No, don't—that's bad," etc. Sometimes it seems that we are so busy trying to promote ourselves that we can hardly afford the time even to learn the names of those who sing in our chorus, let alone make the attempt to understand the thinking and the lifestyles of our choristers. We become obsessed with a goal of making the programs which we conduct better in their sound and content than those performed by our principal competitor who lives either across town or across the state....

In some ways it seems to me at times that this is all rather pseudo and artificial and even downright dishonest. Where is music? Where is beauty? Where is living? (pp. 129–130)

When a mutual and sympathetic understanding of the human spirit is built, people finally become persons. (p. 149)

—Howard Swan
in *Conscience of a Profession*

One of the objectives, or at least by-product, of a rehearsal well lived and well planned is that any choir, regardless of skill level, becomes for lack of a better word *willful*. The more I consider this concept, the more it seems to be the logical outcome of a pedagogically intense and spiritually positive rehearsal.

Willful choirs are those ensembles that not only have the technical tools (both vocally and aurally) to sing a piece of music, but also have received enough information along the way to take responsibility for the music they are performing. Too often, conductors unknowingly accept this incredible burden simply because it is not in their rehearsal "psyche" to shift that responsibility to the singers. Instead, they need to chart a course to "turn over" responsibility for the piece as the rehearsal process progresses. Once charted, this empowerment path should be undertaken from the first rehearsal.

Inherent in this concept is the fact that at some point the conductor must be able to "let go" of the choir and allow the singers to find their own way. The singers must understand that it is their responsibility to sing a musical line, to listen, and to bring all of their individual human spirits to bear upon the music at hand. The rehearsal process, then, should lead the singers to understand their responsibilities and constantly encourage them to take musical risks.

"Letting go" is certainly one of the most profound life issues we have to face. But as conductors, "letting go" of the sound of the ensemble becomes much more than a simple cognitive act; it involves a level of trust that goes beyond the simple facts of the rehearsal. Through all that we do as conductors, the rehearsal process must constantly affirm to every member of the choir that singing a piece is much more than notes on the page—it is a belief in the singers as musicians, and it is ultimately rooted in their own personal affirmation of their own abilities and love of themselves. A successful rehearsal can accomplish all of this, often wordlessly through the actions of the conductor.

How do you know when you have truly "let go" of your ensemble? There will be an exciting and strange "willfulness" living within the sound when the choir sings. You can sense that the singers have assumed most, if not all, of the responsibility for the music, and as the conductor, you seem to be along for the ride. When *will* is operating, it almost seems as though you (the conductor) have lost "control" of the music making. Initially, if not recognized for what it truly is, this feeling can be very frightening. And if you are not aware that this is a normal progression, then you will likely respond by "controlling" more to get back to that comfort zone as a conductor.

If the rehearsal is right and you have done your work well, then the willful choir will emerge. But to accomplish this, you must chart a course in your rehearsal planning that will empower the singers to be musically willful and then choose a rehearsal technique that will enable you to stay that course. To have this concept of "willfulness" in your awareness at all times as you conduct can be powerful enough. Ensemble willfulness will happen if it is allowed to happen—if we as conductors believe that any ensemble is capable of this magical corporate willfulness.

In general, there is a will within us for those things we believe in most profoundly in our lives. In music, singers should be led to believe that part of the ensemble experience is the exercising of *their* individual wills. Musical line is nothing more or less than the want to move a musical sound forward. So if musical line is indeed the movement of sound forward, and musicality is ascertained through musical line, then it follows that musical line will be vibrant and speak directly to people if propelled by the will of the human spirits who sing it.

The most compelling choirs I have heard in my life are those choirs who carry willfulness in their sound, such as the musical will one hears in The Emerson String Quartet, or in the playing of Dinu Lipatti, or in the Bach Cello Suites played by Yo-Yo Ma, or in the singing of Ella Fitzgerald. Out of that willfulness is borne stunning intonation, shimmering sounds, and profound insights into the human condition, exponentially powerful because of the many who contribute to its whole.

Helen Kemp understands the power of young singers who become empowered through her mantra:

Body, Mind, Spirit, Voice....
It takes the *whole* person to sing and rejoice.

That philosophy empowers singers with the will to sing and express themselves through music. Charles Bruffy develops this "willfulness" through empowering the choir to use the text—both the sounds of the words and the deepest meaning—to bring color to the music. Text, in his case, is used as a vehicle for the human will and spirit.

However, musical will, used improperly, transforms itself into its opposite— arrogance with a total lack of humility. I have also observed willful conductors. There is a profound difference between choirs that are willful and conductors who make choirs seemingly willful by the sheer force of their presence. Their musical "will" is in a sense inflicted upon the ensemble, and they are forced to accept it at the risk of muting or even stifling their own human selves. Conductors of this nature are often able to propel a performance to a place of aural significance, but the profound human statement that is embodied in beautiful and honest sound is lacking.

When present, musical will is powerful, yet strangely calm and silent. It creates an aura in rehearsal and most certainly transforms a performance. Willful and honest music making should form the core of your rehearsal technique. And it will, provided you keep this concept of willfulness in your awareness.

Howard Swan understood musical will, admonishing choral conductors in his book *Conscience of a Profession* (Hinshaw Music, 1987): "Our responsibility as choral musicians does not stop with the teaching of music. We must find time and energy for thought and study so that we can help teach people how to live."

An understanding of will leads to more brilliant doors through which we can walk with our ensembles. Perhaps there is no greater gift we can give to our singers than the gift of self-will as learned through the music-making experience in our rehearsals.

Chapter 11

The Rehearsal Room as a Secret Place for Musicians

Phenomenologists insist that one dimension of the self—its private side—is formed within a secret place—that secluded region of lived experience, especially childhood experience which lies "beyond the world of institutionalized life." (Langveld, 1963). Within this margin of experience the child may live in solitude and safety, often losing himself in imagination and fantasy. Feeling at home in a secret place, the child may begin to imagine a self that is singular, distinct from others in the world. He may begin to read between the lines of the script that might otherwise seem impenetrable and closed to scrutiny and question. And for Langveld, this sense of a secret place is retained into adulthood, when it is more likely to be shared with significant others. (p. 135)

—Tom Barone
in *Touching Eternity*

If we add up "sense of rightness," "tranquility," "balance," "catharsis," "expressivity," we begin to approach the meaning of "fun." Add to these "participation," "creativity," "order," "sublimation," and "energy release," and you almost have it. Fun is all the things we find it impossible to say when we hear the Opus 131, or witness *Letter to the World*. (Beethoven and Martha Graham must have had this kind of fun *making* those works.) Fun is the final goal of the collected aesthetic searchings of David Prall, Dewey, Richards, and Santayana. Fun is the "x" of the equation that tries to solve the riddle of why art exists at all. (p. 104)

Every artist copes with reality by means of his fantasy. Fantasy, better known as imagination, is his greatest treasure, his basic equipment for life. And since his work is his life, his fantasy is constantly in play. He dreams life. Psychologists tell us that a child's imagination reaches its peak at the age of six or seven, then is gradually inhibited, diminished to conform with the attitudes of his elders—that is, reality. Alas. Perhaps what distinguishes artists from regular folks is that for whatever reasons, their imaginative drive is less inhibited; they have retained in adulthood more of that five-year-old's fantasy than others have. This is not to say that an artist is the childlike madman the old romantic traditions have made him out to be; he *is* usually capable of brushing his teeth, keeping track of his love life, or counting his change in a taxicab. When I speak of his *fantasy* I am not suggesting a constant state of abstraction, but rather the continuous imaginative powers that inform his creative acts as well as his reactions to the world around him. And out of that creativity and those imaginative reactions come not idle dreams, but truths—all those abiding truth-formations and constellations that nourish us, from Dante to Joyce, from Bach to the Beatles, from Praxiteles to Picasso. (pp. 358–359)

—Leonard Bernstein
in *Findings*

If we would take some time for serious introspection, focusing upon the best rehearsals we have either conducted or participated in, I am sure we would all agree that those rehearsals were truly magical times when the rehearsal room was transformed from a mundane and pedantic collection of rehearsal techniques to a place where you were transported to other places via the music. In considering how we rehearse, we should attempt to analyze and understand the recipe that creates such magic. For it is the creation of that magic that empowers the music to speak to every member of the choir.

Truly great teachers and conductors have an innate ability to say the right things and provide the incendiary spark that ignites human souls to levels of music making that, theoretically, they have no right to be functioning at! To understand how this might be done is perhaps the most valuable "rehearsal technique" we can possess.

Since writing *The Musician's Spirit* (GIA, 2002), I have deepened my convictions about the power of knowing one's own story as a central part of a musician's life. I have experienced rehearsals in which I was transported (as were the singers) both magically and mystically to a higher level of awareness and music making. Those magical moments are the ones that make life worth living to us as musicians. And once we experience them, our musical life is never the same. But careful thought and study must be devoted to how this is done. In examining the conductors who are able to regularly take singers to higher levels of music making (and who are able to do so in a profound, deep, and meaningful way), there are several commonalities that seem to emerge. To borrow a term from Abraham Maslow, such rehearsal spaces transform themselves into "self-actualizing" rehearsals. Weston Noble refers to this environment as "a special world." The quote at the beginning of this chapter speaks of a "secret place." The underlying key to transforming a rehearsal into "a special world" is an understanding of those "secret places" in the souls of our singers.

Storying has taught me that the experiences of our early lives form the music making matter of later life. What I did not totally understand is that (1) those experiences remain with us and can be unearthed only through our re-exploration and re-visitation of our story and (2) these magical moments of early life are stored as deep secret places in young adults and adults, waiting to be retrieved. For many, unfortunately, retrieval never occurs. And strangely, the arts are the only retrieval device (other than psychotherapy) that is available to us. These secrets know no socioeconomic barriers and are common to the lives of all cultures. If we accept that these experiences are retained, then it seems to follow that our work needs to focus on unlocking and bringing into the consciousness the power of those early experiences.

Accessing the Secret Place

There is a statement in Tom Barone's book *Touching Eternity* that has caused me to finally understand magical rehearsal moments. In describing one of his teachers (which is really a case study—and a brilliant one at that!), Barone noted that this teacher "recruited them into his program to equip them with additional resources for maintaining an internal aesthetic playground, for guarding the silence of their secret places against the noisy distractions of larger culture."[1]

Aha! I found it. A powerful paradigm for rehearsal: creating an internal aesthetic playground! Rehearsals must be times when singers are cajoled, or even forced, into that playground, where they will find all of the secret places they have already experienced. It is those secret places that make music making special; they provide depth and interiority to every note of music that is sung or played.

As conductors, we are the catalyst of this process. And we, too, must go to our "secret places" of childhood experiences. Elaine Brown always told her conducting students not to be afraid "to be a fool." The word "fool" is misunderstood in modern living. The fool in medieval societies was a respected member of the community. The town fool, through his acting, would cause people in the town to take journeys to places they would never speak of. If we enter a rehearsal room able to access our secret place, then we will be able to magically through our gesture and words guide our singers to that same place in *their* lives. But to do so, we must first believe that this is an important part of the rehearsal process. By going into rehearsal occupying our "secret place," we transform ourselves into the mystical and magical fool of old, who is able to, with great care, move an entire community to action—in this case, music.

This mode of instruction in rehearsal is subtle, many times indirect, and very persistent. Elaine Brown never gave up "being the fool." Every rehearsal, she expected each one of us to commit and go to "the secret place," and only when the choir could be moved to that secret place did the music live. Most days, it happened wordlessly. You could sense she was in a magical place, and you went to yours because she was in hers. Barone states it so elegantly:

...tactfulness in teaching. Tactfulness means "touching" someone, rousing them from slumber into a greater personal awareness while respecting and preserving their personal space. This kind of

---

1 Quote taken from *Touching Eternity*, Tom Barone, p. 136.

tactfulness can bring coherence to the scattered pieces of a self, prompt the construction of a more integrated worldview, and thereby encourage personal growth. (p. 140)

…a seed planted by an act of tactfulness may itself lie dormant within the consciousness of the student, with growth and learning serendipitously as a propitious moment years hence. (p. 140)

This should become our mantra for rehearsals. The tactfulness Barone speaks of can be re-interpreted as a conductor who operates from a loving and caring place, who is aware of his own secret place. That "spiritual place" in rehearsal is infectious to those around him. His "place," defacto, creates the "re-creation." And each singer's magical "secret place," where the core of all music making lives, should be revisited in every rehearsal.

While every conductor is different, I offer the following suggestions to consider, which may act in such a way to cause you to access your "secret place." Many of these suggestions take place just prior to or upon entering the rehearsal room.

- **Story thyself** – Spend time remembering as much as you can about your life from age two through six. There will be sharp and clear memories of happy times, silly and fun times, and sad times. If you have them, look at old photographs of yourself, which may spark memories. If necessary, write them down in a journal. Place yourself in those situations to reawaken each of the secret places in your life.

- **Access quiet** – This is perhaps the most valuable rehearsal tool for conductors. You need to be able to quiet yourself for many reasons. First, you can only hear outside of yourself if you can hear within yourself! Quiet allows others to experience your warmth and the core of who you are. Second, a moment when quiet takes over allows you to access reference points in your life (as described above). And third, when music making is not at its strongest in a rehearsal, accessing quiet provides a momentary point of clarity where changes of direction can be employed, whether a change of rehearsal technique or an altering of the course of the rehearsal.

- **Story the ensemble** – Many times, shifting responsibility to individual choir members is necessary and can be a very powerful technique in rehearsal. This can be done using the text of the piece. If you have selected a piece with a text (or music) that has profound connection to your life events, then you can use that text to ask individual members to search within their own life stories and sing the piece from that perspective. Ultimately, in all music making situations, it is the singers' responsibility to make these journeys for each piece they perform.

- **Practice quiet in your daily routine** – This is one of the most valuable rehearsal preparation suggestions I can make. It stands to reason that you will not be able to access quiet if you have not had experience in accessing quiet. Some ways to do this include journaling, meditating, or taking walks, as well as Yoga, QiGong, and Tai Chi. Or even allowing time within your day just to sit quietly will form a powerful ritual that will begin to bond you and your being to quiet. As conductors, this ability is necessary when we raise our hands to begin rehearsal. It is at that moment when our inner space needs to be calm. And that calm can only be learned through the practicing of quiet.

The Magic of Listening

Perhaps no other tool is so compelling in rehearsal than the tool of listening. Ensembles love to know they are being listened to! Conductors who are involved in listening in the most profound ways compel a connection between themselves and their singers that is at times very deep. In its purest sense, listening creates a magic, a serenity, and an honesty in the rehearsal room that transforms and elevates the music making experience for all in the room. Listening cements the connection between singers and conductor in the most meaningful way.

If we believe that rehearsals are profoundly moving events, then we need to understand that such profound moments are created from the synergy that listening provides. The ability to listen in life teaches us profound things about life, and listening while making music will lead to powerful connections within ourselves.

Be Not Afraid

Fear in many forms sabotages the rehearsal process. Access to each singer's individual "secret place" cannot be realized if the conductor is fearful of some aspect of the music making process, whether it be a fear of not being able to come up with an immediate answer to a music problem, or a fear of not knowing the score, or a fear of growing apart from the ensemble, or a fear that is brought into the rehearsal from life.

Trusting and caring are effective antidotes to rehearsal fears. We cannot have such fears in rehearsal, for they prevent us from being whole in front of our singers. Fear, when it is present in any form in rehearsal, adds a palatable stench or even darkness to the energy and overall atmosphere of the rehearsal. Rehearsals should be places of great luminescence, light, and brilliance. An absence of fear will ensure that this is truly the case.

Chapter 12

The Energy Dynamic of the Rehearsal

Pacing and Energy

The soul of the human species is sometimes called the *collective unconscious*, but it is not that. It is the soul of humankind. Your soul is a miniature of the soul of the human species. It is a micro of a macro. It has as much energy and power. As part of the micro, you have all the power of the macro calibrated to the individual form of certain frequencies. You form collective energies that help the whole evolve, although they are not themselves souls, and do not have souls. In between the macro and the micro are the various experiences afforded the individual human soul learning within a group, participating in group evolution, such as the evolution of your country, your religion, and the individual personal experiences that comprise the human experience. (p. 117)

—Gary Zukav
in *The Seat of the Soul*

Allow yourself to become aware of what you feel. Give yourself permission to choose the most positive behavior in each moment. As you discharge negative energy consciously and set your intentions according to what your heart tells you, as you challenge and release your fears and choose to heal, you align your personality with your soul and move toward becoming a being of Light, fully whole and empowered and inwardly secure. Humbleness, forgiveness, charity and love, all gifts of the spirit, take root and bloom, and you draw to yourself the Universe's greatest gift: human beings with open hearts. (p. 248)

—Gary Zukav
in *The Seat of the Soul*

It goes without saying that spiritual writing is not about God. It is about the human longing for all that God can mean. It may be possible to be an atheist, but it is probably impossible, once alive, not to respond to the presence of something—soul, spirit, life force, you name it—that the human core from which the cry of anguish and the whoop of joy emanate. The sheer instinct to record these experiences of extremity is, in itself, a spiritual act. (p. xxiii)

Patricia Hampl
in Philip Zaleski, *Spiritual Writing*

Man in his being is derived from, attended by, and directed to the being of community. For man to be means to be with other human beings. His existence is coexistence. He can never attain fulfillment, or sense meaning, unless it is shared, unless it pertains to other human beings. (p. 45)

—Abraham Joshua Heschel
in *Who Is Man?*

Let [the person] who cannot be alone beware of community. Let [the person] who is not in community beware of being alone. (p. 78)

—Dietrich Bonhoffer
in *Life Together*

The use of energy within a rehearsal is one of the more difficult concepts to master. Many conductors tend to "over-energize" rehearsals to compensate for singers who do not put enough of their own energies into the musical processes at hand. But when a conductor takes this approach in rehearsal, such energy outlay usually results in rapidly diminishing returns. Instead, you must strike a balance between work propelled by energy and work propelled through the use of center and solitude.

Pacing a rehearsal is all about the careful and methodological balance of energy and silence. Both should be strategically used within any rehearsal; they empower each other and should be used only to shore up the quality that seems to be missing within an ensemble on a given day.

Reading the Room

Reading the room is one of the most important "gifts" a conductor can possess. When you walk into a rehearsal space, you should be aware and sensitive to the amount of energy in the room at the moment. Rehearsal rooms that are filled with energetic singers demand one approach to rehearsal, and rooms that are filled with singers who are relatively quiet demand another type of rehearsal.

Generally, it is wise to adopt the opposite "energy" as the choir. Energetic choirs require more contemplative conductors, while quiet ensembles at times need an energy "transfusion" that causes them to be more alive in rehearsal. You must be sensitive to the energy needs of your ensemble, both at the start of a rehearsal and throughout the rehearsal process itself. Conductors who are not sensitive to ensemble energies usually conduct rehearsals that seem to be difficult to move forward.

Energy Generated through Awareness

Over the years I have come to believe that energy within rehearsal comes through a total awareness of oneself in a space. Awareness in and of itself creates vibrant energy and is much more powerful within the rehearsal process than energies of the "nervous" type. Awareness of oneself and others seems to build a vibrancy that is quite different from various neurotic energies (i.e., energies for energy's sake).

When you walk into a rehearsal room aware and alive, the perception of that energy is extremely powerful within the choir. It transfers with an intensity into each individual singer within the ensemble and creates a vibrancy that invigorates choral sound in an unmistakable way. On the other hand, to walk into a room and not be aware of the energy within the room will most certainly doom a rehearsal—or at least make it harder to achieve any musical goals. Rehearsals should always be about maintaining inward and outward awarenesses. That, in turn, will create vibrant, exciting, and productive rehearsals.

Efficient But Unaware Rehearsals

In contemporary psychological language, efficiency is a primary mode of denial....Two insanely dangerous consequences result from raising efficiency to the level of an independent principle. First, it favors short-term thinking—no looking ahead, down the line; and it produces insensitive feeling—no looking around at the life values being lived so efficiently. Second, means becomes ends; that is, doing something becomes the full justification of doing regardless of what you do. (p. 39)

—James Hillman
in *Kinds of Power*

As good teachers weave the fabric that joins them with students and subjects, the heart is the loom on which the threads are tied, the tension held, the shuttle flies, and the fabric is stretched tight. Small wonder, then, that teaching tugs at the heart, opens the heart, even breaks the heart—and the more one loves teaching, the more heartbreaking it can be. The courage to teach is the courage to keep one's heart open in those very moments when the heart is asked to hold more than it is able so that the teacher and students and subject can be woven into the fabric of community that learning and living require. (p. 11)

The culture of disconnection that undermines teaching and learning is driven partly by fear. But it is also driven out by Western commitment to thinking in polarities, a thought that elevates disconnection into an intellectual virtue. This way of thinking is so embedded in our culture that we rarely escape it, even when we try. (p. 61)

—Parker J. Palmer
in *The Courage to Teach*

A prevalent problem in rehearsal technique is the overly efficient rehearsal. I have known many conductors who are incredible teachers whose rehearsals are planned down to the last second, with each segment of the rehearsal meticulously timed. The choir efficiently moves from one musical/rehearsal objective to another—certainly a study in efficiency. But there is no time in their rehearsal plan for the human aspect of "living" the music. There is no time for the music to become a part of each member of the choir.

The necessary inward journey is generally not part of the rehearsal plan. The rehearsal becomes an assembly line of rehearsal techniques and teaching procedures that tend to have a chilling effect upon the choral ensemble sound. Words such as "cold," "detached," "disconnected," and "aloof" are often used by choir members to describe a rehearsal. Most choral singers who live in such a world also complain that they feel no connection with the music—and more importantly, little or no connection with the conductor. A balance is needed between the rehearsal paradigm and the knowledge gained from score study and analysis.

PART FOUR
OTHER CONDUCTORS' INFLUENCES
UPON THE REHEARSAL PROCESS

Chapter 13

The Door into Musical Style

Timbre Preferences

In considering the theory of possible timbre preferences of a conductor based upon information gained from a standardized measure, such as the *Instrument Timbre Preference Test*,[1] it seems logical that if a conductor has timbrel preferences that are left unrecognized or undeveloped, then the choir will tend to sing only the timbrel preferences of the conductor. My experience seems to indicate that this is true. Thus, you should consider as a part of rehearsal technique that your ensemble may have a timbre preference, and if left unattended, the result will be monochromatic performances by the ensemble. An awareness of the timbre preferences of your ensemble can inform both your pedagogy and your rehearsal technique.

---

1 Edwin Gordon's *Instrument Timbre Preference Test* (GIA, 1984), which requires less than thirty minutes to administer, objectively assists students nine years of age and older in selecting an appropriate brass or woodwind instrument to learn to play.

Gaining Insight into Your Ensemble's Timbre Preferences

Consider administering the *Instrument Timbre Preference Test* by Edwin Gordon (GIA) to your ensemble. This test will yield an instrument timbre preference and also provide a rank ordering of the timbre preferences for each individual. Time and future predictive validity studies will need to be conducted to validate the theory of using a standardized measure, but in my experience there seems to be a great deal of indirect validity in using such a test for this new purpose.

After you have administered the test and the results are known for each singer in your ensemble, study the results for any unusual or unique trends among all the singers and within each section. For example, you might find the soprano section has a preference for oboe/bassoon timbre. If so, then you need to work with them not only to hear other timbres, but also to be on guard for their default timbre—oboe and bassoon timbres embedded within their sound! Armed with this information, you can incorporate into your pedagogy an awareness that other timbres do in fact exist. The timbrel world of the choir can be expanded through this type of "awareness" pedagogy.

Implications for Musical Style

Timbre has everything to do with musical style. Embodied within the vocal timbres of a choir are the resonances of language via vowels and consonants, which are the carriers of choral style. Choral style should be achieved through diction choices and sound choral ensemble diction pedagogy. And, it should be considered that one's timbre palate can be expanded and deepened through the pedagogy of a rehearsal.

Choral ensemble sounds that are appropriate to a particular style period can be most efficiently achieved through the resonance qualities of the vowel. If your ensemble's timbre preferences are not in line with the stylistic resonance of a work, then you might find it difficult to achieve a stylistically accurate and beautiful performance. The resonances of language are the carriers of musical style. If you leave your singers to their own devices, then they will sing their timbre preference, which may or may not align itself with the musical style at hand. An understanding of the resonance of each stylistic period can be derived from exemplary recordings and musicological research and study. A recommended list of recordings for study follows.

Title/Contents: *Blessed Spirit: Music of the Soul's Journey*. Gregorian chant, Gustav Holst, John Sheppard, Heinrich Schutz, Russian traditional, Sir Henry Walford Davies, and American Spirituals (Collegium).
Ensemble: The Choir of Clare College, Cambridge
Conductor: Timothy Brown
Vowel Shape: Tall/narrow and round
Comments: This is a wonderful recording because it presents a wide variety of choral ensemble colors in one package. I find the sound of Timothy Brown's choir to be flexible, resonant, and stylistically appropriate. Highly recommended.

Title: *Our American Journey* (Teldec)
Ensemble: Chanticleer
Vowel Shape: Tall/narrow
Title: Five Centuries of Choral Music (Clarion)
Ensemble: The Swedish Radio Choir
Conductor: Eric Ericson
Vowel Shape: Tall/narrow
Comments: This stunning recording should be in every musician's choral library. The recording covers five centuries of choral music. Despite the various musical styles, the choral sound remains within the realm of tall, narrow sounds.

Title: *Voices from a Sixteenth-Century Cathedral* (Angel)
Ensemble: The Roger Wagner Chorale
Conductor: Roger Wagner
Vowel Shape: Round
Comments: This recording presents the model for round, resonential sounds in choral music.

Title: *Maurice Duruflé: The Complete Music for Choir* (BIS CD-602)
Ensemble: St. Jacob's Chamber Choir
Conductor: Gary Garden
Vowel Shape: Tall/narrow
Comments: Without doubt, this is one of the most stunning recordings of the choral music of Duruflé. While the choir sings with a beautifully focused and in-tune sound, their tone possesses warmth and flexibility. Vowel colors employed in this recording are exceptional.

Title/Contents: *Sacred and Profane* (Harmonia Mundi, HMC 901734) Benjamin Britten, Edward Elgar, Frederick Delius, and Charles Stanford
Ensemble: RIAS Kammerchor
Conductor: Marcus Creed
Vowel Shape: Round bias
Comments: This wonderful choir, while it possesses a very lean sound, crosses the boundary slightly as far as choral tone is concerned. The ensemble maintains a stylistic integrity for this English music but adds a slightly rounder vowel shape to its production.

Title: *Rachmaninoff: Vespers* (Telarc)
Ensemble: Robert Shaw Festival Singers
Conductor: Robert Shaw
Vowel Shape: Round
Comments: This recording represents some of Shaw's most beautiful work. It is an invaluable recording for the study of round, resonant choral sounds.

Title: *Motets of the Romantic Era* (Cantate)
Ensemble: Westfalische Kantorei
Conductor: Wilhelm Ehmann
Vowel Shape: Round
Comments: Of all the recordings available, this is the one that demonstrates the ideal "romantic" sound. Although it is difficult to find, it is worth the effort.

Title: *Lauridsen: The Complete Choral Cycles* (Fresh Water Records, FWCL 105-2)
Ensemble: Choral Cross Ties
Conductor: Bruce Browne
Vowel Shape: Tall/narrow and round
Comments: This recording demonstrates an ensemble with a flexible sound concept that adapts to various styles of literature.

Title/Contents: *Illumina* (Collegium, COLCD 125) Gregorian chant, William Byrd, Hildegard von Bingen, and Alexander Grechaninov
Ensemble: The Choir of Clare College, Cambridge
Conductor: Timothy Brown
Vowel Shape: Tall/narrow and round
Comments: This CD is a particularly good resource because it presents not only a wide variety of styles but contrasting choral colors.

Title: *Tarik O'Regan*: *Voices* (Collegium, COLCD 130)
Ensemble: The Choir of Clare College, Cambridge
Conductor: Timothy Brown
Vowel Shape: Tall/narrow
Comments: This superb recording should be a must have for all conductors who are students of choral sound. Most noteworthy from a sound perspective on this recording is the consistently produced tall, narrow vowel sounds. On this recording, one should note the different "brighter" vowels in English-speaking choirs. Of particular note is the beautiful "ah" vowel of this choir. The recording also represents on-the-breath singing.

Title: *Love Is Spoken Here* (CFN 0507-2)
Ensemble: Mormon Tabernacle Choir
Conductor: Craig Jessop and Mack Wilberg
Vowel Shape: Round
Comments: This beautiful CD is a wonderful example of round sounds used to lyrical advantage, especially in the context of folk music. I highly recommend track 7. One should make note of the remarkable consistency of vowel sounds in this 300+ member choir.

Title: *A Ceremony of Carols** (Marquis 81327)
Ensemble: The Toronto Children's Chorus
Conductor: Jean Ashworth Bartle
Vowel Shape: Tall/narrow
Comments: All conductors of children's choirs should use this recording as their benchmark of beautifully produced children's singing. The production on this recording is outstanding; vowel sounds are always resonant, free, and on the breath.

Title: *Light of the Spirit* (Collegium, CSACD 902)
Ensemble: The Choir of Clare College, Cambridge
Conductor: Timothy Brown
Vowel Shape: Varied
Comments: Of all the recordings recommended for further listening, this comes with my highest recommendation. The two-CD set covers all styles from Gregorian chant to Heinrich Schutz to Györgi Ligeti to Norman Luboff. There are few recordings that dare to tackle such a broad range of music styles. What is unique about this recording is that each composer is treated with stylistic integrity with regard to sound. This recording is a must-own for choral conductors.

Title: *Parish Anthems* (Gamut Recordings)
Ensemble: The Choir of Clare College, Cambridge
Conductor: Timothy Brown
Vowel Shape: Tall/narrow
Comments: The sounds on these traditional hymns, by and large, employ a relatively tall and narrow approach to singing. As always, the choral singing is exquisite and serves as a great aural model for conductors.

Title: *Dreams** (Ondine, ODE 786-2)
Ensemble: Tapiola Choir
Conductor: Erkki Pohjola, Osmo Vänskä
Vowel Shape: Tall/narrow
Comments: This is probably one of the most outstanding examples of what is achievable with children's voices. The vowel concept is remarkable for pitch clarity and color. Production is phenomenally consistent and at all times breathtaking.

Title: *The Angel Choir and the Trumpeter** (Eastern Mennonite University)
Ensemble: Shenandoah Valley Children's Choir
Conductor: Julia White
Vowel Shape: Tall/narrow
Comments: This recording of Christmas pieces with brass is an example of a natural children's sound with a consistent approach to vowel sound.

Title: *1994 England and Scotland Tour**
Ensemble: Indianapolis Children's Choir
Conductor: Henry Leck
Vowel Shape: Round
Comments: While it is dangerous at times to categorize sounds, the sounds on this recording are perhaps some of the most stunningly natural children's sounds that I have heard on any recording.

Title: *Hear through the Ages** (Mark Custom Recording, 3185-MCD)
Ensemble: Piedmont Choirs
Conductor: Robert Geary
Vowel Shape: Round
Comments: The works on this recording are representative of a rounder approach to resonance applied to a children's choir, used with great artistry.

Title: *Untraveled Worlds** (Pelagos International, PEL 1004)
Ensemble: Chorus Angelicus
Conductor: Paul Halley
Vowel Shape: Tall/narrow
Comments: This beautiful recording is another for resonance study. The sound is open, free, and resonant. There is also appropriate variation in between styles. This recording is a beautiful model. Of particular note is the recording of Orlando Gibbons's "Drop, Drop Slow Tears."

Title: *My Heart Soars** (Marquis Classics, ERAD 199)
Ensemble: Toronto Children's Chorus
Conductor: Jean Ashworth Bartle
Vowel Shape: Tall/narrow
Comments: The remarkably consistent and beautiful sound of the Toronto Children's Chorus is presented on this exquisite recording through a variety of musical styles. Of special note is the singing of the sopranos. Vowel concepts on this recording are worth studying. Bartle achieves a remarkable legato.

Title: *Closing the Century** (Amabile, AM 0020 2231)
Ensemble: Jitro Czech Children's Chorus
Conductor: Jiri Skopal
Vowel Shape: Tall/narrow
Comments: This recording is a stunning example of a children's choir singing with a consistent resonance concept applied to varied choral literature. Vowel concepts on this recording are particularly noteworthy.

Title: *2002 Spring Concert**
Ensemble: St. Louis Children's Chorus
Conductor: Barbara Berner
Vowel Shape: Round
Comments: Of all the recordings suggested on this list, it is perhaps the sound that comes closest to my personal biases concerning tone in children's choirs. The conductor elicits exquisitely natural vocal production with a consistent approach to vowels, all supported with a remarkable honesty of expression within the tone. I highly recommend this recording.

*Denotes a recording featuring a children's choir.

Chapter 14

Breathing New Life into Renaissance Choral Music

Gerald Custer

I have come to realize over the years that a healthy mistrust of written music is the only proper starting point. The page doesn't mean what it seems. It's only a beginning (sight) not an ending (sound)…To understand what I am attempting here, realize that I am trying to balance two antithetical worlds at once—those of eye and ear—and in this case, ear must always triumph not only in the notes, but in the written text where a living voice must be sounding for you to respond in kind. (p. xxii)

—Alice Parker
in *The Anatomy of Melody*

To say that Renaissance harmony is merely the result of combining melodic strands is plainly absurd, even in a contrapuntal texture, since it suggests that the composer had no consideration for the vertical aspect of what he wrote. It would be nearer the truth to say that in sixteenth century polyphony the harmonic progression is directed by the counterpoint, whereas in a wholly tonal composer like Bach, the reverse applies. When it comes to cadences, however, Palestrina and Bach are on something like equal footing, because limited and universally accepted choice of chord progression (the same for both composers) ensures that harmonic considerations must take precedence. The cadence has always been recognized as a door through which music passed from modality to tonality. (p. 21)

—Malcolm Boyd
in "Structural Cadences in the Sixteenth
Century Motet," *The Music Review*

The music of the sixteenth century was for the greatest part conceived within the framework of the church modes. In it we find neither tonality or atonality in the later sense of the terms. Yet we meet with phenomena—indeed, with whole repertories—which do not fit into the traditional system of the eight modes but show, often, in an astonishing manner, prefigurations of tonal, and even atonal thinking. (p. 1)

—Edward Lowinsky
in *Tonality and Atonality in Sixteenth Century Music*

What did Renaissance choral music actually sound like? This question, perhaps above all others, is the continuing challenge that bedevils conductors and singers engaged in recreating this repertoire as faithfully as possible. It is also a question that, sadly, admits of no easy answer, for choral music during the Renaissance was anything but monolithic. Instead, it presented a wide-ranging collection of genres, including such disparate repertoire as the motets of des Pres and Victoria, the chansons of Lassus and Jannequin, the masses of Palestrina and Byrd, the anthems of Batten and Tallis, and the madrigals of Marenzio and Morley.

Yet even if it is physically impossible to determine with absolute certainty the precise sound of choral music as it was first performed in the Renaissance, the presence in relatively large quantities of one particular source material offers an important insight for choral musicians seeking to meet this challenge: namely, the existence of printed scores for much of this choral repertoire.

What did these scores look like? What did they contain—and omit? Why do they now appear so vastly different from their original form in most modern editions? What needs to be done (or undone) to recover their original look? And by extension, what is required to rediscover the sound ideal that Renaissance singers had in their ears when originally singing from them? What consequences for articulation, phrasing, creation of line, and texture arise from such an investigation? And what is the most effective way to share this information with singers in the time-constrained context of a typical rehearsal?

Salient questions all. This chapter will answer them in two ways: (1) by articulating fundamental principles to keep in mind when approaching this repertoire, and (2) by demonstrating their practical value by illustrating their application in preparing the score and a rehearsal plan for the motet *O Magnum Mysterium* by Tómas Luis de Victoria.[1]

The Look of Renaissance Choral Music

The Renaissance was the first era in music history in which choral music was widely available in printed form. Until 1501, when Venetian Ottaviano Petrucci leveraged Johann Gutenberg's 1452 combination of movable type and printing press

---

1 Reference *Metric Flexibility in the Performance of Renaissance Choral Music* by Gerald Custer (Chicago: GIA Publications, 2008) for in-depth exploration of these concepts.

technologies to publish the chanson collection known as *Harmonice Musices Odhecaton A*, music had been captured and transmitted in manuscript form by generations of anonymous monastic copyists. It was something made manually (literally, *per manus*, "by hand"). With a final turn of the screw mechanism that drove his printing press toward the waiting paper, Petrucci literally changed the face of music forever.

So what did these printed scores look like? What notational conventions did they follow, and which did they omit? Fortunately, modern choral conductors no longer have to speculate about answering such questions. The volume of existing printed versions of choral music in the Renaissance era speaks with clarity and a high degree of consistency to both.

Printed Renaissance choral music appeared in formats that would be alien and unfamiliar to most choral singers today. Rather than the ubiquitous multiple-voice "open score" or "choral score" format favored by today's publishers, Renaissance choral music was not actually printed in a score format of any sort. Instead, it was typically given to singers in one of two arrangements: part-book or choir-book form.

Choir-book form likely developed first, presumably as an extension of the format in which the chant manuscripts used by Medieval monks in daily worship were presented. Early printed choir-books emerged from this heritage and, like them, were often dimensionally oversized for easy visual access by a group of multiple singers (thereby perhaps requiring fewer printings). **Printed choir-books** differed from modern scores in one important respect: they placed each voice part in a separate location on a single pair of pages, as in **Figure 14-1.**

As manufacturing costs for paper, type, and presses inevitably declined, a second approach to music printing emerged: publication in **part-book form,** which presented each voice part on a separate page, with those pages bound together in a single volume. This new approach offered several advantages: individual parts could be printed with greater accuracy and clarity; multiple movements of longer compositions could be printed on successive pages; and individual singers could have their own copies of music from which to perform. An example of **part-book printing** is shown in **Figure 14-2**.

Figure 14-1. Example of choir-book printing.

The opening Kyrie of Josquin's *Missa de Beata Virgine*, written during the reign of Pope Leo X (1513–21). The superius part is at the top of the left-hand page, with the altus part directly below it; the tenor part is printed at the top of the right-hand page, with the bassus directly below it. Music printed in this fashion required multiple impressions: one for the staves, a second for the notes, and a third for the text.

Figure 14-2. Example of part-book printing.

The cantus voice of the opening movement (Kyrie–Christe–Kyrie) of Palestrina's *Missa Papae Marcelli* (1567), taken from the part-book of the same name for his *Second Book of Masses*, published in 1598. Note the significant improvement in print quality achieved by the part-book method, just a few generations after the previous example by Josquin.

As these figures illustrate, some standard notational elements are common to music printed in either choir-book or part-book format:

- Five-line staves
- Key signatures
- Time signatures
- Durational indications of both pitch and silence, and text underlay

At the same time, a number of traditional notational elements are surprisingly missing:

- No tempo indications
- No dynamics
- No articulation marks of any kind
- No ties used to combine different durations (although the dotted-note convention is clearly evident)

Perhaps the most glaring omission is the absence of any indication of mensuration in the music. There are no bar lines to either identify or aggregate measures of the musical fabric; no visual cues to imply how individual durations are to be grouped; no compositional signals to suggest which pitches might be expected to receive greater or lesser degrees of weight in performance. As a result, the impact of concepts such as "downbeat," "upbeat," "syncope," and "agogic accent"—all of which presuppose a constant unit pulse that regularly recurs in equal-sized groups—is simply not possible in this musical context. In the absence of this important notational marker (the bar line), such concepts are totally foreign to the musical thinking of this period. They simply did not exist in the ear of the Renaissance age.

If this is so, then some other aesthetic principles must have guided composers and performers of this music. What were they? What provided the fundamental philosophical basis for Renaissance choral repertoire?

The Renaissance Musical Aesthetic

No musical era or style exists in a vacuum. Past practices almost always serve as a prologue to be either creatively reframed or rejected outright, and Renaissance choral music is no exception to this rule. Its roots lie first in the proclamation of the Divine Word by the Church in its daily worship and then in the explication of human words in the secular genres that follow shortly after. It is probably no coincidence that the term used to identify early texted music, *motetus*, shares linguistic origins with the French for "word," *mot*.

The primacy of text and its immediate communication to listeners are central aspects of the aesthetic that governed the music of the Renaissance. Textual primacy drives the prevailing linear, story-telling orientation of this repertoire; textual primacy gives rise to the word painting that abounds in much of it; and textual primacy provides the rationale for that most familiar of all Renaissance composition practices: the introduction of new musical material to match the appearance of each fresh line of text.

At the same time, creative expression in the Renaissance was closely linked to a sincere desire on the part of its intellectual class to restore and follow Greek artistic ideals, especially in drama, dance, and music. When one accepts the Greek premise that drama is established and propelled by conflict, a second key to the Renaissance musical aesthetic comes into focus—the central role contrast plays in creating texture at multiple levels and in multiple dimensions in this music, whether by voice pairing, register and timbre shifts, sectionalization produced by changes in textural density, or similar devices.

But it is the final issue identified by examining notational conventions in Renaissance choral music that concerns us most, precisely because it arises from what is missing in the printed music rather than what is explicitly present there. This is how best to reconcile the enduring influence of dance, with its repeated alternations between patterns of *arsis et thesis*, of stress and release, with the marked absence of bar lines or any other visible system of sensible metrication in this repertoire.

It seems reasonable to believe that those who first composed this music followed a set of guiding principles when performing it. But what were they? And what is the most effective—and least disruptive—way to recapture, present, and apply them in our own time?

Metric Flexibility

Since 1900, numerous attempts have been made to recapture the original look, feel, and sound of Renaissance choral music. Musicologist Friederich Blume (1893–1975), in his pioneering early music series *Das Chorwerk*, placed bar lines between the staves of choral scores, leaving individual lines unbarred and eliminating tied notes altogether, in an approach known as *mensurstrich* notation.

The American conductor Leonard Van Camp (1934–2003) proposed a radically different solution, placing bar lines in each voice part independent of one another in what he called "VariaBar" notation.

In recent years, some conductors have questioned whether Renaissance choral repertoire even contains internal phrase groups unaligned with the prevailing pulse. Those who believe it does favor the so-called "microrhythm" approach; those who do not prefer to emphasize the "oratorical" dimension instead.

Each perspective has its merits, but the passion with which their adherents advance these opposing points of view tends to fracture the discussion, which fosters divisiveness and mutual exclusion. What is needed is an approach that acknowledges the best features of each and synthesizes them. Fortunately, such an approach has been developed and serves as the basis of this chapter's discussion: **metric flexibility.**

Metric flexibility is a way of seeing and hearing that enables modern performers to experience and respond to Renaissance choral music in as close a manner as possible to the intent of the composers who first created it. It recognizes that the primary organization of this music is in the metrical dimension—the deliberate grouping of successive durations in units that can be smaller or larger than the *tactus*, or prevailing pulse. At the same time, it also recognizes that these durational groupings must be informed by the natural syllabic stresses of individual words, by the larger oratorical impulse of the entire text (or significant portions of it), and by the period's accepted aesthetic values, especially dramatic contrast.

Metric flexibility organizes durational sequences in individual vocal lines by viewing them as independent phrases that each have their own unique, inherent metrication. The relative size of these metrication groups often changes during the course of the composition, and frequently metrication decisions do not align with the prevailing mensuration signatures given by the composer at the beginning of the work.

Yet metric flexibility does not focus exclusively on one end of the durational scale at the expense of the other. Unlike "microrhythm," which considers durational groupings only *smaller* than the prevailing *tactus*, metric flexibility recognizes that durations can be grouped in sense units that are either smaller *or larger* than the stated unit of pulse. It accommodates durational divisions and combinations within the same stated metric framework.

Perhaps of greater interest is that more than five years of personal experience testing and refining the implementation of this approach in the real world conclusively validates the premise that metric flexibility renders Renaissance choral music more directly accessible and more easily sung by modern vocal ensembles, producing performances that are fresher, more energized, more nuanced, and more vibrant for performers and audiences alike.

Although it may be tempting to think that metric flexibility can be reduced to simply applying specific techniques or following a set of predetermined rules, experience suggests that unreflecting dogmatism seldom yields flexible or musically satisfying results in the end. Ultimately, metric flexibility rests on five principles from which its particular practices and rules are subsequently derived:

1. **Textual primacy** – Because choral music is by definition *texted* music (and the Renaissance an era more text obsessed than many), the inherent properties of text must always direct and control metrication decisions. The relative weight of individual syllables creates the shape of specific words; the grammatical/functional importance of individual words dictates their relative weight within a specific phrase; the oratorical/meaningful impact of individual phrases establishes their relative importance in the larger meta-context (period or section). Anything that obscures, diminishes, or contradicts the primacy of text—at any layer in the musical fabric—is to be avoided.

2. **Independent linearity** – Renaissance choral music had neither bar lines nor multi-part scores; regular recurrent equal-sized units of measured time were foreign to the eyes and ears of the age. Consequently, metrication decisions must always propel the individual vocal line forward. Agogic stress (a concept unknown to Renaissance composers) must never impede the organic motion of the individual line, which is (except at cadence points) constantly forward. Each voice part must be approached and analyzed on its own merits. The ingrained tyranny of the bar line (a habit of feeling virtually instinctive to modern ears) should be consciously resisted at all costs. Metrication must always reinforce forward linearity.

3. **Embrace of contrast** – Renaissance artists strove to recapture what they understood to be Greek aesthetic ideals, including the important role of conflict, contrast, and change as key agents for creating and sustaining drama. Changes of vocal texture, surface rhythm density, rate of harmonic change, tonal/modal center, vocal register, timbre, and melodic motive—aligned with the sense of the text and the introduction of new textual material—are frequently accompanied by corresponding changes in metrication. Metrication decisions must always align with and support compositional devices that create or highlight musical contrast and dramatic conflict.

4. ***Arsis et thesis*** – Early theorists spoke about the gathering and subsequent release of energy, concepts called *potential* and *kinetic energy* in physics but known to the Renaissance as *arsis* and *thesis*. These came from the primary gestures in dance: raising the foot (a relatively weightless gesture that gathered energy) was called *arsis*; placing the foot (a weighted gesture that released energy) was *thesis*.

   Yet just as inspiration and expiration are two components of the single unified act of breathing, *arsis et thesis*—or *anacrusis* and *crusis*, to use their musical names—are inextricably linked. One inevitably leads to the other. And just as breath cycles can differ in length, *anacrusis* and *crusis* can be established by more than one size of duration. The initial anacrustic breath that precedes phonation at the start of a work, and subsequent anacrustic durations (or groups) that gather energy that is later released, must both be explicitly included in making metrication decisions. Each must be recognized for what it is: an inherent part of the musical flow with its own discrete metrical value.

5. **Cadential inevitability** – Despite its missing bar lines, Renaissance choral music is highly goal-oriented. It does not wander mindlessly; it always moves toward oratorical closure, seeking a point of ultimate repose. Cadences, both internal and final, function as keystones of the musical arch of Renaissance vocal lines, and their structural importance is frequently reinforced by a shift in metrical emphasis, common to groups built from larger durations or meta-rhythms.

   Good analytical practice, practical experience, and common sense all suggest that the best approach to preparing a Renaissance choral score—after first analyzing the text from which it springs and enumerating the implicit compositional expectations it creates—begins with identifying its cadences and understanding their metrical implications.

It is these steps that are considered in the next part of this chapter.

From Words to Music

The counter-Reformation composer Tómas Luis de Victoria (1548–1611) published his motet *O Magnum Mysterium* in Venice in 1572 before returning to his native Spain. The text originally served as the fourth responsorial at the monastic office of Matins on Christmas morning, and is built from three sense units plus a concluding Alleluia, as shown in **Figure 14-3**.

Figure 14-3. Breakdown of text from *O Magnum Mysterium*.

O magnum mysterium	**A**1	O great mystery
et admirabile sacramentum,	A2	and wonderful sacrament,
Ut animalia viderent Dominum natum	**B**1	That animals see the Lord born
jacentem in praesepio.	B2	lying in a manger.
O beata Virgo,	**C**1	O blessed Virgin,
cujus viscera meruerunt	C2	whose womb merited
portare Dominum Jesum Christum.	C3	carrying the Lord Jesus Christ.
Alleluia!	C4	Alleluia!

The text's narrative arc parallels the Incarnation event as it unfolds. First, it contemplates heavenly mysteries (A). Next, it relates a concrete and earthly scene: barnyard animals silently witnessing a birth (B). Finally, it identifies two particular individuals, Mary and Jesus, who nevertheless embody various pairs of complementary archetypes: human and divine, female and male, parent and child, old and young, promise and fulfillment, temporal and eternal (C). What a wealth of meaning and scope of action is contained in these twenty-five words!

Each sense unit of the text has a discrete shape, created by the combined impact of syllabic stresses within words, word stresses within phrase, and phrase stresses within sense units. These multiple levels, and the impact of their superimposition, can be depicted as shown in the graphic in **Figure 14-4**:

Figure 14-4. Levels of sense units of the text.

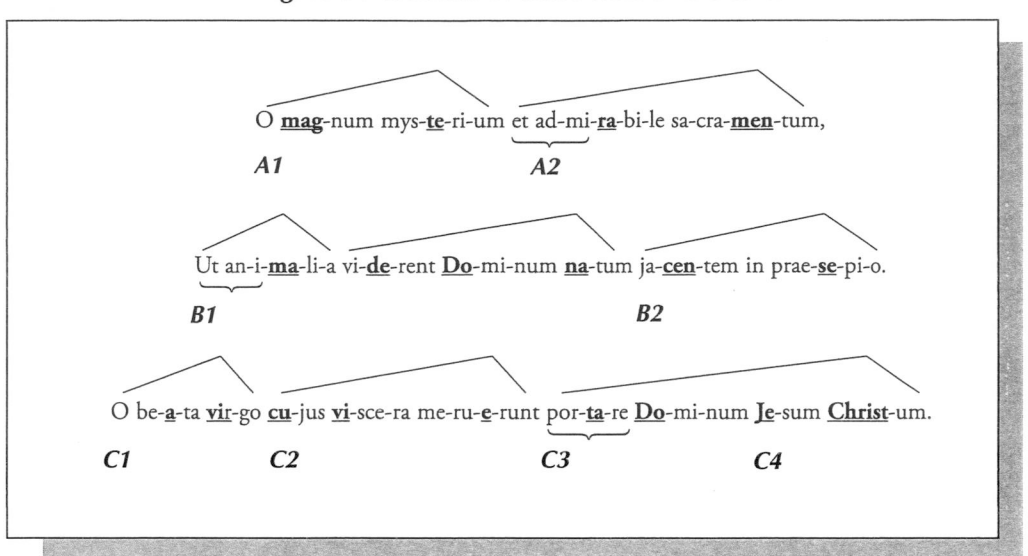

Although each phrase has its own unique peak, these individual phrases jointly "belong forward" to the primary climax of each sense unit. Multiple syllables that act as extended pickups, or anacrustic groups, have been bracketed in the graphic above. Charting the text in this way is useful when later seeking to establish that Victoria, like any competent composer, recognized and interacted with the expectations created by the text. For example, from the graphic in Figure 14-4, we can deduce the following:

- Each sense unit begins anacrustically, and this anacrustic start is holographic: each phrase except for one begins with either an anacrustic syllable or with durations that jointly function as an anacrustic group.

- Each sense unit peaks penultimately (prior to the last syllable), and this shape is holographic as well, repeated in the shape of each phrase in each sense unit.

- Additive construction is consistently evident—subphrase A2 is longer than A1, B2 longer than B1, C2 longer than C1—and this additive process is holographic: the second part of A1 contains more syllables than the beginning, etc.

- Additive construction is also present at the highest oratorical level: sense unit A is one phrase long, sense unit B is two phrases long (B=A+1), and sense unit C is three phrases in length (C=B+1).

- A single exception to the foregoing patterns is found in the last part of phrase C3, which names the subject of the entire motet text: Jesus Christ.

These insights provide a useful starting point from which to determine what musical elements one would reasonably expect to find in a setting that is responsive to the implicit cues created by the text. Such elements include:

- Three large sections defined by cadences on the words *sacramentum*, *praesepio*, and *Christum*
- A strong final climax on the words *Jesum Christum*
- Phrases and sections that begin anacrustically
- Changes of melodic motive, prevailing meter, vocal texture (or some combination of these) to create contrast with the introduction of each new portion of text
- Musical periods in which later phrases are longer (in total number of measures) than earlier ones

What do we actually find in the music? Turning to Victoria's setting (edition reprinted in **Figure 14-7** at the end of this chapter), we see:

- Four large sections defined by cadences on *sacramentum* (measure 19), *praesepio* (measure 39), *Christum* (measure 53), and *Alleluia* (measure 74)
- Two phrases that appear to begin on the beat, *O magnum* (measures 1–2) and *O beata* (measures 40–41), and two that clearly begin anacrustically, *ut animalia* (measures 19–20) and *Alleluia* (measures 53–54)
- Changes of melodic motive (measures 5, 19, 28, 40, 45 and 54), changes of vocal texture (measures 20, 25, 40, and 54), and a shift of prevailing meter (measure 53) used to create contrast and highlight the introduction of new portions of text

Clearly, Victoria has recognized and interacted with expectations created by the text. But before unlocking the internal metrication of his musical fabric, it is worth examining two departures Victoria makes from these expectations—(1) the sectional organization of the motet and (2) the impact of additive musical construction in creating these sections. At the highest level, Victoria's musical setting breaks into four units, which can be mapped as shown in **Figure 14-5**.

Figure 14-5. Map of Victoria's musical setting of *O Magnum Mysterium.*

Text	Sense Unit	Measures	Length
O magnum...sacramentum	A	mm. 1–19	[19]
Ut animalia...praesepio.	B	mm. 20–39	[20]
O beata Virgo...Jesum Christum	C1–C3	mm. 40–53	[19]
Alleluia!	C4	mm. 54–73	[21]

As the table shows, Victoria builds his motet in four sections of roughly equal length, creating the final one by melismatically extending the last word, *Alleluia.* Although this may appear to violate the literal disposition of the text, it does not contradict its essential spirit: the composer has transformed what had been a textual codetta into an emotional response to the meaningful content of the first three lines—a technique that directly harkens back to the ancient Gregorian chant practice known as *jubilus.*

How are these individual sections constructed? As illustrated in **Figure 14-6**, they are actually built by repeating part or all of the text in all but one of the sense units (repeated phrases are shown in italics).

Figure 14-6. Section construction of Victoria's *O Magnum Mysterium.*

Text	Phrases	Measures	Length
O magnum...sacramentum	A1–A2	mm. 1–9	[9]
O magnum...sacramentum	A1–A2	mm. 10–16	[7]
...et admirabile sacramentum	A2	mm. 17–19	[3]
Ut animalia...Dominum natum	B1–B2	mm. 20–24	[5]
...viderent Dominum natum	B2	mm. 25–27	[3]
Jacentem in praesepio	B3	mm. 28–32	[5]
Jacentem in praesepio	B3	mm. 33–39	[7]
O beata Virgo...meruerunt	C1–C2	mm. 40–47	[8]
Portare Dominum Jesum Christum	C3	mm. 48–53	[5]
Alleluia! (triple meter)	C4	mm. 54–66	[13]
Alleluia! (duple meter)	C4	mm. 67–74	[8]

This is not simply sterile analysis or willful deconstruction. These departures matter. Among other things, they indicate that there are not four but actually eleven significant phrases in this motet—and that at least eight of them begin anacrustically: *et admirabile, ut animalia, viderent Dominum, jacentem* (twice), *portare Dominum,* and *Alleluia* (again, twice).

Further, it seems reasonable to expect that Victoria, a practicing Catholic in what was a religiously contentious age, would not repeat text senselessly. His textual repetitions are purposeful; they are chosen not simply to build multiple sections of equal length, but to reinforce substantial points that underscore two key tenets of his faith: Christ's Incarnation and Divinity. Hence, the emphatic repetitions on the themes "wonderful sacrament," "birth of God," "lying in a manger," and "Alleluia." Repeated phrases, of course, will require vocal intensification, and call for careful attention when assessing their metrication.

Metric Flexibility in Practice

Having unpacked the text and determined its overall structure, identified the musical expectations the text creates, and examined how the composer has interacted with these expectations, you can mark the score to identify and highlight the presence of phrases that do not align with the prevailing stated metrication of the piece.

The first step is to negate the tyranny of the bar line and recover the visual linearity of the music while still making it possible for modern singers to find their places in the score. This requires a compromise; most choirs have neither the time nor the inclination to learn how to read from individual part-books. To facilitate this change, small vertical tick marks have been used in place of the bar lines found in earlier editions (my thanks to Dr. James Jordan for sharing this useful technique with me).

The next step is to search the score to locate and resolve issues created by tied notes. Since this notation was unknown in the Renaissance, ties reflect a decision made by some unseen editor, which reinforces a feel of syncopation and agogic accent (again, constructs foreign to the period) when used across bar lines. So for example, the soprano voice at the cadence on the words *Jesum Christum* originally had a half note at the end of measure 50 and a dotted-quarter note at the end of measure 51. How should this be resolved?

Three rules apply in this situation. The first is that larger groups are to be preferred to smaller ones. The second is a derived application of the first: groups of three durations are preferable to groups of two. The third rule specifically applies to cadences: an increase in metrical group size is often found at cadential approaches to emphasize a drive to closure.

Therefore, the best way to group the durations in the soprano voice at measures 51–52 is to visually reconstitute them as three successive half notes (two tied quarter notes that create a C-natural half note, followed by an A-natural half note, followed by the equivalent of a dotted-quarter note on D and an eighth note on C that comprise the final half-note duration). A horizontal metrication bracket is drawn over these six durations to explicitly highlight their membership in this larger metrical group, equal to a measure of 3/2 time.

In the same way, triple meter groups can be detected in measures 51–52 in the alto voice, measures 51–52 in the tenor, and measures 50–51 in the bass, as the brackets on page three of the edition indicate. Note that the rests in measures 49–50 in the bass have also been bracketed to help the basses "think triple" before singing in that meter in measures 50–51 (not a required practice but a wise one, since Renaissance singers would likely have grouped the rests in just that fashion).

Having dispensed with bar lines and ties, let's next examine the shape of individual words and phrases in the text. One of the greatest benefits of metric flexibility is that it helps prevent distortion of the natural pattern of stress and release at syllable and phrase levels. The most effective way to begin this process is to return to the text apart from the music and pronounce it aloud, noting where these stress/release patterns occur.

Anacrustic groups—a series of three shorter durations followed by either one longer duration or by a melisma on a single syllable (the aural equivalent of a longer duration)—should be marked by a dashed metrication bracket to indicate they are to be sung without any weight. They represent a gathering of energy (an *arsis*) rather than its release. So for example, the syllables *et ad-mi* in measures 4–5 (soprano), measure 5 (alto), measure 12 (tenor), measures 13–14 (alto and bass), and measures 16–17 (all parts) function anacrustically, and are so marked in this edition. The word *portare* in measure 48 (upper three voice parts) functions anacrustically in the same way. But beware: Text that looks anacrustic is not always set that way by composers, as analysis of the phrase *ut animalia* (measures 19–20, tenor and bass; measure 21, soprano and alto) makes clear.

Considering the inherent weight of individual words within phrases is a critical part of implementing metric flexibility. Both the opening phrases of sense units A (*O magnum mysterium*) and C (*O beata Virgo*) are anacrustic in their shape and their grammatical function: in each case, the initial exclamation (*O*) is followed by an adjective (*magnum, beata*), which modifies the noun that serves as the destination point for the phrase (*mysterium, Virgo*). Clearly, both *O*s should be sung without any weight—yet both apparently occur on the beat.

The solution in this case is to recall a fundamental truth of singing: that inspiration precedes phonation; that before we sing, we breathe. Since this is so, the breath before these exclamations can (and should) be assigned a specific metric value of its own. Therefore, one deliberate change—the insertion of an additional *tactus*-length's duration breath—has been made to the first measure of this edition, and the rest in the second half of measure 39 has been "added forward" to construct a triple meter grouping.

The final step in this process is to extend the same approach to smaller phrases and individual words. In most instances, the natural shape created by syllabic stress will be the clue to tease out the appropriate metrication (especially when guided by the rules already mentioned). For example, the dotted-quarter/eighth/quarter pattern used for the second half of the word *admirabile* (soprano, measures 5–6; alto, measure 7; tenor, measures 12–13; bass, measures 14–15) readily emerges as a triple meter group (rule: threes are preferred to twos), or the longer phrase *animalia viderent Dominum* (soprano and alto, measures 21–24) finds its natural shape with all the accents in the appropriate places when viewed as two successive triple meter groups based on half notes (rule: larger is preferred to smaller).

One particular advantage that metric flexibility affords is found in the final section of Victoria's motet. By consistently referencing the *tactus* as the unit of pulse throughout the work, the transitions between duple and triple meter at measures 52–53 (and their reversal at measures 66–67) can be negotiated with relative ease. The durational length (time) of the *tactus* remains the same—only its division is changed, broken into two equal units in duple meter and into three equal units in triple meter (half note = dotted-half note = half note).

Rehearsal Strategies

Conductors who program Renaissance repertoire with their choral ensembles face an array of daunting challenges: it is frequently in a foreign language, often features melismatic passages, is sometimes written in tonal and harmonic frames of reference (modes) unfamiliar to most amateur singers, and is usually presented in editions that do little to help promote the natural linearity or the metric subtlety that first characterized this music. Add to this litany the customary problems of limited rehearsal time and the pressure of performance deadlines, it is frankly surprising any music of the Renaissance is performed at all!

Pre-rehearsal preparation of the score along the lines of the principles given above will go a long way in rendering this music easier to learn—especially if presented in a logical rehearsal sequence that builds growth in musical and vocal confidence as well as conceptual retention of the music. To that end, here are some practical suggestions to consider:

- **Start with the text.** Renaissance music is always text driven, so begin there. Chant the text aloud in an exaggerated fashion, emphasizing individual syllabic stresses and destination points for each phrase, until it makes sense as poetry.

- **Investigate interaction.** Have singers engage the text to identify the expectations it creates for the composer. Then find evidence in the score that the composer has interacted with the text. (Overheads are useful for this.)

- **Rehearse cadences first.** If architecture is frozen music, then music is architecture that dances. Learn the major cadences first, preferably in reverse order so your singers can consistently move from unfamiliar into familiar material.

- **Master metrication separately.** Overcoming bar line tyranny will be easier if using editions that omit them and use metrication brackets instead. Years of singing syncopations, ties, and agogic accents create a legacy not easily overcome. Learn the metrication groups first, singing them on a neutral syllable before adding text.

- **Attend to the attention span.** Fifteen minutes is as long as most of my singers can productively focus on a single task (twenty minutes, max). Short but regular rehearsal segments, when done consistently, pay greater dividends.

- **Circle the wagons.** Especially in music, where orientation is independently linear, it is helpful to periodically have singers rehearse in a series of circles, one per voice part. This is a highly effective way to promote consistent vowels and articulation.

Presented below is a typical rehearsal sequence that incorporates these ideas:

Rehearsal Number	Objectives and Activities
Rehearsal #1	Teach text, focusing on syllabic stress and destination words. Have students show shape of each phrase by air drawing it with finger/arm.
Rehearsal #2	Review text emphases. Learn pitches and durations for final and penultimate cadences on neutral syllable.
Rehearsal #3	Chant text once, checking stresses. Review final and penultimate cadences; learn remaining cadences.
Rehearsal #4	Polish all cadences. Explore text (overheads useful), identify major sense units, and discuss what expectations the text creates. Examine score to find evidence of composer/text interaction.
Rehearsal #5	Rehearse pitch/duration content for last sense unit on neutral syllable.
Rehearsal #6	Review pitch/duration content for last sense unit, rehearse pitch/duration content for the next-to-last sense unit on neutral syllable, and run both sections.
Rehearsal #7	Chant text once through, checking stresses. Rehearse pitch/duration content for opening sense unit on neutral syllable. If possible, run all sections in sequence, even if below performance tempo.
Rehearsal #8	Chant text once through, checking stresses and internal metrication. Add text to music at cadences, and then to entire work.
Rehearsal #9	Rehearse entire work in sectional circles.
Rehearsal #10	Run and polish entire work as needed.

Although original printed scores offer no help in determining tempo and dynamics in Renaissance choral music—one must wait until the Baroque to see such indications on a regular basis—the theoretical writings of the day suggest some useful guidance in both areas. In matters of tempo, the healthy human pulse was considered the benchmark to be observed: equal to a tempo between 60 and 72 beats per minute. In this edition, a suggested tempo of 54 mm. has been given. Since Victoria's motet was likely intended to be sung in a cathedral space, a slower *tactus* would be required to ensure clear text declamation in the reverberation created by typical cathedral building materials and architectural practice.

Regarding dynamics, it may help to remember that human voices naturally increase in amplitude as they phonate at successively faster frequencies, due to the combined impact of registration changes (*passaggii*) and the physical laws of acoustics (as frequency doubles, intensity squares). Consequently, ascending vocal lines naturally crescendo, and descending lines decrescendo. In addition, the prevailing aesthetic of the Renaissance era suggests that dynamic changes used to effect or heighten dramatic contrast—the phrase *O beata virgo* (*ff* in measure 40), for example—are appropriate as well.

A final word: It is worth noting that Renaissance choral music is often challenging when first encountered by modern singers. It seems to speak to us from an unknown place, from a time when all things were freshly discovered and everything seemed possible. Yet as those who spend time with it will readily attest, the delights it extends to both singers and audiences far outweigh the challenges that need to be overcome to successfully perform it.

Figure 14-7. Reprint of Victoria's *O Magnum Mysterium*.

5

O MAGNUM MYSTERIUM
SATB Voices, *a cappella*

Fourth Responsory at Matins, Christmas morning

Tómas Luis de Victoria, 1548–1611
Edited by Gerald Custer

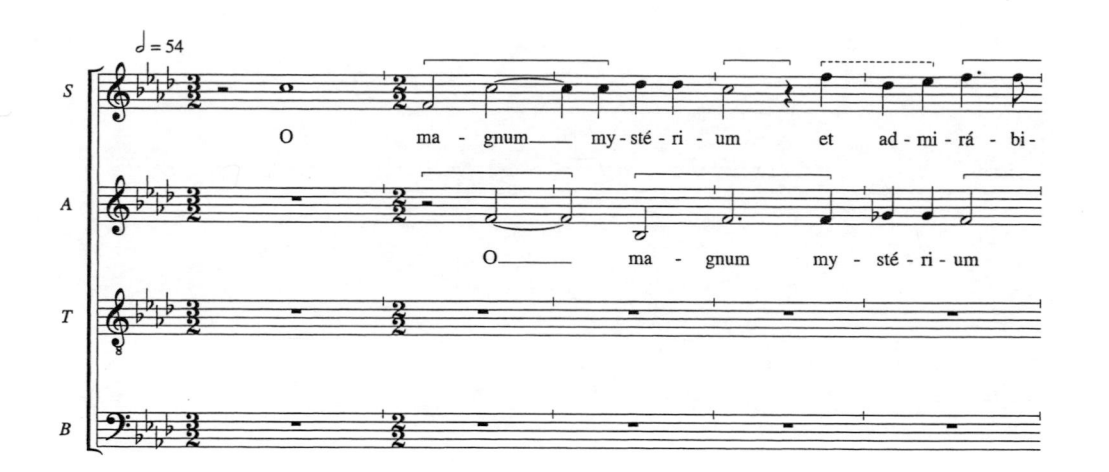

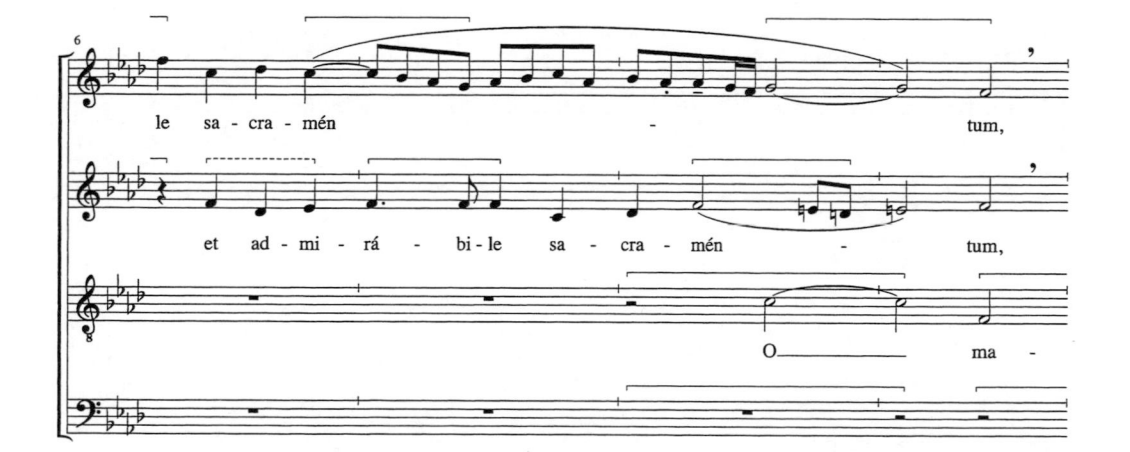

Edition Copyright © 2008 by GIA Publications, Inc. • All Rights Reserved • Printed in U.S.A.
7404 S. Mason Ave., Chicago, IL 60638 • www.giamusic.com • 800.442.1358
Reproduction of this publication without permission of the publisher is a violation of the U.S. Code of Law
for which the responsible individual or institution is subject to criminal prosecution. No one is exempt.

G-7025

Figure 14-7. (Continued)

6

Figure 14-7. (Continued)

num ná - tum, vi - dé - rent Dó - mi - num ná - tum,

num ná - tum, vi - dé - rent Dó - mi - num ná - tum, ja - cén -

num ná - tum, vi - dé - rent Dó - mi - num ná - tum, ja - cén -

num ná - tum, ja - cén - tem in

ja - cén - tem in prae - sé - pi - o,

tem, ja - cén - tem in prae - sé - pi -

tem in prae - sé - pi - o, ja - cén - tem in

prae - sé - pi - o, ja - cén - tem in prae -

ja - cén - tem in prae - sé - pi -

o, ja - cén - tem in prae - sé - pi -

prae - sé - pi - o, in prae - sé - pi -

sé - pi - o, in prae - sé - pi -

Figure 14-7. (Continued)

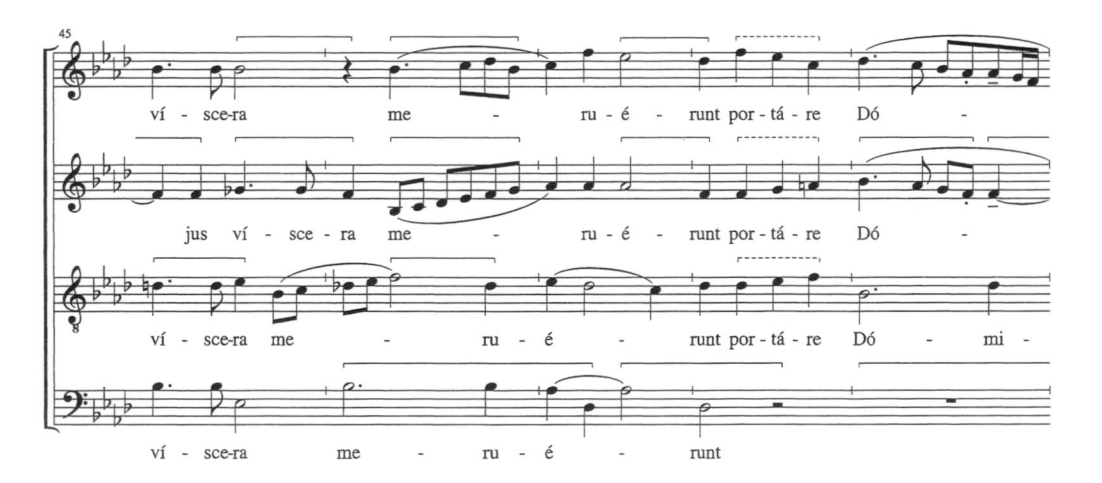

Figure 14-7. (Continued)

Figure 14-7. (Continued)

Bibliography for This Chapter

Aldrich, Putnam. "An Approach to the Analysis of Renaissance Music." *The Music Review*, Vol. 30, February 1969.

> *This article is considered a ground-breaking article concerning the importance of cadential structures within the Renaissance motet and their effects on both interpretation and performance. It is highly recommended reading for all of those conductors confronting the performance issues presented in this chapter.*

Apel, Willi. T*he Notation of Polyphonic Music: 900–1600*. Fifth edition (revised). Cambridge, MA: Medieval Academy of America, 1961.

Boyd, Malcolm. "Structural Cadences in the Sixteenth Century Mass." *The Music Review,* XXX (1969), pp. 1–21.

Butcher, Kenneth. "Choral Partbooks, Then And Now." *The Choral Journal,* September 1985.

Custer, Gerald. "From Mathematics to Meaning: New Perspectives on the Microrhythm Debate." *The Choral Journal*, August 2005.

————. *Metric Flexibility in the Performance of Renaissance Choral Music*. Chicago: GIA Publications, 2008.

————. "Provoking Meaning: Thoughts About Choral Hermeneutics." T*he Choral Journal,* December 2001.

————. "The Conducting Project Paper." *The Choral Journal,* November 2004.

Dart, Thurston. *The Interpretation of Music*. New York: Harper and Row, 1963.

Donington, Robert. *The Interpretation of Early Music*. London: Faber and Faber, 1963.

Hurty, Jon. "Singing Renaissance Music from Partbooks." *The Choral Journal,* March 1996.

Lowinsky, Edward. E. *Tonality and Atonality in Sixteenth Century Music*. Berkeley: The University of California Press, 1962.

Sachs, Curt. *Rhythm and Tempo*. New York: W. W. Norton and Co., 1953.

Shrock, Dennis. "Phrasing in the Music of the Renaissance." *The Choral Journal*, August 1994.

Chapter 15

Determining Tempos for Performance and Rehearsal

No matter how diverse their views on every other topic, most musicians agree that finding the right tempo is at least half the interpretation. Wagner went further, asserting that the right tempo was the interpretation. In his essay, *On Conducting*, he writes: "I am persistently returning to the question of tempo because, as I said before, this is the point at which it becomes evident whether a conductor understands his business or not." Tempo is also the principal feature singled out by critics in commenting on performers. With all this consensus on the crucial importance of tempo, it may seem curious that musicians hardly ever agree on the proper choice of tempo. Accord in theory has never spread into agreement in practice. (p. 101)

—Erich Leinsdorf in
The Composer's Advocate

A metronome is an undependable criterion; the only designation which can't be misapplied is *presto possible*. Tempos vary with generations like the rapidity of language. Music's velocity has less organic import than its phraseology and rhythmic qualities; what counts in performance is the artistry of the phrase and beat within a tempo. A composer is never sure of tempo before a rehearsal, for preoccupation with such detail during composition slackens creative flow. Writing time corresponds in no way to performance time, and intuitions regarding the latter are, at best, approximate. (p. 326)

Tempo indication is not creation, but an afterthought related to performance. Naturally, an inherently fast piece must be played fast, a slow one slow—but to just what extent is a decision for players. If the composer happens to be the performer, so much the better. Rhythm and phrasing, nevertheless, do pertain to composition and are always misconceived (though sometimes beautifully), for as I say, notation is inexact.

When a composer determines his tempo as a final gesture to the product, he does so as an interpreter. Since his tempo varies with the life of the times, his marking is inaccurate, his emotional conjectures will not have authentic translation into sound. The composer will never hear his music in reality as he heard in spirit. (p. 326)

—Ned Rorem
in *Setting the Tone*

I was much concerned, in setting the Psalm verses, with problems
of tempo. To me, the relation of tempo and meaning is a primary
question of musical order, *and until I am certain that I have found the
right tempo, I cannot compose.* (p. 68)

—Igor Stravinsky
in *The Robert Shaw Reader*

I have found that one of the most fundamental problems, especially for
less-experienced conductors, is that not enough careful thought and study is
devoted to determining what is the "best" tempo for a piece of choral music. There
are many factors to consider when determining the appropriate tempo for a piece,
so it would follow, then, that considerable time and study are necessary for any
conductor to make an informed decision regarding musical tempo. Correct tempo
allows a work to "sing," allows for the harmonic language of the conductor to be
heard, and allows for inspirited and technically correct performances. So the choice
of "the" tempo for a piece is one of the most important decisions a conductor can
make, and it is based on four important factors:

1. Performing acoustics
2. Vocal/technical considerations: vocal skill and experience of the singers
3. Rate or speed of harmonic change
4. Historical and performance practice factors

Rehearsal Tempo vs. Performance Tempo

Before discussing the four factors above, there is another factor that must be
considered separately. Tempos chosen for rehearsal must be based solely on
pedagogical factors. One of the first rules of rehearsal procedure for any conductor
should be: **Always introduce a piece slower than its performance tempo.** Rehearsal
tempos should be chosen so singers can hear a piece with care. Teach pieces with
complex harmonic motion at a very slow tempo so every intricacy of harmonic

progression can be both heard and savored. Also take complex passages at a slower tempo for the same reason. Slower tempos in rehearsal also allow for two very important vocal/technical considerations to be implemented: (1) rhythmic breathing and (2) learning the piece "on the breath." It is perhaps because of these two points that slow tempos in rehearsal are most important.

Establish ensemble breathing. By rehearsing at a slow tempo, you can clearly establish one of the most important vocal and musical factors: rhythmic breathing. The breath establishes not only the tempo of a piece but also, perhaps more importantly, the vocal color and dynamic of the piece in addition to the rhythmic quality of the piece. Singers tend to "cheat" at every point a breath is taken, and it is at those points where both tempo and tone color suffer. Insisting on rhythmic and in-tempo breathing does much to repair or avoid other problems that may be encountered when learning a work.

Teach "on the breath." This is perhaps the most important reason for rehearsing a work at a slow tempo, especially for those works that will eventually be performed at a fast tempo. How a piece of music "feels" to singers (in their body), especially for those who are new to singing, is of utmost importance and must be established in the early stages of rehearsal. In fact, I believe there is no more serious oversight in rehearsal technique than learning a choral work "off the breath." How do you know if the choir is "off the breath"? The singing will sound pressed, loud, hard, harsh, edgy, glasslike, and sometimes airy. But how do you hear if a sound is off the breath? You must know how to hear it. *The Choral Conductor's Aural Tutor* (GIA, 2006) was designed for this purpose. Using the workbook and the recordings (included with the workbook), conductors can teach themselves to hear what on-the-breath singing should sound like *within* a choral ensemble. An on-the-breath sound is not only free, but it is also richly resonant, in tune, and gives the aural image of moving constantly forward. The ability to recognize an off-the-breath sound is one of the most important skills conductors can possess.

Performing Acoustics

The acoustic of the performance space will affect tempo considerations. Yet too often, this important factor is not taken into consideration when choosing the music for a concert program or when trying to establish the ultimate performance tempo of a piece.

A reverberant acoustic requires a slower tempo, dependent upon the harmonic motion within the piece. A drier, less-resonant acoustic requires a faster tempo that will allow a piece to "sing" in the less-reverberant space. As you near the ending rehearsal process of a piece, it is important to move the choir toward the actual performance tempo of the piece based upon the performance acoustic of the hall in which the piece will be performed.

Vocal/Technical Considerations: Vocal Skill and Experience of the Singers

Another consideration for determining a performance tempo for any piece should be the age of the singers and their vocal experience. Singers who are younger or vocally less experienced generally cannot sustain slow sostenuto singing. Therefore, tempo should be adjusted slightly faster so the direction and requirements of the musical line can be accomplished. For example, the tempo in some of Brahms's works might have to be altered for a young boys' choir.

To determine whether a tempo adjustment needs to be made, listen for two aural indicators: pitch and musical line. If there is a continuing problem with pitch, increasing the tempo will usually help. Likewise, if a musical line seems to plod forward, and even "get stuck" in places, then an increase in tempo may be justified.

Rate or Speed of Harmonic Change

One of the more important factors for consideration in the selection of tempo is the rate or speed of harmonic change within a piece. If the rate of harmonic change is relatively rapid (i.e., two chord changes per measure) and the work will be performed in a reverberant acoustic, then a more moderate approach to tempo is required. Pieces with slower rates of harmonic change or transformation can tolerate faster tempos, but the performance acoustic must also be able to handle the faster tempos as well.

Although metric structure often can be derived from notation, tempo cannot. It is disturbing to many musicologists and performers to be unable to "prove" this or that tempo for a particular piece, and scholarly literature is full of efforts to give exact, of fairly exact, metronome markings to each dance type. (p. 148)

—Robert Donington
in *Baroque Music: Style and Performance*

Historical and Performance Practice Factors

There is much to learn about tempo from the performing practices of a given period. While this knowledge should not be the sole factor in choosing the performance tempo for a piece, it will certainly enable you to make a more informed decision.

There is little disagreement in the musicological world that pieces from the Baroque were dance influenced.[1] This influence can be found within the underlying rhythm structure of the music. Most, if not all, pieces written in the Baroque period were influenced by the dances of that period.

To arrive at an appropriate performance tempo, search within each piece for the underlying rhythmic structure. Once you determine the structure, you must also understand the specific stepping of the dance to arrive at an appropriate performance tempo. The underlying dance step contained in the rhythmic/harmonic structure is the key to tempo determination in the music of the Baroque.

---

1   The writings of Meredith Ellis Little are considered by many to be the authoritative writings in the use of Baroque dance steps to establish correct performance tempo for Baroque music.

Familiarizing Yourself with Baroque Dance

To supplement the material in this chapter, I highly recommend the following two videos (especially the first) to help you gain practical application and instruction as it relates to determining performance tempo.

- *Introduction to Baroque Dance*, by Paige Whitley-Bauguess
    Volume One: Step Sequences for the Courante, Minuet, Bourée
        and Rigaudon, Allemande, Gavotte and Sarabande
    The Baroque Dance Project 2005
    www.BaroqueDance.com

- *Dance of the French Baroque Theater* by Paige Whitley-Bauguess
        and Thomas Baird
    The Baroque Dance Project 2005
    www.BaroqueDance.com

Also:

- *Dance and the Music of J. S. Bach* by Meredith Ellis Little and Natalie
        Jenne (Indiana University Press, 2001)

- "Choreographies of Baroque Dances" by Meredith Ellis Little, from *Journal of the American Musicological Society* (Spring 1975)

Dance rhythm structures are inherently contained in Baroque works even though the specific dance may not be contained in the title itself. Dances to be considered are listed below. Many of these dances originated as peasant dances but were highly refined for use in the French Court.

Triple Meter Dances
Minuet
Sarabande
Courante
Passepied
Chaconne
Polonaise
Passacaglia

Duple Meter Dances

Allemande

Bourée

Gavotte

Meredith Little provides a helpful list for performance consideration by listing the **Baroque dances from fast to slow**, as shown in **Figure 15-1.**

Figure 15-1. Relative tempi of Baroque dances from fast to slow.

Rigaudon

Passepied

Canarie

French Gigue

Giga II

Bourée

Loure

Forlane

Gavotte

Giga I

Minuet

Chaconne

Passacaglia

Corrente

Polonaise

Sarabande

Courante[2]

---

2 Little, Meredith Ellis, and Natalie Jenne. *Dance and the Music of J. S. Bach.* Bloomington: Indiana University Press, 2001, p. 20.

Treatises and Writings

Many of the treatises by Baroque theorists contained suggestions regarding tempo, which are briefly summarized in **Figure 15-2**. (For more detailed information, reference the original source materials of the theorists that are listed.[3]) Keep the following factors in mind when interpreting these treatises of the period:

- Metronomes did not exist in this period when these treatises were written.

- Theorists differed as to what qualified as "a beat" or *tactus*. Some used the word "pulse" in their writings, while others used the word "step." It is important to note that the language between and among all of these theorists does vary.

- One theorist, Monteclair, wrote in 1736, "Do not confuse time signatures and tempo." This is an important rule to always consider when determining tempo issues in Baroque music.

- These theoretical "ideas" are presented here as a guide only. You must strike a sensible balance with regard to these tempo suggestions and considerations. The suggestions are just that—suggestions.

Tempo Conversions: Half to Dotted Half

Another factor that needs to be understood when determining tempo is tempo conversions. Consider this: A work that is marked half note in one section equals the dotted-half note in another section. Is that an equal conversion? Or is some adjustment on either side possible? In general, common practice seems to suggest that the conversion between half and dotted-half is the same pulse. In practical reality, I feel comfortable suggesting that conversions to triple be taken a bit faster.

Whenever you are considering conversions, "walk" the piece to get a "feel" for the appropriate conversions.

---

3 The material presented in Figure 15-2 was taken from detailed class notes from lectures on "Baroque Performance Practice" by Milton Sutter, an authority on Baroque performance practices who was on the faculty of Temple University.

Figure 15-2. Summary chart of theoretical treatise information.[4]

Theorist	Summary of Suggestions
Muffat (cir.1700)	Differences between "common time" and "cut time" meter signatures. Common-time pieces (C) should be slow or moderate tempo. Cut-time (C-slash) signatures should be twice as fast as common-time signatures. The exception to this is overtures and symphonies, which should be taken fairly slowly. Signatures where numbers are used should always be taken slower.
Muffat	Signatures written in 3/4, generally, are always quicker than signatures written in 3/2.
Quantz	For Sarabande, quarter note = 80.[5] According to chore graphies suggested in treatises, a Sarabande in 3/2 is slower than a Sarabande in 3/4, but in these writings neither Sarabandes or Minuets should be taken slowly.
Quantz	One "human pulse" to every two beats. Passapied should be "lighter and quicker" than Minuets. For those noted in quarter notes or eighth notes (3/4 or 3/8), the eighth or quarter should equal 180.
Brossard	Minuets should be "lively," almost a feeling of 3/8.
Muffat	In general, 3/4 is quicker than 3/2.
Quantz	For Minuet, quarter note = 160. For Gigue, dotted-quarter note = 160. Each measure should receive one pulse. For Courante, quarter note = 80.

---

4   The metronome markings suggested in this chart are not those of the theorist (metronomes did not exist); they are approximations of the dance steps suggested by each theorist in the treatise. All tempo suggestions directly relate to the court dances of the period that can be seen and experienced on the videos.

5   It is generally agreed that Bach Sarabandes are slower because of the harmonic rhythms of those works.

Figure 15-2. (Continued)

Lafilare	For Minuet, dotted-half note = 70. Cautions regarding this tempo if excessive counterpoint is present.
Muffat	No matter what the time signature, Gigue should be taken as fast as possible. Suggested is dotted-quarter note = 160!
Quantz	For Rigaudon, quarter note = 160. Bourée should be taken at a faster tempo. For Gavotte, quarter note = 120 (with four quarters to a bar).
Lully	For 4/4, quarter note = 126. For 2/2, half note = 63.

Indications of Tempo by Composers

While many composers indicate tempos for their compositions, I have found that in some cases those tempos should only be considered as suggestions. Experience has taught me that at times the tempo markings are incorrect! For example, the tempo markings in the motets of Poulenc are inaccurate, and this information is gleaned from Poulenc himself! Many composers set tempos in their minds without considering other factors such as the level of experience of the choir or the performing acoustic. However, other composers are extremely specific concerning tempo indications, and their suggestions should be followed.

Three examples of this are the markings of Benjamin Britten, Igor Stravinsky, and contemporary composer Morten Lauridsen. I have always found Lauridsen's tempo markings to be highly informed and thoughtful regarding the technical aspects of his music. Stravinsky was known to decide the tempo of a piece before he ever started to compose the work! For him, the tempo was germinal to his conception and compositional style. Benjamin Britten, an astute choral musician and a composer extremely knowledgeable of the voice, always gives accurate tempo indications for his compositions.

By and large, the tempo markings of composers should be seriously considered. More often than not they contain valuable interpretive "clues" concerning the music and its performance.

Chapter 16

A Voice Teacher's View of the Rehearsal

From the Perspective of a Voice Teacher

Lynn Eustis

Like other ensemble musicians who aspire to become soloists, singers quickly learn to cooperate with the conductor's wishes. They keep their opinions to themselves, at least when they're not sharing them with their closest friends. Thus, I approach this topic with some trepidation. I have worked with many wonderful choral conductors, and I consider myself extremely fortunate to have learned so much from these wise, compassionate, talented human beings. I have grown immeasurably as a solo singer due to these musical and often very personal experiences. Everything I say here is borne out of respect for the demands of the choral conducting profession and the desire to communicate honestly on behalf of the many students singing in choirs today.

Music schools of all sizes and levels offer choral experiences, and most require the vocal students to participate. Voice teachers continually debate the dangers versus the benefits of choral singing for students. Most recognize the musical benefits—developing musicianship skills, learning to sight-read—even as they fear the potential for vocal conformity. In my view, this conformity (also described as "blend") is positive for students in ways far beyond the vocal and musical aspects. Singers tend to possess larger-than-life egos about the sounds they are able to make. Learning to sing as part of a group is essential to developing healthy awareness of and respect for other singers.

When voice teachers and choral conductors work together, everyone wins— most particularly the students. At times this seems like an impossible goal. It is certainly not productive for voice teachers to blame all of their students' vocal problems on choral singing, nor is it effective for conductors to divorce themselves from the needs of the singers in their capacities as soloists. Both sides can benefit from a better understanding of each other's process. Perhaps the easiest place to begin is in the area of basic vocal technique.

Vocal Technique

What do voice teachers wish for in choral conductors? The obvious first response is attention to vocal technique. Does the conductor strive for a healthy sound, characterized by free production? Does the conductor allow the students to "sing" while being careful not to make them over-sing?

My work in the vocal studio is greatly affected by the aesthetic of the university's choral conductor. These students spend one hour per week with me as opposed to upwards of four hours per week in rehearsal with the choir. The way they sing during these rehearsals has an enormous impact on the way they sing their solo repertoire.

When conductors concern themselves with the use of breath, vowels and intonation, and beauty of tone, they complement the singers' work in the vocal studio. In an ideal world (or at least in my ideal world), all choral conductors would devote at least a small portion of each rehearsal to warm-up exercises. Many conductors are so pressed for time that they skip this crucial step and move directly into the repertoire for an upcoming performance. In doing this, however, they decrease the effectiveness of the rehearsal tenfold. The singers are not ready to sing, vocally or aurally, and they take far longer to find their corporate sound. The omission of preparatory exercises also encourages the poor but common habit many singers have of jumping immediately into difficult repertoire during their own practice sessions. Done repeatedly, this ultimately compromises vocal health in all areas of the singers' work.

I keep a quote on my studio door—my sincere thanks to its unknown author:

"In the beginning there was breath..."

—Unknown

The breath is the most important aspect of vocal technique, as its function impacts everything else a singer is trying to accomplish. As I say to my students, it does not matter whether you are driving an old Buick station wagon or a new Porsche; if there is no gas in the car, you aren't going anywhere. New seat cushions, a softer steering wheel, and even a new engine will not make the slightest bit of difference.

As a conductor, you can help by developing free use of breath to keep the sound buoyant. Many young singers fear choral singing because they don't feel they can "sing out." I believe this is a fallacious concern for smart singers. The breath should spin freely through the sound at all dynamic levels; singers should never create a *piano* sound by stopping the breath.

I must say a few words here about straight tone and its proper production. Blend, intonation, and style often require a straighter tone at particular points. To accomplish this, singers too often clamp down on the vowel space and use less breath. In my experience, straight tone is best found by keeping the vowel as spacious as possible and spinning the breath at a faster (more narrow) speed to keep the sound afloat. The best conductors I know are vigilant about the way singers produce the desired sound and reject any obvious compromises in vocal technique. Results tend to be better all around when singers employ the same basic vocal technique in both choral and solo settings.

One of the other concerns I encounter as a voice teacher is vowel production, particularly as it relates to intonation. Some of my singers seem to think vowels should be formed differently in choral singing, typically with less space and distinction. They think they are creating a smoother line by using what I call the "uni-vowel." True legato line is made by a series of minute adjustments in the space, with the goal of matching resonance from vowel to vowel. In this way, singers maintain a purer vowel throughout the range and, as a result, stay in tune. When the singers in a group fail to create and match pure vowels, the group will not sing in tune. Group intonation depends heavily on listening and the use of breath flow, but in my experience the single most important factor is vowel production. It is important to understand this as a conductor and to encourage attention to the formation of clear vowels.

There are probably as many different preferences for tonal quality as there are musicians. Nevertheless, conductors should consider the aesthetic of the tone they are making with their choirs. In my college choir, under the immensely talented William Payn, I learned what constituted a beautiful tone, and I also learned that a whisper could be just as powerful as a shout. Many young singers learn more about musical phrasing in choir than they do anywhere else. They learn the essential skills of musicianship, and under inspired conductors they learn much more about the art of music.

Repertoire

The repertoire a conductor chooses has an enormous influence on the budding artistic personalities of young singers. The conductor has an important opportunity to introduce students to particular composers and styles in a different way than the students experience in their solo work. The students are also forming opinions about choral singing in general through the selection of repertoire for the group. One of the most common complaints I hear from my voice students about their choral experiences, when they're not happy in their assigned group, is that they don't respond well to the music. This usually means the music is either too difficult musically or too taxing vocally. On the positive side, my students often come to their lessons excited about the new work they're learning in choir. "We're doing this great piece by Sibelius. Do you know who he is?" Their enthusiasm is contagious. Sometimes they will even ask me whether a particular composer wrote anything for solo voice.

As a voice teacher, I hope my singers will be exposed to a well-balanced diet of "meat and potatoes" repertoire along with some unusual selections. Young singers are well aware when conductors (both choral and opera) choose obscure, seldom-performed works to gain public attention. However, I think young singers need to learn to respect the music as bigger and more important than they are, and this is often best achieved through familiar repertoire. They know they are part of the larger musical tradition, temporary custodians of the music before the new generation takes its turn. In choir, they can either learn the importance of this responsibility, or they can learn that the pursuit of music is driven by the pursuit of personal glory and public recognition. As educators, we choose each and every day which model we will present to our impressionable young students.

Many people respond positively to the excitement of several hundred voices singing together at full volume. As a singer, I have felt the thrill of sharing in that kind of experience as one of those voices. It is important to remember, however, that clear intonation and beauty of tone can be the most impressive qualities in a choir of any size. So as a conductor, one should make every attempt to balance the repertoire with big chestnuts, new oddities, and music of varying difficulty levels. Rare pieces are sometimes chosen because we ourselves have grown weary of the more standard repertoire; I am tempted all too frequently to do this as a studio teacher. But we must remember that most of our students are experiencing these pieces for the first time, and we owe it to them to let them know that fresh joy. I will never forget the anticipation with which the late Mary Nell Saunders opened our first rehearsal on

Orff's *Carmina burana* at the Brevard Music Center, turning directly to the "Veni, veni, venias" to spark our own new love affair with this piece. As the saying goes, variety is the spice of life—our students need to sing the big works as well as lots of other pieces.

Caring for the Personal Growth of Students

The common thread I see in my favorite choral conductors is a sense of humanity and dignity, coupled with an ability to create an environment in which all of the singers thrive, both as individuals and as members of a tightly knit group. And so I assert that a student's personal and educational needs are the most important consideration for any choral conductor. What do conductors teach the students about why they sing?

I have always believed that true confidence comes from the realization that one's own talents are unique and special. If confidence is defined by comparison to others, then it can be easily shaken. I think it is unhealthy for young singers to be overly competitive with one another and to be motivated by the desire to be better than others. In sports, this type of motivation is essential, due in large part to the objective nature of evaluation. But in music, which is an art form first and foremost, any ranking of artists is highly subjective. Singers must have pride in personal excellence for its own sake.

The most effective, artistically sound choirs sing because they love the music and they are humbled by the opportunity to participate in the larger tradition. The singers in these groups all experience a sense of ownership that is both individual and corporate. When conductors ask the singers to be "the best" in the school (or county, state, etc.), they are teaching the singers to evaluate their artistic worth solely as others see it in relationship to other choirs. As a motivational tool, this approach has limited value. Inevitably a choir encounters a "better" (more highly regarded) choir, and the group loses its basis for confidence. While all artists inevitably face comparison with other artists, students may be healthier if they avoid focusing on it.

In my studio I encourage students to put their best efforts forth at all times and to refrain from too much direct competition with other singers. In this way, the singers learn that I respect them as individuals, and in turn, I hope they will learn to respect other singers as well. If each voice is truly unique, a conductor can choose one singer for a solo without the others feeling too rejected. They understand that when an apple is required, an orange simply would not be the right choice. I have found that "competitive edge" too often finds its way into vocal sound, usually leading to a tight, aggressive tone. It is difficult to produce a relaxed, natural, beautiful sound when singers are fueled essentially by anger and the fear that someone else will get the credit that is rightfully theirs.

As a conductor, how can you show respect for the individual singers in your choir? You can identify unique qualities in each singer while acknowledging that all of the singers have value to the group. When conductors single out one singer as the model for the rest of the section, they demonstrate a lack of respect for the individuality of the other instruments. This is particularly true when such a distinction is made within an atmosphere of fear: "Sound like this person or else don't bother singing" is sometimes what the other singers perceive.

I would also caution against making status distinctions between performance majors and music education majors. These students are all voice majors, and each one is an equally valuable resource for the group as a whole. If anything, music education majors tend to have both a greater respect for the choral art form as well as a greater likelihood of continuing involvement in making choral art. Their work should be an example for the performance majors in terms of discipline, attention to detail, and typically positive attitude.

Working with Colleagues

The way conductors relate to and speak about a program's voice teachers sets a powerful example for students. Students learn and define their future professional behavior through what they see in teachers and conductors as leaders, so we must always be aware of that when we interact in front of them. This can be an especially sensitive issue when faculty members serve as soloists for choral concerts. The students are always watching, and if we do not practice what we preach in terms of how to treat other artists, then we lose all credibility with the students. We must also be careful not to fight our battles with each other through comments to students, tempting though that is at times.

In talking with voice teachers about this topic, I have found that the need for improved communication seems to be one of the biggest concerns between voice teachers and choral conductors. Voice teachers hope conductors will solicit their input when appropriate, acknowledge their contribution to the success of the choir, and keep them informed about what the students are doing. All too often it is the small things, like changing schedules without informing the faculty, that breed resentment. I think it is important for conductors to understand that voice teachers are generally not in a position of ensemble leadership in any area of the program, and this often leaves them feeling neglected or vestigial. I teach at a very large university in which my students participate in the various choirs, the opera, the early music program, contemporary music concerts, and the jazz program, in addition to any work they may be doing outside the College of Music. Nothing makes me more distressed than to learn basics of repertoire and scheduling from the students rather than from my colleagues who lead in these areas. Applied faculty members may get testy at times because they have relatively little control over the larger projects in which their students perform. Conductors can help by keeping this in mind and letting voice teachers know that they play a vital role in the life of the program. A little bit of kindness can go a long way toward smoother relationships and, consequently, a healthier educational environment for students.

I have attempted here to articulate the voice teacher's general point of view in working with choral conductors. I realize conductors may also have their own thoughts and desires for working with voice teachers, and it is my hope that this will help to open up the lines of communication across the divide. My students benefit more than I can say from their work in both school and professional choirs.

I would like to close by offering my most sincere thanks to the many choral conductors who have shaped my own professional life in music, especially William Payn, James Jordan, David Hayes, Kevin Jones, David R. Davidson, and C. David Keith.

PART FIVE
APPROACHES TO SCORE ANALYSIS

Chapter 17

Score Preparation
A Kaleidoscopic Process

The conductor is looking at the painting and painting it at the same time. (p. 15)

—Pierre Boulez in
Eugene Corporon, *"The Quantum Conductor"*

While correctness is one of our goals, we must realize that "making right" is not necessarily "making music." The objective elements in music are much more easily observed and modified than the subjective feelings that music is about. It is important to understand that simply eliminating error is useless unless we find expression in the process. An over-concern for accuracy may drain the spontaneity of a group, and spontaneity is the ally of great music making. At some point we must stop correcting the grammar and start reading the story. The process must be about creation, not mindless repetition. Without discovery and discussion there can be no insight. (p. 13)

—Eugene Corporon
in *"The Quantum Conductor"*
Teaching Music through Performance in Band, Vol. 1

The time spent on score study and score preparation for rehearsal is the most valuable time we can spend with the music we are going to make and with ourselves. Score study needs to be an almost sacred process and ritual for each conductor. It is our time alone with ourselves so the music we are studying can begin to enrich our spirits and inform our rehearsal process.

As a rule, I find that choral conductors spend much less time on score study than our colleagues in the wind and orchestra worlds. The great teachers and conductors of our profession, such as Shaw, Hillis, and Ehmann, are somewhat unique exceptions.

Kaleidoscopes have become a relatively recent fascination for me. There is an art gallery in Sedona, Arizona,[1] that has one of the largest displays of kaleidoscopes. Each year I go there and leave fascinated by my experiences of looking into each of the remarkable visual worlds. Through some physical twisting of the apparatus, the contents of each kaleidoscope through the miracle of refraction and lenses are transformed into a magical visual world.

As conductors, our score study process needs to be such a kaleidoscopic activity. It should allow our musicianship to view the piece we are about to rehearse from many angles so each view from a different perspective is a new one!

In that spirit, I present many different angles of score preparation. The work of Julius Herford has inspired many, including the young Robert Shaw and the young Elaine Brown. I worry that this central tool for choral analysis is not always in our score preparation "peripheral" vision. The work of Margaret Hillis also deserves our constant awareness as conductors. Frauke Haasemann taught me how to study a score "vocally." And finally, one of America's great wind conductors, Eugene Migliaro Corporon, provides us with another kaleidoscopic angle from which to examine a score.

So in the chapters to follow I present to you a kaleidoscope of score preparation. I believe that not one but all of these approaches should be employed when studying a score so we can arrive at rehearsal not only informed, but also deeply inspired by the music we have just studied.

---

1   The Scherer Gallery is in Sedona, Arizona, on Highway 89A.

Chapter 18

The Quantum Conductor

Eugene Migliaro Corporon

Note from the author of this book:

This chapter first appeared in Teaching Music through Performance in Band, *compiled and edited by Richard Miles (GIA, 1997). I came across it as I searched the resources GIA Publications had published for band and orchestra conductors; I was hoping to find relevant information for use in this book, knowing that choral conductors might not necessarily be aware of the contributors to those volumes or their ideas. What struck me is something we all know and believe: Good teaching and good conducting is not genre specific. It is clear that many of GIA's publications have valuable score study and rehearsal tips for choral musicians. I have long admired the work of Eugene Migliaro Corporon. His work embodies all things I believe a conductor should be and do. When I came across this chapter, it provided me with a fresh perspective and viewpoint for the rehearsal process—a viewpoint I wanted to share with my colleagues in the choral profession. I want to thank Eugene Corporon for agreeing to be a part of this book and for allowing this chapter to be reprinted. His work and music making hold a wealth of knowledge for the choral profession.*

—James Jordan

Informed Learning

The act of learning a piece of music involves a never-ending process of exploration and discovery that turns ideas and feelings into actions. Acquiring knowledge and sensitivity creates a constant interplay of energy and information. Energetically collecting and sharing information can be compared to going on a firefly hunt in the woods on a summer evening at twilight. Because all of their lights never come on at once, success depends on being able to focus on a single firefly at a time. The challenge is to cautiously capture each light source and put it in the jar without damaging it. With care, patience, and persistence, the container is eventually filled with enough fireflies to create an incredible hive of living light. At the end of the evening, the release of the collected illumination can be as inspiring and fulfilling as the search. While the illusive product is miraculous, in the end it is the process that we carry in our memory and treasure the most.

I am a strong advocate of the importance of approaching learning as a process, not a product. In music especially, the process becomes the product. A process-oriented approach must be thorough, effective, thought-provoking, enlightening, expressive and, above all, creative. Music is designed to be innately enjoyable. It is incumbent upon us as teachers of music to amplify that joy! Tim Galway, author of *The Inner Game of Tennis*, has said, "The teaching of music should be more musical..."—I could not agree more. The ultimate goal is to connect with the work of art and with the people who bring it to life.

In most settings, the amount of time we have to devote to a project is finite. It seems as though there is never enough time to accomplish all that needs to be done: it invariably takes as much time as you have and sometimes even more. I remember once saying to my colleague and mentor, Robert Fountain, that I wished I had "just one more rehearsal." His response was filled with wisdom: "You've already had it; you just didn't use the time very well." His point was well taken. Very often the amount of time we waste is equivalent to at least one full rehearsal. We must investigate ways to use our time as efficiently and effectively as possible while producing quality work that is painstakingly thorough! Above all else, it is essential that we teach musicianship.

A **balanced learning process** should focus on the technical, intellectual, musical, and personal growth of the musicians, as represented in **Figure 18-1**.

Figure 18-1. Balanced learning process.

Craft *Objective* Knowledge	Technical / Work for the Body Intellectual / Work for the Mind	Teach Skill
Inspiration *Subjective* Feelings	Musical / Work for the Soul Personal / Work for the Heart	Develop Musicianship

Whether an instrumental conductor or a choral conductor, we must allow all four of these areas to grow equally and evenly. The growth environment should be nurturing and facilitate the goal of teaching musical concepts that create knowledgeable and "feelingful" performers. The process has to encourage creativity and stimulate curiosity. Transferring some bit of knowledge every day is paramount, as is connecting to the feelings inherent in the work. The conscientious accumulation of meaningful information can lead us to our expressive selves. There can be no room in the teaching environment for anger or sarcasm because they create fear and self-doubt. Replace these non-productive, dehumanizing actions with patience and understanding, and you will build confidence and accountability in your musicians. It is so important to avoid forced response and move towards natural learning. This must be accomplished in an atmosphere that is safe and encouraging.

As a teacher, strive to be a person of vision, imagination, persistence, humor, and discipline. In addition, self-control and honesty will help to develop your singers' commitment to personal responsibility and accountable actions. Of course, your singers must also bring something to the party: they should be attentive, involved, interactive, thoughtful and, above all, understand the importance of contributing. Everyone involved contributes continually to everyone else. That's one of the beautiful things about music: making it establishes a community.

The key to success is understanding the importance of developing individual responsibility—"no deposit, no return." If you are not contributing, you are taking away. Consider this description from *Flow: The Psychology of Optimal Experience* by Mihaly Csikszentmihalyi (Harper Perennial, 1991):

Every relationship is one of give and take. Giving engenders receiving, and receiving engenders giving. What goes up must come down, what goes out must come back. In reality, receiving

> is the same thing as giving because giving and receiving are
> different aspects of the flow of energy in the universe. And if you
> stop the flow of either, you interfere with nature's intelligence.

There is no neutral position. It is incumbent upon us to find ways to help individual musicians become partners in the firm, assume ownership, and make daily deposits for the good of the community or ensemble. Your singers should be encouraged to turn good intentions into thoughtful actions. There must be a consensus, an understanding, that progress must be made and that the process must involve moving forward, no matter how slowly! Imagine that every musician represents one cell in the body that is the ensemble. In that light, the analogy from *Flow* of the law of giving is a perfect metaphor for what it means to be a member of an ensemble:

> A cell is alive and healthy when it is in a state of balance and
> equilibrium. This state of equilibrium is one of fulfillment and
> harmony, but it is maintained by a constant give and take. Each cell
> gives to and supports every other cell, and in turn is nourished by
> every other cell. The cell is always in a state of dynamic flow and
> the flow is never interrupted. In fact, the flow is the very essence of
> the life of the cell. And only by maintaining this flow of giving is
> the cell able to receive and thus continues its vibrant existence.

In addition to generating energy, conductors often function like a solar energy collector, drawing energy in and storing it when things are sunny, and then dispersing it when things get dark or cloudy. Because the energy of the rehearsal or performance is continually cycling through the conductor, it is important that we learn to control and guide its flow. We empower and excite; we detonate and ignite. We cause things to happen. Above all, we facilitate the learning process by being non-defensive and eliminating interference. The goal is to create a state of relaxed, focused concentration in the musicians so they can succeed and fulfill 100 percent of their potential. Our primary job as conductors is to make the musicians' job easier as we fulfill the composer's dreams.

While correctness is surely one of our goals, we have to realize that "making right" is not necessarily "making music." The objective elements in music are much more easily observed and modified than the subjective feelings that music is about. It is important to understand that simply eliminating error is useless unless we find expression in the process. An over-concern for accuracy may drain the spontaneity of a group, and spontaneity is the ally of great music making. At some point we must stop correcting the grammar and focus on reading the story. After all, the process is about creation, not mindless repetition. Without discovery and discussion, there can be no insight. It is necessary to discover the feelings, ideas, and patterns contained in the music, remembering that we are the translators of the message that is encoded in the composer's symbolic language, called *notation*.

We can bring understanding to the listeners only if our work is clearly perceivable. Clarity is a primary factor in transmitting ideas. Being sensitive to the smallest ingredient and perceiving it as a major event will produce clarity of purpose as well as artistic depth. Subscribing to the **four principles** (in order) shown in **Figure 18-2** will help establish ensemble clarity and aesthetic value in the music making process.

Figure 18-2. Four principles (in order) for establishing ensemble clarity.

In Tone	producing characteristic quality sound (imagination and moving air are the allies)
In Time	internalizing cumulative pulse (traveling together in and through time)
In Tune	audiating and matching pitch (an aural illusion created by stopping the beats)
In Touch	perceiving emotion and meaning (a fluid and natural connection that serves the music)

Physically   Technique   Facility
(portray the music with the **body**)

Mentally   Thought   Intellect
(understand the process with the **mind**)

Emotionally   Feeling   Inspiration
(intuit the message through the **spirit**)

The learning process should reveal emotion as well as meaning. Show your singers what to listen for in the music. Help them hear what you hear in your mind's ear, feel what is in your heart, and discover what is in theirs. Keep in mind that instrumental musicians perform from a single line of music while conductors are privileged to work from a full score. Conductors have the advantage of seeing the entire work of art throughout the process; instrumentalists only see an extracted part. Finding creative ways to help musicians hear what the conductor sees in the score is the challenge. Actually, choral musicians have a distinct advantage in this regard for very often, if not always, they sing from a complete score, allowing them to observe the entire composition every time they sing. I believe the great musicality that so many choirs achieve has much to do with working from a complete representation of a composer's creation.

Another goal of the learning process is to compress the margin of error: develop accuracy and consistency, both within the individual and throughout the ensemble. The difference between a young artist and a professional is often a matter of consistency. A professional may have only a 5 percent margin of error while a student's margin may vary drastically. Defining your goals early in the process is very important. Clarifying the difference between planning, practicing, rehearsing, and performing is essential; each serves a very different function in the music making process.

One purpose of the rehearsal is to determine what needs to be practiced. I cannot stress enough how crucial it is to the success of an ensemble for its individual members to practice outside of the rehearsal. Do not assume your singers know how to practice. Help them set short-term and long-term goals that give direction and purpose to practice sessions, and enable them to achieve their objectives. The amount of practice time invested does not need to be overwhelming, but it does need to be regular and focused. Great performances are facilitated by good planning, practice, and rehearsal habits.

A conductor's role in the music making process has a lot in common with an archaeologist's approach to a dig. Sometimes machinery can be used to clear away large amounts of superfluous material until the location of the hidden treasure is exposed, while at other times careful hand work is required to avoid damaging the precious artifacts. As one gets closer to the find, extreme care and delicate tools are used to unearth the valued object of the search. Eventually, time on hands and knees is needed to brush away the dust and reveal the minute details of the discovery. The more intricacies we bring to light and make audible in a work of art, the more reverent and respectful we become of the composer's artistry, process, and achievement.

Stages of Development

The progression of learning and then teaching a piece can be diagramed in a way that represents what I call the **Quantum Conductor Sphere** (shown in **Figure 18-3**). All stages appear as part of a whole; they are connected to each other and interact with each other simultaneously and continuously. Because any single stage is in constant communication with the other three, improvement in one stage informs all the others. Each stage contributes equally to the growth process, and the process becomes incomplete if any stage goes missing or is unattended.

Figure 18-3. Quantum conductor sphere.

CREATING
physical activity realize
the sound image

CONCEPTION
"score reading"

CONCEIVING
mental acitivity build
the sound image

PRESENTATION
"performance"

PREPARATION
"score study"

TRANSFER
feelingful intelligence

IMPLEMENTATION
"rehearsal"

DEVELOP
informed intuition

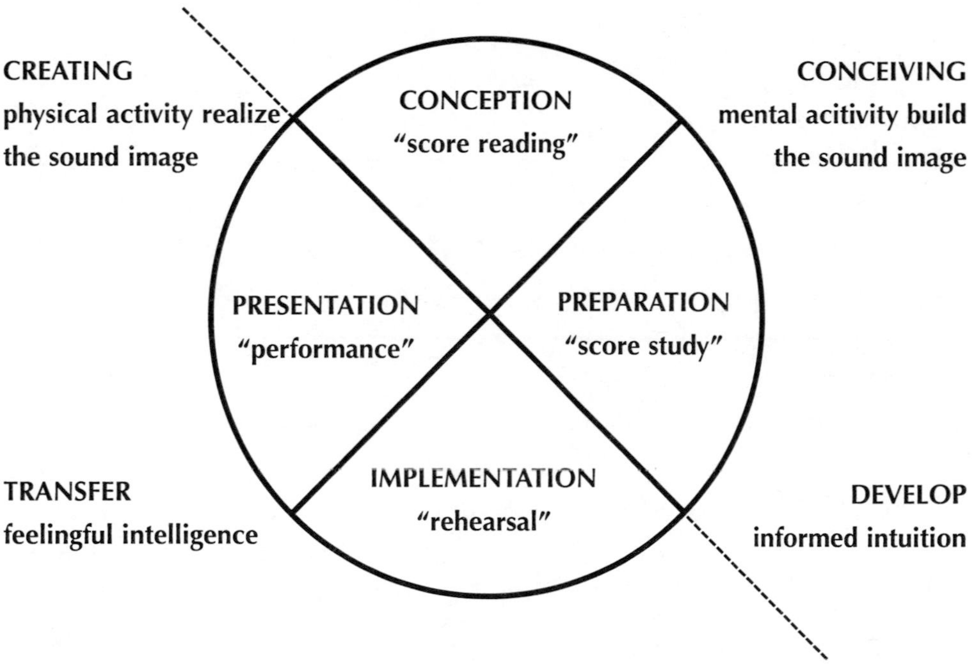

Conception

In the conception stage, we develop the imagined ideal of the work. Pierre Boulez has said, "The conductor is looking at the painting and painting it at the same time." Every piece of music begins in the mind, moves through the spirit, and reflects the soul of its creator. The composer conceives the sounds and organizes them into ideas that, in turn, are presented by some system of notation. Our job as conductors is to translate and make clear that system of notation. This requires imagination (seeing the music in our mind's "eye") and audiation (hearing the music in our mind's "ear"). We learn to hear in our mind what we see with our eyes. This, in fact, becomes the pressing question when we work. Do we hear what we see on the page? When converting what we hear into a physical presentation or specific conducting motion, remember that the character of the desired sound determines the quality of the gesture. No gesture can have meaning without conception. You must conceive the sound before you reference a gesture. All gestures begin with a sound image conceived in our mind that will be expressed by our spirit. Conducting is, after all, showing how sound looks and feels. Great conductors create the illusion of swimming in the sound. They convince us that the air is "thick with sound."

Using a recording to facilitate or accelerate the conception development process can be beneficial. However, be aware of the danger of being overwhelmed by a single interpretation. The goal is to develop your own unique expression of the artwork that is faithful to the composer's intentions (or at the very least, in the range of the composer's intentions). If you use a recording, it is better to sample a number of different ones to allow for personal musical growth that is free of imitation. It is critically important to develop an opinion without becoming opinionated. The music must come from you—and no one else.

At this stage of the process, we are score reading much the way we would read a magazine. We keep our eyes moving and do our best to hear the music in our mind. Alternating between audiating and actually listening to the work facilitates our ability to hear the piece in our "inner ear." In a very real sense at this stage, our mind is our instrument.

Preparation

In the preparation stage, we devote time to studying and analyzing the score. The goal is to develop a uniform memory of the piece. To quote Walter Piston, "The bringing to light of the inevitable deviations from the commonplace on the part of every composer is perhaps the most interesting and profitable result to be obtained through analysis." It is necessary to introduce the ensemble into the equation and begin thinking in terms of designing a distinctive rehearsal plan that will facilitate problem solving and musical growth for your group. Unlike the conception stage, stop often while going through the score and zoom in on the details of the music, noting the compositional, structural, formal, and expressive elements that create an understanding of the relationships that exist in the music.

Developing a concept of the skeletal phrasal shape will help you make observations about the composer's plan of presentation. Begin to determine what choices the composer has made, and think about why the composer may have made them. Since every composition represents a series of choices, there is much to be gleaned from observing and acknowledging those choices. Pondering the potential choices that went unused can also be enlightening. Thinking about why the composer made a specific choice over the others often yields great insight. David Elliot, author of *Music Matters*, suggests that a composition is "a thought generator." I believe it is also "a feeling instigator." Learning how a piece is put together will enable you to take it apart, and you must be able to disassemble the music in order to rehearse it. Understanding and being clear about how it goes back together is paramount; otherwise; you will be left with a collection of cleaned parts laying on the podium with no hope of reconstructing the work of art in a way that reveals its emotions and meanings.

Great preparation will yield a great rehearsal plan. Your level of achievement will be directly related to your mastery of the score, the flexibility and effectiveness of your rehearsal plan, and your ability to communicate. Knowing and being able to show what comes next in the music is essential. Become aware of where you have been, where you are, and where you want to go. In this regard, conductors are like time travelers, moving freely at will through the past, present, and future of the work. Preparation will allow you to develop this ability. Score study is an ongoing process of filling out the substance of the work, much like packing clay on a skeleton to recreate the shape and contour of a body. Study is to conducting what practice is to playing. We must do our work in order to succeed!

Implementation

In the implementation stage, the imagined ideal of the piece meets up with the reality of the ensembles' ability. As Richard Bach wrote in *Illusions* (Arrow Books, 2001), "You are never given a wish without also being given the power to make it true. You may have to work for it, however." While the first two stages involve mental activity, the next two require physical action. The time has come to turn ideas into sound. We have moved from *conceiving* the work of art to *creating* the work of art. The goal of the first two stages was to develop informed intuition. Now you must transfer it to your singers as feelingful intelligence. In other words, you can now realize your intentions. The stuff that makes conductors and performers different from theorists and musicologists can be found in the implementation and presentation stages. Studying and audiating a piece is not enough; performing artists must make the music come to life in order to feel complete. The rehearsal and performance are truly their "reason for being"—the ultimate reward for doing all of the detailed preparatory work. The conception and preparation stages were done in the quiet solitude of your "study place." It is now time to enthusiastically share your vision with living, breathing musicians. Through diligent study, you have earned the right to act as the composer's advocate and representative.

The rehearsal goals are clear: make it better every time you work on it, recreate the composer's intentions to the best of your ability, and be uniquely and creatively expressive in the process. Transcending technique is key to connecting with the composer's inspiration. Get past the problems of the individual parts to discover the significance of the entire piece. Your goal is to give the gift every composer dreams of: a performance that goes beyond his or her own conception of the work.

As conductors we must illuminate concepts not just fix problems. The rehearsal provides the perfect opportunity to help musicians learn to target their powers of attention, creating an awareness that allows them to focus more and more on the subtle details of the music. This laser-like "relaxed focused concentration" helps us listen and perform with depth and intelligence. We cannot perform without knowing how to listen or what to listen for. Good listening skills are a prerequisite to successful performance! Our challenge as conductors is to create a collective uniform memory of the work in the minds of our musicians while teaching them to listen. A process that is natural, effortless, focused, and relaxed will produce music that is the same. We can only make it work if we understand the score and communicate what we know and feel in a positive and caring way.

Presentation

In the presentation stage, we culminate our work on a given piece of music and share its wonders. To quote Edward T. Cone, "The convincing performance is one that absorbs the listener so deeply into the flow of the music that even though he may know perfectly everything that lies ahead, he can still savor each moment as if for the first time." If a composition is of serious artistic merit, and we perceive it as being so, we most likely will add it to our repertoire and repeat it at some point in the future. In this moment, we realize the assimilation of the work has become a lifelong project. Our study of the piece becomes a work in progress. If our approach in each of the previous stages has been thoughtful, thorough, and heartfelt, then the presentation cannot help but be successful.

Throughout all of the stages, the goal is to teach the whole piece to everyone and to share our feelings about the work with anyone who hears it. We want to experience the music—not just perform it. We want to be connected to one another as the music unfolds, making the vision and intent of the composer clear. It is important that self-expression not be distorted and turned into self-exposure. The music must come before the ego of the conductor and the performers. Music must be honored as an end in itself—not a means to an end. The hope is that body, mind, and spirit will work together, and that feeling and knowing will combine to express and communicate ideas and emotions in a transcending way.

Even though we know perfection is an unattainable idealized goal, we continue to pursue it with a passion. Can a work be performed musically and not be 100 percent correct? Can a performance be absolutely correct and have nothing musical to say? These questions will help you remember the importance of balancing craft and inspiration in your performances. As conductors we must do more than teach band, orchestra, or choir. We must teach musicianship. Our purpose should be to take what we have made right and turn it into something significant and feelingful. A great performance is one that uses uncompromising craft to create inspirational, soul-to-soul music making.

Steps to Success

Step 1: Planning

Conductors need to provide a firm but flexible rehearsal plan that captivates the musicians. It is always better to have a plan and not need it than to need a plan and not have it. Beginning work on a composition is very much like turning over an hourglass. Consider that the process is represented by the sand in the container. When you flip it, the sand (which is finite) begins to flow, giving you a limited amount of time to complete your work. The rehearsal provides an opportunity to bring your imagined ideal of the sound image to life. An **overall plan with a sample timing** can be diagramed as shown in **Figure 18-4**:

Figure 18-4. Sample overall plan with timing.

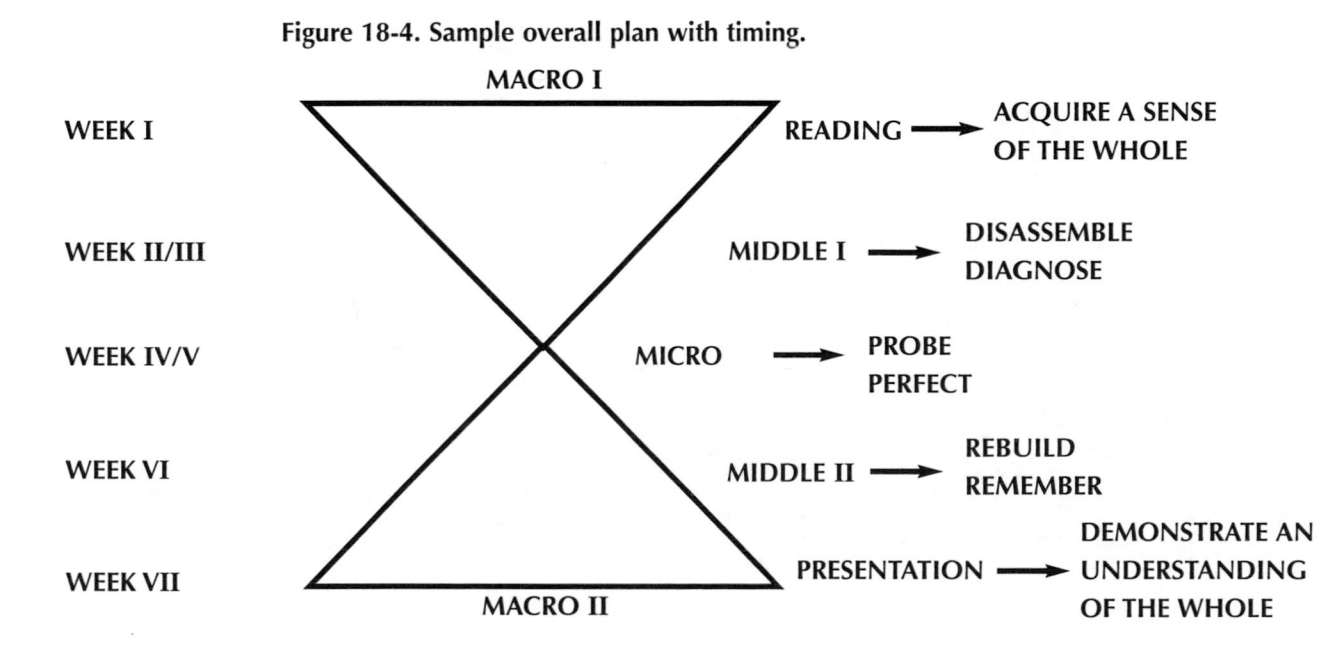

185

You will notice that the process begins with allowing the group to not only experience but also become familiar with the whole piece before starting to deal with the more specific middle- and micro-level issues. You can lose a great deal of the energy and excitement that surrounds a first encounter by beginning detailed work too soon. Give your singers time to buy into the project and experience the sounds. It is during the Middle I and Micro stages that you will do the majority of your intricate work. You might at times zoom in on a middle- or micro-level issue not because it needs to be fixed, but because you simply want your singers to notice the musical significance of the fragment being investigated.

The sand in the hourglass can also represent the fluidity of the composition itself. As the piece works its way from top to bottom of the hourglass, your singers will develop skill while learning more and more about the music. This provides insight into the workings of the composer's mind and connects everyone to the composer's feelings. Your singers learn about the composer (who), the historical circumstances (when) surrounding the creation of the composition, and the cultural environment (where) influencing its conception. They grasp the theoretical aspects (how) and become aware of the interaction of the **compositional, structural, and formal elements** (what), as shown in **Figure 18-5**.

Figure 18-5. Compositional, structural, and formal elements.

Compositional Elements	Structural Elements	Formal Elements		
Pulse	Work	Unity	Statement	New
Melody	Movement	Contrast	Digression	Repeated
Harmony	Section		Return	Varied
Timbre	Sub-section			Developed
Texture	Double period			
Form	Period			
Scoring	Phrase			
	Sub-phrase			
	Motive			
	Note			

Monitoring, controlling, and adjusting the **expressive elements and musical goals** shown in **Figure 18-6** creates style and character, and allows conductors to become the composer's advocate and ally when designing an interpretation:

Figure 18-6. Expressive elements.

Sound		Silence
Energy	(low to high)	Thought
Volume	(soft to loud)	Impact
Speed	(slow to fast)	Effect
Length	(long to short)	Quantity
Timbre	(dark to bright)	Quality
Texture	(thick to thin)	Clarity
Resonance	(wet to dry)	Reflection
Morphology	(how sound or silence begins/sustains/ends)	Morphology
Growth	(vertical shape/horizontal movement/ diagonal process)	Purpose
Note grouping	(inflection within the phrase)	Punctuation

Musical Goals

Direction/Repose

Tension/Release

Anticipation/Resolution

Preparation/Execution

As we work to realize the ideal sound image, a great deal of time and energy is spent revealing the implied meaning that is hidden in the written symbol. We rely on memory, expectation, illusion, suspense, and surprise to create a musical experience. Discovering what is in the music, developing a genuine feeling for it, and communicating its meaning is crucial. Rather than just isolating and fixing tones, we must highlight the relationships between the tones to make an impact.

A great way to promote your singers' involvement in developing a rehearsal plan is to ask questions. This could be done informally on a regular basis throughout rehearsals or formally with a questionnaire. You could distribute a **"learning goal survey"** (a sample is shown in **Figure 18-7**) to involve your singers in the process of planning. The questions would help your singers develop short-term goals, which lead to long-term solutions. Hand the questionnaire out at the first rehearsal. Let everyone know they will be filling out the questionnaire at the completion of the first reading. Once filled out, have your singers sign and date the questionnaires, and then collect them. A few weeks later, hand out the questionnaires again. Allow your singers to evaluate their progress and review their initial reactions and evaluations, amending them as needed. Repeat the exercise and compare the answers.

Figure 18-7. Sample questionnaire.

1. Is this the best you can sing this piece?
2. What passages went well?
3. What passages will need the most work?
4. How will you practice the difficult passages?
5. What makes the passage difficult?
6. What is the general style of this piece?
7. What is the form of this piece?
8. Describe this piece in one or two word phrases.
9. Will this piece be difficult to learn?
10. How long will it take to learn this piece?
11. Is this a good piece? Why?

The stages of transformation that musicians go through can be very exciting. There are many more questions you could ask. Add questions that are significant to you. Be inventive and inquisitive.

The simplified goal of the rehearsal is to "transfer ownership" from you to your singers. The idealized goal of the rehearsal is to discover how a piece works—the goal is not to fix problems. The discovery process will expose problems, which in truth, can only be solved by the singers. You can facilitate that process by offering solutions. Your singers must take the action to implement the change; that is the only way to improve. It is important to understand that the rehearsal is the place to do the work together that cannot be done alone.

You can achieve your goals in rehearsal by engaging your singers in the project. Capturing their attention is paramount. Activity and responsibility are the two things that will keep your singers connected. They need to feel they are getting an aesthetic return on their investment of time and energy. Sharing the insights and information you have gleaned through your preparation and study is most important. The goals are many, but primarily you should strive to establish an emotive link with others through your performance. The process is not about being the best; it is about doing your best. Consider the following performance goals:

- **Engage** and **Impact** the listeners/singers.
- **Affect** and **Reach** the listeners/singers.
- **Move** and **Enrich** the listeners/singers.
- **Elevate** and **Captivate** the listeners/singers.
- **Challenge** and **Reward** the listeners/singers.

With a comprehensive approach, it becomes apparent we have the ability to make a wonderful contribution as conductors. In a world that has become so quantity oriented, our art is uniquely suited to improve the quality of the lives of those who are touched by what we do while bringing equality to all who participate in the process.

Step 2: Pacing

We can use the same diagram of the hourglass shown in Figure 18-4 to illustrate rehearsal pacing. When laid on its side (as shown in **Figure 18-8**), the hourglass becomes a useful visual for describing the flow of the rehearsal. Great rehearsals should include a series of multiple zooms (in and out). They can also begin with very detailed work and progress to the whole. Avoid getting caught doing detailed work with a select few as rehearsal time runs out.

Figure 18-8. Rehearsal pacing.

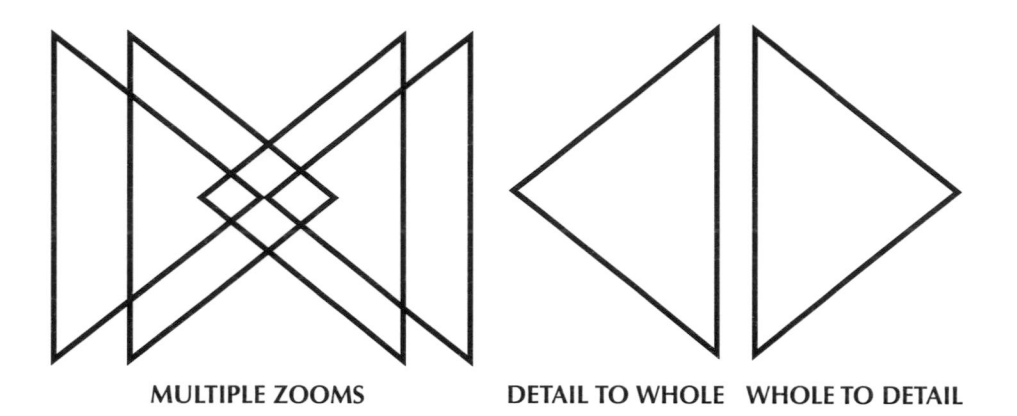

MULTIPLE ZOOMS   DETAIL TO WHOLE WHOLE TO DETAIL

Consider the following:

- Keep the tempo of the rehearsal moving.
- Change the dynamics of the rehearsal as well as the mood to appropriately reflect the qualities you hope to extract from the music.
- Use instructions that are simple and doubt-free.
- Avoid confusion by giving instructions that focus on one primary issue at a time.
- Let your singers know why you stopped and what to do to make it better.
- Avoid letting the rehearsal lapse into a practice session.
- Be clear about whether you are dealing with an error of preparation or an error of concentration before you begin to fix a problem. After all, it may not be broken, only out of focus.
- Remember that thought must be present for change to occur.
- Make sure time spent acknowledging accomplishment is, at the very least, equal to the time spent calling attention to a problem.
- Let your singers know you appreciate their good work. As the leader of the process, showing appreciation is one of your primary responsibilities.

The most successful rehearsals usually involve a series of quick raids on problems, separating out an issue and working on it in a way that involves those who are not singing as well as those who are. Getting stuck in one place can quickly bring a rehearsal to a grinding halt. Continually monitor the atmosphere and attitudes in the room. If you think you are beginning to lose your singers, then you probably already have. Take the following steps to accomplish a change:

1. **Identify** the problem.
2. **Recommend** a solution.
3. **Experience** a change.
4. **Remember** the feeling that created the solution to the problem.
5. **Acknowledge** the accomplishment.

Be persistent with the understanding that not all problems can be solved in one rehearsal. Before you move on, be sure your singers know what to do and how to practice to make it better. There is no shortcut to improvement. You and your singers come together as individuals to form an ensemble that has as its purpose the recreation of a work of art. Everyone should think of the rehearsal as an artistic assembly plant. The music gets put together at the plant. It is assembled each day and you listen to it work, all the while noticing where improvement is needed. At the end of the rehearsal, you disassemble the artwork and send a part of it home with every singer. Your singers agree to work on their parts so they will fit better the next time the piece is reassembled. Obviously, when a part is missing or not being sung well, the composition is less than whole and progress is impeded. In a very real sense, all musicians have the opportunity to bring a gift to rehearsal, something they make themselves at home...a beautiful part.

As conductors, we are responsible for using the time we have wisely. Some of the most effective rehearsal approaches are those offered by Barry Green in *The Inner Game of Music* (Doubleday, 1986). With this concept, our **will** is used to create **trust** and **respect** and increase **awareness**. Issues cannot improve without first increasing awareness. Trying often fails. Avoid using the word "try" in rehearsals. Instead, ask your singers to "think about," "look for," "focus on," "listen to," "make clear," or "bring out." Such a request creates failure-proof instruction.

Good rehearsals develop feeling as well as skill. Most rehearsal instructions are based on one of the **six skills of awareness** listed in **Figure 18-9**. To have a well-balanced rehearsal, it is important to give as many subjective instructions as objective ones. David Perkins suggests that ensembles will become more and more musical as they learn to identify and understand the relationships of the different aspects of playing (also listed in Figure 18-9). Both objective and subjective directions can lead us to improving their ability to identify and understand musical relationships.

Figure 18-9. Six skills of awareness.

OBJECTIVE INSTRUCTIONS +	SUBJECTIVE INSTRUCTIONS =	UNDERSTANDING RELATIONSHIPS
SEE	FEEL	CAUSE — EFFECT
REMEMBER	HEAR	WHOLE — PART
UNDERSTAND	IMAGINE	FOREGROUND — BACKGROUND
		FORM — FUNCTION
		UNITY — VARIETY
		LINES — LAYERS
		HORIZONTAL — VERTICAL — DIAGONAL
		COMPARISON — CONTRAST
		SUCCESSIVE — SIMULTANEOUS
		REPLICATE PRODUCT —
		CREATE INTERPRETATION

A primary goal is to assist your singers in fulfilling their potential by eliminating anything that interferes with the process. You can accomplish this by giving simple instructions that elicit an immediate response and create change. Remember to work on one issue at a time, simplify the instructions, avoid fear and confusion, and encourage your singers to become a part of the solution.

Step 3: Evaluating

While it is necessary and productive to critique and review your work, avoid becoming overly critical of your students as well as yourself. Acknowledging accomplishment is equal in importance to suggesting improvement. Develop ways to monitor your singers' progress during the process rather than focusing on an evaluation of the product at the end. In *Music Matters* (Oxford University Press, 1994), David Elliott reminds us that "it is imperative that we help our students to assess and evaluate their own developing musicianship." His options to help students map their progress include:

- **Compiling a "musical process folio,"** which can include audio and video tapes of students' efforts in group rehearsals and individual practice sessions; tapes of solo and small group performances during class and outside of class; students' self evaluation of their progress; lists of future rehearsal goals; written or recorded feedback from peers, teachers, or outside guests.

- **Writing an "ensemble rehearsal critique,"** similar to the many standardized evaluation forms used at festivals throughout the country. Additionally, students could write comments as they listen to or observe a recording of a rehearsal or performance.

- **Keeping a "practice journal or diary,"** which is the student's personal record of plans, achievements, and self-reflection that can be shared with peers and teachers for feedback and coaching. This is a terrific means of setting short-term and long-term goals as well as organizing practice time.

- **Notating a "listening log,"** which encourages students to listen to recordings of works they are learning to interpret and perform. Listening more widely to other works by the same composer or from the same style period can also be helpful. This process might also involve making interpretive comparisons of the same piece performed by different conductors or performers. Reading reviews can also be interesting and thought provoking.

In addition, structured debriefing sessions following rehearsals or performances can be beneficial. Here are some sample questions you could use to help your singers focus on their achievements and set new goals:

- What did you like about your performance?
- Is there still room for improvement?
- Do you think any performance can be absolutely perfect?
- If perfection is an impossible goal, what is the goal?
- Did you experience something in this performance that was new?
- Did you hear something in the music that was new?
- Did you see anything that you hadn't noticed before?
- Did you remember things you forgot you knew?
- Did you use your imagination to create images?
- Were you moved by this experience?
- Do you think you moved the audience?
- Did you feel connected to the music?
- Did you feel connected to your fellow musicians?
- Do you have any other comments or thoughts about this experience?

- What do you think you will remember most about this experience ten years from now?

Often in this setting the responses can be sensitive, perceptive, expressive and, quite simply, overwhelming. Providing a forum in which your singers can articulate their ideas, acknowledge their feelings, and share pride in their accomplishments will lead to many new discoveries!

In leading a closure session of this sort, we become immediately aware of David Elliot's premise that "music education is a unique and major source of several fundamental life values which include self-growth, self-knowledge, self-esteem, and musical enjoyment." Additionally, we recognize the value in his belief that "understanding and feeling music is achievable, accessible, and applicable to all students, not just the talented few."

Step 4: Closing

An educational approach that emphasizes the development of comprehensive musical knowledge while teaching musicianship will lead to broader and more meaningful experiences for everyone involved. At the very least, participation in a music program should create feelingful people who understand and enjoy music. Music creates a pathway to the center of our souls and provides a renewable resource for exploring and expressing our emotions. There is no doubt that music has the power to strengthen and enhance the human condition. In truth, music defines what being human means.

Music captures moments and preserves the essence of the various paradigms in the world that we call *culture*. As teachers and professionals, we must be careful not to limit ourselves to the most familiar or comfortable paradigms. The truth of the matter is that our limitations are too soon passed on to our students. If we make an eternal commitment to growth and remain open and curious, music can provide a unique way of knowing and experiencing each other and the world we share. Mary Anne Radmacher offers the following: "A key to a vital life is an eagerness to learn and a willingness to change." While music is not a language, it can express the thoughts and emotions of a culture or an individual in a way nothing else can. Music is and has always been multicultural because it exists within a context of people and places. It is wonderfully diverse, and if we are to continue to learn and grow, we must embrace that diversity.

Music is a primary condition of the human experience. In the history of man on earth, many civilizations have been identified that could not read, write, or calculate. None have been discovered that did not make music. It is also interesting to note that of all the species, only humans purposefully engage in making music. There are so many feelings in our hearts and images in our minds that can only be accessed through creating, performing, and audiating great music. When those thoughts and feelings are activated and engaged, we can experience the profound impact of music making as an endless source of inspirational energy that flows continually through our lives: elevating, expanding, and deepening our spirits.

Our interaction with music as performers and teachers is both cognitive and intuitive. The profession has coined phrases like "informed intuition" and "feelingful intelligence" in an attempt to explain this phenomenon. Increasing the depth of our musicianship gives us the ability to express our feelings while leading others to discover theirs.

As conductors and teachers, we have found that teaching and performing music is not something we do to make a living; it is something we do to make a life. It is important to understand that musicing is not about building a career; it is about living our purpose. I have heard it said that if you want to be known as a good conductor, you should only conduct good players (or singers). However, in the world of education, if we want to conduct good musicians, then we must become good teachers.

Chapter 19

Begin with Aural Study
Ear Before Eye

It might sound like only a game with words when one says that there is a difference between "learning about things" and "learning things," just as there is a difference between "speaking about religion" and "speaking religion" or "speaking about music" and "speaking music." However, we know that it is easier to have an opinion about life than it is to live wisely. It is also considerably easier to have an opinion about great music than it is to bring it to life. There is a subtle difference between intelligent, even sensitive interpretation and bringing music into existence: in the case of intelligent interpretation, the emphasis is on the opinion of the interpreter, but when music comes into existence, it speaks for itself. (p. 23)

Some of our greatest and deepest enjoyment as conductors can come not in performance, but in the quiet and intense process of learning during which the simple but profound truths of the score reveal themselves. We must constantly strive to come closer to the simple truths so that we may stimulate our singers (and audiences) toward such a search of their own. Our great subject is actually the search for those values which caused Bach's (or Mozart's or

Stravinsky's) work. If they are discovered, it is hoped that we might re-conquer them in order to possess them, so that they may become the cause of a more basic life of our own and be shared with those whom we conduct. (p. 24)

—Julius Herford
in *The Choral Journal*

No matter how diverse their views on every other topic, most musicians agree that finding the right tempo is at least half the interpretation. Wagner went further, asserting that the right tempo was the interpretation. In his essay *On Conducting*, he writes: "I am persistently returning to the question of tempo because, as I said before, this is the point at which it becomes evident whether a conductor understands his business or not." Tempo is also the principal feature singled out by critics in commenting on p erformers. With all this consensus on the crucial importance of tempo, it may seem curious that musicians hardly ever agree on the proper choice of tempo. Accord in theory has never spread into agreement in practice. (p. 101)

—Erich Leinsdorf
in *The Composer's Advocate*

Musical analysis, then, is the attempt to comprehend the
composer's musical language tonally and temporally. It asks: what is
his vocabulary?—what are his materials?—what are the metric
motifs?—what are the melodic motifs?—how does he organize
those pitches which sound simultaneously?—which sound
successively?—what tone "colors" are uniquely his?—how does he
deal with loudness and quietness? And finally, what materials are
"structural" (and important) and what are "accompanimental"
(and subsidiary)? pp. 57–58

—Robert Shaw
in *The Robert Shaw Reader*

Many will be somewhat familiar with the score study techniques addressed in
later chapters. However, I have found it very useful to begin the score study
process from a slightly different perspective. I have long believed that musical
notation at times misrepresents the rhythmic structure of a piece. In other words,
notation introduces strong interpretative biases that are based on how the score
appears to the person viewing it.

Consider the following: Would you interpret the same musical example
differently if it were in triple meter but notated in 3/4, or 6/8, or 9/8, or 12/8? From
an aural point of view, we should not interpret the above meters in most situations
different from one another. However, depending upon instruction and experience,
for some reason we do.

I have found it useful to begin the score study process by listening to a fine
recording of the piece I am going to study—and to listen to that recording multiple
times without a score! Then when I look at the score, it is always surprising to
discover that the score (from a rhythmic point of view) looked nothing liked I had
anticipated it would.

When studying a score, it is important to first study how the piece moves
forward. Conductors, through gesture, relay how a piece of music moves forward.

Your gesture reflects the large macrobeat structure, which is in direct relation to how the piece feels in your body. Sometimes notation either interferes with the larger rhythmic intent or, in some cases, works in opposition to it. And in some situations, the rhythmic structure is accurately reflected in the notated score.

What I am advocating is to learn the rhythmic structure of a score first, not the specific tonal and pitch elements of the score. I believe every score has its unique kinesthetic. It is important to know first how a score feels in your body as you perform it. I also believe that kinesthetic understanding unlocks many of the musical secrets of each score and should be the first element of a musical c omposition that is studied.

A recording can also be helpful in becoming familiar with the harmonic language of a score. Aural familiarity of harmonic structure is a prerequisite to learning the tonal specificities of a score.

Rhythmic Organization and Breath

I have found that many young or inexperienced conductors begin learning scores by studying them visually. They mark the scores dutifully, and even attempt to learn some of the sound aspects of the score. Instead, score study needs to begin with the study of two mutually dependent factors: **the quality of rhythmic motion and breath.**

Rhythmic motion (or phrasal inertia) in music is set in motion by the breath. The arch of a phrase and its trajectory is charted solely by the energy of the breath and the temporal time allotted to that breath. Ironically, these two elements hold the keys to the central understandings of any piece of music. And those understandings can only be acquired aurally. Visual study of a score can only provide cursory information. For the essences of phrase motion, sounds must be heard, experienced, and sensed by the conductor.

William James, the great American psychologist of the nineteenth century, had a fascination with rhythm perception. How we learn, or rather acquire, rhythm was the focus of much of his observational research and writing. One of the most fascinating insights his writings provide rests in his theory that all rhythm learning occurs kinesthetically—and that all rhythmic information enters through the sensations in the joints of one's body. It was his contention that if we could not move, we could not acquire rhythm. For James, rhythm was an experience migrated by rhythm sensations acquired through joint movement. Applying this to music, it would follow then that if rhythmic information is channeled through our joints, then that information concerning the movement of the musical phrase could only be acquired through movement. Movement of the joints of the body provides kinesthetic markers.

One of my teachers, Elaine Brown, always used to quote her favorite description of music:

"Music is silent screaming, motionless dance."

"Silent screaming" refers to the joy and human emotion in music, and "motionless dance" clues us into one of music's most fascinating paradoxes: sound that portrays and relays motion.

Emile Jacques-Dalcroze has informed generations of teachers and students of the importance of body kinesthetic in understanding the musical phrase. Rudolf von Laban informed our body sensitivities one step beyond Dalcroze by bringing attention to the factor of weight. In a number of experimental studies in the 1980s, using the theory of William James, I became fascinated with the singular role that weight displacement held in *all* rhythmic learning. Those studies convincingly proved that feelings of weight inform one's rhythm performance and, in point of fact, dramatically improve it. I suspect Dalcroze knew this, as did Kodaly and Orff. While movement and the awareness of weight displacement are somewhat commonplace these days in classroom teaching and studio teaching, I have found that conductors are a reluctant audience—at least from the waist down!

Approaching the Score as a Kinesthetic Experience

If we use movement as the first litmus test in score study, such information not only provides insight into the musical matters at hand, but also deeply and profoundly informs the rehearsal process—and the conducting gesture that is then used to sound the score.

In this age of the iPod, score study has placed a musical world in our pockets. My iPod has become my most valuable score study tool. The first aspect of my score study is to listen to the work I am about to prepare *without looking* at the score. I usually listen to the work several times, and at some point, I move to what I hear. That movement always informs my decision about both conducting and teaching the work.

Measure Signature vs. Meter Signature

One of the initial problems in score study, and subsequently rehearsal pedagogy, begins with the misunderstanding of the numbers that appear at the start of a score. Many of us refer to these numbers (e.g., 3/4, 6/8, 5/8, 12/8) as meter signatures. In many cases, these numbers have no aural significance. They simply inform the printer where to draw the bar line! Composers take care to make certain the meter signatures they choose reflect the rhythmic structure; however, for larger phrasal movements, these signatures are, at best, inadequate. Renaissance composers knew this all too well and avoided the use of bar lines; they left the displacement of accents to the role of the text and the performers. But it is also important to realize that Renaissance rhythm structures and most, if not all, Baroque rhythm structures were directly informed by dance.[1]

The work of Laban, discussed in Chapter 28, "Using the Principles of Laban Movement Score Analysis (LMSA)," leads us to the understanding that all musical style is related to weight displacement: styles in musical sound are achieved either through the withholding of weight or the direct displacement of weight. This displacement of weight, and the intimate kinesthetic understanding of the displacement of that weight, is key to the score study process.

As mentioned, for me the first stage of score study is to listen to the music without a score, and then move my entire body to the music. I initially begin by stepping the music to understand the large beat structure. After I kinesthetically move to the beat structure, I will then move my body to the musical phrases in the performance I am listening to. Only when I am comfortable with moving to the music I hear through my iPod do I look at the score! It is fascinating to discover how many times the measure signature is in conflict to what my body has led me to believe. When such a conflict arises, I always go with my kinesthetic information for both teaching and conducting.

---

1   One of the most exhaustive studies of rhythmic phrase structure and tempo in Baroque can be found in the work of Meredith Ellis Little.

To summarize, here are the steps for iPod rhythm score study:

1. Listen to the music through an iPod. On first listening, begin to find the large beat structure.

2. On repeated listenings, move around the room to the music, first by stepping to the music.

3. After you have stepped to the music to uncover its rhythmic structure, then move your entire body to the score to discover where and how much weight to displace to mirror the phrase direction and phrase structure.

4. Throughout the movement process, make sure you are breathing for each phrase *and* releasing air as you move through the phrase.

5. Finally, continue to move while you moan in a deep, almost primal moan to each of the phrases of the music.

Learning to Breathe a Piece

One of the most valuable aspects of score study is to learn how a piece "breathes." The breath informs all matters musical both for the conductor and the ensemble. The duration, depth, and quality of breath directly affect the motion of the phrase that follows. As you move to the sounding of a piece during score study, you should also study the breath in conjunction with how the piece moves. Phrase motion and breath form one organic unit and, thus, need to be studied as such.

While the study of tonal materials is important, obviously to understanding a composer's harmonic language, it is the interrelationship of breath and the resultant rhythmic motion that provide the keys to the basal and most important organic elements of the score. It is most often these elements that are entrusted with the human message of the score.

It is important to also remember that while taking a breath informs the initial energy of a phrase, your exhalation as conductor allows for the natural trajectory of the phrase. Inhalation and exhalation are vital elements in the score study process.

Overall Principles of Aural Metric Organization: Duple vs. Triple

Perhaps we can more easily accept the above-mentioned conflict between measure signatures and meter signatures if we revisit rhythmic structures of the Renaissance. In the Renaissance, there were but two meters: **duple** and **triple**. The "large" beat could only be divided into two or three. From an aural perspective, this is the only possibility, unless the beat is indivisible, in which case it is both large beat and its own subdivision (e.g., 3/8 followed by 1/8 followed by 5/8). From a score study perspective, decisions must be based upon aural and kinesthetic input regarding how the music moves. Remember that the written measure signature is usually in conflict with what is actually being sounded in a piece of music.

Acquiring Harmonic Syntax

It is generally accepted that conductors "know" a score only when they have learned each of the individual parts in the score. I am a strong advocate of the use of *la*-based minor solfege to acquire such understanding. However, again using an iPod or similar listening device, there is an understanding that needs to be in place *before* you begin the tedious and necessary process of singing each part with solfege. After moving to the work you have just begun studying, I strongly advocate repeated listenings to immerse oneself in the harmonic language and harmonic motion of the composer. This process is best accomplished without notational influence! Depending on our background and experience, notation moves us from the organic experience of the score to a theoretical realm. Theory helps us to understand the inner workings of the score but often clouds our clear perception of what is really happening harmonically within a work. It is important for conductor/teachers to work *first* from the perspective of sound.

Chapter 20

Analysis of Tune and Text

Ordinary musical experiences are gratifying largely because they organize an aspect of human existence that generally comes to us as chaos: time. These ordinary musical experiences may also evoke pleasing memories, suggest touching characters (hope, sadness, grandeur), or set into motion a complex network of thoughts.

There is also, however, an extraordinary experience available though music. The greatest Western art music, well performed, can lead to no less than a spiritual experience, an experience that transcends the physical parameters of time and space. It is the feeling of becoming lost—of losing oneself in the experience. It is losing the self and becoming the sounds. It is the rare and magical experience of the entire work filling a single moment. This is the ultimate, highest, experience of musical beauty. (p. xv)

—Markand Thakar
in *Counterpoint: Fundamentals of Music Making*

I have spent most of my life working with melodies, singing continuously as a child and in formal and informal groups as I grew older, concentrating in organ and composition in college, and then majoring in choral conducting at Juilliard with Robert Shaw, which gave my life its direction. In working with him, I felt as though I'd never really listened before, never been aware of the subtleties of living sound, of the incredible variety of sounds the throat can produce. We began working on arrangements for albums recorded by the Shaw Chorale, and I spent hours, days, and weeks in the New York Public Library sifting through thousands of songbooks. I began to get a sense of what melodies would work for me, for us, which would produce a wonderful arrangement or which would lead to okay but uninspiring results. (p. 3)

The answer was always within the single line itself—not the setting, the harmonies (actual or implied), or any of its elements separately. The tune itself (text + rhythm + pitch) contained, like a seed, all the elements needed for its growth. If something was missing, one might try to replace it with cleverness, but never with profundity. Over the twenty years Robert Shaw and I worked together, I came to have a profound respect for any melody that lasted, any melody that successive generations have sung and loved and kept in their hearts and passed onto the next. (p. 4)

I sometimes think of song as an invisible presence always around us, an ever-present possibility hovering like a cloud above us. The song is implicit until it is sounded—then it begins to pulse and glow, come to life, flourish, and fade away. The first sound released into the room either conjures forth the melody or makes it impossible for it to live. The first sound followed by others that never break the chain creates a structure as sturdy—and as fleeting—as a tree, a leaf, or a flower and as flowing as water. (p. 7)

—Alice Parker
in *The Anatomy of Melody*

The chapters that follow present an overview of several different systems of analysis relating to harmonic structure, harmonic motion, and cadence structures. Phrase lengths are studied and charted, and large forms achieve a visual representation so a work's superstructure can be realized. Instrumentations, dynamics, and translations of texts are analyzed in an effort to seek their deeper meaning through the language of the composer. Many of us, however, fail to look at the most obvious of musical materials: the tune that binds all of these elements together into an organic whole. We study harmonic structure but at times seem to ignore the one aspect that might provide the most clues in our musical search— melody. There have been many courses on analysis for conductors. Yet Robert Shaw was often heard to remark that we have courses in everything else, so why don't we have any in melody?

While writing this book, I was given a copy of just such a "course" in the form of a new book on melody entitled *The Anatomy of Melody* by Alice Parker (GIA, 2006). This is a book I enthusiastically recommend to conductors, and I thank Alice Parker for sharing her insights with us. In that book, she identifies some characteristics of our musical search concerning melody. She writes:

The issue here is not originality, but inevitability. Our society's preoccupation with originality has been one of the great misapprehensions of these times. Novelty is certainly a welcome component in art, but surely not the *sine qua non* of artistic achievement. Pushing back the boundaries is often the role of the young and the reckless, but profundity more often seems to look inward rather than out. The greatest art can arise from the simplest and most timeworn materials. (p. 122)

Regarding the score study process, I am suggesting that you perform an analysis of the melody alone and search for all its rich inner components that will, in turn, inform your music making. And I am recommending the process that Alice Parker suggests in her book, which is presented in Figure 20-1. I also suggest two ancillary and supporting approaches to assist in this process: (1) the interpretation of text as either narrative or first person, as discussed in Chapter 25, "Understanding the Journey of Texts," and (2) the "day-tay" system of Weston Noble.[1] I encourage you to read both of these chapters in conjunction with this chapter to gain a broad overview of the possibilities of melodic analysis.

In the score study process, it is extremely important to view the melody and its internal dynamics alone. Analysis of the shape of the melody, in addition to its organizational length, is important. Carefully examine the relation of text to the musical elements to look for hidden secrets. Refer to **Figure 20-1** for **Alice Parker's recommended guidelines for melodic analysis**, as contained in her book.[2]

Figure 20-1.
List of elements to consider when analyzing and/or performing a melody.

Voicing: Who is singing?

solo/group

high voices/low voices

old person/young person

man/woman

child/grown-up

Text: Who is speaking?

color/idiom

tone of voice

meaning

form (verse structure)

loaded syllables

metaphors

alliteration, etc.

Rhythm: Who is dancing?

free/metric

duple/triple

steady/changing

fast/slow

quality of beat (accent, dance)

tempo

---

1   The "day-tay" system of Weston Noble is covered in Chapter 31 of Volume 1 of *The Choral Rehearsal* (GIA, 2007).

2   Parker, Alice. *The Anatomy of Melody*. Chicago: GIA Publications, 2006, pp. 136–137.

Figure 20-1. (Continued)

Pitch

mode/scale

home/cadence

range/tessitura

sonority

phrase curves

Articulation

legato/non-legato

marcato/staccato

Dynamics

soft/loud

sudden/gradual

Mood/sonority (Can you find the right word?)

swinging

bouncy

firmly

swaying

forceful

with humor

tenderly

teasing

floating, etc.

Form

phrase structure

question/answer

parallel/opposite

endings/connections

repetition/variation (exact or partial)

beginning/middle/end

climax/resolution

Can you add to this list?

When examining a tune, Alice Parker submits the melody to a careful analysis. In examining the melody *Teach Me the Measure*, she details the following:

Melodic Analysis of *Teach Me the Measure*[3]

Text:

Source: Isaac Watts, Psalm 39 II, 5 vs.

Form: 8.6.8.6

Rhyming: *abab*

Mood: somber meditation on the brevity of life

Voice: formal English

Color words/dynamics/changing moods:

(1) measure, maker, narrow space, frail ***mp*** sad

(2) span, boast, inch, vanity, dust, flower, prime ***mf*** regret

(3) vain, mortals, shadows, rage, strive, desire, love, noise, vain ***f*** firm

(4) wish, wait, creatures, earth, dust, expectations vain, disappoint trust ***pp*** lost

(5) forbid, hope, recall, give up mortal int'rest, my God my all ***mf>p*** stern, then acceptance

Music:

Source: *Kentucky Harmony*, 1816

Time: Suffield

Pitches: modal e minor (all seven notes), range D to F-sharp (a tenth), demands good voices

Rhythm: 3–2/2–2, slow, quiet, relentless, coiled energy, half-note pickups, parallel durations 1–3 and 2–4, whole-note endings.

Phrases, range and endings:

(1) gentle curves up and down; fifth, E to B to E;   home

(2) up a third, then stepwise down; fourth, G to B to F-sharp;   away

(3) down from B to E, then dramatic leap up, climax; B up again to F-sharp alt, then back to B tenth B to E to F-sharp to B;   away

(4) up a second, then stepwise down to E; sixth, B to C to E;   home

---

3 Alice Parker, *The Anatomy of Melody* (GIA, 2006), p. 141.

The idea is not to do *the* perfect performance, but to keep the melody alive, the song singing, and the energy refreshing to everyone within hearing. And when we have to stop—the song is there, ready to be picked up the next time.

This kind of music-making is transformative. It should be just as much in tune, in time, and in style as we can make it, but it's much more than that. It is merging with the creative energies that propel the universe, absorbing us all into the stream of life. (p. 126)

—Alice Parker
in *The Anatomy of Melody*

Chapter 21

Vocal Score Study

Analyzing the Vocal Requirements of a Score

Whenever you are planning to teach a piece to your choir, there are three separate processes of score analysis you must consider: (1) analysis of the overall structure and harmonic movement and phrase structure using the Herford style of analysis (presented in Chapter 26), (2) harmonic solfege analysis to determine solfege for each individual part within the choir (presented in Chapters 15 and 16 of *The Choral Rehearsal*, Vol. 1) and (3) vocal technique analysis of the score, to be covered in this chapter.

Some of the best advice I received from a former colleague when I began my teaching career admonished me to "try to predict ahead of time every vocal technique mistake the choir might make before you even hear the piece." Examining the score in this way not only deeply informs the pedagogy needed to teach the piece, but it may also give insight as to the technical difficulty of the piece.

A listing of the **elements of vocal technique** (in order of pedagogical importance, from the most fundamental elements to the more challenging elements) is presented in **Figure 21-1**. Frauke Haasemann gave me this list years ago when I asked her if her teaching had any "order" to it. Her belief was that vocal technique in a choral ensemble is built sequentially through the effective planning of the choral warm-up.[1] Dr. Haasemann always told her students that "choirs need vocal tools" (i.e., vocal technique that is built in a logical and consistent process). A potpourri approach to choral training does achieve results, but it is not healthy or efficient over the long term. A pedagogical "roadmap" is necessary. This roadmap can be slightly different depending upon the vocal requirements of the pieces to be taught in any rehearsal. Therefore, it is important that you spend considerable time analyzing the

---

1 In support of that belief, this author developed detailed procedures and pedagogy for teaching voice and planning an efficient choral warm-up in *The Choral Warm-Up* (Chicago: GIA, 2005).

pieces to be taught for the vocal elements you would need to teach to the choir. Your lesson plans need to be developed around the vocal technique that needs to be taught in rehearsal, as well as the tonal and rhythm aspects of the score.

Figure 21-1. Elements of vocal technique in order of pedagogical importance.

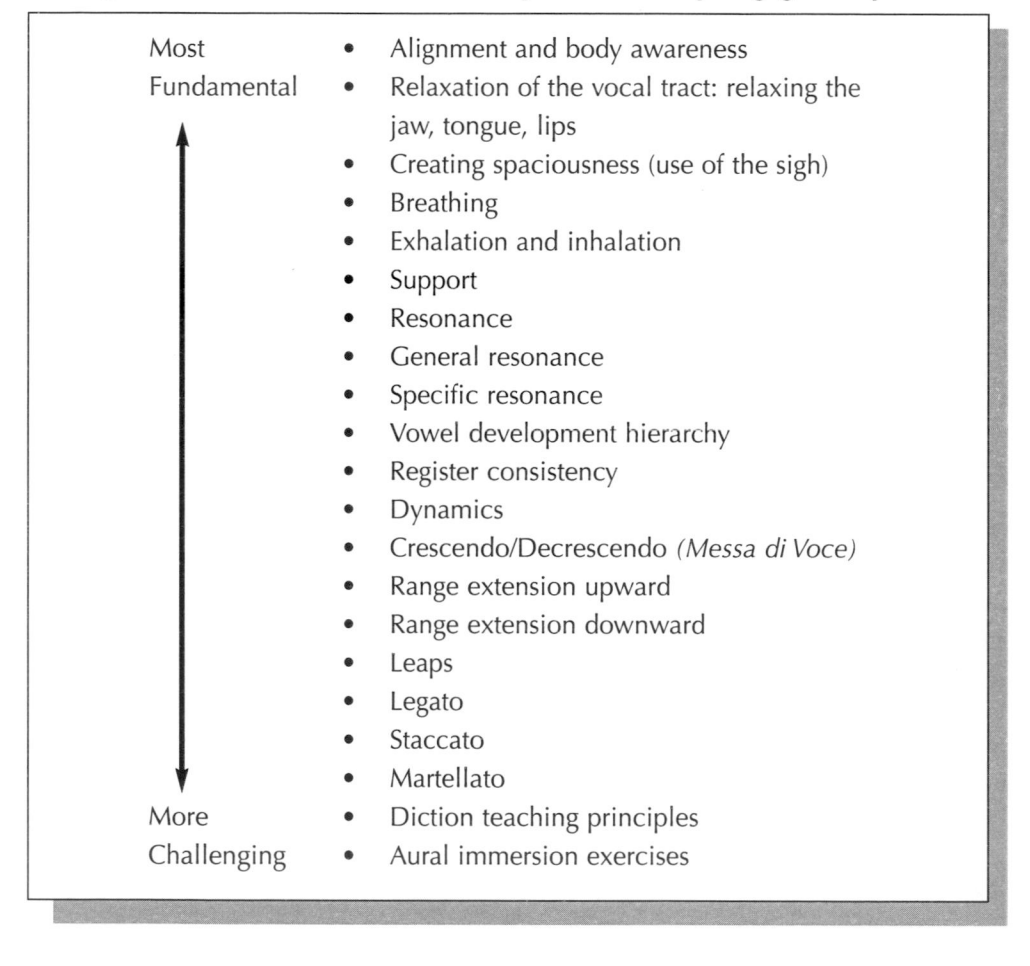

Most	• Alignment and body awareness
Fundamental	• Relaxation of the vocal tract: relaxing the jaw, tongue, lips
	• Creating spaciousness (use of the sigh)
	• Breathing
	• Exhalation and inhalation
	• Support
	• Resonance
	• General resonance
	• Specific resonance
	• Vowel development hierarchy
	• Register consistency
	• Dynamics
	• Crescendo/Decrescendo *(Messa di Voce)*
	• Range extension upward
	• Range extension downward
	• Leaps
	• Legato
	• Staccato
	• Martellato
More	• Diction teaching principles
Challenging	• Aural immersion exercises

Example 1:
Venite Exultemus Domino **Jan Pieterszoon Sweelinck**
Evoking Sound Choral Series (GIA, 2004) G-5930

The first step in proceeding with a vocal analysis is to make the following determinations:

1. Choral "resonance" required from the historical performance practice of the work
2. Appropriate vowel resonance for the musical style
3. Appropriate tempo that allows for the best "singing" of the piece, which is dependent upon (a) the experience and age of the singers and (b) the acoustic

Resonance for the Piece: tall, narrow vowel sounds
Tempo: half note=72

I recommend using the Elements of Vocal Technique in Figure 21-1 as a guideline to examine a piece for its inherent vocal problems. I have completed such an analysis on the first thirty measures of **Venite Exultemus Domino** to illustrate how to proceed through such a vocal analysis. In looking at the score, shown in **Figure 21-2**, I circled and numbered each part.

Figure 21-2. Sample analysis of *Venite Exultemus Domino*.

VENITE EXULTEMUS DOMINO
For SSATB Voices and Keyboard

Psalm 95:1–3

Jan Pieterszoon Sweelinck (1562–1621)
Edited by James Jordan

*Come, ring out our joy to the Lord;
hail the rock who saves us.
Let us come before God, giving thanks,
with songs let us hail the Lord.
A mighty God is the Lord,
a great king above all gods.*
—The Grail

Copyright © 2004 by GIA Publications, Inc. • All Rights Reserved • Printed in U.S.A.
7404 S. Mason Ave., Chicago, IL 60638 • www.giamusic.com • 800.442.1358
Reproduction of this publication without permission of the publisher is a violation of the U.S. Code of Law
for which the responsible individual or institution is subject to criminal prosecution. No one is exempt

Figure 21-2. (Continued)

Figure 21-2. (Continued)

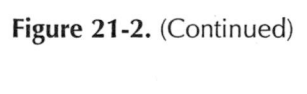

Figure 21-2. (Continued)

Next I created a running "**key**" for the numbers assigned (shown in **Figure 21-3**). This chart includes not only a description of the problem but also a possible solution. Use the chart in conjunction with the sample marked score (Figure 21-2).

Such a completed analysis can serve as the foundation of your planning for warm-ups; it clearly charts the vocal/pedagogical course of the work as it proceeds through the rehearsal process. You gain an umbrella overview of all (or at least the most important) vocal issues within the score. This important pedagogical overview will make your rehearsal process more efficient and pedagogically sound.

This analysis process is especially helpful, and somewhat necessary, for beginning teachers or conductors, or others who are new to the vocal pedagogical procedures of a choral rehearsal.

Figure 21-3. Sample analysis chart of *Venite Exultemus Domino*.

Analysis No. as marked in Figure 21-2	Problem	Solution
1 (soprano)	Upward leap	Start with bright, forward vowel; make sure tongue position is high enough for "eh" vowel; close "ee" vowel on upward leap; make internal space on upward leap (represented by circles).
2 (soprano)	Repeated vowel sounds	Re-sing vowel on each pitch; maintain high tongue position for each re-sung vowel; make sure vowel sounds do not open.
3 (soprano)	Same as measure 1	
4–5 (soprano)	Same as measure 2	
5 (soprano)	Rhythmic breath	Make sure breath is in the tempo of the piece and occupies a full quarter note value.
6 (soprano)	No diphthong	Sing only the first vowel sound and make sure vowel is sufficiently closed.
7 (soprano)	Rhythmic breath	Make sure breath is in the tempo of the piece and occupies a full quarter note value.
8 (soprano)	Vowel consistency	Make sure tongue stays high for both vowels and that both vowels have some degree of closure.

Figure 21-3. (Continued)

Analysis No. as marked in Figure 21-2	Problem	Solution
9 (soprano)	Register consistency	Make sure sound remains high and forward on downward leap; make sure breath is rhythmic.
10 (soprano I, soprano II, tenor)	Insert breath	Change half note value to quarter note and quarter rest to ensure clean phrasing.
11	Register consistency and breath	Make sure sound remains high and forward on downward leap—no crescendo on downward leap!
12	Upward leap/ register consistency	Make space on upward leap and maintain a closed vowel at top of leap; to have a more separated leap, place "n" consonant on top note of leap; if a legato leap is desired, place "n" consonant on bottom note of leap.
13	*Messa di Voce*	Give choir technique for singing crescendo/decrescendo on one pitch; use vowel opening and closing to assist with crescendo/decrescendo process.
14	Martellato/ repeated vowel sounds	Use martellato articulation technique on sixteenth note passage; re-sing vowels on repeated notes.
15 (tenor)	Non-legato leap	Place "n" consonant on top note of leap; make space on upward leap; keep vowel closed on "ni."

Figure 21-3. (Continued)

Analysis No. as marked in Figure 21-2	Problem	Solution
16 (soprano II)	Register consistency; upward leap	Maintain high and forward sound in lower tessitura; make space on ascending leap; keep vowels closed on upward leaps!
17 (alto)	Lower register issues; phrasing	Maintain high and forward sound; do not allow for crescendo; if not enough sound, instruct singers to open the vowel sounds; can also cue in a few tenors for color.
18 (alto, tenor, bass)	Register consistency and upward leaps	Maintain high and forward space in lower register; make internal space for upward leaps; keep vowels closed on upward leaps; make sure all breaths are rhythmic and in character of piece.
19 (tenor)	Register consistency	Maintain high and forward sound; do not allow tenors to crescendo; if more sound is needed, cue baritones.
20 (bass)	Repeated vowel sounds	Re-sing the vowel on each repeated note.
21 (all parts)	Vowel issues; register consistency	Make sure vowel sounds between "eh," "oo," "ee," and "oh" are accomplished with quick changes of tongue position to ensure good intonation; make sure "eh" vowels are high and forward; make sure diphthongs are not sounded!

Figure 21-3. (Continued)

Analysis No. as marked in Figure 21-2	Problem	Solution
22 (all parts)	rhythmic breath	Because of the slight change in articulation in the next section, a breath must be taken in the new rhythmic character and spirit of the piece; make sure singers breathe in the vowel shape of the first pitch.
23 (bass)	repeated tones	Make sure each note is articulated and the tongue position does not change as each note is sustained; also make sure vowel sounds do not open as notes are repeated; maintain high and forward sound throughout entire passage.
24 (soprano I, II)	Diphthong	Sufficiently close final vowels to achieve a muted, reduced text stress on last syllable; allow no diphthongs!
25 (soprano I, II)	Breath	Make sure breath is in tempo of piece and occupies a full quarter note duration!
26 (alto/tenor)	Diction	No diphthong; stay on first vowel sound.
27 (soprano I, II)	Articulation	Make sure the choir springs to each vowel sound; marcato articulation for rhythmic quality.

Figure 21-3. (Continued)

Analysis No. as marked in Figure 21-2	Problem	Solution
28 (alto)	High and forward sound	Because of the low tessitura of this part, maintain a high, forward vocal sound; may need to use physical gesture to maintain this "placement."
29 (bass)	Diction/ register consistency	Make sure singers do not change the vowel as they sustain longer tones; also make sure the vocal sound remains "high and forward" when the octave leap occurs.
30 (bass)	Breath/diction	Insist on a rhythmic breath that is the value of the half rest; make sure the tongue position is high enough on the "eh" vowel to bring enough resonance to the vowel.
31 (alto, tenor)	Breath/diction/ dynamic	Make sure the breath is rhythmic in this measure; make sure the tongue position is high enough on the "eh" vowel to bring enough resonance to the vowel; make sure the vowel is sufficiently closed and spacious to produce a resonant *piano* sound.
32 (soprano I, II)	Resonance	Make sure the singers maintain a spacious sound throughout all the vowels.
33 (tenor, bass)	High/forward	Make sure all vowels are kept high and forward.

Figure 21-3. (Continued)

Analysis No. as marked in Figure 21-2	Problem	Solution
34 (all parts)	Breath	Make sure all breaths are rhythmic.
22–34 (all parts)	On-the-breath singing	In quasi-marcato passages such as these, the choir will be inclined to sing such passages "off the breath"; be vigilant to listen for on-the-breath singing at all times.
35 (alto)	Rhythmic breathing	Make sure a rhythmic breath is taken in the proper dynamic.
36 (tenor, bass)	Rhythmic breathing, rhythmic clarity, diction	Place the "s" of the "mus" on the first beat of the measure and breathe at the same time; make sure the vowel of "faciem" occurs on the beat; have the choir eliminate the eighth note that is tied to the quarter note for rhythmic clarity.

Example 2:
Geistliches Lied, Op. 30 Johannes Brahms
Evoking Sound Choral Series (GIA, 2004) G-6480

As in Example 1, the first step in proceeding with a vocal analysis is to make the following determinations:

1. Choral "resonance" required from the historical performance practice of the work
2. Appropriate vowel resonance for the musical style
3. Appropriate tempo that allows for the best "singing" of the piece, which is dependent upon (a) the experience and age of the singers and (b) the acoustic

Again, understand that these decisions are made first but are often changed after the score study is completed.

Resonance for the Piece: round vowel sounds
Make sure all breaths that are taken in this work are round and deeply seated.
Tempo: half note= ca. 64

When doing this type of vocal analysis, there are many more problems than perhaps could be circled in any passage or score. So you should become skilled at selecting the most significant problems your choir will likely encounter. Remember that this process is aimed at your ability to predict the vocal problems of your choir before the ensemble ever sings the work. You will be better prepared for rehearsal if you can anticipate what problems are likely to occur in rehearsal before they actually occur. Vocal "prognostication" is perhaps the most helpful rehearsal preparation tool. Time is always well spent when this analysis is done on each piece to be rehearsed.

Figure 21-4. Sample analysis of *Geistliches Lied, Op. 30*.

For the Inaugural Season of the Williamson Voices of Westminster Choir College, James Jordan, Conductor.

GEISTLICHES LIED, OP. 30
LASS DICH NUR NICHTS NICHT DAUREN
Let Nothing Ever Grieve You
For SATB Voices and Organ
Major

Text: Paul Flemming (1609–1640)

Johannes Brahms (1833–1897)
Edited by James Jordan

Copyright © 2004 by GIA Publications, Inc. • All Rights Reserved • Printed in U.S.A.
7404 S. Mason Ave., Chicago, IL 60638 • www.giamusic.com • 800.442.1358
Reproduction of this publication without permission of the publisher is a violation of the U.S. Code of Law
for which the responsible individual or institution is subject to criminal prosecution. No one is exempt.

Figure 21-4. (Continued)

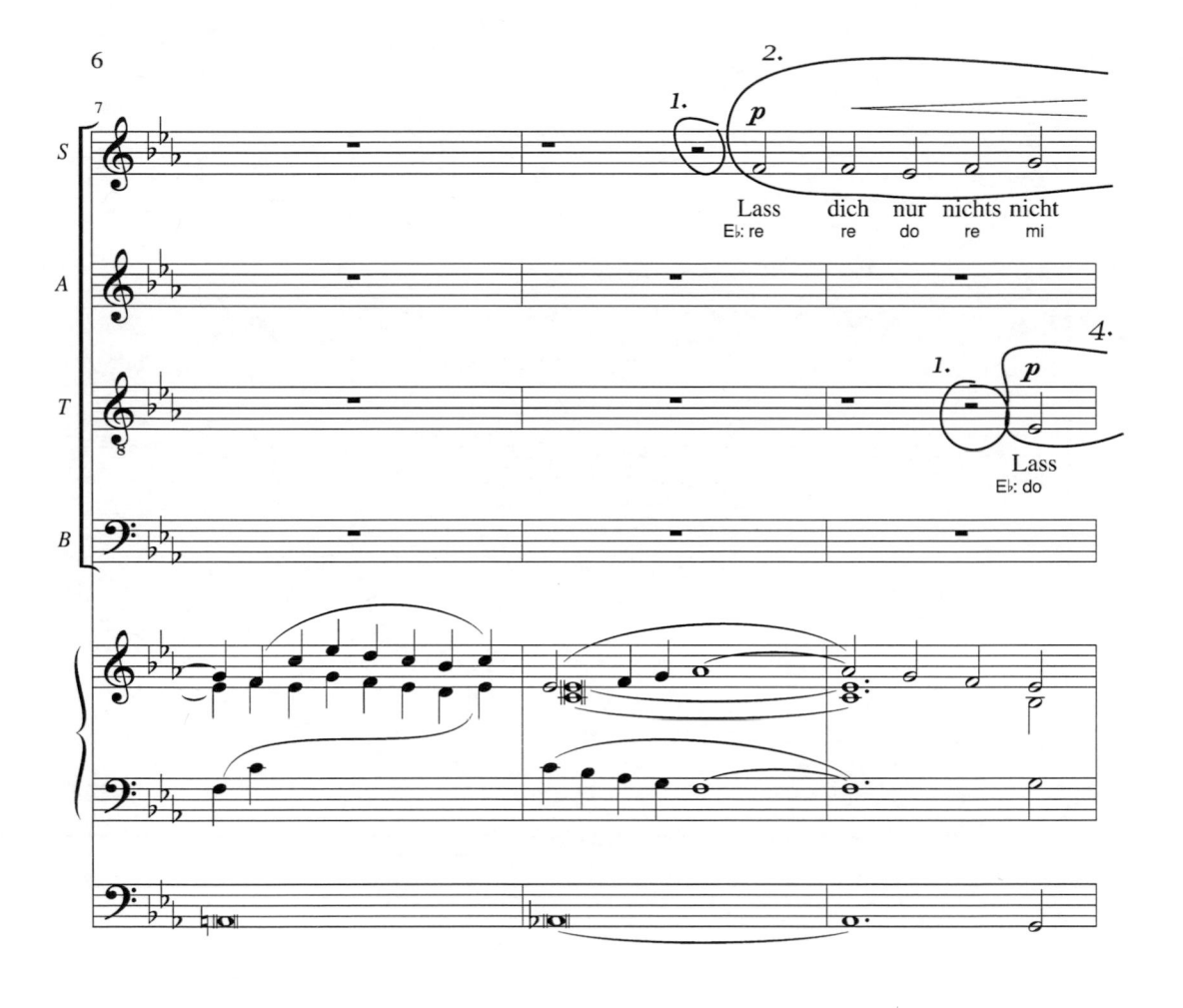

Figure 21-4. (Continued)

Figure 21-4. (Continued)

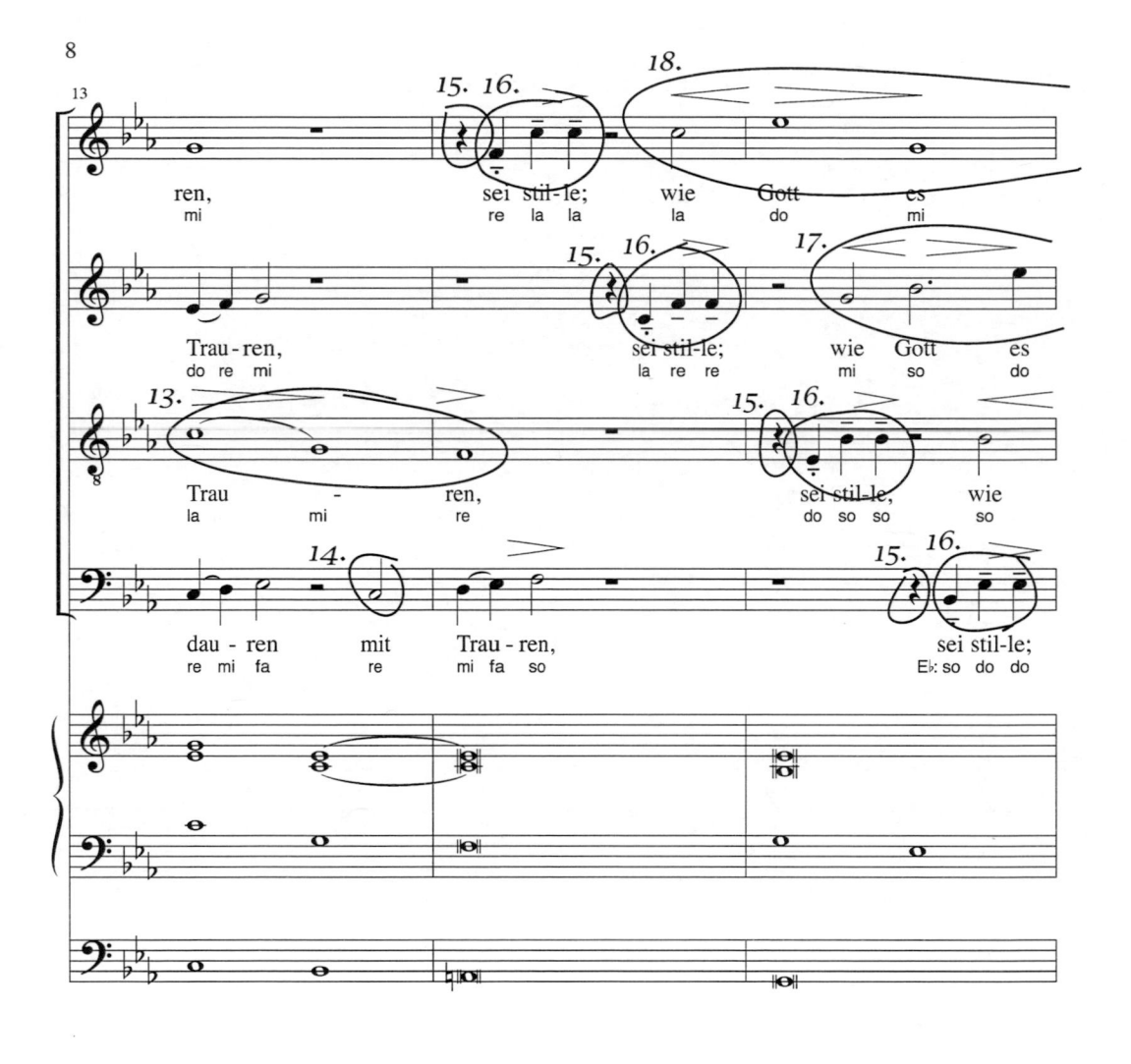

Figure 21-4. (Continued)

Figure 21-5. Sample analysis chart of *Geistliches Lied, Op. 30*.

Analysis No. as marked in Figure 21-4	Problem	Solution
1 (all parts, initial entrance)	Breath	The key to this work is to make sure the breaths are as deep and low as possible, and are seated within the body as deeply as possible; it is the depth and interiority of the breath that establishes the vocal color of this piece.
2 (soprano)	Resonance	Because of the low tessitura of this piece, make sure the sopranos keep their sound high and forward at all times.
3 (soprano)	Diction	It is important that all unaccented, unstressed syllables be muted by wrapping lips around the vowel.
4 (tenor)	Resonance	Because of the low tessitura of this piece, make sure the tenors keep their sound high and forward at all times.
5 (alto)	Resonance	Because of the low tessitura of this piece, make sure the altos keep their sound high and forward as they begin this line.
6 (alto)	Upward leap	While only a third, it is important that the singers maintain support and make more space for the sound as they ascend.

Figure 21-5. (Continued)

Analysis No. as marked in Figure 21-4	Problem	Solution
7 (alto)	Downward leap	This downward octave leap is treacherous; make sure as the altos descend the octave, they keep the sound high and forward and do not increase volume as they descend.
8 (alto)	Lift/passagio issues	In the area of pitches B–C, many altos experience "lift" or "break" problems; if the singers do not maintain supported, on-the-breath singing, out-of-tune singing will result.
9 (bass)	Downward leap	This downward octave leap is treacherous; make sure as the altos descend the octave, they keep the sound high and forward and do not increase volume as they descend.
10 (soprano)	Spacious	Because this line starts in the upper middle range of the soprano, it is important that the note is sung with space and grows out of the breath before; make sure there is sufficient head tone contained in the resonance of the pitch.
11 (soprano)	Downward leap	Make sure sound is maintained high and forward as the downward leap is executed.
12 (tenor)	Initial attack	Make sure tenors sing their entrance on the breath.

Figure 21-5. (Continued)

Analysis No. as marked in Figure 21-4	Problem	Solution
13 (tenor)	Downward leap	Make sure sound is maintained high and forward as the downward leap is executed.
14 (bass)	Lower register attack	Begin sound high and forward.
15 (all parts)	Rhythmic breath	Make sure singers are breathing in quarter rest value and the breath is rhythmic.
16 (all parts)	Upward leaps	Make sure these leaps are begun high and forward, and support is increased before the leap is executed and internal space is made as the leaps ascends.
17 (alto)	Upward leaps	Make sure these leaps are begun high and forward, and support is increased before the leap is executed and internal space is made as the leaps ascends.
18 (soprano)	Upward leap followed by downward leap	Make sure these leaps are begun high and forward, and support is increased before the leap is executed and internal space is made as the leaps ascends; on the downward leap, maintain the space achieved on the upward leap; make sure they simply close the vowel as they descend and maintain a sound that is high and forward.

Figure 21-5. (Continued)

Analysis No. as marked in Figure 21-4e	Problem	Solution
19 (bass)	Upward leap	Make sure these leaps are begun high and forward, and support is increased before the leap is executed and internal space is made as the leaps ascends; make sure the lips are wrapped around the vowel on the ascending leap.
20 (soprano, tenor)	Upward leap	Make sure this leap is begun high and forward, and support is increased before the leap is executed and internal space is made as the leaps ascends; make sure the lips are wrapped around the vowel on the ascending leap.
21 (alto)	Descending leap	Make sure the sound remains high and forward on the descending leap.
22 (soprano, tenor)	Singing in lower register	Maintain high and forward sound on descending leap.

Biography—Frauke Haasemann

Frauke Haasemann was born on November 25, 1922 in Rendsburg, Schleswig-Holstein, Germany. The German contralto, Frauke Haasemann, studied music (particularly church music) at the Evangelischen Kirchenmusikakademie (Evanglist Church Music Academy) in Herford (Westphalia), where she passed her examinations as a church musician. She further studied singing at the Folkwang College of Music Essen and at the College of Music Hanover. In 1951 she began her career as an international concert and (above all) oratorio soloist, whereby she dedicated herself especially to the music of the Baroque period. She was soloist of the Westfälischen Kantorei, with extended tours in Europe, North America, and Asia, under conductor Wilhelm Ehmann. Frauke Haasemann did not draw only as an oratorio and a Lieder singer, but she was also considered the authority on choral voice building. She joined the faculty of Westminster Choir College in 1979, where she conducted The Westminster Chapel Choir and was Assistant Conductor of the Westminster Symphonic Choir. She prepared the Westminster Symphonic Choir for its appearances with the New York Philharmonic and The Philadelphia Orchestra, and collaborated with prominent conductors of her artistic generation. She worked in Hannover and St. Moritz as well as in the United States in various educational institutes. She published several works in this area, including Handbuch der chorischen Stimmbildung (1984), Voice Building for Choirs (1981) with Wilhelm Ehmann and translated by Brenda Smith, and Group Vocal Technique (video, book, and vocalise cards) (1990) with James Jordan.

Chapter 22

The Rite, Passage, and Necessity of Score Marking for Conductor and Choir

There is a vitality, a life force, an energy, a quickening, that is translated through you into action, and because there is only one of you in all time, this expression is unique. And if you block it, it will never exist through any other medium and will be lost. (p. 75)

—Martha Graham
in *The Artist's Way,* Julia Cameron

Play is the exultation of the possible. (p. 198)

—Martin Buber
in *The Artist's Way,* Julia Cameron

A metronome is an undependable criterion; the only designation which can't be misapplied is *presto possible*. Tempos vary with generations like the rapidity of language. Music's velocity has less organic import than its phraseology and rhythmic qualities; what counts in performance is the artistry of the phrase and beat within a tempo. A composer is never sure of tempo before a rehearsal, for preoccupation with such detail during composition slackens creative flow. Writing time corresponds in no way to performance time, and intuitions regarding the latter are, at best, approximate.

Tempo indication is not creation, but an afterthought related to performance. Naturally, an inherently fast piece must be played fast, a slow one slow—but to just what extent is a decision for players. If the composer happens to be the performer, so much the better. Rhythm and phrasing, nevertheless, do pertain to composition and are always misconceived (though sometimes beautifully), for as I say, notation is inexact.

When a composer determines his tempo as a final gesture to the product, he does so as an interpreter. Since his tempo varies with the life of the times, his marking is inaccurate, his emotional conjectures will not have authentic translation into sound. The composer will never hear his music in reality as he heard in spirit. (p. 326)

—Ned Rorem
in *Setting the Tone*

Although one can agree that a composer begins with a text, and that it is his inspiration to a certain respect, it is the responsibility of the performer, it seems to me, to satisfy as nearly as he can the composer's language and then seek what the inside of the composer sought, how he might have felt about the text rather than arriving at a textual, philosophical relationship with the text that is one's own personal interpretation and forcing that upon the composer. I can remember once that somebody said that Bach was the greatest witness to the crucifixion of Jesus; not that he happened to be present, but because he was a witness to the meaning of the crucifixion.

—Robert Shaw
in *Preparing a Masterpiece: The Brahms Requiem* (video)

To become truly immortal, a work of art must escape all human limits: logic and common sense will only interfere. But once these barriers are broken, it will enter the realms of childhood vision and dreams. (p. 84)

—Giorgio De Chirico
in *The Artist's Way,* Julia Cameron

When I teach conducting I always start with score study. It is what determines everything the conductor will do—from rehearsal procedures to gestural technique. First, I have the student make sure he sees everything on the page. It's amazing how many things can be missed if one doesn't follow a procedure to get all the information that is on a score. Also, it's amazing how many mistakes can be found in scores—accents or symbols used indiscriminately. And, there are frequent inconsistencies of markings on musically identical material. (p. 7)

Once a score has been totally marked—signifying your thorough study—it is basically memorized. You have your score in front of you, but you don't have to look at it. (p. 9)

—Margaret Hillis
in *An Interview with Margaret Hillis*, Dennis Shrock

Many years ago, I had my first encounter with Margaret Hillis. She was (and remains) the master guru in teaching conductors about both the discipline and the inherent value of tediously marking a score. For her, marking a score with tedious detail, in color, was a necessary rite of passage for every conductor. A marked score illuminated the important aspects of the score so information could come alive in rehearsal. Through the courtesy of the Chicago Symphony Orchestra and The Rosenthal Archives, the **score marking system** advocated by Ms. Hillis[1] is presented in **Figure 22-1**, as prepared by Don Horisberger.

---

1 This summary of the Hillis color score marking system was prepared by Don Horisberger, a former student of Miss Hillis and a CSC associate conductor) and provided courtesy of the Chicago Symphony Orchestra Archives and Robert Villeya.

**Figure 22-1. The Margaret Hillis color-coded score marking system
from Don Horisberger, CSC Associate Conductor.**

*Note: A color version of this chart is available for download at
www.giamusic.com/jordan/hillis.*

When I studied with her, there were different types of marks reinforced by color (using colored pencils). (Incidentally, she used to compare colorizing a score to the difference between maps printed in color vs. black and white.)

Dynamics:

pp (& less) . . . . boxed in green
p. . . . . circled in blue
mp and *mf*. . . . . boxed in brown
f. . . . . circled in red
ff, sf, etc. . . . . boxed in red
cresc., etc. . . . . underlined with red
dim., etc. . . . . underlined with blue
hairpins marked over with
red (cresc.) or blue (decresc.) . . . . Miss Hillis also added red or blue
hairpins (neatly, with a ruler), especially
when a "cresc." or "dim." indication led
to a printed dynamic.

Articulation:

Marcato, accents, etc. . . . . underlined with red
Dolce, espressivo, etc. . . . . underlined with blue

Score/bar line analyses:

Bar line reinforced with black fully down the score. MH also indicated "extra" bars that broke regular bar patterns.

Figure 22-1. (Continued)

Tempo markings:

Slower tempo . . . . blue
Moderate tempo . . . . brown
Faster tempo . . . . red
accel., etc. . . . . underlined or boxed in red, with added
    red arrows to right
ritard., etc. . . . . underlined or boxed in blue, with added
    blue wavy lines

Thematic analyses (often using highlighters):

Principal themes . . . . yellow
Secondary themes . . . . green
Tertiary themes . . . . orange
Other thematic ideas . . . . blue (or other colors as needed)

Beat patterns were generally indicated in brown with graphic representation of the beat rather than numbers (e.g., "V" for two, "+" for four, etc.).

Cues were marked with red (inverted "L" shape), with instrument or voice part to the cue's left (e.g., "FL," "TIMP," "S1").

The Hillis System as a Rehearsal Archive

Upon visiting the Archives of the Chicago Symphony Orchestra, I discovered several facts about Ms. Hillis's approach to score preparation that might provide some food for thought for all of us.

In addition to the scores Ms. Hillis prepared for rehearsals with the Chicago Symphony Orchestra Chorus, there is also a collection of other scores I found fascinating. Once her preparation with the choir was complete, as the choir moved to piano rehearsals with Maestro Solti, Ms. Hillis took a fresh, unmarked score into the rehearsal. She marked musical issues that came up in that rehearsal in the fresh score. For the first full orchestra rehearsal, she again took another blank score into the rehearsal and made markings pertaining to that rehearsal. Her practice of marking a "fresh" score continued throughout the "run" of that particular work.

A similar procedure was used in recording sessions, with a new score being marked for each of the recording sessions. Ms. Hillis then took all of the scores from all of the recording sessions to the mixing session with the engineers and Maestro Solti. Having all of those marked scores allowed her to not only pinpoint problem places for Solti, but because of her meticulous markings, she could locate better passages to use where the choir had difficulties.

By doing this, she created a "musical archive" of sorts—a step-by-step documented process through marked scores of how the chorus sang in each rehearsal and each performance. This procedure would be a wise one to consider as you prepare your choruses for large performances.

To view an archival example of two pages of Ms. Hillis's score, see **Figure 22-3** at the end of this chapter (p. 254). Also a color version of the score pages is available for download at www.giamusic.com/jordan/hillis.

Another Approach to Score Colorization

In the remainder of this chapter, I present my adaptation of Ms. Hillis's color-coding system. Without doubt, this is a vital step in the score study process. It is a step often overlooked amidst all our diligent preparations. The time you spend on this tedious process will reap benefits when you enter the rehearsal room.

The first step in this process must be the material presented in Chapter 26, "The Historical and Structural Analyses of Choral Works: Julius Herford's Study Procedure." Herford analyses provide a visual representation of structure and function. Detailed marking of the musical score illuminates finite details within the score and provides awareness of musical details that provide points of clarity in the final realization of the score.

Marking the Score[2]

The first step in preparing for rehearsal is the obvious step of preparing and marking the score. Learning the notes and rhythms of all of the parts is a prerequisite to the other levels of score preparation. The following steps are recommended:

1. **Hum or moan through the piece.** Intensely hum the overall piece (following its principal rhythms) on the consonants "mm" or "nn" at a *mezzo forte* or *forte* level. Breathe for as many of the entrances as possible. This technique allows you to actively participate in and make decisions concerning the phrase directions of the work. The humming or moaning establishes a connection between the notes on the page and the sound of a musical line in motion. It is during this activity that you should also establish breath locations.

2. **Play and sing all parts.** Play and/or sing all parts individually. Then play one part and sing another until all combinations of parts have been experienced. Finally, begin by singing one part and then switching immediately to another part. This procedure is especially helpful in contrapuntal music.

3. **Reinforce Alexander-based alignment sensations and thoughts.** When preparing a score, always prepare it from a sitting or standing position that is reflective of the singing process. There is an intimate but unseen connection between body posture and the music learning process. When a piece of music is performed, the body's "muscle memory" will recreate the posture and body alignment that was in evidence as the score was being learned. View score preparation as both an aural and a kinesthetic exercise. The kinesthetic attitude of the body is established at the time the initial note learning takes place. Constantly reinforce all of the Alexander-based alignment issues.

---

2 Apart from the processes described in this chapter, there is a choral score reading program available that gives conductors feedback concerning their ability to detect errors within a choral performance. That program, *The Choral Score Reading Program* by Richard Grunow and Milford Fargo (GIA), includes a self-study workbook to help improve one's ability to detect errors.

4. **Mark the score.** One of the most obvious aids in rehearsal technique is often overlooked by both experienced and novice conductors. Marking the score in an organized manner will assist in the preparation for rehearsal and serve as a visual reminder for you in rehearsal. While such score marking may be time consuming, you will find that it hastens the score learning process.

The key to score marking is to establish a consistent procedure. Establish standard color codes for the most important aspects of the score. Refer to **Figure 22-2** for a **suggested color-coding system** that may be used as a model. (Unless otherwise indicated, colors refer to colored pencils.)

Figure 22-2. Model color-coding system suggestions from James Jordan.

red . . . . .circle all *forte* dynamics

green . . . . .circle all *piano* dynamics

dark green . . . . .circle all *mezzo forte* dynamics

light green highlighter . . .trace over all crescendos and decrescendos

orange . . . . .enlarge all meter changes

yellow highlighter . . . . . .trace and track thematic and imitative material

blue . . . . .indicate textual words that receive stress

purple . . . . .connect notes between voice parts that are in suspension or create a dissonance

pink highlighter . . . . .trace over accents

maroon . . . . .place harmonic analysis underneath the score; use highlighter to draw attention to unusual harmonic progressions

turquoise . . . . .circle thirds in triads and other intervals that may cause intonation problems

light green . . . . .underline all tempo changes

pencil . . . . .indicate necessary possible vowel modifications above the voice parts and trace over with blue highlighter; draw arrows where necessary to track entrances

247

Figure 22-2. (Continued)

Score Marking Color Key

1) Numerically mark each measure.
2) Observe rule of all breaths on tactus of piece.
3) Mark all breath impulses in ORANGE.
4) Numerically mark all breath impulse beat numbers in BLACK.
5) Mark all text (syllabic stresses = points of energization) in BLUE.
6) Mark all schwas (unstressed syllables) with RED circles.
7) Circle all dynamics as follows: *pp* in TURQUOISE, *f* in RED, *p* in GREEN, *mf* in DARK GREEN.
8) Mark major entrances with brackets larger than the stave and with a large arrow in BLACK.
9) Highlight in YELLOW any musical direction (e.g., cantabile, etc.).
10) Trace over all crescendos and decrescendos with LIGHT GREEN highlighter.
11) Underline tempo changes in LIGHT GREEN.
12) Mark harmonic analyses in MAROON.

---

5. **Conduct while humming or moaning through the piece.** Now conduct and intensely hum the overall piece on the consonants *mm* or *nn* at either *mf* or *f.* Breathe for as many of the entrances as possible.

6. **Study and experience the breath of the piece carefully.** When learning scores, it is important to have a clear sense of where the singers will breathe within the phrase structure and between phrases. Conductors often alter the consistent tempo of a piece because they do not breathe with the singers and, hence, rush the tempo. One of the most important factors in maintaining consistent tempo is to make sure the singers' breath process is rhythmic. In the initial stages of the score preparation process, it is very important for the conductor to not only breathe where the choir breathes but also exhale air constantly in the motion of the piece to simulate the forward motion of the phrases. You could also moan or hum in a monotone. Regardless of the rhythm of the work, the humming or moaning should be *continuous* and not simply echo the melodic rhythm (exact rhythm) of the piece. This encourages you to always be connected with the "sound" of the piece while learning the score.

When learning a piece of music, always connect yourself and your singing mechanism to the ongoing rhythmic motion and flow of the work. This will help to free your conducting gesture.

7. **Conduct the piece while inhaling and exhaling constantly.** Continually inhaling and exhaling while conducting a piece is a valuable score preparation technique. Conducting gesture is often totally unrelated to the sound and line of a piece; that is, the conducting gesture is not directly connected to both the energy of the body and the energy of the breath. Connecting the gesture to the body and to the breath is essential to good rehearsal technique. Much can be taught to a choir without words if the gesture is connected in such a fashion. By inhaling and exhaling on *tss* or *shh* (or any consonant combination that provides a resistance), you can establish this connection between gesture, body, and breath.

8. **Breathe the color of the style and effect of the piece.** While programmatic approaches to music making can be dangerous, it is very helpful to consider the character of the breath for each piece you conduct and rehearse. Establishing a sense of textural color was introduced in Chapter 13, "The Door Into Musical Style," through association of colors with the music. Since the vocal "color" of a piece is set through the inhalation process, you must predetermine the color and mood of the breath that is taken to start phrases so the color of the ensemble is set in the breath the singers take. If you "hear" a particular passage as purple, it is often effective to ask the choir to "inhale" the color purple. Such a technique will elicit a darker sound than if one asks the choir to "breathe" red, and so on.

9. **Study and experience the breath process that connects phrases.** When teaching a piece, take special care to teach how the breath begins simultaneously with the end of a phrase. Amateur singers tend to finish the phonation of the tone and then begin the breath process for the start of the next phrase. In examining the process as a singer, the inhalation of breath happens at the same moment as the finishing of the tone. When conducting, do not conduct the end of the phrase; rather, simply breathe for the next phrase—cue the breath. By doing so, the previous phrase ending will take care of itself, and the tone color, pitch, and forward rhythmic motion of the phrase will be maintained.

Preparing the Tonal Materials of the Music

After gaining an understanding of the rhythmic life of a piece, you must establish a procedure for learning the tonal aspects of the score. Many conductors play through the score at the keyboard. This certainly will give you an idea of the harmonic movement but will actually do very little to establish the direction of individual parts within the piece. Instead, begin by first singing the soprano part. On subsequent repetitions, sing and conduct the soprano part. After it becomes very familiar to you, then move ahead and do the same with the alto, tenor, and other parts.

The time you spend singing and conducting individual parts is perhaps the most valuable aspect of score preparation. If you know each of the parts, the musical mind is then able to combine them. As you are conducting the work, your ear will easily be able to switch between parts while continuing to track the parts you are not focusing on. If instrumental or keyboard parts are present, you should also learn those parts in a similar fashion.

Anticipating Vocal Problems Within the Score

Aside from preparing the tonal, rhythmic, and harmonic aspects of the score so you can "hear" the score you are to conduct, it is valuable to study the score with respect to vocal technique problems an amateur choral singer may encounter. For example, a tonal or rhythm error might be caused by a singer's inability to correctly execute the pitch being heard.

Below you will find a list of possible vocal problems to look for in any score. In some cases, short solutions or "tools" are offered.[3]

1. **Maintaining posture for correct singing: the foundation for the inhalation process** – Examine the score meticulously for those points where a breath must be taken. Rehearse the inhalation process as you count through the work. Make sure the breath is being taken low enough and is not shallow. Make sure the choir is able to set the sound with the breath. This can only be done if the body is able to accept air through correct posture and alignment.

---

3 Obviously, the space allotted here does not allow for detailed explanations or solutions for all problems. For further pedagogical answers, the reader is referred to *Group Vocal Technique* by Frauke Haasemann and James Jordan (Hinshaw Music, 1991).

2. **Diaphragm activity (for diction and for articulation of the rhythm)** – The process of using the breath for singing should be taught to the choir as a two-step process. Diaphragm activity is not support; it is used only for cleaner, sharper diction and accents. If air is only taken into the body to the perceived level of the diaphragm, shallow breath will result. Moreover, if the diaphragm is used to propel the air through the vocal mechanism rather than through the lower "support" mechanism, a harsh, pushed sound will certainly result.

3. **Breathing (exhalation, inhalation, and support)** – You must establish the manner in which the breath is allowed to fall into the body and the sensation of support for the particular piece of music to be rehearsed. The singers need to "feel" what the support sensation is like for each piece of music, and they need to connect the feeling of support for each piece to their bodies.

4. **Appropriate resonance for the style of the music** – As conductor, you must hear within yourself an appropriate color or sound for the particular piece to be rehearsed before your singers enter the rehearsal room. That sound is borne out of your own experience and tone preference. You must make an initial decision concerning whether the piece to be rehearsed will require a bright tone color or a dark one.

5. **Five pure vowels (without diphthongs) to maintain pitch and tone color** – Do not use diphthongs when rehearsing a piece; always rehearse the piece using the five pure vowels. Because the choir is not skilled in diphthongs, poorly executed diphthongs will manifest themselves as a veiled or unusual tone color, or a variance in pitch. After the choir has learned the piece on neutral syllables, then move the choir to the text of the piece. Locate all diphthongs in the text and be prepared to teach the proper performance of the diphthong.

6. **Finding head voice (yawn-sigh) to maintain proper tone color** – As conductor, you must be vigilant to maintain the appropriate amount of head tone in each respective voice part, regardless of the tessituras of the work. Often, parts that lay low in the tessitura for a voice part, sung without the proper amount of head tone, will immediately result in pitch difficulties, inability to perform a wide range of dynamics, and obvious inconsistencies in tone color.

7. **Expanding the vocal tract to ensure a free, open singing sound** – If a variety of vocal ranges are required to perform the work, maintaining a free vocal tract will likely present some problems.

8. **Range extension and register consistency required by the piece** – If extremes of tessitura are required for a particular work, you should address range extension and, more importantly, register consistency needs. In fact, a choir's ability to maintain register consistency (the same relative color throughout the entire range) is a major determinant of choral tone.

9. **Flexibility (runs)** – For certain styles of music, especially from the Baroque and Classical periods, the ability to execute runs is important to the rhythmic clarity of a piece. In this case, teach your choir the technique of singing *martellato*, and you will find your choir is able to sing extended melismas with ease.

10. **Resonance and placement to execute a specific style** – You must determine the color or shape of vowels to be used to reflect a certain sense of style in the sound of the work.

11. **Rhythmic style** – In studying the score, you will make a determination based upon your concept of the piece and the inherent rhythmic style included in the piece. Much can be accomplished toward that end through the correct choice of neutral syllable and consonant combinations when the work is introduced and taught. Rehearse the inherent rhythm style of the piece, focusing on staccato, legato, dynamics, and accents (*sforzatos*).

12. **Crescendo, decrescendo, and *messa di voce*** – This may seem like an over-simplification, but amateur choirs need instruction on the proper execution of crescendos and decrescendos as required by the score. Most amateur choral singers will provide more air (support) to sing a crescendo without dropping the jaw, which results in a harsh, unrealistic crescendo. The use of *messa di voce* (crescendo and decrescendo on one pitch) will heighten the choir's expressive color and range of emotional expression. Make your singers very familiar with *messa di voce* and how it is produced. This technique is especially necessary in contrapuntal music.

13. **Execution of leaps** – Locate leaps within all voice parts. Then be sure to give the choir the "tools" they need to execute the leaps. Basically, you should teach the choir to drop the jaw and "fish mouth" for every ascending leap. This technique is also the foundation for vowel modification.

14. **Vowel modification (for blend and intonation)** – Singers will need help when their voice parts approach extremes in range. This is especially important in both female and treble parts. Failure to deal with vowel modification issues will result in poor tone color as well as pitch difficulties. In many instances, what seems to be a problem of inaccurate pitch is simply a vowel modification issue.

When preparing a score for rehearsal, sing each vocal part and search for technical problems. By familiarizing yourself with these problems and the proper solutions before rehearsal, you will be able to keep the rehearsal moving by providing the singers with the "tools" they need to fix these problems.

Preparing and Studying the Text

In addition to making yourself aware of the vocal technique aspects of a score, take considerable time to understand the diction issues of the work you are going to conduct. To understand the diction is to understand the inherent color of the work. For English diction, reference *The Singer's Manual of English Diction* by Madeleine Marshall (G. Schirmer, 1963), and for other languages, reference *Diction* by John Moriarty (E. C. Schirmer, 1975).

Biography—Margaret Hillis

Margaret Hillis was born in 1921 in Kokomo, Indiana, and died on February 6, 1998, in Chicago, Illinois. The American choral conductor, Margaret Hillis, learned to play piano, trumpet, horn, saxophone, and string bass. She studied at Indiana University, Juilliard, and with another of America's choral innovators, Robert Shaw. By the age of eight, Margaret Hillis knew she wanted to be an orchestral conductor, but since the field was entirely male at the time, she was advised (not entirely tactfully) to try her hand at choral conducting. Eventually, she did get to conduct some major orchestras, if only by accident. At a 1977 Carnegie Hall concert when Sir Georg Solti (the scheduled conductor) became ill, she stepped in to lead Mahler's gigantic Eighth Symphony, and received a standing ovation. She was the first woman to conduct the Chicago Symphony Orchestra. She also put together the Chicago Symphony Chorus, the first American professional symphony chorus. For thirty-seven years, she was director laureate of this group, which came to be recognized as one of the world's great choral organizations.

Figure 22-3. Archival example of a Hillis score.

A color version of these score pages is available for download at www.giamusic.com/jordan/hillis.

Excerpt from Walton's *Belshazzar's Feast* from Margaret Hillis Collection, Rosenthal Archives, Chicago Symphony Orchestra. Used with permission.

Chapter 23

Deciphering the "Code" of Renaissance Composers

Cadential Analysis and Application to the Performance of Renaissance Music

How far Palestrina and his contemporaries reacted to the pull of the dominant in the wider context of musical form is more a matter of speculation. (p. 1)

—Malcom Boyd
in *The Music Review*
"Structural Cadences in the Sixteenth Century Mass"

To say that Renaissance harmony is merely the result of combining melodic strands is plainly absurd, even in a contrapuntal texture, since it suggests that the composer had no consideration for the vertical aspect of what he wrote. It would be nearer the truth to say that in sixteenth century polyphony the *harmonic progression* is directed by the counterpoint, whereas in a wholly tonal composer like Bach, the reverse applies. When it comes to cadences, however, Palestrina and Bach are on something like equal footing, because limited and universally accepted choice of chord progression (the same for both composers) ensures that harmonic considerations must take precedence. The cadence has always been recognized as a door through which music passed from modality to tonality. (p. 21)

—Malcolm Boyd
in The Music Review
"Structural Cadences in the Sixteenth Century Motet"

The music of the sixteenth century was for the greatest part conceived within the framework of the church modes. In it we find neither tonality or atonality in the later sense of the terms. Yet we meet with phenomena—indeed, with whole repertories—which do not fit into the traditional system of the eight modes but show, often, in an astonishing manner, prefigurations of tonal, and even atonal thinking. (p. 1)

—Edward Lowinsky
in *Tonality and Atonality in Sixteenth Century Music*

There were long periods when art did not seek out the new but took pride in making repetition beautiful, reinforcing tradition, and ensuring the stability of a collective life; music and dance then existed only in the framework of social rites, the Masses and the fairs. Then one day in the twelfth century, a church musician in Paris thought of taking the melody of Gregorian chant, unchanged for centuries, and adding to it a voice in counterpoint. The basic melody stayed the same, immemorial, but the counterpoint voice was a new thing that gave access to other new things—to counterpoint with three, four, six voices, to polyphonic forms even more complex and unexpected. Because they were no longer imitating what was done before, composers lost anonymity, and their names lit up like lanterns marking a path toward distant realms. Having taken flight, music became, for several centuries, the history of music. (p. 168)

—Milan Kundera
in *The Curtain*

Regarding Edward Lowinsky's ideas presented in this chapter:

Professor Lowinsky's new book is a study in the harmonic logic of those sixteenth century maestri whose musical explorations led them beyond the musical confines of modality and to the discovery of the "free" harmonic world, however cut and patterned, is still the harmonic field of the composer today. The subject matter of Professor Lowinsky's study is for me perhaps the most exciting in the history of music, his method is the only kind of "writing about music" that I value. (p. ix)

—Igor Stravinsky, 1961
from the Foreword to Edward Lowinsky
Tonality and Atonality in Sixteenth Century Music

The Renaissance: Exploration, Innovation, and Realignment

The Renaissance was an incredibly fertile musical time. Moving from the Medieval period, composers began to explore new frontiers of the miracle of confluent musical lines. One approach to understanding this music is to conceptualize and even adopt the philosophy that triadic "tonality" as we know it did not exist, and harmonic structures are merely the coincidences of contrapuntal lines that need to be brought to resting points at important points in the text. As composers explored the possibilities of counterpoint, they began to discover ways to change the "emotional colors" of a piece through modal modulation. The first acknowledged piece to explore this modal modulation practice was Josquin des Prez in the monumental *Miserere Mei Deus*. The first point of "emergence" of triadic tonality was given birth in cadential structures of Renaissance motets. In fact, individual composer style, personal musical syntax, and the progression of musical development can be studied almost exclusively through cadential structures.

Many conductors approach the performance of Renaissance music armed with an aesthetic sense, usually gained from recorded performances and based on some musicological study of performance practices of the period. I often find, however, that the most helpful device to assist with interpretation lies within the individual cadential structures of the work.

A common performance problem with Renaissance choral music lies in the fact that most of a composition is contrapuntal in nature. This makes it possible for the music to "glide along," and the listener perceives a beautiful, forward-moving structure. However, because the cadences are treated democratically, the listener is not made aurally aware of the compositional intent of the composer.

Humanism and Natural Expression

The aesthetic of the Renaissance is one of objective reality. Musical tones as well as the art of the period are vivid and expressive. Human experiences are transferable into the visual and sound art of the period. Because of this aesthetic, you must be able to search the musical language of each composer for what I refer to as the expressive life realities of a piece. Profound insights into life were contained within the counterpoint, the metric structure of the work, and the cadential structures of the compositions.

The remainder of this chapter will deal with the codes contained within cadential structures. The metric codes in these works are addressed in detail in the next chapter, "Breaking the Renaissance Code," in which Gerald Custer discusses understanding the metric code and provides these guidelines:

1. Primary of text is paramount throughout.
2. Durations support delights.
3. Horizontal trumps vertical.
4. New text, new music, new meter.
5. Imitation follows suit.
6. Three of a kind beats a pair.
7. Bigger is better.
8. Longer is stronger.
9. Honor the anacrusis.
10. Breathing takes time.
11. Expect entrophy.

Greek Drama and Conflict: Understanding the Composer's Code

The ideals of Renaissance musical language is rooted in the ideals of Greek drama. Conflict disguised as resolution of drama is inherent in the pairings of voices, contrasts between voices, and cadential structures! The secret of Renaissance music is understanding the musical expressive language of the period, and understanding that its seemingly simple "musical drama" to our musical ears is actually a quite sophisticated system of musical expressiveness hidden within simple musical structures. A sort of "Da Vinci Code" is contained within every work. As conductors, our understanding of the codes of these Renaissance composers has everything to do with our ability to both interpret and perform Renaissance music.

The Code of the Tenor

Conductors would do well to begin unlocking the code by tracking the tenor. Few could argue the profound influence of the *cantus firmus* motet upon the compositional processes of composers. While it can only be a theory, it is a safe assumption in most situations that contrapuntal constructions began with the tenor (or perhaps the alto in some situations because of the range). You must search for the cadential code—that is, those voices that carry the essence of the cadential structure are the voices that need to be "brought out" of the texture so the listener can hear the true structure of the work. In the cadential charts that follow, this is a vital part to the analysis process of determining the musical shape of any Renaissance work.

Modal vs. Keyal Music: The Code of Cadences

Your first challenge as a conductor is to change how you analyze and hear the music you are going to conduct. While Renaissance music could be analyzed with commonly used methods of harmonic analysis, it is not wise to do so. In his landmark book entitled *Emerging Tonality in 16th Century Music*, Edward Lowinsky makes the convincing case that prior to the system of harmonic analysis, it appears Renaissance composers paid unique and particular attention to how their contrapuntal and modal lines would meet in cadential structures. According to Lowinsky, not all cadences were created equal in the eyes of Renaissance composers. There appears to be a distinct hierarchy of cadences that relate directly to textual importance.

Cadential structures are listed in **Figure 23-1** in order of importance. Lowinsky arrived at this hierarchy after examining the works of Renaissance composers.

Figure 23-1. Chart of cadential strengths.

Strongest . . . . .Cadences containing only perfect octaves
Middle strength . . . . . . .Cadences containing only the perfect fifth
Weakest . . . . .Cadences containing thirds, either major or minor

Many conductors tend to analyze Renaissance music in terms of vertical chord structure. And you could superimpose modern analytical methods over the top of Renaissance pieces. However, to do so ignores both the aesthetic of the period and the way Renaissance composers conceived their music. Music of the period was conceived horizontally, not vertically. If harmonic structures familiar to us make an appearance (I, IV, V, etc.), it is Lowinsky's point of view that this is mere coincidence.

It is better to track the movement of concentus, or gravitational pitch areas within a piece. It is then helpful to construct a "cadence chart," which compares concentus with strengths of cadences and relates text at the moment to these structures. To demonstrate how effective this analysis system is, I have chosen the Josquin *Ave Maria* to demonstrate these principles.

Weighting Cadences

Before we study the Josquin and construct what is known as a cadence chart, let's consider cadential weight. A synonym for cadential weight might be "finality." Not all cadences are created equal, although many conductors perform them as if all cadences are equal in both musical strength and importance. Cadences that are weaker in strength should not be allowed to settle as much as cadences that are stronger. Stronger cadential structures should clearly arrive at a point of definite repose or rest. Cadences that are weaker should have a restlessness and want to move toward the next phrase.

Also consider the two voices that carry the harmonic color of the cadences. In weaker cadences arriving at chord structures with thirds, you will usually find that the tenor voice is in a relationship with another voice part and contains some degree of dissonance to draw you toward the cadential structure. Because the approach to cadence contains this dissonance that moves sound forward, that particular cadence is often mistakenly considered more important. However, the aesthetic of the Renaissance usually means this is a weaker cadence! Cadences that arrive at a perfect octave are the ones that deserve finality, rest, and a sense of musical closure to a musical idea.

Another way to view this approach to cadences is that for weaker cadences, you should *withhold* weight from your conducting gesture as you move toward cadence. Stated in another way, cadences that have weaker voices should not be accorded so much musical weight, stress, or finality. Finality is reserved only for those cadences that have textual importance and textual imperative. Conversely, you should add weight[1] to your hand on cadential structures that are strongest. Cadential structures that middle these extremes are open to subjective interpretations.

Work for Musical Study: Josquin des Prez *Ave Maria*

One of the works I feel is essential for understanding the "code" of the Renaissance period is the Josquin *Ave Maria*. Study the work shown in **Figure 23-2** before proceeding and determine its major compositional devices and overall construction.

Figure 23-2. Marked score of Josquin *Ave Maria* for musical study.

KEY:	V	=	cadence point.
	___	=	lines used to indicate cadential voices (i.e., voices that create the cadential structure at that point in the work) and their resolution. Cadences appear in shaded areas in the score.
	(E)	=	The bracket at cadences is used to indicate the concentus at that point in the work—that is, the note around which the counter point and cadential structures seem to arrange themselves. Remember, this is not to be considered a "key" but simply a summary of the coincidence of the contrapuntal activity to that point. The letter contained within the parenthesis is the pitch around which the concentus is centered.

---

1 When I instruct students to add "weight" into the cadence, that added weight should be applied only to the palm area of the hand. Weight should never be added throughout the entire arm structure through muscular tension. In general, weight should be withheld from the gesture and only used at points of cadential need.

Figure 23-2. (Continued)

AVE MARIA

Josquin des Prez

Figure 23-2. (Continued)

Figure 23-2. (Continued)

Figure 23-2. (Continued)

Figure 23-2. (Continued)

Figure 23-2. (Continued)

Figure 23-2. (Continued)

Adding Weight to Conducting Gesture at Cadential Points

While I have addressed adding weight to gesture in a general sense, I would like to specifically address the issue of weight and conducting gesture as it pertains to the conducting of Renaissance music. Understanding where to displace weight at cadences is central to understanding the "code" of this music. And technical development of the conductor involves understanding how to provide the "illusion" of adding weight into the gesture.

Velocity + Speed = Renaissance Line

The beginning point of all conducting gesture for much of the choral music of the Renaissance lies in understanding the use of velocity and speed in the conducting gesture.

The primary rule to remember:

***Velocity devoid of weight is the starting point
for all gesture for Renaissance music.***

Also, velocity and speed can only be deployed within the horizontal part of the conducting gesture. In chironomy (an art that seems to be lost in the understanding of this music), there is almost no vertical gesture. Remember that vertical gesture slows the forward movement of sound (i.e., musical line). In his book, *A Gregorian Chant Handbook* (GIA, 2005), William Tortolano visually depicts the **chironomic conducting gesture** for the chant shown in **Figure 23-3.**[2]

---

2 Other examples are contained in Tortolano's *A Gregorian Chant Handbook* (GIA, 2005) on pages 28–29.

Figure 23-3. *O Filii et filiae* **from William Tortolano:**
A Gregorian Chant Handbook. **Chicago: GIA, 2005, p. 58.**

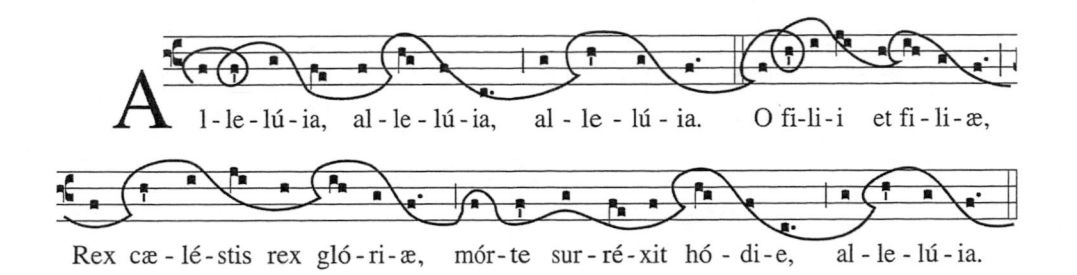

Much can be learned from the study of this example and can be directly applied to the conducting of Renaissance music. While as a conductor you must stay within the framework of a conducting pattern, it is your responsibility to decide which parts of the conducting gesture should be minimized and which should be maximized. Points of minimalization should always be within the vertical beat structure. In studying the example in Figure 23-3, the vertical gesture is difficult to find, and it occurs only at points of musical accent. Velocity is accomplished (1) by increasing speed, which is indicated by thicknesses of the drawn lines in the score, and (2) by increasing velocity, covering more physical horizontal space with the gesture. The desired end musical product is a musical line that moves forward with premeditated ascents and descent.[3]

The Shape of the Renaissance Musical Line

Contrary to common belief, it is important to remember that regardless of the changes of direction in musical line, the overall performance aesthetic is one of gentle ascent and gentle descent. The trajectory of Renaissance lines is always a longer rather than a shorter temporal event. Downward or upward leaps are *never* accompanied by changes of musical weight in the line. For example, many performances of the *Victoria O magnum mysterium* carry weight into the opening leap of a perfect fifth. That unnecessary weight not only slows the forward movement of the line but also tends to create serious intonation problems brought about by the change of color in the sound created by the additional weight brought into the sound, usually because of improper pedagogy or, more likely, through the conductor's gesture. Vertical beats, when used in this music, must be devoid of

---

3 To see this practice, I highly recommend viewing the DVD by Paul Salamunovich: *Chant and Beyond* (Quaid/Schott Media). The principles discussed here can be seen throughout this DVD.

weight. When an ictus needs to be employed, it needs to be used to deploy *energy* into the ensemble, not weight.

As conductors, we too often assume the spoken text accents that we experience are the same when examining the original chant source. While many times conductor instinct agrees with the precedent of the chant, sometimes there are subtle surprises.[4] Recite the text of *Ave Maria*. Now look at the **translation** in **Figure 23-4**, noting where the text rises toward. Notice the *word* accent was not used. The Renaissance aesthetic is to rise toward the *note* of "accent" and then gradually rest as one moves away.

Figure 23-4. Translation of *Ave Maria.*

Ave	María,	grátia	pléna:		**Hail Mary, full of grace,**
Hail	**Mary**	**of grace**	**full:**		**the Lord is with thee,**
Dóminus		técum,			
Lord		**with you,**			
benedícta	tu	in	muliéribus,		**blessed art thou among women,**
blessed	**you**	**among**	**women,**		**and blessed is the fruit of thy**
					womb, Jesus.
et	benedíctus	frúctus	véntris	túi,	Jésus
and	**blessed**	**fruit**	**of womb**	**your,**	**Jesus.**
Sáncta	María,	Máter	Déi,		**Holy Mary, Mother of God,**
Holy	**Mary,**	**Mother**	**of God**		**pray for us sinners,**
					now and at the hour of our death. Amen.
óra	pro	nóbis	peccatóribus,		
pray	**for**	**us**	**sinners,**		
nunc	et	in	hóra	mórtis	nóstrae. Amen.
now	**and**	**at**	**hour**	**of death**	**our. Amen.**

---

4 I strongly recommend using *Translations and Annotations of Choral Repertoire* by Ron Jeffers (Earthsongs, 1988) as the resource for correct text stress in all musical matters that are chant based.

The Superimposed Ictus

Movement of sound forward can usually be accomplished primarily by applying velocity and speed of gesture to the horizontal part of the beat pattern and minimizing vertical aspects of the pattern. However, because of the need for vertical or textual clarity, it may be necessary to add point (or **ictus**) *onto* a legato beat pattern. The operative word here is "onto." In music of the Renaissance, sometimes mistakenly when an ictus is added into the beat, it disrupts the forward and smooth continuity of the pattern, which affects not only the musical line but also the breath support of the singers.

Constructing a Cadence Chart for Renaissance Music

Cadential charts are valuable because, like any method of analysis, they allow for connections to be made between various elements of the musical score and may, at times, illuminate aspects of the score that may not have been apparent without the analysis. Structural details of a piece, as well as connections between musical materials and text, are more easily studied in this format. Using the Josquin *Ave Maria* reprinted in Figure 23-2 earlier in this chapter, **a sample "cadence chart"** has been constructed in **Figure 23-5** for illustration of this analytical procedure. As a conductor, you must complete this aspect of score study before you enter into the rehearsal process with your choir.

Figure 23-5. Sample cadence chart for Josquin _Ave Maria_.

Measure Number	Text	Concentus	Cadence Voices	Cadence Structure and Strength
				S = Strong M = Medium W = Weak or Elided cadence
1–9	Ave Maria, Gratia Plena	Ionian on C	T–B	8va; Strong
9–13	Dominus Tecum	C	TB	P5; Medium/Elided
13–14	Virgo Serena	C	SA	3rd; Weak and Elided
14–16	Virgo Serena	C	TB	8va; Strong
16–18	Ave cujus conceptio	E	SA	8va; Strong; SA duet
18–20	Ave cujus conceptio	E	AB	P5; Medium; Trio of ATB
20–22	Solemni plena gaudio	G	SB	3rd; Weak; elides into coelestia section that follows
22–27	Coelestia, terrestria, Nova replete laetitia	C	SB	3rd; Weak; ornamented cadence voice in alto
27–30	Ave cujus nativitas	C	SA	8va; Strong
30–33	Nostra fuit solemnitas	C	TB	3rd; Weak and Elided
33–39	Ut Lucifer lux oriens verum solem praeveniens	C	SB	8va; Strong
39–41	Ave pia humilitas	G	SA	8va; Strong; elided over TB entrance transforming sound at point of cadence to a P5–Medium duet
41–42	Ave pia humilitas	G	TB	8va but within an elided cadence transforming to P5; Medium; duet
42–44	Cujus annumciatio	C	SA	P5; Medium; elided cadence; **unusual approach to cadence**
44–47	Nostra fuit salvatio	C	TB	8va; Strong; sectional division
47–49	Ave vera virginitas	C	AB	3rd; Elided
49–51	Immaculata castitas	C	AB	3rd; Elided
51–53	Cujus purificatio	C	TB	3rd; Weak and Elided
53–57	Nostra fuit purgatio	C	SB	8va; Strong; sectional division
57–61	Ave prae clara omnibus	G	TB	5th; Medium
61–65	Angelicis virtutibus	G	TB	8va; Strong
65–68	Cujus fuit assumptio	C	TB	3rd; Weak and Elided
68–72	Nostra Glorificatio	C	AB	P5; Medium; GP two-beat rest
CODA **(homophonic)**				
73–74	O Mater Dei	C	TB	3rd; Weak
75	Memento Mei, Amen	C	SB	8va; Strong

In examining such a chart, broad tendencies in the music tend to emerge clearly from the "code." Using such a chart, you should be able to answer the following questions:

1. What is the relationship of the strength of the cadential structures to the text?
2. Is there a "code" within the shifts of concentus and their relationship to the text?
3. What is the dramatic role of counterpoint vs. homophonic passages?
4. How does the shift or change of concentus relate to an overall structural form of the piece?
5. Is there a pattern to the voices that were employed as cadential voices?
6. What is the role of the various dramatic melodic devices and their relationship or interaction with the cadential structure and changes in concentus?
7. Is there any symbolism buried within the change of concentus as it relates to text?

Questions for Conductor/Interpreter to Begin Score Study

As you examine a score for the first time, you should seek answers to the following questions:

1. **Text:** Length? Overlapping? Repetitions of text? The endings of sections of text must be clearly identified to the singers in your ensemble. Overlapping or elided textual ideas are especially important to point out. Singers must be aware when one textual idea ends and a new line of text begins.

2. **Expressive chromatic devices:** Plorant semi-tone; octave leaps, etc. Identify all expressive "codes" for the singers and have them mark the codes in their scores. Then have the singers relate the codes to the text at the moment.

3. **Rhythmic groupings determined by text:** Examples include 2s, 3s, and 2s and 3s going on simultaneously. It is important for the singers to understand when a type of "rhythmic counterpoint" is taking place. Largely determined

by textual matters, how the music is rhythmically organized has everything to do with structural clarity. The clarity of such rhythmic details is important to the interpretative/performance process.

4. **Polyphonic vs. homophonic:** These structural elements carry with them implications for interpretation. Generally, homophonic statements carry a stronger musical message than contrapuntal textures. Modern ears would probably incorrectly reverse their importance.

5. **Cadential hierarchy:** Identify the three categories of cadences (Strong, Medium, Weak) and compare them within the confines of a cadence chart to discover interrelationships contained within the score.

6. **Concentus.** Concentus are pitch center areas. Changes of concentus (i.e., c–e) carry a great amount of significance for the interpretative code of a work. Since there is not the sophisticated harmonic language of later musicing, such shifts of concentus carry great significance, and generally coincide with text meaning.

7. **Form:** How is the work arranged with regard to text. Is text repeated? Are fragments of the text repeated? What is the relationship of changes of text to changes of cadence and voicings?

8. **Tempo:** Conversions from triple to duple meter are important to the understanding of this music. Generally, the accepted rule is that the tactus, or primary beat, is maintained throughout. It would follow that if this rule is observed, sections in triple meter would be faster than those in duple.

9. **Tessitura:** Does the tessitura have anything to do with text painting or text meaning? The range of a part has everything to do with the "code" of a work. Parts that move out of accepted ranges carry great interpretative significance.

10. **Thematic relationships:** Are there any thematic relationships between sections?

11. ***Cantus firmus:*** Is a *cantus firmus* used? If so, in which voice is it contained?

12. **Counterpoint:** Identify all contrapuntal devices used in the composition. In the case of early works, it is important to identify both tonal and rhythmic canons! It is the rhythmic canons that often carry significant textual relationships.

Melodic Formulae that Form Expressive and Symbolic Language

The melodic "codes" of Renaissance music are, at least to modern ears, quite simple. Because this music grew out of chant and various folk idioms, melodic content was generally straightforward. But as composers began to explore the relationship between text and tones, a "code" emerged that attempted to imbed a newfound "symbolism" within the melodic formulae of both the tunes and the counterpoint. While one could compile quite a list in examining the practice of Renaissance composers, certain early tendencies, birthed in the music of Josquin, seem to maintain their expressive power throughout the period. Recognition of the following "codes" can bring a new expressive power to both ensemble and conductor.

- **Plorant semi-tone** – Commonly known as the "sighing" motive, this half-step movement, usually downward, was placed upon text that carried either a sighing or crying quality. This highly expressive device was used sparingly but always noted moments of great textual and human significance in the text. Usually found in the upper (or superius) parts, it also appeared in inner parts and lower parts. It is important for these sighing semi-tones to be identified and then voiced according to the interpretation of the ensemble.

- **Octave leap** – Perhaps no device in the "code" of renaissance composers carried more expressive significance than the octave leap, especially within a homophonic framework. While octave leaps were rare in contrapuntal textures, they did occur. However, when composers used octave leaps upward, they were usually reserved for the climax or musical high point of the entire work. The final phrase of the Josquin *Ave Maria* is a classic example of this highly expressive device.

- **Changes of texture** – Before contrapuntal procedures were explored and codified, canon was one of the principal compositional devices in the "code" that was used to provide variety from homophonic textures. For variety, and to perhaps more accurately reflect changes in the text, changes of texture were combined with various canonic devices to create new sounds. Pairing voices, as well as grouping various combinations of voices in threes, provided new expressive freedom to composers. With these changes of texture came the ability to vary the inherent color within a specific work. Viewed today as a simple device, the re-allotment of textural forces opened up a new expressive possibility within the Renaissance "classic" aesthetic. The strictness of the new rules of canon meshed perfectly with the period aesthetic.

- **Rhythmic canon** – One of the expressive devices often overlooked as a symbolic device is the rhythmic canon that is devoid of melodic canon material. People often confuse these highly intricate rhythm devices with the rhythmic modes of the period and dismiss them as such. When used, these intricate rhythm canons carry great significance for the interrelationship of text and music. The most complex structures in much of the Renaissance music is contained within these highly sophisticated rhythmic figures.

In looking at the Josquin *Ave Maria*, we see the use of **pivotal expressive devices** (see **Figure 23-6**). Once these codes are identified, it is left to the discretion of the conductor and the singers to determine the textural emphasis they should or should not receive.

Figure 23-6. Chart of pivotal expressive devices or "codes" in Josquin _Ave Maria_.

Measure Number	Expressive Device or Code	Possible Symbolic Interpretation
1–15	Downward moving sequence	Downward moving sequence a "code" for the humanness of Mary.
31–35	Duet in upper parts	Simple dueting code for tone painting symbolizing the Immaculate Conception.
40	_Tutti_ rest	The _tutti_ rest is a highly dramatic part of the "code." Out of the rest grows the text referring to the solemnity of the event.
43	Pitch B-flat introduced in bass part	The B-flat is a melodic code for "joy" in this Ionian mode.
44–50	Upward moving sequence	Code for the rising morning star.
51	B-flat–A–B-flat rhythmic figure	Melodic depiction and code for joy.
78–80	Homophonic pairing	Code for humility encoded within fifths and small step movement.
130	Ascending stepwise motion	Code for word painting.
133–141	Hemiola	Code for blessings and angelic virtues of Mary.
145–146	Plorant semi-tone in tenor: B–C	Code for imploring Mary to hear the human prayer.
142	_Tutti_ rest	Rest causes dramatic pause and emphasis for next line of text. Full measure rests are highly expressive devices in the code.
147–148	Octave leap in bass	Octave leaps are one of the most expressive devices within this "code."

Using the Metronome to Define Rhythm Parameters

As Igor Stravinsky often said, to be expressive, one needs not to be expressive at all. Spoken by a true neo-Classicist, the restrictions imposed by the classic aesthetic created an expressive language born out of the strictest of parameters, whether form, rhythm, melodic constructions, or harmonic structures. Yet I have found that many younger conductors believe the Renaissance was a period of Romantic expressivity. However, the aesthetic of the period, both in music and in art, was quite the opposite. Clarity and restraint were hallmarks of the expressive aesthetic of the period. Expressivity was built into the musical "codes" of the period. The type of expressive lyricism generally associated with more Romantic aesthetics has no place in the interpretative framework of Renaissance music. The adage "less is more" could certainly be considered a mantra for Renaissance music.

While the musical structure takes into account many of these aesthetic principles, it is the rhythm, or more specifically the nature of the rhythmic pulse, that in the end betrays the aesthetic of the period. Consistent tempo with few fluctuations needs to be the *sine qui non* of every performing ensemble. Stated another way, a strict rhythm discipline needs to be a part of every rehearsal and performance of music of this period.

I have found that the use of a metronome consistently through the rehearsal process defines quite sharply the strict parameters that accompany singing within a consistent tempo. For the musical elements to be clear in any performance of Renaissance music, the aural palate must be one of absolute tempo consistency and stability. When consistent tempo is established and then maintained by an ensemble, a remarkable expressivity begins to emerge through the music. If tempo is allowed to fluctuate, the musical details are aurally hidden from both the performers and the listeners. A metronome quickly establishes a "communal" tempo which, because of its inherent "rigidity," creates the magical aesthetic of this period.

Chapter References

The "codes" of Renaissance music that composers hid in the cadential structures and melodic devices provide valuable tools for understanding Renaissance scores, and such knowledge will help any ensemble bring this music to a more realistic and alive musical level. While the devices appear simple, viewed in the context of the musical developments of the time, they were revolutionary in their courage to explore new sound worlds for musicians. For further exploration and study of the analysis procedures presented in this chapter, consider the references provided below.

Aldrich, Putnam. "An Approach to the Analysis of Renaissance Music." *The Music Review*, Vol. 30, February, 1969.

> *This article is considered a ground-breaking article concerning the importance of cadential structures within the Renaissance motet and their effects on both interpretation and performance. It is highly recommended reading for all conductors confronting the performance issues presented in this chapter.*

Apel, Willi. *Gregorian Chant*. Bloomington, IN: University Press, 1958.

———. *The Notation of Polyphonic Music: 900–1600*. Fifth edition (revised). Cambridge, MA: Medieval Academy of America, 1961.

Boyd, Malcolm. "Structural Cadences in the Sixteenth Century Mass." *The Music Review,* XXX (1969), pp. 1–21.

Butcher, Kenneth. "Choral Partbooks, Then and Now." *The Choral Journal*, September 1985.

Custer, Gerald. "From Mathematics to Meaning: New Perspectives on the Microrhythm Debate." *The Choral Journal*, August 2005.

———. *Metric Flexibility in the Performance of Renaissance Choral Music*. Chicago: GIA Publications, Inc., 2008.

———. "Provoking Meaning: Thoughts About Choral Hermeneutics." *The Choral Journal*, December 2001.

———. "The Conducting Project Paper." *The Choral Journal*, November 2004.

Dart, Thurston. *The Interpretation of Music*. New York: Harper and Row, 1963.

Donington, Robert. *The Interpretation of Early Music*. London: Faber and Faber, 1963.

Horsley, Imogene. "Improvised Embellishment in the Performance of Renaissance Music." *Journal of the American Musicological Society*, Vol. IV, pp. 3–19.

Hurty, Jon. "Singing Renaissance Music from Partbooks." *The Choral Journal*, March 1996.

Kundera, Milan. *The Curtain*. New York: HarperCollins, 2005.

Lowinsky, Edward. E. *Tonality and Atonality in Sixteenth Century Music*. Berkeley: The University of California Press, 1962.

Meier, Bernhard. "The Musica Reservata of Adrianus Petit Coclico and Its Relationship to Josquin. *Musica Disciplina*, Vol. 10, 1956, pp.67–105.

Sachs, Curt. *Rhythm and Tempo*. New York: W. W. Norton and Co., 1953.

Shrock, Dennis, "Phrasing in the Music of the Renaissance." *The Choral Journal*, August 1994.

Chapter 24

Breaking the Renaissance Code

Metric Flexibility Exercises for Singers

Gerald Custer

Conductors who embrace the principles of metric flexibility in performing Renaissance choral music have particular tasks to accomplish when preparing scores for rehearsal. To successfully identify various changing metrical groupings inherent in this music, you must carefully analyze the relationships between text and music, melodic line and texture, and harmonic rhythm and cadential formulae, to name three among many such considerations.[1]

Young singers and adult amateurs face a different set of challenges when performing music that contains continually shifting meters. One reason choirs experience this difficulty is that the bulk of the music they sing was composed between 1600 and 1850 (roughly encompassing the Baroque, Enlightenment/Classical, and Romantic periods). This repertoire shares three characteristics:

1. **Relentless metric consistency** – Music that begins in a given meter usually remains in that meter (duple is always duple, triple is always triple, etc.).

---

1 For a detailed explanation of the rationale, principles, and practices referenced here, see *Metric Flexibility in the Performance of Renaissance Choral Music* (Chicago: GIA Publications, 2008) by the author of this chapter.

2. **Bar line tyranny** – The first note in any measure (e.g., directly right of the bar line) almost always receives perceptively greater stress (the "downbeat" convention).

3. **Presumptive syncopated stress** – Durational shifts, both across bar lines and within measures (i.e., "against the beat"), are almost always sung with an accent.

These three conventions generally governed the metrical organization of music for almost three hundred years. They are your singers' preset defaults, the ingrained habits they follow unconsciously. Your singers have heard music structured along these lines for most of their lives, and it is what they have come to expect, as even a cursory sampling of popular offerings would quickly confirm. Consequently, music that does not conform to these ingrained expectations, regardless of period of style, "sounds wrong."[2]

Therefore, the first step in unlocking the Renaissance code, from the singers' perspective, involves deliberately breaking the power of these subconscious defaults. Lecture alone is insufficient. Telling your singers that Renaissance musicians neither encountered bar lines nor felt agogic stress or syncope, while useful, is not enough. Why? We are all creatures of habit, predisposed by past experiences, accumulated over millennia, to identify (and expect) patterns that repeat. While Leonard Meyer correctly observed that affect is created when a tendency to respond is inhibited,[3] most of us instead prefer to operate under the rubric of consistency. If we sing three successive bars in duple meter, for example, we typically expect that the next measure would be organized in exactly the same way, and this is a degree of metric consistency that Renaissance choral music violates on a regular basis. Visceral, direct encounter is required to break free from the pull of such expectation.

One effective way to introduce singers to performing unmeasured music with constantly shifting metrical groupings is to make plainsong, or Gregorian chant, a regular part of the rehearsal process. Since this is likely the same musical materials that Renaissance musicians encountered in their own studies, singing it today allows us to experience a degree of musical solidarity with our choral ancestors across the ages. More importantly, repeated use of plainsong helps choristers learn to think and

---

2   A similar sort of "metric myopia" must be overcome to successfully sing music of the modern age, which frequently employs irregular and changing meters (Stravinsky, Messiaen, etc.). Choirs who learn to perform Renaissance music correctly are, therefore, better prepared to sing modern repertoire as well—but without initially facing the additional challenges of harmonic, melodic, and rhythmic complexity that such music frequently presents.

3   Meyer's book, *Emotion and Meaning in Music* (University of Chicago Press, 1956), while sometimes challenging, remains a highly recommended text for conductors and performers alike.

sing anticipatorily, looking ahead to see how each successive group of pitches is organized metrically, rather than expecting the past to predict or dictate what comes next.

Another way is to sing (on a neutral syllable such as *voo* or *vee*) exercises built around shifting metric groups, such as the three examples shown in **Figure 24-1**.

Figure 24-1. Exercises built around shifting metric groups.

When performing these exercises (and similar ones that can and should be invented), it is important to observe the following three caveats:

1. Bar lines must be omitted. Renaissance composers did not typically use them, and Renaissance singers did not customarily see them. Their presence reinforces the very thing we seek to eliminate: the tyranny of the bar line.

2. Metrication brackets must be included. They provide the key visual cue modern singers use to identify and perform metrically flexible groupings. Recognizing and responding to them are essential skills that must be mastered.

3. Singers should give slightly more weight—but not an audible accent—to the first duration in each metric group under the bracket.

Although optional, experience suggests that the following techniques may also prove helpful when performing these exercises:

1. Singers should physically track the first division of the prevailing pulse, or *tactus*. In the exercises shown in Figure 24-1, the *tactus* is typically a half note (in modern notation). Singers should tap quarter notes (the first division of the pulse) with their fingers into the palm of the opposing hand, with their fingers on their sternums (or with their hand into the thigh, if seated).[4]

2. Conductors and choirs familiar with the eurhythmic methodologies of Jaques-Dalcroze are strongly encouraged to leverage the advantages of bodily movement when performing these exercises.

3. For variety, the choir could be divided into two groups (male/female, high voices/low voices), with one group performing the exercises as written and the other singing the first division of the prevailing *tactus*.

4. As an added challenge, every other singer should perform either the exercises or the first division of the *tactus,* switching off at the conductor's discretion.

Metrical Combinations

Three particular metrical combinations—short to long, long to short, and the metricated breath—were consistently used by Renaissance composers. The remainder of this chapter discusses these conventions, illustrated by excerpts from period literature. Once your singers can successfully perform the type of exercises as shown in Figure 24-1 consistently and with a high degree of accuracy, then they should sing these excerpts regularly until they are mastered. (For maximum access by all voice parts, some excerpts have been transposed from their original key.)[5]

---

4   On no account should singers be allowed to tap their feet on the floor, since this action short-circuits the intended kinesthetic effect by "giving away" the pulse to an inanimate receptor. If singers are not using individual music stands, then these exercises should be projected on a screen (or printed large enough on a single sheet of paper) so all are able to read and perform them simultaneously.

5   A growing number of sacred and secular Renaissance choral works, edited by this author to reflect metric flexibility principles, are now available as part of the *Evoking Sound Choral Series*, edited by James Jordan, available from GIA Publications (www.giamusic.com).

Short to Long

Renaissance composers frequently shifted from shorter (smaller) to longer (larger) metrical groupings, especially at cadence points. This shift created the impression of ritardando without changing the actual tempo of the music, but simply by slowing the surface rhythm of the music. A typical example from Thomas Weelkes's madrigal **Hark, All Ye Lovely Saints** is shown in **Figure 24-2**. Note how syllabic stresses in the text—not the time signature—determine its true metric organization.

Figure 24-2. Excerpt from *Hark, All Ye Lovely Saints* by Thomas Weelkes.

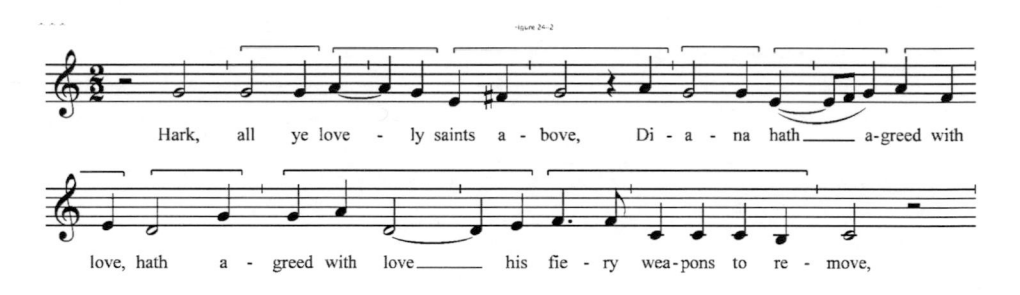

A second example, from Adrian Batten's anthem **O Sing Joyfully**, is shown in **Figure 24-3**. This example shows that although Renaissance composers used time signatures to indicate *tactus*, they did **not** intend them to govern the meter of individual phrase groupings. Clearly, the excerpt shown in Figure 24-3 is about triple groupings, not syncope.

Figure 24-3. Excerpt from *O Sing Joyfully* by Adrian Batten.

Long to Short

Greek dramatic ideals fueled Renaissance thinking and artistic imagination. Drama, the Greeks believed, was created and sustained by conflict. Renaissance composers typically expressed dramatic conflict by deliberately emphasizing a heightened degree of contrast among various musical elements (voicing, texture, motivic figures, and so forth).

One favorite method frequently used to establish contrast was to alternate long and short metrical groups, as in the opening of John Farmer's wonderfully alliterative madrigal *Fair Phyllis*, shown in *Figure 24-4*.

Figure 24-4. Excerpt from *Fair Phyllis* by John Farmer.

Another typical example[6] occurs during a moment of word painting in the middle of John Bennet's madrigal ***All Creatures Now*** (shown in **Figure 24-5**).

Figure 24-5. Excerpt from *All Creatures Now* by John Bennet.

---

6 Figures 24-4 and 24-5 are more than just long to short metric pairs, even if they do represent typical examples of metric complexity in Renaissance choral writing. In Figure 24-4, the actual progression is {L, 3S, L}, a metrical series that could be notated using modern time signatures as [3/2 (3/4, 2/4, 3/4) 3/2]. In Figure 24-5, the progression is actually {L, 6S, L} or [3/2 (3/4, 3/4, 2/4, 3/4, 3/4, 2/4) 3/2]. This complexity results from using the conventions above in sequence—a L/S (long to short) pattern to heighten dramatic contrast followed by a S/L (short to long) pair to create cadential elongation. If this explanation does not help to clarify matters, feel free to ignore it.

Metricated Breath

A particular problem arises when well-intentioned modern editors needlessly insert superfluous bar lines neither envisioned nor used by Renaissance composers— namely, emphasis is often mistakenly placed on a word that in the original oratorical context was meant to be unstressed. The solution to this problem is twofold: first remove the bar lines that create this artificial problem, and then rewrite the opening measure, assigning specific duration to the metricated breath that precedes the initial onset of sound.[7]

Two examples of this process in action are shown in **Figure 24-6** and **Figure 24-7**. In each case, the metricated breath in the opening bar requires a compromise: the one-time use of a different time signature. The first excerpt[8] comes from the beginning of the anthem *If Ye Love Me* by Thomas Tallis.

Figure 24-6. Excerpt from *If Ye Love Me* by Thomas Tallis.

The second example is from Tomas Luis de Victoria's motet *O magnum mysterium.*

Figure 24-7. Excerpt from *O magnum mysterium* by Tomas Luis de Victoria.

---

7 A discussion of the causes of this problem and methods for resolution can be found in my article, "From Mathematics to Meaning: New Perspectives on the Microrhythm Debate," *The Choral Journal* of the American Choral Directors Association (ACDA), Oklahoma City, August 2005.

8 This example conflates the initial superius entrance with material that follows directly after it in the tenor voice.

Like any skill, acquiring the facility to sing music characterized by metric flexibility requires time and patience. Breaking free from centuries of ingrained habits will not happen instantaneously. But in the end, the reward of performing Renaissance choral music in all its complex linear beauty more than compensates for the effort invested in the process.

Chapter 25

Understanding the Journey of Texts

The Artist and the Search for Meaning

A human life is the most complex narrative of all; it has many layers of events which embrace outside behavior and actions, the inner stream of the mind, the underworld of the unconscious, the soul, fantasy, dream and imagination. There is no account of a life which can ever tell this. When telling her story all a person can offer is a sample of this complexity. The best stories suggest what they cannot name or describe. They deepen respect for the mystery of the events through which identity unfolds. (pp. 137–138)

At the deepest level, creativity is holiness. To create is to further the dream and the desire of the creator. When the world was created, it was not a one-off, finished event. Creation is a huge beginning not a finished end. Made in the image and likeness of the Divine Imagination, human creativity helps us to add to creation. The unfinished is an invitation to our imagination. (p. 142)

The imagination offers revelation. It never blasts us with information or numbs us with description. It coaxes us into a new situation. As the scene unfolds, we find ourselves engaged in its questions and possibilities, and new revelation dawns. Such revelation is never a one-off hit at the mind. The knowing is always emerging. The imaginative form is graced by gradualness. (p. 147)

—John O'Donohue
in *Beauty*

Then there is the cultivation of being. It is through this that legends of the soul's journey are retold with all their gaiety and their tragedy and the bitterness and sweetness of living. It is at this point that the sweep of life catches up to the mere personality of the performer, and while the individual (the undivided one) becomes greater, the personal becomes less personal. And there is grace. I mean the grace resulting from faith: faith in life, in love, in people, and in the act of dancing. All this is necessary to any performance in life which is magnetic, powerful and rich in meaning. (p. 86)

—Martha Graham
in "An Athlete of God"
from Jay Allison, *This I Believe*

Abraham Joshua Heschel wrote a book entitled *Man's Search for Meaning*. In which he explores with the elegance and depth of his thought and language how the search for meaning is intimately bonded to the identity of each of us as human beings and how each person must empower himself or herself to search for life's meanings through the awe and wonder in all things. As artists, we bear a burden of privilege to seek that awe and wonder in each piece of music we perform.

Our musicing needs to be about the search for such meaning, which will enable our choirs to find beautiful tone and intonation that adds a shimmer and depth to all they sing.

As choral musicians, we can search for "meanings" within the text to help us interpret a composer's intent. Texts provide a direct insight into possible meanings of the musical sounds we sing. However, I have always found it intriguing to attempt to delve deeply into not only the words of the music, but also their profound implications for our own lives from varying perspectives. In examining the work of composers, you will soon discover that the text not only offers a kind of meaning, but also choices about the point of view of that text. Looking at a text under such a microscope is as different as viewing the text in black in white or in color—or even high definition.

There are several approaches you might employ for such study. I have marveled at the journeys Helmut Rilling is able to take an ensemble on, which merge the spirit, beliefs, and gifts of Johann Sebastian Bach into performances that change not only the lives of the singers, but all those who hear the performances as well. Robert Shaw taught us all lessons on how text is wedded to musical sounds, and if we choose to study and listen close enough, he also offers up to all of us ways of living our lives. Elaine Brown made texts meaningful to the lives of her choirs through what I refer to as "meaningful storying." The study of text should not only occupy a special place in the score study process, but it should be completed before the first rehearsal with a choir. A conductor's deepest understanding of text not only informs the conductor's rehearsal techniques and approach to teaching the piece, but also determines the conductor's way of "being" in front of the choir as the piece is being born in sound from the first minutes of rehearsal.

This chapter will present several approaches to studying text. Explore these approaches, and use the one that provides you and your singers with the most depth of human connection.

Surface Interpretations

The imagination may be compared to Adam's dream—he awoke and found it truth.

—John Keats
22 November 1817
in a letter to Benjamin Bailey

When I began in this musicing business, I seemed satisfied to merely arrive at what I term "a simple and literal surface translation of the text." For some odd reason, I never needed or wanted to delve into any deeper meaning of text. Or perhaps I was so captivated by sound that the sound of the choir was my motivation for rehearsing and conducting. While the choirs performed well with this "music only" approach, I am certain higher levels of music performance could have been achieved had I taken the time to consider the deeper meanings of the texts.

Composers with a Non-Expressive Message

If we study the lives and writings of composers, we might gain insight into certain works or knowledge about the composers' "philosophy" of composing. Sometimes the findings are illuminating, and sometimes they are surprisingly sobering.

Studying the writings of Igor Stravinsky will provide considerable insight regarding not only his compositional style, but also his compositional aesthetic! Stravinsky wrote on many occasions that he would not compose a note until he had firmly decided on a tempo for the work. In his mind, rhythm and tempo were central to the genesis of every piece. But one idea drawn from quotes of Stravinsky is both surprising and illuminating: Stravinsky believed that the highest level of expression was not to be expressive at all. If conductors know and believe this, they would approach interpretation with a sense of both directness and detachment as never before. As a neo-classicist, some degree of clarity and directness in interpretation and sound would be expected, but Stravinsky provides all who perform his music with a more direct approach to the *sounds* that he writes, which makes all the difference in both the interpretation and the conducting of his pieces. If you closely examine Stravinsky's setting of texts, you will see that words are taken out of their natural word stress context and are used instead as carriers of sound.

Interpretations with Life Implications

The Imagination is like a lantern. It illuminates the inner landscape of our life and helps us discover their secret archaeologies. When our eyes are graced with wonder, the world reveals its wonders to us. There are people who see only dullness in the world because their eyes have already been dulled. So much depends on how we look at things. The quality of our looking determines what we come to see. Too often we squander the invitations extended to us because our looking has become repetitive and blind. (p. 145)

—John O'Donohue
in *Beauty*

When looking at text, it is often necessary to examine the text to ascertain whether it was chosen by the composer for any particular reason. Is there contained within the text itself any life lesson that may be rooted in the composer's life experiences that the composer is trying to communicate through both the music and the words? Knowledge of the composer and the events surrounding a composition can sometimes cast a different hue upon the music. For example, Morten Lauridsen composed much of the *Lux Aeterna* during his mother's battle with cancer. He wrote much of the piece as a way of helping himself endure her illness. Knowing that small fact certainly places that masterpiece in another light.

Frank Martin never intended (or wanted) his virtuosic *Mass for Double Choir* to be performed by any choir. He believed the music was not deserving of any performance. Knowing this, as conductors we might choose to bring a sense of inwardness, gentleness, and shyness to the piece. Or perhaps after considering this fact, a conductor's interpretation could (and probably should) reflect the humbleness of this great man.

Zoltan Kodaly composed the *Missa Brevis* while he was taking refuge from the bombing of Budapest. Kodaly wrote that he believed he might never see the light of day. With an understanding of both physical and spiritual entrapment, the music would carry within its sound the desperation and helplessness of persons in that situation. Also contained within the music would be moments of great spirituality and hope, as is so often the case when human beings are confronted with such hopeless and dire life situations.

Occasionally, composers will respond, if asked, to the deeper inner meanings of a work. As I was writing this book, I was asked to record a new work for choir entitled *Innisfree* by American composer Gerald Custer. In my opinion, this is one of the finest pieces of the last decade; the text by Yeats spoke to me immediately in certain ways when interpreted on a pastoral level. When I asked Jerry to write about his piece, he responded with a compelling verbal explanation (see below). The lesson to be learned in what follows is that composers ponder their choice of texts with great care. As conductors, we owe it to them as interpreters and transmitters of their music to try to take a glimpse into their souls to help others who hear our choirs sing experience the deeper inner meanings of the music.

As Gerald Custer wrote to the choir...*William Butler Yeats was born in 1865 in Dublin to Irish painter John Butler Yeats. He spent his childhood in County Sligo, where his parents had been raised, and in London, where he was educated. He returned to Dublin to study painting but quickly discovered he preferred poetry. Yeats became deeply involved in Irish culture and politics, and after the Easter Uprising was named a senator of the Irish Free State in 1922. He is rightly regarded as one of the very greatest poets—in any language—of the twentieth century. Yeats was awarded the Nobel Prize for Literature in 1923 and died in 1939 at age seventy-three.*

Innisfree is a real place, located in Lough (Gaelic for "lake") Gill in County Sligo, an area Yeats loved and knew well. Written mostly in hexameter (six stresses in each line) in a loosely iambic pattern, "The Lake Isle of Innisfree" was published in Yeats's second book of poems, The Rose (1893). It is one of his first great poems, one of his most enduring, and its final line—"I hear it in the deep heart's core"—is a crucial statement for Yeats, not just in this poem but in his career as a whole. The belief that truths dwelling deep within us are essential to life was one that guided Yeats always, and the struggle to remain true to the deep heart's core was, in the opinion of many, his primary undertaking as a poet. Two aspects of Yeats's poem are intriguing. The first is the remarkable economy of its vocabulary. All but twenty of the words in this poem are monosyllabic, and of these, only two use more than two syllables. The second point of interest is the change of tense at the end of the poem. Although most of the work employs future tense, the last three lines shift into the present—a subtle and incredibly powerful bit of craft. The linnet is a small variety of finch, popular because of its melodious song and found in areas of shrub, in hedges, or in low trees. Even if a dwelling of clay and wattles was not as chic as one built from wood or stone, possession of enough land on which to plant nine full rows of beans and be surrounded by beehives was to enjoy a life of reasonably comfortable self-reliance.

What is your deepest longing? What secret lives in your deep heart's core? Where is home for you? Are you there now, or still searching for it? Whatever your answers to these questions turn out to be, if you put them into how you sing Innisfree, the result will be true and honest music making that releases real healing into a broken world that desperately needs it—and that is all any composer could hope or ask for.

—Jerry Custer

The Lake Isle of Innisfree

I will arise and go now, and go to Innisfree,
And a small cabin build there, of clay and wattles made:
Nine bean-rows will I have there, a hive for the honeybee,
And live alone in the bee-loud glade.

And I shall have some peace there, for peace comes dropping slow,
Dropping from the veils of the morning to where the cricket sings;
There midnight's all a glimmer, and noon a purple glow,
And evening full of the linnet's wings.

I will arise and go now, for always night and day
I hear lake water lapping with low sounds by the shore;
While I stand on the roadway, or on the pavements grey,
I hear it in the deep heart's core.

—William Butler Yeats (1865–1939)

Having a Viewpoint: Narrative or Being?

For many years, I have been fascinated by an approach to interpretation that I had encountered with one of my teachers, Gail Poch, in dealing with two works: Gian Carlo Menotti's *The Unicorn, The Gorgon and Manticore* and the *Mass* of Leonard Bernstein. On two occasions, I have also heard Charles Bruffy speak both compellingly and eloquently on this approach to interpretation. While I am sure both would write about this approach differently, I will attempt to synthesize their perspective on the interpretation of texts.

As conductors we have the option in interpretation of selecting a voice or voices for the choir. That is, we can choose based upon the interpretation of the text, the perspective from which the choir would sing. This approach has its roots in Greek drama and the role of the chorus: Would the chorus simply stand back and comment on the action at hand, or would the chorus *be* the event and speak from that perspective? If the choir would actually *be* the event at the moment, this would provide us with a whole new world of sound possibilities.

On several occasions, I have heard Charles Bruffy speak on this approach to interpretation. I find his compelling viewpoints inspirational, and I find the singing of his choirs likewise when his "narrative versus first person" approach is employed in interpretations. Composers adopt these changing perspectives within a single work; the choir sings from two perspectives: one as narrator, simply commenting on events as observers, and one as a voice that is actually the event at hand. A piece that demonstrates this oscillation from narrative to first person is the Benjamin Britten *Hymn to the Virgin:*

A Hymn to the Virgin

Of one that is so fair and bright
    As the star of the sea,
Brighter than the day is light,
    Mother and maiden.
I cry to thee, thou see to me,
Lady, pray thy Son for me,
    So holy,
That I may come to thee,
    Maria!

All this world was forlorn
    Through Eve's sin,
Till our Lord was y-born
    Of you, his mother.
With *ave* it went away:
Darkest night, and comes the day
    Of salvation,
The well springeth out of thee
    Of virtue.

Lady, flow'r of ev'rything
    Rose without a thorn,
Thou bare Jesu, heaven's King,
    By divine grace:
Of all thou bear'st the price,
    Lady, Queen of Paradise,
    Chosen:
Maid mild, mother *es Effecta.*
Effecta.

—Benjamin Britten (1913–76)

In my mind, three distinct voices are assigned to the choir. The first voice is commenting on the event from a distance. "Of one that is so fair and bright" and "Brighter than the day is light" could be viewed as text that describes the birth of the child as an objective and "reported" event. The role of the second choir in Latin provides another voice to the composition. This choir speaks only in Latin, almost from a perspective after the life of Christ as knowing the profound impact that His birth and the role of Mary have had upon civilization. This remarkable juxtaposition of perspectives provides the basis of color changes between the choirs. But the miracle of the work rests in one tiny fragment of text: "...that I may come to thee." Just as in the Yeats *Innisfree* poem presented above, the choir is switched dramatically to a first person existence, the third distinct voice in this piece. At this remarkable musical moment, the choir is transformed from commenting on the event to actually being the newborn child, the actual voice of the Christ child. It is one of the remarkable moments in twentieth century choral music—one that I fear has passed many of us by. Ascertaining the voice of the choir provides a kaleidoscopic view into the human experience and brings a deeper and more profound meaning to both singers and audience.

Interpretations that Require Additional Life Information

There is yet another approach to music that deserves serious consideration. How necessary are actual life experiences (of both conductor and singers) to an honest and insightful performance of any work? Do we have an obligation as conductors to provide for such an immersion for both ourselves and our choirs before we perform pieces in which text and music is drawn from life experience? The answer is a resounding and emphatic "Yes." Any music that is not part of our personal culture, upbringing, and life experience requires experiential validation. To perform such music any other way would be a bit dishonest and would ultimately fail those of us with the best of intentions.

While it is not perhaps always possible to have firsthand experiences with all types of music, we can certainly make a concerted effort to both inform and educate ourselves as a viable and legitimate substitute for this experience. Let me share two experiences to try to illustrate this point:

Moses Hogan

I had the unique fortune of meeting this great man in the spring, before he took ill, via a series of Masterclasses on the Westminster campus. As part of that Masterclass series, all of the choirs prepared some of his music for him to "workshop." I was assigned his arrangement of *Wade in the Water.* So I dutifully prepared it. I must admit the choir sang it well enough, but something clearly was not "right." So when Moses arrived, I "fessed" up and explained that I was a bit embarrassed, that something wasn't right with it. So he asked me to conduct the piece while he listened. After I was done, he took me aside and I asked him what I was doing "wrong." With great kindness, he said, "You haven't been to a black church, have you? You don't know 'the sway.'" I sheepishly answered no, and he walked toward the choir and began to work his magic.

That magic was simply explaining his life in the church and how *he* learned what he called "the sway." He got the entire choir to sway and then began *Wade.* The secret was in the sway: the sway set the tempo and, more importantly, the spirit of that work. That spirit was borne out of life experience. The lesson learned? An understanding of the real-life experience with music that is borne out of cultures and the collective experience is central to any real, meaningful and, if I might be so bold as to say, "legitimate" interpretation. Once I understood the cultural roots of *Wade in the Water,* it was able to have its own unique voice.

Past Life Melodies

Many of you are probably familiar with the work of Sarah Hopkins (published by Morton Music), which uses melodies styled on Aboriginal folk tunes and overtone singing. Sarah created a CD that teaches conductors how to sing her work. While the CD is quite informative and well done, I decided to seek out the help of an Australian who might be able to better teach the work. Her ability to talk about the culture of the Aboriginals and her understanding of the sound of the work transformed the performance of the piece from a good performance to an inspired and great performance. Knowing the culture and understanding the texture of the music of the Aboriginals provided valuable insight for the performance of the piece.

While many singers can negotiate the waters of much of the music that comes from around the world, the experience of the music can be deepened and enhanced for singers by exposing them to others who have lived within the culture who can bring those life experiences to the music.

Chapter 26

The Historical and Structural Analyses of Choral Works

Julius Herford's Study Procedure

Tony Thornton

The historical analysis stresses the fact that a musical work originates at a certain time and place and not in a vacuum. It deals with external evidence and informs the student about up-to-date research. The structural analysis deals with internal evidence. It strives for a conception of the unique *Gestalt* of the work under discussion.

—Julius Herford
from *The Julius Herford Collection*

Following the selection of singers and literature for a choral ensemble, score study is the most important activity for conductors. Yet because of the myriad of responsibilities required of us—recruiting, auditioning, attending board and faculty meetings, scheduling tours and recording sessions, rehearsing, teaching, and performing, to name a few—it is not surprising that many take shortcuts in their musical preparation.

The effort to balance personal and family lives with a musical career, spiritual growth, and physical and mental wellbeing could cause even the best organizer to "short circuit." As a servant of the music, an advocate for the composer, and a responsible teacher of singing and language, you should not shortchange yourself, your singers, or the audience because of a lack of knowledge of the score.

So how do you find the time for focused score study? By calling upon the same time management and goal-setting skills you use to schedule rehearsals, produce concerts, program a season, or create a budget. Plan the time and then prioritize to focus your study.

The goal of this chapter is to provide conductors with a practical score study process, beginning at square one. This process can be applied to any piece of music, whether unaccompanied, with piano or organ accompaniment only, or with a few instruments or voices, a chamber orchestra, or a full orchestra. It may be necessary to invest more time initially as you learn the process. However, the musical results for you and your ensemble will be well worth the additional time spent. The more music you analyze, the more proficient and confident you will become. As with everything in music, it takes practice, practice, practice.

The Score Study Process

Score study involves much more than placing breath marks in a score or listening to a recording to learn a musical work. In this process, we will explore two major levels of analysis: a historical analysis and a structural analysis.

The **historical analysis**, or information-gathering process, provides insight into editions of the piece, chronology, style features, performance practice, and the life and works of the composer and poet or lyricist.

Julius Herford, the teacher of Robert Shaw, Margaret Hillis, Roger Wagner, Lukas Foss, and many of the most respected choral conductors active in the field today, describes **structural analysis** in the following way:

> Structural analysis is a study in depth (internal evidence). It examines the technique of composition, the composer's musical vocabulary, and the spirit and soul of the work. It deals with the work as a whole (the overall structure) and the form of single movements. To know a work of art, we must have a concept of what it means as an entity. Our judgment should be based upon the form as a whole. In this process, we should know as much as possible about the physical shape of the composition.[1]

The score provides us with most everything we need to know. Historical information surrounding a work, combined with a thorough structural analysis, will strengthen your knowledge of a composer's language and style, inform your rehearsal and performance planning procedures and conducting gestures, and allow you to hear the score and the re-creation of the score in rehearsal and performance with heightened abilities. You will build a database of knowledge that you can call upon again and again. As more composers and works are studied, you begin to connect the dots between the various style periods, forms, compositional techniques and influences, and harmonic language.

Nänie, Op. 82, by Johannes Brahms, will be used to demonstrate the historical and structural score study process. (To maximize learning, consider following along using a full score as this piece is discussed. Refer to "Editions in Print" later in this chapter for a list of full score editions. Order a copy for your personal library, or check out a copy from your local music library.) It is not within the scope of this chapter to provide a note-by-note analysis of *Nänie*, but rather to explore larger concepts that can be successfully employed to guide your private study. Then, calling upon your past and current studies in vocal technique, and choral and orchestral conducting (keyboard, music theory, orchestration, music history and performance practice, ear training, research classes, and language), the intimate details of the score will be revealed to you. A checklist at the end of each section will guide you step by step as you study other works.

Before you begin, the following guidelines for success will aid you in creating a new model for studying choral repertoire.

---

1 Herford, Julius. *The Julius Herford Collection*. William and Gayle Cook Music Library, Indiana University.

Guidelines for Successful Score Study

1. Schedule a time for score study and keep it sacred.

2. Prioritize the focus of your score study to avoid procrastination. Creating a to-do list can be a powerful focusing tool. Placing your ideas on paper relieves the stress of juggling a variety of tasks in your head and allows you to develop a list of attainable goals, achieving them one step at a time in a logical order.

   I use a simple ABC method when preparing my to-do list. Tasks placed in the A category are the most important and should come first. The B category tasks are of medium importance, and the C category tasks are the least important at the moment. Items in the B and C categories move up in priority as you accomplish tasks from the A list. While everything you do in your score study process is essential, every task is not an A. Demote the less-critical activities to B or C initially, and they will eventually become an A.

3. Always use a full score when studying and performing choral-orchestral works. The orchestra will often introduce the main themes of the piece. For small-scale works with organ or piano accompaniment only, analyze the keyboard part thoroughly.

4. Study in stages. Last-minute cramming will not serve the learning process, nor will it allow you to gain a thorough understanding of the score. Begin your score study at least two or three months before the first rehearsal. Larger works will require even more time. Those conductors who are popular on the workshop and festival circuit often plan two years in advance. In any case, you should complete the bulk of your work before the first note is sung. Note that you may find it necessary to make small adjustments to your planning following the initial rehearsals.

5. Study in a place that is comfortable, yet appropriate for an academic endeavor. You will need materials to mark your score, so a desk in your home or school office is probably the best bet. You will also need room to spread out your research and score marking materials.

6. Whenever you have a mental block—as we all do at times—take a break from your study. Take a walk, stretch, or meditate for a few minutes, and you will return to the score mentally refreshed.

7. Find a mentor in your area. An experienced conductor willing to spend an hour or two discussing a score is an invaluable resource. A conductor who has many years of service to the choral art will most likely have conducted the piece you are studying and can offer suggestions that will greatly enhance your understanding of the piece. In addition, you could exchange programming ideas for future concerts or call on the expertise of your mentor for conducting or rehearsal technique questions.

8. After you have completed a thorough historical and structural analysis, listen to a respectable recording of the work. You will be amazed by what you hear. Again, this may take a little more time in the beginning, but the payoff will be tremendous.

Cursory and shallow score study will only provide you with a surface-level understanding of the music. You will not gain a deeper understanding of the work studied, which will most likely result in a surface-level performance. Without knowledge gained from thorough score study, an appropriate interpretation of the music might be indistinguishable from a poor one.

Our growth as conductors depends on our ability to look deeply inside a score to understand the language the composer uses and the appropriate gestures and sound concept necessary to convey the composer's message. Our goal is never to merely interpret the music, but to discover and represent the "voice" of Bach, Brahms, and Mozart, and to determine what they are trying to communicate expressively through their music.

Historical Analysis: The Information-Gathering Process

Prior to beginning the study process, you need to select appropriate literature for the ensemble in line with your organization's budget. Once literature is selected, you should then begin your study of the required vocal and instrumental forces, editions in print, composer and poet biographies, historical information on the work and style period, and an in-depth analysis of the text and a translation.

A wealth of information is available online today and in the form of articles, books, class lectures notes, and workshop notes. However, your local music library may prove to be your most valuable resource. Perhaps there is a dissertation or recording available through Interlibrary Loan, or an article on JSTOR that is critical to your research. Music librarians are quite helpful, so do not hesitate to ask for help.

Required Vocal and Instrumental Forces for *Nänie*

The vocal and instrumental forces are placed under the category of historical analysis because the number of singers, the voicing, and the makeup of the orchestra for the particular style period are historical considerations. You will note, for instance, the pairing of instruments below, a common feature of the classical-romantic orchestra—and certainly for Brahms:

- 2 flutes
- 2 oboes
- 2 clarinets in A
- 2 bassoons
- 2 horns in D
- 3 trombones
- Timpani
- Harp (if possible, several)
- SATB chorus – Except for two measures of easy divisi in the bass line in measures 174–175, the chorus is SATB only.
- Violin 1
- Violin 2
- Viola
- Violoncello
- Contrabass

The performance time for *Nänie* is approximately 13 minutes. In programming your concert, you would need to determine other works that utilize similar instrumentation. Michael Rosewall's *Directory of Choral-Orchestral Music* (Routledge, 2006) discusses more than 3,500 works written for chorus with orchestra. Each entry includes instrumentation and voicing, timings, languages, publishers and editions, and composer information. Another resource is Jonathan D. Green's *A Conductor's Guide to Choral-Orchestral Works* (published by Scarecrow Press in multiple volumes). Both of these valuable resources contain much of the background materials needed for the historical analysis.

Editions in Print

When comparing editions of a work, there are two main types:

1. *Urtext* **(or historical) editions** – The *Urtext* edition is created from primary sources, including the autograph copy, a first-edition correction copy with corrections made by the composer, and copies made by the composer's pupils or assistants. A critical commentary or preface is generally supplied by a scholar of the particular work or the composer.

2. **Performance (or interpretive) editions** – Performance editions include editorial markings (generally in brackets), such as dynamics and ornamentation, in an attempt to provide the performers with the scholar's "best guess" as to how the music should be performed.

Another type of edition that is highly beneficial to conductors in preparing a score for rehearsal and performance is the **critical study edition**, such as *Norton Critical Scores*. Along with the score, critical editions often provide historical background information, an analysis of the work, views and comments from scholars, and a bibliography for further study. A critical study score of *Nänie* does not currently exist, hence the choice of this work for our analysis.

Brahms's earliest works were published by Breitkopf & Härtel. He served as an advisor and editor for Breitkopf & Härtel's *Sämtliche Werke* (complete works) editions of the works of Bach and Mozart, among others. But after a falling-out over his *String Sextet*, Op. 36, in 1865, Brahms published with Johann Rieter-Biedermann in Winterthur (who first published *Ein deutsches Requiem*, Op. 45) and Nikolaus Simrock in Bonn, a hornist, publisher, and promoter of Beethoven's music. Yet Brahms allowed Dr. Max Abraham, who founded C. F. Peters in Leipzig in 1800, to publish *Nänie* as part of his Edition Peters, which Abraham established in 1867 to provide inexpensive access to the great musical works of the time. Edition Peters and Breitkopf & Härtel full scores are available for purchase.

Kalmus publishes a full score of *Nänie* as a reprint of the Breitkopf & Härtel edition and a miniature study score of three choral works by Brahms: *Alto Rhapsody* (Op. 53), *Schicksalslied* (Op. 54), and *Nänie* (Op. 82). Historical and analytical information is not included in the miniature study score, however. Dover also publishes an authoritative Breitkopf & Härtel edition that includes *Alto Rhapsody, Nänie, Schicksalslied,* and *Gesang der Parzen* (Op. 89) in full score.

Once the full score edition has been selected and the instrumental parts have been ordered or rented from the publisher, you must determine the edition to be used by the chorus. Breitkopf & Härtel, C. F. Peters, Kalmus, and G. Schirmer publish piano/vocal scores. Order single copies of each edition. Once the copies arrive, compare the vocal parts to those in the *Urtext* edition or the *Sämtliche Werke*. Most major music libraries will own the complete works of the key composers.

If you plan to perform more than one work included in the Dover edition, you may consider purchasing full scores for the singers. The price of a Dover edition compared to individual copies of the four titles may be more cost-effective, and you would have four of these pieces in your library for future programming instead of one.

Composer and Poet Biographies

A general knowledge of the life events of the composer and the poet, especially those events that led to the creation of the text and the music, is necessary to fully understand the creative process and the circumstances—a festive occasion, for a patron, for a funeral, and so forth—under which the piece was composed. Much of this information will be needed as you prepare program notes and may be recycled, with necessary improvements, for future use.

Johannes Brahms (1833–1897): Johannes Brahms was born in Hamburg to Johann Jakob Brahms and Christiane Nissen. Brahms received his earliest musical training from his father, a town musician, a horn and double bass player. Brahms began piano lessons with Otto Friedrich Willibald Cossel at the age of seven, supplementing his family income by playing at bars, restaurants, and theaters. Following his studies with Cossel, he continued lessons with Eduard Marxen, who had studied in Vienna with a pupil of Mozart. In his early teens, Brahms developed a love for choral and orchestral conducting. Conducting choirs and instrumental ensembles helped to develop his musical skills.

At age nineteen, Brahms embarked on a concert tour with respected Hungarian violinist Eduard Reményi. On this tour, he met famous violinist Joseph Joachim in Hanover and Franz Liszt at the Court of Weimar. It was

Joachim who introduced Brahms to Robert and Clara Schumann. Robert Schumann was so impressed with Brahms's talent that he published an article entitled "Neue Bahnen," or "New Paths," in *Neue Zeitschrift für Musik* (*New Journal of Music*, which was founded by Schumann). In the article, Robert Schumann proclaimed that Brahms was "destined to give ideal expression to the times."

While Brahms never married, he became quite close to Clara Schumann, who was fourteen years his senior. It is interesting to note that Brahms's mother was seventeen years older than his father. His relationship with Clara seems to have been a platonic one, despite Brahms's intense feelings for her. He wrote to her, "I regret every word I write to you that does not speak of my love for you."[2] He stood beside Clara after Robert Schumann's attempted suicide and confinement to a psychiatric hospital in 1854. Schumann died two years later. After Schumann's death, Brahms held two positions—at a women's chorus in Hamburg and as the court music teacher and conductor at Detmold. He was appointed conductor of the Vienna Singakademie in 1863, but resigned the following year. However, he did make Vienna his home, becoming the Director of Concerts at the Vienna Gesellschaft der Musikfreunde from 1872 to 1875.

Brahms's largest and most famous choral work, *Ein deutsches Requiem*, premiered in Bremen in 1868. The overwhelming success of the premiere gave the often self-critical Brahms the confidence to complete his cantata *Rinaldo*, four symphonies, several cycles of piano pieces, including *Piano Concerto No. 2* of 1881, clarinet quintet and two clarinet sonatas, and *Four Serious Songs (Vier ernste Gesänge)*, among others. Beginning in 1881, the same year Brahms completed *Nänie*, Hans von Bülow, a former student of Friedrich Wieck (father of Clara Schumann) and one of the most famous conductors of the nineteenth century, began to premiere the works of Brahms with the court orchestra of the Duke of Meiningen.

Throughout his life, Brahms frequently participated in the performances of his works as soloist, accompanist, and conductor. He died of cancer in April 1897.

---

2 Mussgrave, Michael. *A Brahms Reader*. New Haven, CT: Yale University Press, 2000.

Friedrich von Schiller (1759–1805): German poet, dramatist, philosopher, and historian Johann Christoph Friedrich von Schiller was born in Marbach, Württemberg (north of Stuttgart) on November 10, 1759. The son of a military officer and surgeon for Duke Karl Eugen of Württemberg, Schiller was ordered to enter the duke's military academy, the Karlsschule, at the age of thirteen. He studied law and medicine at the Karlsschule. In 1780, he was appointed to the position of army surgeon at a Stuttgart regiment.

Schiller's first play, *Die Räuber (The Robbers)*, was published in 1781 and performed the following year in Mannheim. Focusing on the ideas of liberty, the play made Schiller an overnight sensation. Verdi's opera *I Masnadieri* is based upon *Die Räuber*. Upon learning that Schiller left the regiment without permission to attend a performance in Mannheim, the duke placed him in prison for two weeks and forbade him to publish anything except medical treatises.

Schiller fled to Mannheim, moving through Leipzig and Dresden to settle in Weimar in 1787. In 1789, he was appointed Professor of History and Philosophy in Jena, a small town in central Germany. However, to be closer to his friend Goethe, Schiller returned to Weimar in 1799. Both were major figures in German literature's *Sturm und Drang* (storm and stress) movement, which was distinguished by its stress on emotion and passion, subjectivity, and the unease of man; its theme of youthful genius and the all-powerful individual in rebellion against accepted standards; and the affirmation of nature.

Schiller completed *Nänie* in 1799, shortly after completion of his masterpiece, the Wallenstein cycle, a trilogy that follows the life of a commander during the Thirty Years' War. Goethe and Schiller founded the Weimar Theater, where many of their works were performed. Schiller died of tuberculosis at the age of forty-five in Weimar.

Schiller's *An die Freude (Ode to Joy)* (1785) was set by Beethoven as the "Finale" from Symphony No. 9. Brahms set another Schiller text, *Der Abend (The Evening), No. 2*, as part of his Op. 64 *Quartette für vier Solostimmen mit Pianoforte*. *An die Freude, Der Abend,* and *Nänie* all contain references to Greek mythological subjects.

Historical Information on the Work and Style Period

Nänie (Song of Lamentation) was named for Nenia, the Roman goddess of dying, mourning, and lamentation. The Romans used the word *nenia* to describe a funeral dirge in honor of the dead. The nenia was sung by relatives, accompanied by flutes, and later by hired mourners called *praeficae*. Completed in the summer of 1881, *Nänie* (note the German spelling) is one of the least known of Brahms's many choral works. This piece was written to honor the memory of his friend, painter Anselm Feuerbach (1829–1880), whom Brahms had been instrumental in attracting to the Vienna Academy of Visual Arts. In the spring of 1881, Brahms traveled to Venice (where Feuerbach died), Rome, southern Italy, and Sicily to familiarize himself with sites of classical antiquity, a subject dear to his friend Feuerbach, whose paintings were often based on subjects from Greek and Roman antiquity. The choice of Schiller's poetry, illuminating his shared love of classical antiquity with that of Anselm Feuerbach, was a stroke of genius. Brahms dedicated the piece to Henriette Feuerbach, the painter's stepmother.

The premiere took place in Zürich on December 6, 1881, with Brahms conducting. Brahms had tried out the orchestral sections of the work in Meiningen with Bülow earlier, but stated in a letter to his publisher, Dr. Max Abraham of C. F. Peters, that "it would not be possible to try the chorus because in North Germany people do not sight-read as well."[3]

In addition to composing and publishing *Nänie* in 1881–82, Brahms also completed his *Piano Concerto No. 2 in B-Flat,* Op. 83; *Romanzen und Lieder*, Op. 84; and *Gesang der Parzen*, Op. 89, during this period.

Analysis of Text and Translation

Unlike our orchestral counterparts, choral conductors and singers work with text on a daily basis. Yet the text is often treated as a second-class citizen; the tendency is to jump right into the music when learning new repertoire. We must remember, however, as often stated by my dear friend and respected colleague James Mulholland,

> The poetry is the mother of the music. It dictates both the form and the style of the composition and it should act as a musical thesaurus for appreciation and understanding of the text. The music provides the poem with an instant replay in slow motion, repeating lines and phrases and drawing out important words and syllables through longer note values or dramatic pauses. Proper lighting is necessary in order to supply a great painting with the perfect ambiance. The composer's setting of the music gives the poem a perfect ambiance, illuminating the text as to not miss anything the author has intended.[4]

---

3 Thym, Jurgen. *Two Brahms Letters*. Online resource accessed September 21, 2007.
   memory.loc.gov/ammem/collections/moldenhauer/2428117pdf
4 Mulholland, James. Permission for use granted January 6, 2007.

A complete understanding of the text is one of our greatest responsibilities as conductors. If we do not understand the text, how are we to explain its message to our singers? Failure to communicate a common understanding of the text in rehearsal will eventually send mixed messages to the audience, as singers may interpret the text in a way that is not consistent with the true meaning of the poetry. While certain texts, such as those of the Mass, are well known and perhaps more about the composer's **musical** expression than the text, many— including *Nänie*— may be less familiar to the performing artist.

In either case, the composer begins with the text—and so should you as you prepare for the first rehearsal. Not only will a poetic analysis of the text provide you with a deeper understanding of the music overall, but it will also help to reveal the structure of the piece, much in the same way the composer "sectionalizes" the text prior to beginning a musical composition. Many resources are available online to help you achieve a greater understanding of common terminology and approaches to analyzing poetic texts. A search using the keywords "poetic analysis" or "literary terms" will yield several results.

As the first step in your textual analysis, separate the text from the music. Type the poem and include a word-by-word translation below if the text is in a foreign language. Again, you will reuse this information for the concert program. Copy and paste the text into a new document and change the spacing from single to double. Read the text aloud several times to develop an understanding of the structure, rhyme scheme, and scansion of the poem. If you are not fluent in the language you are studying, prepare an International Phonetic Alphabet (IPA) edition of the text to help you approximate the exact sound of the language as it is sung. In addition, you may consider employing a language expert to assist you as you prepare to teach the diction, to provide a word-by-word translation, or to teach the diction to the chorus. However, it is in your best interest to become proficient in the major sung languages, as adjustments will need to be made to accommodate the vocal needs of the singers and to clarify the text. I authored an easy-to-understand and very practical "Crash Course in Singers' Diction" in *The Choral Singer's Survival Guide* (2005, Vocal Planet),[5] and Joan Wall's *Diction for Singers* (1990, Pst Records) and *International Phonetic Alphabet for Singers* (1989, Pst Records) provide very detailed insight into the pronunciation of major languages as they are sung.

---

5 Also available from GIA Publications, Inc. (Chicago).

The larger structure of *Nänie* is an elegy (a poem that laments or depicts sadness) written in sonnet form (a lyric poem of fourteen lines). The rhyme scheme of the Schiller text is a–b–a–b c–d–c–d e–f–e–f gg, composed of three quatrains (four-line stanzas) and a final couplet, which—typical of the sonnet—offers a summary of the poem. Each pair of lines resembles the form of ancient Greek and Latin elegiac distiches, couplets made up of one line of hexameter (a line of verse consisting of six metrical feet, the patterns of stressed and unstressed syllables) and one line of pentameter (a line of verse consisting of five metrical feet). You will notice, however, through scansion of the text (the process of identifying the rhythms of each line by locating and counting the stressed and unstressed syllables) that each line contains six stressed syllables. While *Nänie* does not represent a textbook example of elegiac distiches, the couplets and caesuras (breathing places or pauses in a line) found in the middle of each odd-numbered line may be seen as a modified version of the form. A familiar example illustrating the *caesura* (pronounced *say-zooh-rah*) is present in the first line of Elizabeth Barrett Browning's sonnet, "How do I love thee? Let me count the ways." The *caesura* follows the question mark, creating a natural pause or breath in the line.

Scan each line of the text below, noting the stressed (/) and unstressed (⌣) syllables, and mark them accordingly. It is helpful to read each line aloud as you do so. Note the *caesuras* in the odd-numbered lines. In line two, the *caesura* occurs between the words "Brust" and "rührt"—two stressed syllables in a row. In this structural analysis, you will discover how Brahms sets these caesuras musically to highlight the text, a difficult task since the lines consist of irregular patterns of stresses.

Nänie
Nenie von Friedrich Schiller

Auch das Schöne muß sterben, das Menschen und Götter bezwinget!
  Nicht die eherne Brust rührt es des stygischen Zeus.
Einmal nur erweichte die Liebe den Schattenbeherrscher,
  Und an der Schwelle noch, streng, rief er zurück sein Geschenk.
Nicht stillt Aphrodite dem schönen Knaben die Wunde,
  Die in den zierlichen Leib grausam der Eber geritzt.
Nicht errettet den göttlichen Held die unsterbliche Mutter,
  Wenn er, am skäischen Tor fallend, sein Schicksal erfüllt.

Aber sie steigt aus dem Meer mit allen Töchtern des Nereus,
    Und die Klage hebt an um den verherrlichten Sohn.
Siehe, da weinen die Götter, es weinen die Göttinnen alle,
    Daß das Schöne vergeht, daß das Vollkommene stirbt.
Auch ein Klaglied zu sein im Mund der Geliebten ist herrlich,
    Denn das Gemeine geht klanglos zum Orkus hinab.

Translation:
Even the beautiful must die. That which subdues mortals and gods
    does not touch the unyielding heart of the Stygian Zeus.
Only once did love soften the ruler of the shades,
    and, yet, at the threshold, sternly he recalled his gift.
Aphrodite does not soothe the wounds of the beautiful boy
    whose delicate body the boar cruelly tore.
The immortal mother does not rescue the divine hero,
    when, at the Scaean gate, falling, he fulfills his destiny.
But she rises out of the sea with all the daughters of Nereus,
    and begins the lament for her glorified son.
Behold, the gods weep, all the goddesses weep,
    because the beautiful perishes, the perfect dies.
Even to be a lament on the lips of a loved one is glorious,
    for the common ones go down to Orcus unsung.[6]

—Translation: Earthsongs
Used with permission.

As a general guide, look up in a dictionary or online anything you do not understand. You must comprehend the meaning of every word to convey the meaning of the poetry clearly to your singers, who will communicate the text to the audience. One misunderstood word can change the entire meaning of a work.

Some research into Greek mythology will be required to fully comprehend the text of *Nänie*. The poem begins with "Even the beautiful must die." The gods and goddesses lament those mortal youths (Euridice, Adonis, and Achilles) who have died. Perhaps Brahms chose this particular text because he felt that Feuerbach was taken too early from life. "That which subdues mortals and gods" refers to the certain death of mortals and the inability of immortals to change the course of death. The "Stygian Zeus" and "ruler of the shades" refers to Hades, the god of the

---

6 Jeffers, Ron, and Gordon Paine. *Translations and Annotations of Choral Repertoire.* Volume II: German Texts. Corvallis, OR: Earthsongs, 2000.

underworld. Lines three and four recall the story of Orpheus and Euridice. Euridice, who was bitten by a serpent, died and descended into the underworld. Her husband, Orpheus, went to the underworld and softened the heart of Hades through his music, convincing him to allow Euridice to return with him to earth. The only condition of this agreement was for Orpheus to walk in front of her and not look back until they reached the upper world. In his excitement, however, Orpheus looked back and Hades "recalled his gift." Of interest, a painting of Orpheus and Euridice was completed by Feuerbach in 1869.

Aphrodite is the goddess of love, beauty, and sexual rapture. Her lover, Adonis, was fatally wounded by a wild boar. The goddess was unable to "soothe the wounds of the beautiful boy." Following, Thetis, one of the Nereids (or daughters of Nereus, a Titan and sea god), mourns the death of her son, Achilles. He was killed by Paris and Apollo when fighting in the Trojan War (Scaean gate) by an arrow, which wounded his heel. The immortal mother rises out of the sea to lament the death of her son, Achilles. All of the gods and goddesses join her, expressing grief over the death of these beautiful youths and their inability to alter the outcome.

The final couplet, containing a summary of the poem, provides both a moment of consolation and a reminder that the common ones (*Gemeine*) descend into the underworld (*Orcus*) unsung. While the poem seems to end on a note of doom and gloom, one may interpret it as a glorification of those mortals included in the poem (**uncommon** beings) who have, in a sense, achieved immortality through their heroic acts.

Historical Analysis Checklist

Before proceeding to the structural analysis, review the **Historical Analysis Checklist** shown in **Figure 26-1**. Helpful questions and additional information are included below some of the items in the checklist to guide you as you undertake the historical analysis of a work.

Figure 26-1. Historical Analysis Checklist.

✔ Determine the required vocal and instrumental forces of the composition.

✔ Research the various editions that exist and select the most historically accurate edition for your score study, rehearsals, and performance.

✔ Using class lecture notes, books, articles, and online reference resources, research the life events of the composer and poet, and create a concise biography. You will reuse this information for the concert program and for future study, so this brief undertaking is well worth the time.

  – Discuss the nationality, dates, employment history and patrons, and distinguishing features of the poetry and music.
  – What inspired the poet to write the poem/composer to set the music?
  – Is the poem/music part of a larger collection?

✔ Using the same resources, locate information about the particular work.

  – When was it composed?
  – Who first performed the work?
  – Identify pieces by the composer that surround the composition. Major works composed by contemporaries during the same period are also important historically.

✔ Begin to compile a list of general style features, including tonal considerations (quality and color), distinguishing features of the composer, geographic area, and composition. You may come across several examples in your initial research. Many of the salient style features will become apparent in the structural analysis of the composition. However, begin the list now and fill in information as you examine the work structurally.

  – What are the major performance practice issues of the style period?
  – How should stylistic markings be interpreted?

Figure 26-1. (Continued)

✔ Undertake a complete poetic analysis of the text. Using online resources or the help of a professional poet, become an expert in analyzing poetic structure, as it is one of your most important responsibilities as a choral conductor. Before you begin, look up any words, phrases, or people included in the poem that are unfamiliar to you. Read the poem aloud several times.

- What is the overall form of the poem?
- What is the rhyme scheme?
- Locate the stressed and unstressed syllables in each line and mark them (scansion).
- Who is speaking in the poem and to whom?
- Where and under what circumstances? What is the specific location or situation?
- What is the tone of voice of the writer? (happy, angry, bitter, reflective, other)
- What is the dominant mood? Is there a subordinate mood?
- What is the overall message of the poem?
- Are there unusual or difficult features of the poem (irregular stress patterns, for example) that may present challenges to the composer as he or she sets the words to music?

Imagine how much knowledge you will accumulate in just a few years by studying composers, poets, and styles in this manner. Add to this a detailed structural analysis of each work, and the artistic growth potential is mindboggling.

Structural Analysis: The Musical Blueprint

The second part of the analysis process—the **structural** analysis—will reveal the overall structure of the work and the relationship of text and music. Full scores may look quite intimidating at first glance, especially to those with little experience in analyzing them. You may become so overwhelmed that you begin to miss even the most obvious features within the score. However, as you begin to relax into the process of score analysis and build experience with a variety of composers and their works, you will find that aspects of a particular work jump right off the page at you. You will become more confident with practice.

Review the guidelines for successful score study as a refresher. To gain an understanding of a score's structure, proceed by studying in layers. Since learning takes place in layers, this makes the most sense. It is easy to become overwhelmed by attempting to study everything at one time. The first rule in performing a structural analysis is to start big, go small.

Layer 1 of the Structural Analysis: The Framework of the Composition (Larger Units of Structure)

Before you begin the analysis, number each measure in the score. This is recommended for the sake of efficiency, as counting measures in rehearsal wastes valuable time.

Score Analysis of *Nänie*

You will find that *Nänie* contains 181 measures of music. While numbering the measures, look for obvious features, such as key signatures, meter and tempo changes, rehearsal letters, changes in texture, and the double bar lines at measures 85 and 141. Does the music appear to be major, minor, modal, or atonal? Is the meter standard, asymmetric, or changing? What is the difficulty level? Is the music primarily homophonic or polyphonic? What might you expect to see and hear in the music of this particular composer? Just make a mental note of these features as you number the measures.

Next, thumb through the piece. Without setting any decisions in stone, notice where the larger sections end. Perhaps the end of a section is marked by a tempo change, a key change, a metric change, or double bar lines. Whatever you do, try not to impose a structure on the piece that is not there. Allow creative ideas to flow easily as you move from page to page. Don't "try" too hard. Look for the obvious and simply jot down your ideas. Look up any terms with which you are unfamiliar, and write the translation above the foreign terms in the score.

The first large unit ends on the downbeat of measure 25, when the voices enter. The second unit begins at measure 25 and ends at measure 84. The beginning of the third unit of structure in measure 85 is highlighted by a key change, a meter change, a tempo change, triplet figures in the harp, pizzicato upper strings, and unison entrance of the voices. Double bar lines again mark the close of this unit and the beginning of a new unit in measure 141. A return to $\frac{6}{4}$ and the direction of *Tempo primo* launches this section of music, which will look quite familiar.

As you may have already noticed, the sections overlap, creating elision from one section to another. A repetition of line 13 of the text, highlighted by a D pedal and bass entrance (beginning with the same material first seen in the soprano voice at measure 25), sets off the last section of the composition. The **Chart of Structure** would look similar to that shown in **Figure 26-2**.

Figure 26-2. Chart of structure.

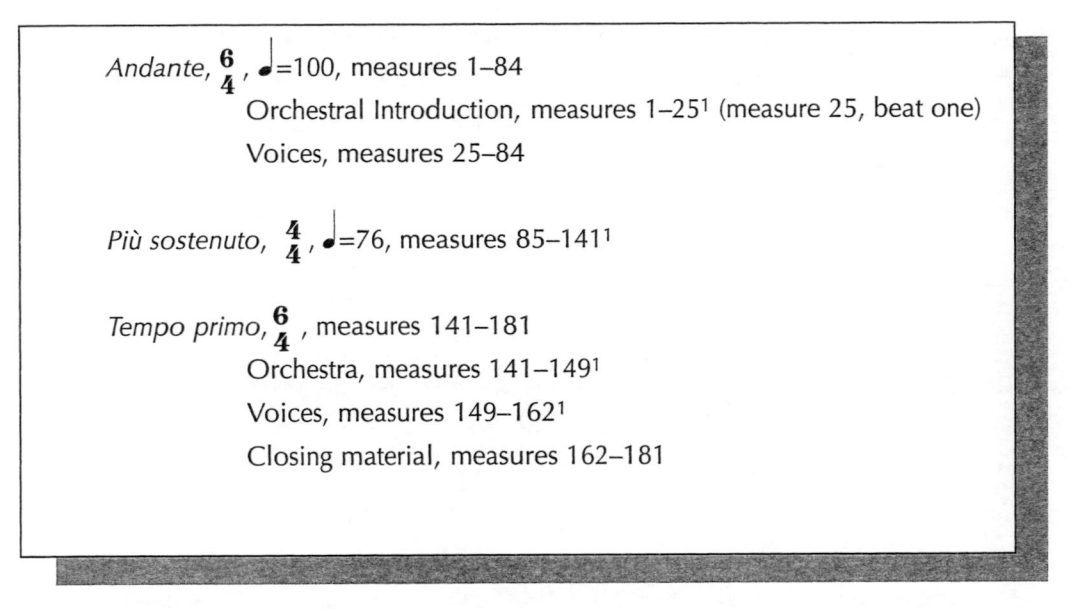

Andante, $\frac{6}{4}$, ♩=100, measures 1–84
    Orchestral Introduction, measures 1–25[1] (measure 25, beat one)
    Voices, measures 25–84

Più sostenuto, $\frac{4}{4}$, ♩=76, measures 85–141[1]

Tempo primo, $\frac{6}{4}$, measures 141–181
    Orchestra, measures 141–149[1]
    Voices, measures 149–162[1]
    Closing material, measures 162–181

The first step is that simple. For multi-movement works, you would repeat the same process for each movement.

As you continue your analysis of the larger units of structure, try as much as possible to focus on one layer at a time. Just look for the obvious in the first reading, using markers such as poetic structure, key, meter, tempo changes, double bar lines, rehearsal letters or numbers, and changes in texture as your guide. This will help you gain an understanding of the overall framework of the piece without clouding your mind with the fine details too early. Addressing the minute details of the score too early will overwhelm you, especially when analyzing difficult works. The process is much like building a house: first create a foundation, then set the frame of the house, and finally fill in the subtle details of the framework.

There is much to discover from performing a scan of the larger units of musical and poetical structure. You now have a greater understanding of the framework of the composition. And with a clear understanding of the framework, you can now determine that the piece is in ABA[1] form. The first A section includes an extended orchestral introduction, and the final A section includes a coda.

Andante (measures 1–84)

You may be tempted to address the voice parts first. However, always begin your score study with the instrumental parts. As is the case with *Nänie*, main themes often appear in the orchestra first, especially in extended introductions.

Look at the first page of the score. You will notice that the piece begins in $\frac{6}{4}$ in D major. The instruments are in pairs, a typical feature of the classical-romantic orchestra. The oboe contains the melodic material. It is important to note the function of the horns, which serve more as wind instruments than brass instruments here. The strings alternate *pizzicato* and *arco* passages, sometimes imitating the melodic material found in the oboe. The strings rest for several measures at a time and re-enter in a quasi-antiphonal exchange with the winds. The harp does not play in the introduction, and the trombones play only for a few measures, beginning at measure 22.

The entrance of the voices is marked by the end of the oboe melody. The voices enter polyphonically in pairs (SA/TB). This is a typical feature of Brahms's music; as you study his works, always look for the duets in his music. The soprano and alto entrances are four measures apart, while the tenors and basses enter only half a measure apart. The soprano and tenor voices enter on the pitches d–a, while the tenors and altos enter on a–d. The strings are the primary accompaniment at measure 25.

Begin to notice when instruments double the voices as you scan each page. For instance, the clarinet in A doubles the tenor voice at measure 33, and the bassoon doubles the bass voice. The string of imitative entrances ends at measure 40. At measure 41, the texture becomes more homophonic, and the chorus is sparsely accompanied or unaccompanied until measure 46. Notice how Brahms handles the *caesura* in measure 44. The basses and tenors sing a syncopated line below the *hemiola* in the soprano and alto lines. Brahms includes a *hemiola* in the next measure in all voices to further highlight the text, "Stygian Zeus."

The bass voice enters in measure 47 with melodic material similar to measure 25. The strings anticipate the bass entrance in measure 46, creating an overlapping phrase (or elision) in the measure. The bass voice is doubled by the clarinet in A and bassoon in measure 47. Measures 47–59 are similar to measures 25–40. The upper voices enter polyphonically in measures 52–53. Notice how the tenor voice enters in contrary motion of the other three voices.

Measures 59–64 are a musical repetition (with some variation) of measures 41–46. The harp enters for the first time in measure 65. It is interesting to note, with the exception of the last five measures, that the harp plays only when the text speaks of the gods and goddesses. At measure 65, the voices once again enter in pairs and the key center shifts to F major. Following a cadence on A major in measure 74, the key once again shifts, this time to f-sharp minor. Make a mental note to cue the timpani at measure 74.

The trombones join in at measure 75. A cadence on C-sharp major (V/F-sharp) closes the A section in measure 83. Two measures of extension create a smooth transition into the next large section of the work. You should note that Brahms set the first two quatrains (total of 8 lines) of text in the *Andante* section.

Più sostenuto (measures 85–141[1])

In this section, Brahms sets the third quatrain (lines 9–12) of the poem, dealing with the lament of the gods and goddesses. The key center shifts to F-sharp major and alternates with the dominant of the key (C-sharp major), the key at the beginning of this section. The first clear cadence in the key of F-sharp does not occur until measure 129. In addition to the key change, the tempo slows in this section and the meter changes to $\frac{4}{4}$.

Overall, the texture is more homophonic. Note the rising motion of the orchestra and voices to depict Thetis rising out of the sea at measure 85. The harp is not orchestrated when the text speaks of the gods and goddesses weeping. In measures 101–104, Brahms expresses the grief of the immortals through the use of extreme chromaticism and a deceptive cadence at measure 104. The instrumental and vocal lines in this section are generally less lyric to depict the sadness of the immortals.

Following a three-bar bridge in measures 104–106, the voices resume in measure 107 in a homophonic, hymn-like texture. Measures 107–108 are voices alone to highlight the text "because the beautiful perishes." Measures 119–141 are similar to measures 85–118. This is the first and only time in the piece that Brahms repeats an entire couplet of the poem (lines 11–12). Measures 119–129 are a repeat of measures 85–95, this time ending in F-sharp major. The harp is included in the orchestration this time.

A re-transition begins in measure 130, musically returning to the key, meter, and melodic material first seen in the *Andante* section. The voices are unaccompanied in measures 138–140. An elision is created on the downbeat of measure 141 (141[1]) as the *Più sostenuto* section ends and the *Tempo primo* section begins.

Tempo primo (measures 141–181)

The recapitulation of material from the *Andante* section, beginning in measure 141, contains 8 bars of musical material from the orchestral introduction in measures 1–25. Once again, the oboe plays the main melody and the key center shifts back to D major. As in the *Andante* section, the voices enter polyphonically. The sopranos and basses sing the opening melodic material, while the alto and tenor voices serve as harmonic support to highlight "ist herrlich" (is glorious). Measures 141–144 are structurally similar to measures 1–4, and measures 149–152 are structurally similar to measures 25–28. Note the duets in measures 158–160, the setting of the chorus without accompaniment in measures 159–161, and the descending melodic lines to symbolize the descent into the underworld (*Orcus*) in measure 161.

The final unit of the piece is highlighted by the D pedal, especially in the timpani and lower strings. Brahms chose to repeat line 13 of the text to honor the memory of his friend Anselm Feuerbach, "Auch ein Klaglied zu sein im Mund der Geliebten ist herrlich" (Even to be a lament on the lips of a loved one is glorious)—a more comforting sentiment—rather than ending with the final line of the sonnet.

The bass voice initiates the closing section, singing a variation of the main melody (this time beginning on the tonic rather than the dominant) from measure 25. Following the entrance of the tenor, alto, and soprano voices, the texture becomes homophonic. The harmonic rhythm (the speed of the chord changes) quickens beginning at measure 170, and the chorus appears without accompaniment to illuminate the text "im Mund der Geliebten" (the lips of a loved one). This text is repeated three times, increasing in intensity until reaching the climax of the piece in measure 172. The harp enters in measure 177. All instruments and voices come together for the final three measures of the piece.

The Conductor as Music Editor

Before progressing to the next level of analysis—the subtle details of the framework—it is necessary to discuss the role of the conductor as music editor when preparing the score.

Those who have worked with Robert Shaw or Margaret Hillis (both of whom studied with Julius Herford) are well aware of the attention they placed on every note. Shaw was legendary for his editions of major works, which addressed every single detail of the music. Each member of his chorus received a copy of the piano-vocal score with his markings, or copied the markings into the score from master copies or rehearsal notes.

As you move from layer to layer in your analysis, eventually focusing on the function of every note in the musical phrase, begin to notice potential balance issues, areas where the ensemble may need to articulate in a different way to communicate the text over the orchestra. Beethoven often wrote triple *forte* in all parts. Imagine the horrible balance issues you would face if everyone played or sang triple *forte*. Reasonable adjustments must be made to account for the size of the orchestra, the number of singers, and the performance acoustic, as composers often do not indicate subtleties in the score.

Following the exact tempo, dynamics, and articulation indicated by a composer may not work for your ensemble or in the performance space. Editing the score and making these critical decisions in advance of the first rehearsal will save hours of valuable time. Of course, you must edit the score with the performance venue in mind, not the rehearsal venue.

Score Marking 101

Conductors mark their scores in a variety of ways. Some prefer few markings in the score, while others mark scores so heavily they look somewhat like a coloring book. Using the resources in this text, develop a system that works for you.

The **suggested markings** shown in **Figure 26-3** come from studies with Margaret Hillis. While you may choose not to use all of them, they will serve as a starting point in developing your own system for marking your score.

Figure 26-3. Suggested score markings.

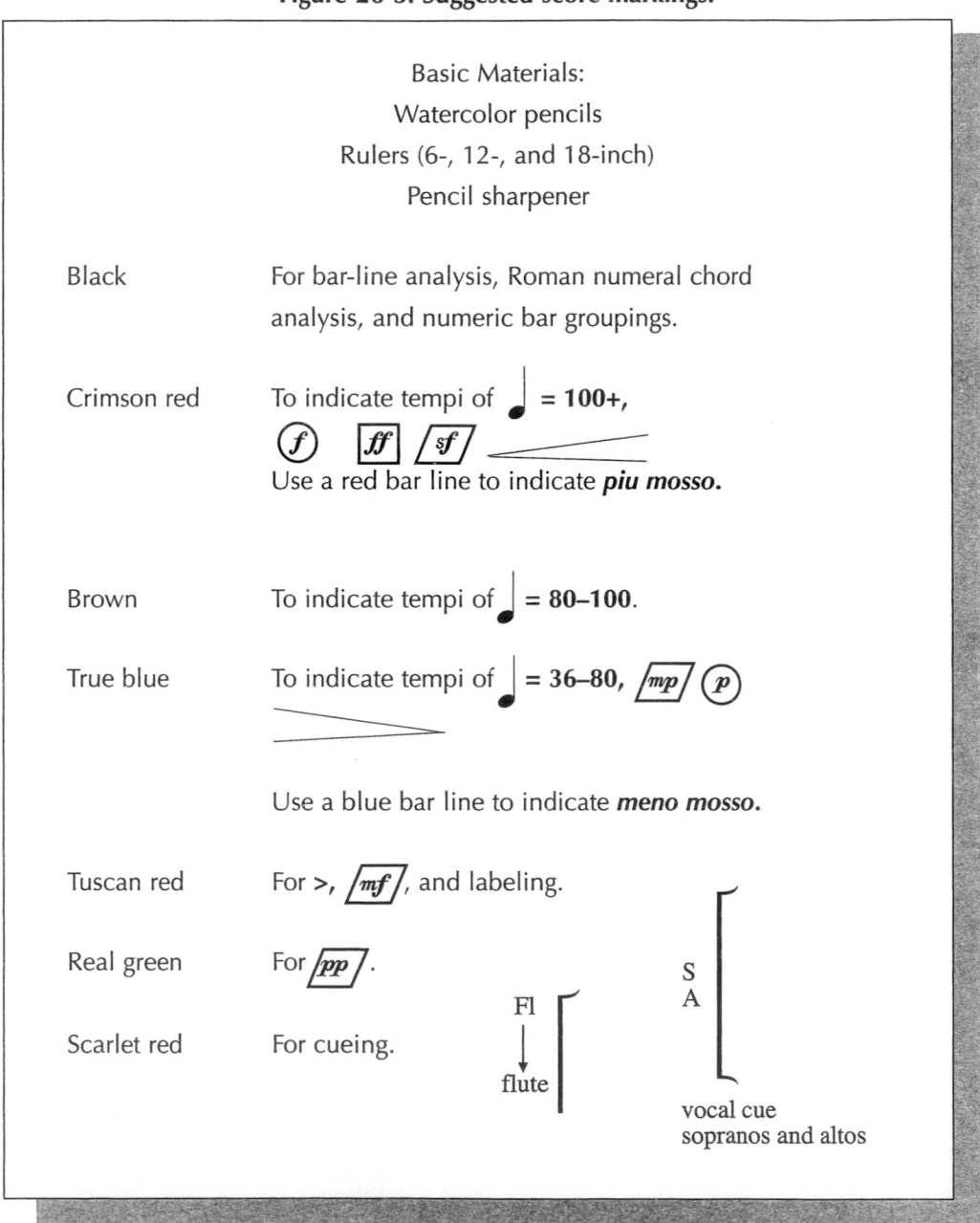

Basic Materials:
Watercolor pencils
Rulers (6-, 12-, and 18-inch)
Pencil sharpener

Black	For bar-line analysis, Roman numeral chord analysis, and numeric bar groupings.
Crimson red	To indicate tempi of ♩ = 100+, ⓕ ⧸ff⧹ ⧸sf⧹ ◁══════ Use a red bar line to indicate **piu mosso**.
Brown	To indicate tempi of ♩ = 80–100.
True blue	To indicate tempi of ♩ = 36–80, ⧸mp⧹ ⓟ ══════▷ Use a blue bar line to indicate **meno mosso**.
Tuscan red	For >, ⧸mf⧹, and labeling.
Real green	For ⧸pp⧹.
Scarlet red	For cueing.

Fl
↓
flute

S
A

vocal cue
sopranos and altos

This system uses **red** to indicate louder dynamics, faster tempi, crescendos, and accents, and **blue** is used to indicate a slowing of tempo, softer dynamics, or decrescendos. The bar-line analysis, indicating the smaller and larger phrase units by placing structural bar lines in the score, is highly recommended. A single line down the page may be used to indicate smaller units of structure, while double bar lines indicate the end of a larger section. Some conductors prefer to place numeric bar groupings (e.g., 4+4) in the score instead. Including both in the score is visually helpful, and you will be able to select appropriate starting places in rehearsal that make the most sense. You will not have to search for a place to begin because the structure of the music will be crystal clear to you. Above all, make the material your own. Do what makes the most sense for you.

A more detailed discussion of Hillis's method may be found in Chapter 22, "The Rite, Passage, and Necessity of Score Marking for Conductor and Choir."

Layer 2 of the Structural Analysis: Subtle Details of the Framework (Smaller Units of Structure)

Now that we have an understanding of the framework of the composition, the role of the conductor as music editor, and a score marking system in place, follow the guidelines below to discover the subtle details of the score. Remember...wait to listen to a recording, study in stages, and take breaks to refresh your mind.

1. Using the black pencil, include bar lines in the score to indicate the larger structural framework. Draw double lines to indicate the end of major sections. In *Nänie*, these are already present, so it is not necessary to draw them here.

    However, draw a single line with the black pencil through the bar line in the instrumental and vocal parts at the end of measures 24, 148, and 161 to highlight the subsections of the ABA[1] framework (as shown in Figure 26-2). Note that the lines appear at the end of the measure before the new section begins.

2. Beginning with the orchestral introduction, determine the smaller phrase groupings. Dividing the orchestra into choirs, focus only on the string choir, analyzing each line horizontally at first and then vertically. Approaching heavily orchestrated scores in this manner is especially helpful.

    For works with piano or organ accompaniment, analyze the keyboard parts just as carefully as you would a score with orchestral accompaniment.

    *   Play the parts on the piano, sing the individual lines, or play one line and sing another, remembering to transpose instruments as necessary. Match the orchestra parts to the full score. Inconsistencies are quite common.

- Are the lines conjunct or disjunct? Diatonic or chromatic? Are dissonances created between the various lines? Are the lines ornamented? Note awkward leaps, sequences, repeated motifs, and imitation. In the voice parts, how does the language affect the contour of the lines?

- Note major themes, fugal passages, phrase lengths, changes in texture, and structural devices such as cadences, crescendos, decrescendos, or dynamics that may illuminate the phrase.

- Analyze the rhythm. Is it simple or complex? How does the composer use rhythm to develop or unify the piece? Look for repetition, *ostinati*, syncopation, augmentation, diminution, *hemiola*, unusual note groupings, use of silence, and so forth.

- Follow the same procedure with the winds, brass, percussion, and voice parts.

- Looking at the score vertically, compare all the various "choirs" with one another. Which part contains the primary material? Which instruments accompany? Note when instruments double the voices. Are there duets? Is an adjustment of dynamics necessary to clarify the melody? Perhaps the accompanimental instruments will need to reduce the volume by one dynamic level.

- At this point, the phrase structure should become apparent. As an example, the opening 24 measures of *Nänie* seem to be grouped 10 (6+4) + 8 (4+4) + 6. Interpret this as a ten-bar phrase further broken down into two smaller phrases of 6+4, plus 8 bars further broken down into two smaller phrases of 4+4, plus 6 bars.

  When first uncovering the smaller units of structure within the larger sections, place a checkmark (✔) in pencil above the bar line where a new phrase begins (e.g., measures 10 and 18). Continue through the score in this manner. When you are completely certain of the phrase units, draw a single line with the black pencil through the bar line in the instrumental and vocal parts.

  Write the phrase grouping (e.g., 10 (6+4)) in pencil at the beginning of each new phrase. You may wish to draw a single line through the voice parts only (or the string choir in orchestral passages) to illuminate the smaller phrase grouping within the larger phrase (the 6+4). This will prove quite helpful in rehearsal when you are searching for an appropriate starting point.

3. Place appropriate markings in the score, including breath marks, using the text as your guide. Use scarlet red to indicate cues (as suggested in Figure 26-3).

4. Trace the harmonic rhythm through a Roman numeral analysis of each measure. Identify the tonal center of each section. Why did the composer choose this key center? Is the harmonic language primarily triadic, modal, or atonal? Do chords appear in open or closed position? Look for key changes, relationships of key areas, and odd doublings of chords. Do unstable harmonic units appear in the music?

    The harmonic analysis of the piece allows you to discover the logical musical plan, to establish relationships between sections or movements, and to anticipate potential intonation and balance issues.

5. Prepare a list of salient style features for each piece and composer you study. In your historical analysis, you will certainly come across many features in your research.

    Some of the style features discovered in *Nänie* include pairing of instruments, duets in the voices, the use of *hemiola*, and a rich, colorful harmonic language. Add to the list and retain it for future use.

6. Following the same process, move to the next large unit of structure in the piece. What are the moments of greatest intensity? Where is the climax of the piece? Does the composition depart from or expand upon traditional forms (sonata form) or expected key centers? If so, where and why?

7. As you continue the analysis, keep a list of rehearsal ideas, potential vocal challenges and remedies, difficult leaps, awkward voicings, and difficult transitions or seams in the music. These notes will come in handy as you develop your rehearsal plan.

8. Once you have completed your detailed analysis, construct an analytical graph of the piece or each movement of larger works.

Editor's Note: The following material, until now unpublished, is taken from the Julius Herford Collection, which is housed at the William and Gayle Cook Music Library at Indiana University. Future volumes of historical and structural analyses of major choral-orchestral works, compiled and edited by Tony Thornton, are currently in development.

Creating an Analytical Graph

Analytical graphs are designed to present the salient structural features of the work in a format quickly and clearly understood by the conductor. Studied carefully, the graphs become concise and useful tools that aid not only in analysis but also in structural memorization.

The graphs present a structural analysis based on measure groups. In each case, the largest measure group appears at the top of the chart; subdivisions into shorter bar groupings appear in successive levels below. Beneath the bar groupings, the textural, textual, tonal, harmonic, and dynamic elements that contribute to the structure are notated. Use abbreviations for the sake of clarity; see **Figure 26-4, Symbols and Their Meanings.**

Figure 26-4. Symbols and their meanings.

Symbol	Meaning of Symbol
1————4 ⏝ 4	Bar grouping spans measures 1–4 and is 4 measures in length.
1————4 ⏝ 4 (2+2)	Bar grouping spans measures 1–4 and is internally subdivided into 2+2 measure units.
1————4 ⏝ 4 (2×2)	Bar grouping spans measures 1–4 and is internally repeated into 2-measure units.
1^2	Second beat of measure 1.
5,6	The phrase goes to the downbeat of measure 6.
40,41	The phrase of measure 41 begins in measure 40.
5–8=1–4	Measures 5–8 are structurally similar to or identical to measures 1–4.

Figure 26-4. Graph of *Nänie* by Julius Herford.

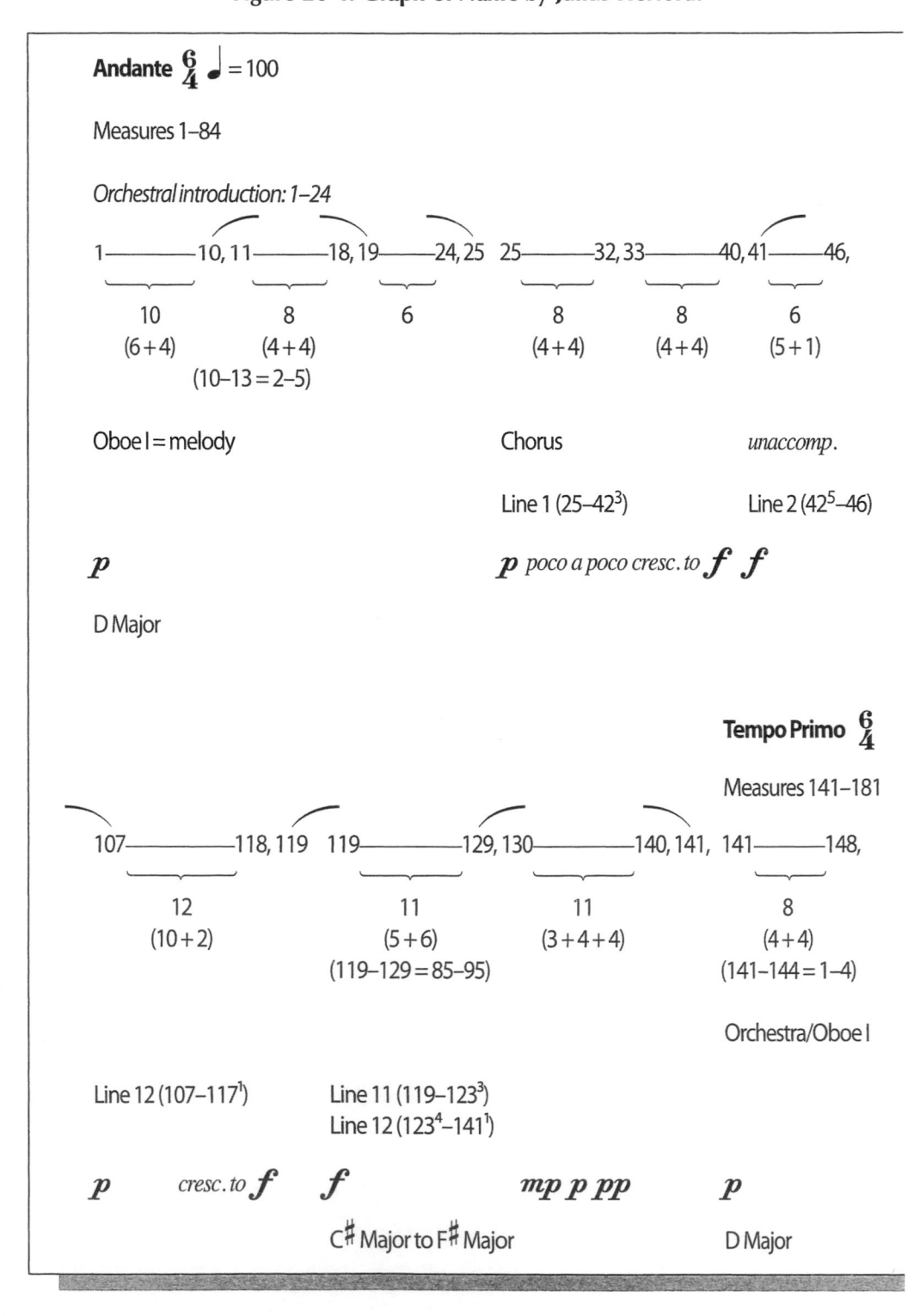

Figure 26-4. (Continued)

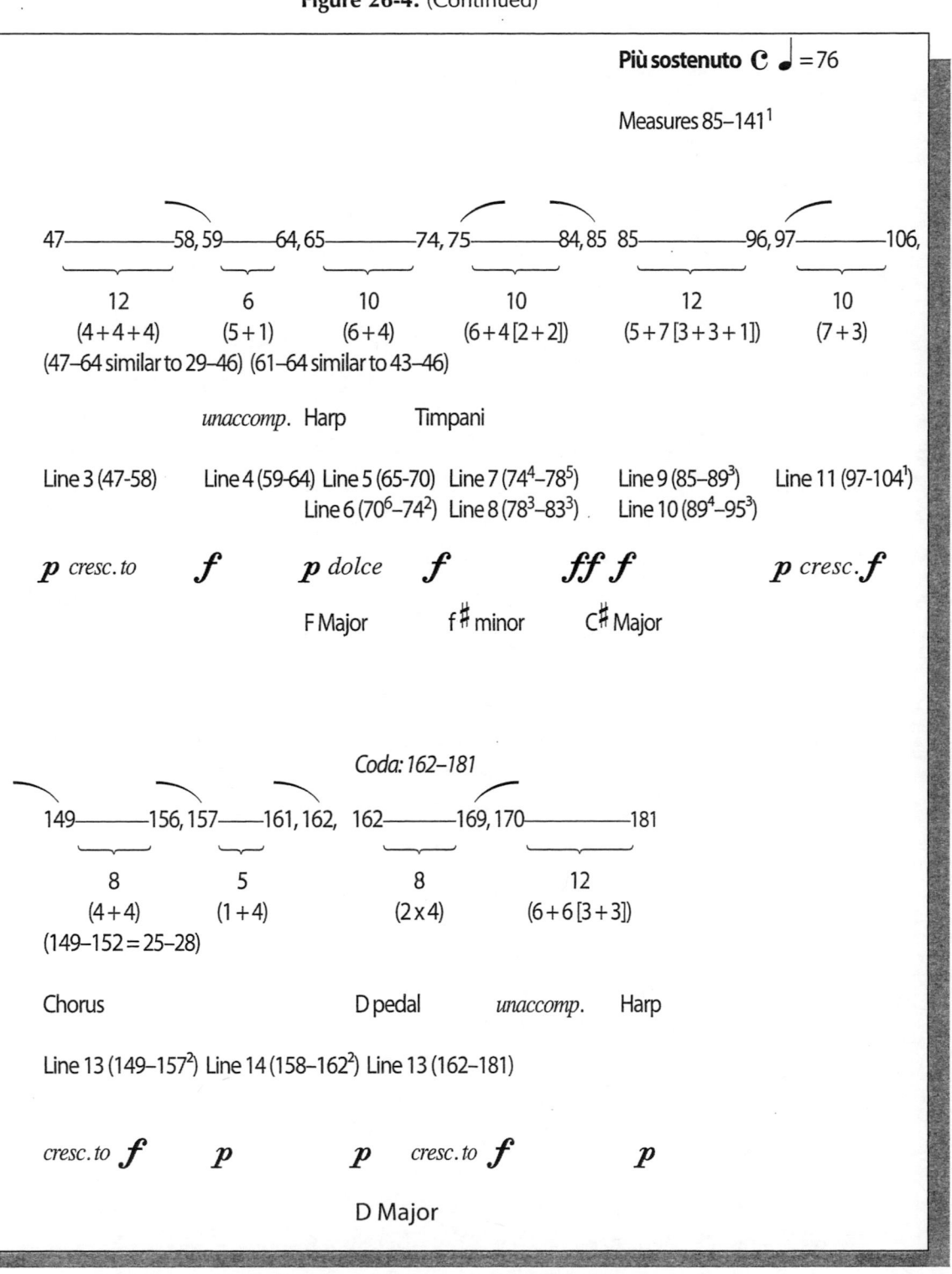

Più sostenuto C ♩ =76

Measures 85–141[1]

47————58, 59————64, 65————74, 75————84, 85 85————96, 97————106,

12	6	10	10	12	10
(4+4+4)	(5+1)	(6+4)	(6+4 [2+2])	(5+7 [3+3+1])	(7+3)

(47–64 similar to 29–46) (61–64 similar to 43–46)

unaccomp. Harp   Timpani

Line 3 (47-58)   Line 4 (59-64) Line 5 (65-70) Line 7 (74⁴–78⁵)   Line 9 (85–89³)   Line 11 (97-104¹)
                  Line 6 (70⁶–74²) Line 8 (78³–83³)   Line 10 (89⁴–95³)

p *cresc. to*   **f**   **p** *dolce*   **f**   **ff f**   **p** *cresc.* **f**

F Major   f♯ minor   C♯ Major

Coda: 162–181

149————156, 157————161, 162, 162————169, 170————181

8	5	8	12
(4+4)	(1+4)	(2×4)	(6+6 [3+3])

(149–152 = 25–28)

Chorus   D pedal   *unaccomp.*   Harp

Line 13 (149–157²) Line 14 (158–162²) Line 13 (162–181)

cresc. to **f**   **p**   **p**   *cresc. to* **f**   **p**

D Major

Excerpts from *The Choral Lectures and Analyses* of Julius Herford.
Reprinted with permission from Peter M. Herford.
© Estate of Julius Herford.

The method for structural analysis and the final analytical graph will change depending on the style of the music. Pre-tonal and some contemporary music does not lend itself to this type of structural analysis. Instead, you would need to identify points of imitation, church modes, or tone rows, for example. Many of the same questions exist, and new ones will arise in every piece you examine. Create a practical and workable graph that makes sense to you, yet captures the details of the piece you are studying.

Exploring your creativity and courage is part of the beauty of what you do as a conductor—those who accept the responsibility of serving the arts are constantly challenged to grow in the understanding of many creative, diverse, yet connected, areas.

The Finishing Touches

Now, following your analyzed score, graph, or both, listen to a recording of the piece. You will probably be amazed at how much more you hear the overall structure and the subtle details of the composition. Other musical ideas will surface as you listen, such as the phrasing of a line in a certain way you wish to consider or a vocal sound you would never have considered before. "Fill in" the missing gaps.

You can certainly learn a great deal from a recording, especially those of the legendary conductors and ensembles admired by all. Yet waiting to listen as a **final** step instead of the first step enables you to sharpen your own skills first.

After you complete the historical and structural score analysis of the work, place any final markings in the score and begin to mark the parts for the orchestra. If you need help marking the instrumental parts, especially the string bowings, consult the concert master or mistress for guidance.

As you plan for the first rehearsal with the singers and eventually with the orchestra, begin to consider conducting gestures that will evoke the most beautiful and appropriate tone, dynamics, articulation, phrasing, diction, and emotion. Prepare a detailed yet flexible rehearsal plan, and create warm-ups to address the vocal demands of the piece. Use the list of ideas you generated during the analysis. As you become a true reflection of the score through a profound understanding of the history and structure of the music you perform, you will inspire your singers, the orchestra, the audience—and certainly yourself—toward artistic greatness. The insight into the text, music, and history, which you are able to share with others with absolute confidence and integrity, becomes a vehicle for extraordinary growth.

I challenge you to analyze the literature for your next concert historically and structurally. You are guaranteed a very different experience—one that will elevate you and your ensemble to new heights musically, spiritually, and organizationally.

Chapter Bibliography

Brahms, Johannes. *Three Choral Works*. Kalmus Study Scores 1160. Melville, NY: Belwin Mills Publishing Corp., n.d.

Clive, Peter. *Brahms and His World: A Biographical Dictionary*. Lanham, MD: The Scarecrow Press, Inc., 2006.

Colles, H. C. "Brahms's Shorter Choral Works." *The Musical Times* 74:1083 (May 1933): 410–12.

Decker, Harold A., and Julius Herford. *Choral Conducting Symposium*, 2nd ed. Englewood Cliff, NJ: Prentice Hall, 1988.

Fulton, Kenneth. Class notes from The History and Development of Choral Music, Louisiana State University, 1991–92.

Garretson, Robert L. *Choral Music: History, Style, and Performance Practice*. Englewood Cliffs, NJ: Prentice Hall, 1993.

Green, Elizabeth A. H., and Nicolai Malko. *The Conductor's Score*. Englewood Cliffs, NJ: Prentice Hall, 1985.

Herford, Julius. *The Julius Herford Collection*. The William and Gayle Cook Music Library: Indiana University. Unpublished (used by permission).

Hillis, Margaret. Workshop notes from Choral Score Analysis, Westminster Choir College, Summer 1993.

Jeffers, Ron, and Gordon Paine. *Translations and Annotations of Choral Repertoire*, Volume II: German Texts. Corvallis, OR: Earthsongs, 2000.

Kross, Siegfried. "The Choral Music of Johannes Brahms." *American Choral Review* 25:4 (October 1983): 5–30.

Moses, Don V., Robert W. Demaree, Jr., and Allen F. Ohmes. *Face to Face with an Orchestra*. Princeton, NJ: Prestige Publications, Inc., 1987.

Poultney, David. *Studying Music History: Learning, Reasoning, and Writing About Music History and Literature*. Englewood Cliffs, NJ: Prentice Hall, 1983.

Sharpe, Lesley. *Friedrich Schiller: Drama, Thought and Politics*. London: Cambridge University Press, 2004.

Thornton, Tony. *The Choral Singer's Survival Guide.* Los Angeles: Vocal Planet Publishing, 2005.

Thurmond, James Morgan. *Note Grouping.* Galesville, MD: Meredith Music Publications, 2000.

Chapter 27

Schenkerian Analysis as an Analytical Tool for Performance Preparation

Matthew J. LaPine

Inferior instinct and (often) complete lack of secure knowledge on the part of today's performing musicians are the reason that the masterworks—how bitter a truth!—have not been heard in our time in their authentic shape. (p. xviii)

—Heinrich Schenker
in *Counterpoint*

Note from the author of this book:

Schenkerian Analysis, while not widely used by choral conductors in their score analysis process, is an approach you should consider as another method to provide a different vantage point of the scores you are going to teach. Consider the analysis methods presented in this book as a type of musical kaleidoscope because they offer ways of viewing the same piece from various perspectives, and the Schenkerian Analysis as another method by which you could understand the organic and germinal points of the structure of a piece from a very unique vantage point. By understanding the essential elements of a score as defined by Heinrich Schenker, you may be able to place other details of the score's construction in a shaper and more musical perspective.

—James Jordan

When choral conductors first encounter a score, it is their job to study the score to best understand the composer's intention, both musically and aesthetically. The aesthetic affect often comes from a thorough understanding of the musical material, text, and circumstances for which the work was written. The preceding chapters focus on musical and textual considerations of score study, in particular the notion of score analysis. This chapter will provide a different view of analysis—and possibly open up new doors of possibilities for choral conductors.

When I first encountered Haydn's *Missa Brevis No. 7 in B-flat* (nicknamed *Kleine Orgelmesse*), I found it aurally simple to understand. Upon further evaluation and score study of the *Kyrie* movement, using the techniques of Julius Herford as outlined in the previous chapter, I noticed an irregular phrase structure. This is an unusual phenomenon because we know Haydn frequented symmetrical and regular phrases. The difficulty with irregular phrases is that the singers must figure out how the irregular phrases fit into a classical style. To do this, it is appropriate to find the similarities between this piece of music and other tonal pieces of music. With that said, it would be most appropriate to perform a Schenkerian Analysis of the movement. The purpose of this type of analysis is to find how the music (which Schenker called the *foreground*) is developed from the fundamental structure, or *Ursatz* (the *background*), through multiple levels of prolongations (the levels of the *middleground*). This can be seen through the **analysis graph of the *Kyrie* movement** presented in **Figure 27-1**.

Figure 27-1. Analysis graph of the *Kyrie* movement of *Missa Brevis No. 7 in B-flat*.

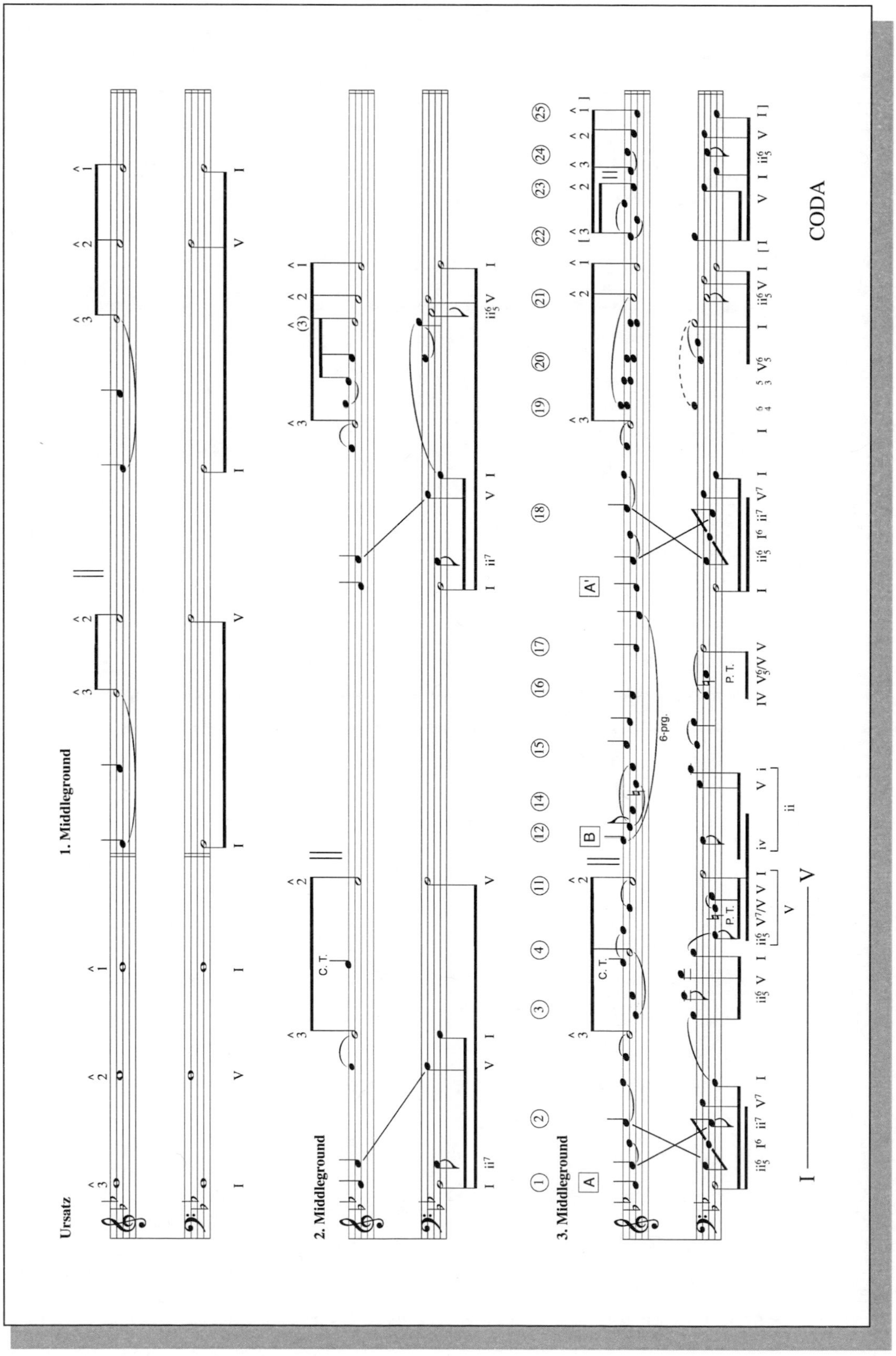

In the graph, the *Ursatz,* or the *fundamental structure* (the *background*), begins with the primary tone, or head tone. In the case of this movement, the primary tone is the third scale degree (D). The first manifestation of this pitch occurs at the resolution of the dominant chord on the fourth beat of the second measure. One might argue that the head tone of this movement is the fifth scale degree, as the second phrase begins on F in the soprano voice. However, I am considering this F to be a cover tone[a] to the D, as it quickly moves down to the D through the use of an anticipatory tone, which further emphasizes the structural importance of the D over the F. Further evidence for naming D as the primary tone is in the first and second violin parts during the cadential extension of measures 3 and 4. In measure 3, the second violin emphasizes the B-flat, while the first violin emphasizes the C, moving through a scale passage that ascends and then descends to the D, yet further emphasizing the primary tone of D.

It is important to note that this movement is broken into three basic sections, with the third section being an altered return of the first. The first section concludes by tonicizing the key of the dominant, while the second section continues in this key area. The second section ends with a half cadence in the key of the tonic, is where the third section begins and ends. This results in a sectional form of A–B–A[1].[b] Neither the first nor the second sections are independent entities, since they both end either by tonicizing the dominant or with a half cadence (on the dominant) and rely on the following section to act as a conclusion and ending. Since the B section is not a contrasting section nor truly independent of the other sections, the form cannot be considered ternary. Thus, the form should be considered rounded binary.

This rounded binary form can first be seen in the graph's first level of the middleground, where an interruption at the second scale degree is employed. Schenker believed that a fundamental line beginning on the third scale degree can only move through scale degrees 3–2–1 in a direct fashion—except in the case of an interruption. In the case of an interruption of a fundamental line whose primary tone is the third scale degree, the interruption occurs at the second scale degree. This second scale degree is accompanied by a dominant harmony. After the interruption, the fundamental line begins again and then completes the descent through the second scale degree to the first. In Haydn's score, we see the movement to the dominant before the interruption (which is continued through the B section) and the return to the tonic key area just after the interruption (at the A[1] section).

---

[a] A *cover tone* is a tone of the inner voice that is suspended above the primary upper-voice material. For further discussion about the concept of the cover tone, see Schenker *Free Composition*, §267.

[b] Sectional letters are marked on the graph at the third level of the middleground in boxes.

Now that we have examined the *Ursatz* and the first level of the middleground (which shows the earliest stages of the form), the remainder of this chapter will focus on how each subsequent level of the middleground shows that the pitches of the previous levels are prolonged. To do this, we will examine the unique features of the lowest level of the middleground (literally, the level toward the bottom of the graph) and relate them to the previous levels. During the initial ascent[c] (which is B-flat and C moving to the primary tone, D), we see prolongations occurring in the melodic material, as well as in the harmonic context. Melodically, the initial ascent quickly moves from B-flat through C, but then continues moving above the primary tone to F. The F is a modifier to the E-flat, which is already in the service of prolonging D (the primary tone). Harmonically, there is a basic I–ii^7–V–I progression, in which the ii^7 chord is prolonged from the first inversion (ii$^6_5$) through a passing I^6 chord to the goal harmony (a ii^7 chord). Through this harmonic movement, there is a direct relation to the melodic material in the form of a voice exchange[d] between the pitches E-flat and C. We could look at this entire figure as being in the service of prolonging I, thus prolonging the I chord, which continues to sound through the arrival of the primary tone.

In the next segment of the graph, the goal is to move to the interruption: The upper voice will move from the third to the second scale degree, and the bass will move from tonic harmony to dominant harmony. Though this is a typical protocol for an interruption, it is important to note how this section is prolonged, which gives the movement its unique qualities. When the primary tone is sounded, there is movement from an inner voice back to the primary tone (B-flat–C–D). Not only does this emphasize the necessity to label the primary tone as D, but it also reflects the initial ascent (as can be seen in the first level of the middleground). Throughout this, there is a cover-tone (F) that appears a third above the restatement of the primary tone. Though the fifth scale degree may initially be considered the primary tone, it is clear from the musical context of Haydn's work that the cover tone (F) is being used to serve as an embellishment to D. The first time we reach this F (looking at the soprano line in measure 4), it immediately descends to D (with an anticipatory sixteenth note D), further delineating the importance of D over F. When F is finally made prominent in measure 6 (through the use of a chromatic neighbor note), the supporting harmony is a dominant chord in first inversion. For this tone to be the primary tone, it must be supported by tonic harmony.

---

c An *initial ascent* is an ascending, stepwise motion to the primary tone. Schenker refers to this initial ascent as the *ascending linear progression*. For further discussion about the concept of the initial ascent, see Schenker *Free Composition*, §120.

d A *voice exchange* is contrapuntal motion between outer voices; it serves to prolong a specific harmony. For further discussion about the concept of a voice exchange, see Schenker *Free Composition*, §236–37.

At this point, we are already working toward a harmonic shift to the structural dominant; this is accomplished through the tonicization of the dominant key. The harmonic movement of this section is exactly the same as the previous section: I–ii$\frac{6}{5}$ –V^7/V (which occurs at a micro level at measure 3, beat 4, though is it not notated in this graph) –V–I in the key of the dominant. At this point there have been three separate occurrences of this I–ii$\frac{6}{5}$ –V–I harmonic progression, in two different keys. After reaching the cadence in the dominant and the second scale degree in the upper voice, we come to the interruption.

After the interruption, there is movement to continue the prolongation of the dominant reached at the interruption. This is done through the tonicization of ii, followed by a tonicization of V (which is shown in the graph at IV, V$\frac{6}{5}$of V, V).[e] Above this harmonic movement, further prolonging the key of the dominant, is a linear progression of a sixth (F–E-flat–D–C–B-flat–A). It can be looked at as a linear progression[f] because the first tone (F) and the last tone (A) are both members of the goal harmony, which is a dominant chord.

Following this short section, which is an extension of the dominant, the A section returns (as is required of rounded binary form). The motion of the ascent and subsequent harmonies to the primary tone is exactly the same as is found at the beginning of the movement (which includes both the unfolding and the voice exchange). The structural material that follows this initial ascent and primary tone is basically the same as in the opening section; however, it is more direct and truncated, thus contrasting the material found in the initial statement of the A section. For these reasons, the third section requires the designation of A^1. The goal of this section is for the upper voice to move through the fundamental line (3–2–1) and the fundamental harmonic structure of tonic–pre-dominant–dominant–tonic. To do this, there is a series of descending thirds that anticipate the second scale degree. This is accomplished because the upper voice of the thirds comprises a descending linear progression of a fifth (G–F–E-flat–D–C). This is justified because both the first and the last notes of the linear progression (G and C) are part of the goal harmony, which is a ii chord (C-minor chord) in first inversion. This chord is the fundamental predominant harmony, which moves through the dominant to the tonic. This harmonic movement of I–ii$\frac{6}{5}$–V–I is the exact same harmony that occurs three times before the interruption (twice in the key of the tonic and once in the key of the dom-

---

[e] The term *tonicization* is being used to describe a temporary shift of tonal center.

[f] According to Schenker, a *linear progression* is the most fundamental way of creating melodic content. A descending linear progression (as in this case) represents motion from a structural outer voice to a structural inner voice. To be classified as a linear progression, the linear progression's first and last tones must have a key relationship, must span at least the size of a third, and must contain passing motion. For further discussion about the concept of a linear progression, see Schenker *Free Composition*, §203–20.

inant) and during the ascent to the primary tone after the interruption (in the key of the tonic). Thus, it may seem like this movement is made up of the harmonic movement I–ii$^6_5$–V–I.

Following the close of the fundamental structure, there is a coda that further exemplifies Haydn's use of this fundamental structure, as the final notes in the soprano are D–C, D–C–B-flat (which is an exact replica of the fundamental line), supported by the harmonic structure I–V, I–ii $^6_5$–V–I, which also imitates the fundamental harmonic structure. Further, this coda includes the same interruption that is found throughout the entire movement.

In this particular movement, a Schenkerian approach to analysis was able to show important relationships between sections, which could possibly explain its use of phrase length and regularity. This analysis also shows what is structurally important, whereas the phrase structure analysis left me confused and questioning my analysis. What I discovered for this particular movement was that while the unusual phrase structure was an important, unique feature, understanding how the piece developed from the *Ursatz* through a series of prolongations better helped me to understand the movement.

When analyzing a piece of music, it is important to use the method that best fits the musical situation. It is important to complete multiple types of score analyses before venturing into rehearsal, and there is probably an order in which they should be done. I would argue that you should always complete an analysis based on the system of Julius Herford, as well as a score colorization analysis of Margaret Hillis; however, sometimes an extra step must be taken to understand a piece. Remember that having a rainbow of colors on a score does not always indicate a depth of knowledge about the score, nor does an elaborate tome of graph paper to show phrase structure or even a beautiful Schenkerian graph.

As conductors we must take the time to live with the music, analyzing it using multiple modes of analysis. It is our responsibility as conductors to do whatever analyses are necessary, no matter how many, to truly understand a piece of music. It is also up to us to discover what type of analyses best fit our musical understanding. It is through this sort of preparation that we can begin to master a score.

The author of this chapter would like to thank Dr. Anthony Kosar, Professor of Music Theory at Westminster Choir College of Rider University, for his guidance and support in writing this chapter.

—Matthew J. LaPine

PART SIX
COMPLETING THE PROCESS

Chapter 28

Using the Principles of Laban Movement Score Analysis (LMSA)

Preparing for the Kinesthetic Rehearsal

Music is silent screaming; motionless dance.

—Elaine Brown
Alumni Lecture
Westminster Choir College, 1989

An impulse is an activating, energizing force. A sound or group of sounds resulting in an increase in energy yields impulse. In a succession of tones of equal rhythmic value, impulse tends to result from ascending motion. Ascending motion by leap tends to result in greater impulse than ascending motion by step.

A resolution is a retracting, de-energizing force. A sound or group
of sounds resulting in a decrease of energy yields resolution. If the
energy gathered by the tightening of a spring is impulse, the
dissipation of the energy effected by the release of the spring is
resolution. Because resolution is a decrease or playing out of energy,
there can be no resolution if there has been no energy gathered.
(p. 13)

Imagine a motion that describes a circle (such as the motion of a
person riding on a Ferris wheel). Beginning at the lowest point, the
first part of the motion is an ascent. The motion continues upward
along the arc on the left side until the highest point. At the highest
point it has nowhere else to go but down; it returns downward
along the arc on the right side, until it connects with the original
point. When it connects, the circle is an indivisible unity. The
whole unit is formed only when the arc of the descent matches the
arc of the ascent. The boundaries are formed by the matching of
the descent with the ascent. (p. 14)

—Markand Thakar[1]
in *Counterpoint: Fundamentals of Music Making*

---

1 Among the two finest books I have ever read on the subject of musicianship and the development of
   musical phrasing is this book by Markand Thakar (Yale University Press, 1990). This book is a "must
   have" for any conductor; it presents an aural approach to counterpoint. Moreover, Dr. Thakar is able
   to articulate in the most accurate language the intricacies of teaching and understanding the musical
   phrase. A former colleague of mine at The Pennsylvania State University, Markand artistically translates this book into sound when he is on the podium. The other book I highly recommend is *Note
   Grouping* by James Morgan Thurmond (Meredith Music Publications, 1991). Robert Shaw
   recommended this book to many throughout his career.

In a previous letter we have remarked that when a melody rises
it marks in general an intensification of energy, when it falls it
signifies a relaxation. Therefore, we must look for melodic
fragments which bear an upward thrust, and balance them
sensitively and minutely with those fragments which signify respite.
(p. 70)

Convey the inner and hidden dialogue, the ying and yang, the up
and down, the question and answer, male and female, boy-girl,
tension and relaxation.

Be considerate of the text. It might just coincide with melodic or
harmonic accentuation—and this moment is the Pentecost of song.

Cultivate the forward look. Melody is a vagabond, incorrigibly
searching the world for a place "really" to settle down. Even
punctuation is not a period of retrospect, but of marshaling strength
and scanning the horizon. The last note we sing is the one to which
all others lead. (p. 71)

—Robert Shaw
in *The Robert Shaw Reader*

One of the areas of score analysis that is often overlooked has to do with the
forward movement of a piece. Many of us take for granted our kinesthetic
gifts—that is, understanding how a piece of music feels in our body. What we fail to
either recognize or appreciate is that our singers do not always come equipped with
fantasies of how music moves and feels in our bodies as we bind those sensations to
the musical sounds we produce. For many of us, this is a natural, almost intuitive,
process.

For vocalists, I have found that these decisions are of paramount importance. Inappropriate weight applied to musical line can directly inhibit vocal production. Vocal technique and the movement of musical line are intimately bound in the music-making process. Not to mention the "fantasy" of musical line confounds the music-making process. Moreover, if this analysis is approached with forethought, the "kinesthetic" study will transfer directly to appropriate conducting gesture—a by-product of the score study process.

While our musical intent is good, too often our gesture sends conflicting information to the choir. Our conducting gestures should match the Laban Movement Score Analysis (LMSA). That is, we should be very clear in our minds just how the music moves forward. LMSA (or some type of study and analysis of the motion and shape of musical line) should take place before gesture is employed in either rehearsal or performance. Such analysis and the understandings it provides are central to the score preparation and musicing process.

Presented below are general rules for LMSA, followed by an explanation of each rule:

1. Make arsis/thesis decisions about the overall shape of the musical line.

2. Add weight to slow musical line; take away weight to add velocity and speed to the forward movement of the musical line.

3. Use direct gestures and efforts to propel musical line. Indirect gestures tend to slow the forward velocity.

4. Always complete movement analysis of a score before applying gestures to the movement. Then imagine yourself conducting the piece while audiating it, but do not move (imaging).

5. Mark the score with several possible analyses (LMSA) that are reflective of your desired musical intent.

6. Give the LMSA to your singers and have them mark the Efforts in Combination in red in their scores.

7. Remember that LMSA should reflect the rate of harmonic movement within any piece.

8. Have your singers speak the voiced and unvoiced LMSA syllables.

Rule #1 – Make arsis/thesis decisions about the overall shape of the musical line.

Use the Day-Tay system of Weston Noble or the Note Grouping principles of James Thurmond as a guide. In Baroque music, knowledge of the underlying dance steps contributing to the rhythmic structure is essential.

Deciding where musical lines move to—their "towardness"—is at the heart of LMSA. Use brackets labeled with "A" for **arsis** and "T" for **thesis** to mark the phrasal direction of every musical line in a score. In contrapuntal music, careful analysis is crucial to rehearsal planning and subsequent teaching. However, as conductors we tend to be too rigid in our thinking as we analyze because we believe the anacrustic part of the phrase is simply assigned to a rhythmic value, such as a pickup note. However, upon closer inspection, we often discover that the "rise" in the musical phrase occupies one or more beats and, in some situations, several measures. Text stresses combined with melodic shape and harmonic movement often provide definitive answers of a composer's intent.

To consider how phrases move in advance of the rehearsal/teaching process should become central to the rehearsal preparation process. Note, however, that many of the decisions made concerning forward movement of sound in a score are products of experience *and* an individual's innate musical instincts. Thus, an awareness of what is happening within your own body is central to this decision-making process.

Rule #2 – Add weight to slow musical line; take away weight to add velocity and speed to the forward movement of the musical line.

The Laban Efforts in Combination show that in many (if not all) situations, the addition of weight changes (or rather "transforms") the combinatory effort. The addition or subtraction of weight is one of the strongest determinants of Flow. Stated in Laban terms, the addition of weight into any movement changes the quality of Flow of the forward motion.

With score analysis in mind, it is important to revisit the **Laban Efforts in Combination** (see **Figure 28-1**).

Figure 28-1. Laban Efforts in Combination to describe movement.

Laban Action Verb	Qualities (Elements)	Movement Examples
FLOAT	indirect (S) light (W) sustained (T)	• treading water at various depths
WRING	indirect (S) heavy (W) sustained (T)	• wringing a beach towel
GLIDE	direct (S) light (W) sustained (T)	• smoothing wrinkles in a cloth, • ice skating
PRESS	direct (S) heavy (W) sustained (T)	• pushing a car
FLICK	indirect (S) light (W) quick (T)	• dusting off lint from clothing
SLASH	indirect (S) heavy (W) quick (T)	• fencing • serving a tennis ball
DAB	direct (S) light (W) quick (T)	• typing • tapping on a window
PUNCH	direct (S) heavy (W) quick (T)	• boxing

The Laban principle is quite direct. Changing the amount of "weight" in Punch, for example, changes the "type" or "quality" of Punch. Subtle changes in weight have profound effects on musical phrasing. Allowing an ensemble to subjectively apply weight to a musical phrase diminishes the musical effectiveness of the ensemble. Instead, use your musical experience and musical instincts to provide the raw material for these important phrasing decisions.

Rule #3 – Use direct gestures and efforts to propel musical line. Indirect gestures tend to slow the forward velocity.

Once you have made decisions that coincide with the forward movement of the musical line, the next stage of LMSA is to explore the qualities of gesture that will directly reflect the musical decisions your analysis has yielded. Conducting gesture that is more direct (i.e., angular) will always propel musical line forward, provided the gesture is physically released after the ictus. Indirect gesture, by its very nature, implies that less weight is involved. The withholding of weight inherent in indirect movement tends to allow the musical line to decelerate. After LMSA of any score has been completed, carefully consider the efforts that should be superimposed over your chosen conducting patterns.

Rule #4 – Always complete movement analysis of a score before applying gestures to the movement.

Gesture should always grow out of careful movement analysis of the musical materials at hand. While it is possible to omit the particulars of LMSA, you will find that without LMSA, you may become handicapped in the rehearsal process because of an inability to objectively describe to your singers the subtleties of the forward motion of the musical line. Without such guided instruction, singers apply their own movement instincts to the musical materials at hand: some will supply little, and others will contribute powerful movement ideas. However, the lack of a clear movement "profile" for a piece will undoubtedly lead to a mediocre rhythmic performance as a result of conflicting musical ideas within the ensemble.

Rule #5 – Mark the score with several possible analyses (LMSA) that are reflective of your desired musical intent.

Mark directly on your score the specific Laban Efforts in Combination (e.g., Float, Glide, Press, Dab, etc.) that reflect your kinesthetic feeling of how the phrase moves forward based upon your musical instincts and experience.

Rule #6 – Give the LMSA to your singers and have them mark the Efforts in Combination in red in their scores.

After you have made decisions concerning the "broad stroke" Efforts in Combination, mark the Efforts in Combination directly on the score (as shown in **Figure 28-4** and **Figure 28-5** at the end of this chapter).

At first glance, it might appear as though LMSA is a choreographic method, or a system that choreographs each movement of the conductor. It is not. The Laban Effort Elements represent a movement system that allows conductors to communicate their "feelings" or kinesthesia of movement through carefully chosen vocabulary. The Efforts in Combination are words that represent the energy within each movement in an attempt to verbalize the inner dynamics of movement. Hence, LMSA is a symbolic system designed to approximately represent all of the factors involved with the kinesthesia of a musical phrase.

Rule #7 – Remember that LMSA should reflect the rate of harmonic movement within any piece.

The rate of harmonic change often provides valuable insight into phrasal ideas of the composer. Yet many conductors fail to pay close attention to the rate or speed of harmonic chord changes. Harmonic motion is integral to most, if not all, phrasing decisions. Moreover, the individual "style" of a composer is highly dependent upon the composer's harmonic language, or harmonic syntax.

Remember that music has no grammar, but each composer possesses individual harmonic syntax. And while harmonic syntax has no strict rules, you can see common patterns that, in turn, define a composer's individual style.

Rule #8 – Have your singers speak the voiced and unvoiced LMSA syllables.

After you have selected the Efforts in Combination, you must be able to "translate" inherent motion into sounds. Sometimes musicians find it challenging to relate movement to sound, but this can become a valuable rehearsal technique.

Theoretical understanding of movement is one thing, but kinesthetic connection of movement to sound will enhance both rehearsal and musical performance. A **modified chart of the Laban efforts** is shown in **Figure 28-2**. This chart combines descriptions of each action from Philip Burton's Expressive Movement course taught in conjunction with Dalcroze training, to which Marilyn Shenenberger has added voiced and unvoiced sounds that mirror the general qualities of Float, Flick, Press, Dab, etc. I have found that the use of these syllables immediately binds kinesthetic movement ideas to musical sounds in the most effective ways. In the right-hand column of the chart, Shenenberger suggests musical structures that most often can be associated with the musical sounds (e.g., diminished chords, staccato, marcato, etc.).

**Figure 28-2. Laban Efforts in Combination
to describe movement and resulting sound.**

Laban Action	Time	Gestural Conducting Translation	Weight	Descriptive Syllable	Musical Sound Analogies
Float	Sustained	Indirect	Light	f	Whole tone No weight Repetitive
Wring	Sustained	Indirect	Heavy	**zh, [ʒ]**	Diminished Chords Chopin Prel., Op. 28, No. 20
Glide	Sustained	Direct	Light	s	Line Phrase
Press	Sustained	Direct	Heavy	v	Bagpipes Feminine
Flick	Quick	Indirect	Light	pft	Grace notes Textures requiring lightness
Slash	Quick	Indirect	Heavy	**z**	sfz
Dab	Quick	Direct	Light	t fast tempo	Staccato
Punch	Quick	Direct	Heavy	CH, [tʃ]	Accents (with some degree of sustainment) that are not tenuto
Dab/ Press*	Sustained	Direct	Light-Heavy	m	Tenuto
Punch/ Press*	Sharp attack, sustained	Direct	Heavy	hwh a la Lamaze breathing	Marcato

* Hybrid combination of Laban efforts to simulate movements needed to play tenuto and marcato.

Choosing Appropriate Efforts in Combination

While all of the musical factors presented in this chapter contribute to the decisions regarding which Efforts in Combination to use to propel musical line, the amount of weight selected may be affected by the vocal/technical requirements of a piece. When conducting, I have often found it necessary to add more weight than originally envisioned to maintain a supported, on-the-breath sound from the singers. Fuller dynamics (resonances) sometimes also require more gestural weight than originally conceived. The deciding factor rests with the sound of the ensemble. As conductors we must constantly react to the sound and vary Laban efforts to achieve the desired musical result.

Where is weight applied to the conducting gesture? The most common misconception is that weight is added *muscularly* to the conducting gesture. However, weight added through increased muscular tension actually creates an undesirable response in the sound. The result is a sound that is out of tune, rigid, and hard. Instead, from an Alexander Body Mapping perspective, consider adding weight in the wrist, which is actually located in the palm of the hand. Imagine that your hand is holding a heavier object. The muscles in your arms should remain released at all times, as should the free motion in your scapulae or "shoulder blades." The weight, then, should be added and subtracted from your gesture through the addition or subtraction of weight in the palm of your hand.

Figure 28-3. Key to LMSA phrase markings.

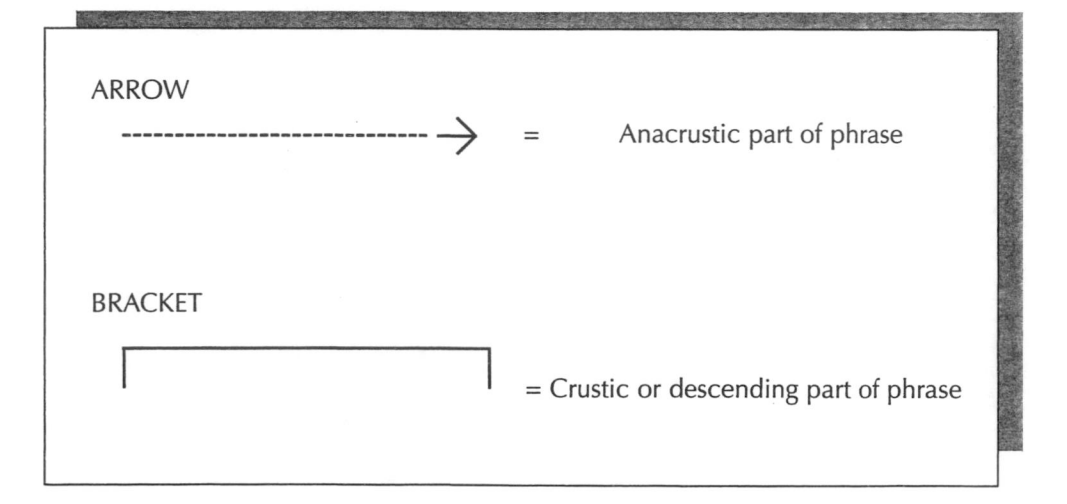

Figure 28-3. (Continued)

Effort Combination Label	Effort	Symbol for Score Marking
FLOAT	indirect (S) light (W) sustained (T)	F
WRING	indirect (S) heavy (W) sustained (T)	W
GLIDE	direct (S) light (W) sustained (T)	G
PRESS	direct (S) heavy (W) sustained (T)	P
FLICK	indirect (S) light (W) quick (T)	FL
SLASH	indirect (S) heavy (W) quick (T)	S
DAB	direct (S) light (W) quick (T)	D
PUNCH	direct (S) heavy (W) quick (T)	PN

Figure 28-4. Example of Efforts in Combination marked in excerpt of
***Innisfree* by Gerald Custer (GIA).**

Note that this is only one LMSA approach to the musical elements in this piece; there may be many more. Also, remember that the *size* of the symbol is directly related to the amount of weight to be added to the conducting gesture.

Winner of the 75th Anniversary Alumni Composition Competition,
Westminster Choir College of Rider University.

INNISFREE
For SATB Voices and Piano

"The Lake Isle of Innisfree"
William Butler Yeats, 1865–1939

Gerald Custer

Figure 28-4. (Continued)

*No breath

Figure 28-5. Example of Efforts in Combination marked in excerpt of
***When Spring Is Born at Last* by Jackson Hill (GIA).**

Note that this is only one LMSA approach to the musical elements in this piece; there may be many more. Also, remember that the *size* of the symbol is directly related to the amount of weight to be added to the conducting gesture.

Copyright © 2005 by GIA Publications, Inc., 7404 S. Mason Ave., Chicago, IL 60638
International Copyright Secured • All Rights Reserved • Printed in the U.S.A.
Photocopying of this publication without permission of the publisher is a violation of the U.S. Code of Law
for which the responsible individual or institution is subject to criminal prosecution. No one is exempt.

G-6525

Chapter 29

Audiation and Imaging

The Key—
"Practicing" Conducting[1]

Don't fly your plane anywhere where your mind has not been first.

—John McDonald, a flight instructor
in a private flying lesson

Man moves in order to satisfy a need. He aims his movement at
something of value to him. It is easy to perceive the aim of a
person's movement if it is directed at some tangible object. Yet there
also exist intangible values that inspire movement. (p. 129)

—Rudolf von Laban
in *Beyond Words,*
Carol-Lynne Moore and Kaoru Yamamoto

---

1 The author of this book would like to thank Eugene Migliaro Corporon for sharing his insight on these principles.

Following one another in movement sequences, the consecutive efforts will build up a kind of melody or sentence-like structure, the collective mood of which is an important part of movement experience. (p. 46)

—Rudolf Laban
in *Modern Educational Dance*

Kinesthesis (the "muscle sense" or "sixth sense") is defined as the sensual discrimination of the positions and movement of body parts based on information other than visual, auditory, or verbal. Kinesthetic perception involves judging changes in muscle tension, body position, and the relative placement of body parts. (p. 48)

Human body movement is an ever-present, complex, and yet an elusive part of our lives, subject to "tune out," simplification, and other perceptual maneuvers. The first task facing the movement observer is to find ways to enhance awareness and to sharpen and crystallize motion perception. (p. 65)

Since body movement leaves no artifacts or traces behind, reconstructing this leap requires some imagination. (p. 74)

In a sense, movement awareness is often the victim of tune-out. As you recall, our perceptual systems are designed to cease to register a stimulus that is repeated again and again. (p. 85)

Yet another view is manifested in the metaphor, "Movement is a private code." Here, movement is seen to have neither panhuman nor even culture-specific meanings, but only unique and individualistic senses to it. That is, each person uses body movement somewhat idiosyncratically, thus conveying meanings that are unique to him or her. (p. 114)

—Carol-Lynne Moore and Kaoru Yamamoto
in *Beyond Words*

One must learn to understand that one thinks not only with the brain but also with the little finger and the big toe. (p. 67)

—Rudolf Steiner
in *Beyond Words*,
Carol-Lynne Moore and Kaoru Yamamoto

Sound itself is not music. Sound becomes music through audiation, when, as with language, you translate sounds in your mind and give them meaning. The meaning you give to these sounds will be different depending on the occasion and will be different from the meaning given them by any other person. Audiation is the process of assimilating and comprehending (not simply rehearing) music we have just heard performed or have heard performed sometime in the past. (pp. 3–4)

Imitation is learning through someone else's ears. Audiation is learning through one's own ears. Imitation is analogous to using tracing paper to draw a picture, whereas audiation is analogous to visualizing and then drawing a picture. Imitation is like painting a canvas; it deals with both the essential and nonessential. Audiation is like sculpture; it emphasizes the essential. Just as you must think for yourself, so must you audiate for yourself. You imitate when you repeat what you heard just a few seconds ago, which is immediate imitation, or when you repeat what you heard a while ago, which is delayed imitation. In either case, they are reactive responses and have only initial and limited value for learning, because unless we audiate what we have just imitated, we soon forget it, as is so often the case, for example, with the names and dates children learn in school. However, audiation is a different kind of learning because when you audiate, you retain, instantiate, and "think about" what you heard seconds, minutes, hours, days, weeks, months, or even years ago. Audiation is an active response. When we imitate we know what to perform next in familiar music by remembering what we just performed. It is a process of looking backward. However, when we audiate we know what to perform next, without negating memory, by anticipating in familiar music and predicting in unfamiliar music what is to come. It involves forward thinking. What is audiated plays a formidable role in how one learns. What we audiate is never forgotten. It becomes a component of more complex audiation. In cognitive terms, the structure of audiation is deep and serves in background conception. The structure of imitation, on the other hand, is superficial and serves simply as foreground perception. (p. 10)

—Edwin E Gordon
in *Learning Sequences in Music* (2007 Edition)

Mr. Fleischer describes the performer as three people in one. "Person A hears before they play. They have to have this ideal in their inner ear of what they're going to try and realize. Person B actually puts the keys down, plays and tries to manifest what person

A hears. Person C sits a little bit apart and listens. And if what C hears is not what A intended, C tells B to adjust to get closer to what A wanted. And this goes on with every note you play, no matter how fast you're playing. It's a simultaneous process that advances horizontally. When it works, when it all meshes, it's a state of ecstasy." (p. 27)

Life knocks the corners off; age, or experience, accounts for some degree of transformation in every artist. One hears new implications. I think one has a tendency to take more time. One listens and takes more time to listen. One is not afraid to more deeply characterize certain ideas. Silence is not the absence of music. Play, judiciously, as late as possible, without being late. (p. 25)

Mr. Fleisher is convinced that he is a better pianist for having become a conductor, as he would probably not have done had his career stayed on course. He may also be, he says, a better teacher…with his remarkable ability to articulate musical ideas in images. He describes a tune as "rising the way a balloon does, at an ever-decreasing rate of speed, to the point where the pressure out-side equals the pressure inside, and it stays suspended." He talks about conducting an orchestra around a curve in the musical line and generating the sort of centrifugal force that causes the driver of a car to lean to the left as he turns his wheels to the right. (p. 27)

—Leon Fleischer
in "A Pianist for Whom Never Was Never an Option"
Holly Brubach
The New York Times, Sunday, June 10, 2007

I believe that it is accurate to say that most Alexander teachers regard the Technique as one bright strand in the large braid of somatics, but some do not. Some want to claim a status for the

Technique as unique, outside somatics, and rightly understood only in contrast to other disciplines. In this argument the teachers look not to the results (they acknowledge that many techniques result in greater freedom and ease of movement and the recovery of body awareness) but to the means. No other method features constructive conscious control, the cognitive process that Alexander used to recover his freedom.

Constructive conscious control exploits the brain's vast potential for consciousness of self and for choice. Some prominent neuroscientists believe that self-consciousness (in the good sense) and choice depend on the size and structure of the human brain. Both the size and structure make it possible for the brain to process its own functioning (creatures with smaller, differently structured brains cannot do this), resulting in consciousness. Alexander's Technique uses the brain consciously for self-observation of habitual use of the organism, for conscious inhibition of habitual use, for conscious observation of an emerging, more integrated use, for conscious cooperation with the more integrated use, and even for conscious observation of the more integrated use, all this depending surely on the conscious linking of conceptual and motor functions in the brain, by choice. Rather than creating a split, as some might expect, all this consciousness instead has a profoundly integrating effect, healing the split many people experience between thinking and being, of mind and body, or consciousness and functioning. It is this integration that is the great good the Technique offers, with freedom and ease as by-products, according to this argument.

—Barbara Conable
from article on www.AlexanderTechnique.com

The term somatics was first introduced into modern psychology by
Thomas Hanna with his book *Bodies in Revolt*. The Greek word
soma is defined as "the body experienced from within" and reflects
the efforts of modern bodywork practitioners and somatic movement therapists to move away from the dualistic splitting of mind
from body, towards a model of integrated functioning of the whole
person, psyche and soma. (p. 11)

—Linda Hartley
in *Somatic Psychology*

The term *audiation,* coined by Edwin Gordon to describe the process by which
we hear and recall music, has become part of the vocabulary for all who
believe that the teaching of listening is fundamental to music learning.
Briefly stated, the broad definition of audiation is the ability to hear sound in all its
dimensions without the sound being physically present. Dr. Gordon details both the
types and stages of audiation in two of his books, *Preparatory Audiation, Audiation,
and Music Learning Theory* (GIA, 2001) and *Learning Sequences in Music* (GIA,
2007). To thoroughly understand the audiation process, which is part of becoming
an *aware* conductor, it is helpful to be familiar with the types and stages of
audiation so you can appreciate the many dimensions of hearing. To simply call
this complex process "inner hearing" can cause us to hear in a very shallow or
incomplete manner. Becoming aurally facile with the depth of the audiation process
is part of "becoming aware."

As a conductor, no one would likely argue that "hearing" a score is the product
of careful score preparation. But the question I find interesting is: How do we as
conductors transfer what we hear, or rather have learned to hear through score study
and subsequent audiation, to gestures that communicate our intent to an ensemble?
I believe that process occurs when we *simultaneously* audiate and image our
conducting as part of our regular practice routine.

Consider this: Athletes in certain sports rely on imaging to practice. For example, because it may not be convenient to do repeated ski runs, skiers might practice mentally, imagining their movement (i.e., practicing through a sort of movement audiation). As another example, dancers imagine themselves moving when they are not practicing. The science of somatics has informed our knowledge of how the brain maps, in a cognitive way, the motion of our body and how we move. The skill we must develop as conductors is to merge sound audiation with what I call **kinesthetic imaging.** We must be able to move while audiating and listening. To imagine our conducting movement separate from audiation will not help us master this important skill.

In psychology, the perception of movement (more particularly, the self-perception of movement) has not been experimentally studied because it is difficult to come up with a research design that provides objective data. While there have been many hypotheses on how we perceive our own motion while moving, studies have not yielded valid objective data.

There is an important principle to understand about conducting. The process of conducting is one that, in essence, occurs before sound actually occurs in the ensemble. Ensemble sound ideally occurs slightly after the sound is birthed through breath and gestural impulse on the part of the conductor. The process becomes more complex when a conductor reacts to the sound he or she is hearing—which is, in essence, after the sound was created, or in its past! If we do not practice audiating and imaging simultaneously, then in rehearsal we are merely reacting to sound "in the moment." Conducting that is not informed by audiation/imaging is essentially conducting without the creative or germinal musical impulse present! The result is a series of reactions that lack the creative initiation of sound that can only be birthed by an impulse before each sound is created. Instead, we should consider the initial marriage of gesture and sound to be born out of multi-dimensional forethought rather than afterthought. Consider a visual paradigm of this process, shown in **Figure 29-1**.

Figure 29-1. Paradigm of score study and the rehearsal process.

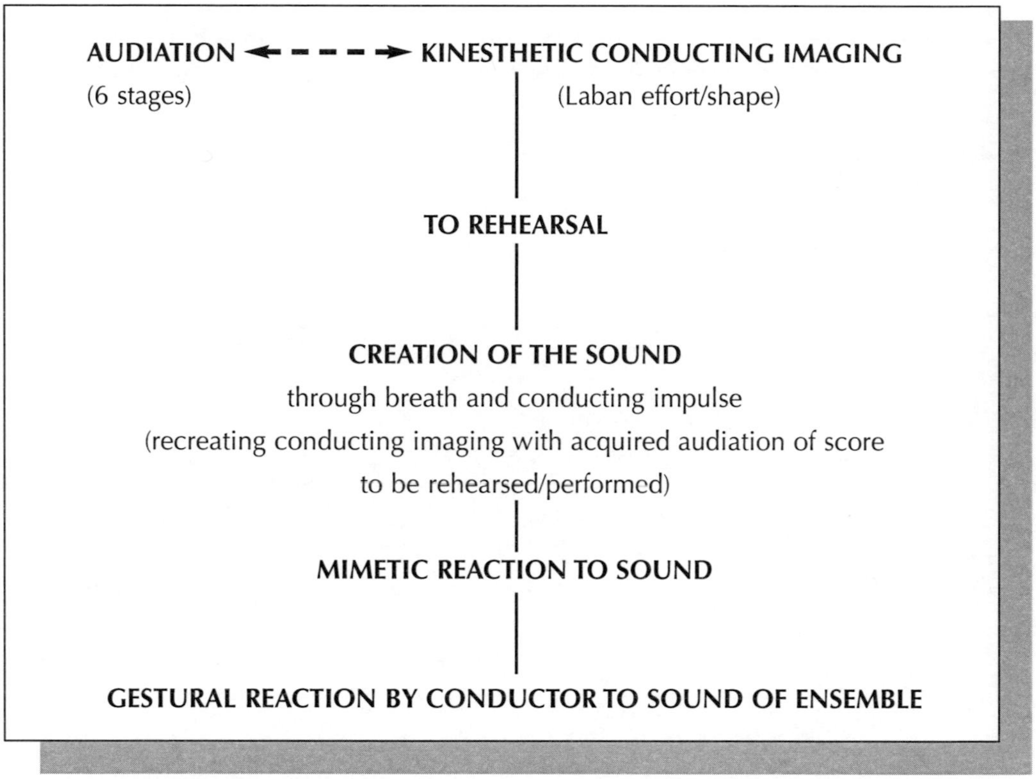

AUDIATION ◄ - - - ► KINESTHETIC CONDUCTING IMAGING

(6 stages)   (Laban effort/shape)

TO REHEARSAL

CREATION OF THE SOUND

through breath and conducting impulse

(recreating conducting imaging with acquired audiation of score

to be rehearsed/performed)

MIMETIC REACTION TO SOUND

GESTURAL REACTION BY CONDUCTOR TO SOUND OF ENSEMBLE

Kinesthetic Audiation: Movement Imaging

We can imagine ourselves moving; however, this is probably one of our least used perceptual gifts. By understanding the use of Laban effort/shape, we awaken our perceptions (or awarenesses) regarding how we move, and we have a vehicle by which we can *recall* what it feels like to move without actually moving in space! Just as the audiation of music can be developed, the imaging of one's movement must also be learned and practiced.

The marriage of sound to movement is a unique process for conductors that must be an integral part of the score preparation process. We cannot assume that by "knowing the score" we will automatically and intuitively make the connection between how the work "moves" and how we would move with the sound present. The perception of one's moving self is powerful. Audiation is powerful. But they must be bound to each other in some way that makes them a symbiotic, interdependent whole before we enter rehearsal!

Mimetic Intuitive Response to Sound

Another factor that could sabotage a conductor's careful thought and study of a score is the theory of mimetics, or in other words, the "envy of the perfect sound" that is omnipresent in our own personal musical world.[1] If we do not stay in "the right place" when things go wrong in rehearsal, most often the first thing to change is our gesture, which carries both our conscious and subconscious musical intent. Instead, if we continue to "image" the movement we envisioned in our score study process, then we can ensure a correct mimetical environment in which the choir can musically grow and listen. In other words, we must stay in awareness as a conductor.

Listening, audiating, and imaging must occur concurrently for musicing to be transformed through our conducting to a level that transcends our music from mundane group parody to the creation of a personal experience with a work of art. We must believe it to be so. That is, we must trust that our ensemble will follow us on our journey so our audiation and imaging can continue to lead the way in our rehearsal process.

A Symbiotic Process

Score preparation must contain equal parts of score study and kinesthetic imaging. The process of imagining how you will move after you have studied the score and have an audiational sense of the score will move your score study and your rehearsals to new levels. Conducting, then, becomes an active recreation of what you have studied in sound and imagined in movement. Simply studying the score will not ensure you can move to the score with gesture that is musically meaningful. While reaction to sound in rehearsal is certainly spontaneous, the basic boundaries of how we move as conductors cannot be. Our self-perception of movement must precede the act of moving in union with music by imaging our movement while concurrently audiating the score in all its dimensions. We can indeed practice conducting prior to rehearsal by audiating the score and imagining how we will conduct the score.[2] Do not underestimate the power of this type of somatic preparation and its effectiveness as part of the score preparation process.

---

1 For more on mimetics, the reader is referred to *The Musician's Soul* (GIA, 1999) and *The Musician's Walk* (GIA, 2006) by this author.

2 As part of this "visualization" process, it is important for conductors to correctly imagine how the bodymoves as one conducts. For more in-depth study, reference the DVD, *The Anatomy of Conducting*, by James Jordan and Eugene Migliaro Corporon (GIA, 2007).

Approaching the unconscious through attending to the body,
we gain access to a great range and depth of sensory and emotional
experience. We begin by listening inwardly to the flow of
sensations, images, feelings, sounds, memories, and movement
impulses which emerge into awareness. (p. 62)

—Linda Hartley
in *Somatic Psychology*

One may be said to "own" or "possess" one's body—at least its limbs
and movable parts—by virtue of a constant flow of incoming
information, arising ceaselessly, throughout life, from the muscles,
joints, and tendons. One has oneself, one is oneself, because the
body knows itself, confirms itself, at all times, by this sixth sense.
(p. 47)

—Oliver Sacks
in *Beyond Words,*
Carol-Lynne Moore and Kaoru Yamamoto

Chapter 30

Rehearsal Planning Checklists

Covering All the Steps

The art of communication is one means by which a concerned teacher will make his contribution to the sound of the music at the present time. If this sound is to be honest and satisfying and splendid it will be so because he is willing to teach himself much of the technical, the historical, the appreciative and the aesthetic principles which are embodied in every musical score (p. 117)

If the conductor is attempting to teach others to be appreciative of beauty, what of his own endowment? Does he respond with enthusiasm to form and design and color—to babies and flowers and people? How long has it been since he has seen a collection of fine paintings or read a book of poetry? (p. 126)

—Howard Swan
in *Conscience of a Profession*

That must have been very nearly my first consciousness of the conductor's art as synonymous with the art of hearing, of listening (Re: a performance of Singet dem Herrn).

It is a work of frightening difficulty…And a couple of weeks prior to the concert we had rugged rhythm and a fair-to-middling sonority—but very little Bach. What we had was not a motet—but a contest.

Fortunately, we also had friends—among them musicians, and among the musicians, Julius Herford. He attended a rehearsal, and after we had sung it through, I turned to him. "It seems to me," he said kindly, "that if we all did a little less singing and a little more listening, we'd have more Bach." (p. 63)

—Robert Shaw
in Joseph Mussulman,
Dear People…Robert Shaw

(Hindemith—Requiem for Those We Love)
And the thing that has been fresh and exciting to those who have been studying and rehearsing it has been the discovery of the vitality and spiritual eloquence of form itself. What we have faced—many of us for the first time—is the awareness that logic does not militate against the expressiveness of music. The fact that music is built with mind and craftsmanship and a sense of order…does not in any way decrease the degree of its "inspiration" or leave it emotionally sterile. For there is a spiritual quality to

pattern itself, the awareness of which may be one of the chief qualifications of the mature artist. (p. 154)

—Robert Shaw
in Howard Swan,
Conscience of a Profession

Great, transforming rehearsals are improvisational and based on a deep and passionate knowledge of the score. They are not solely based on a conductor's personality, although personality shapes everything conductors do. We are, most often, true to ourselves, and we seldom act in ways contrary to our personalities. Great, transforming rehearsals are successful, however, when the conductor is constantly thinking ahead of the ensemble, analyzing what is working and what is not, and coming up with three or four possible solutions for each problem. Boring and unproductive rehearsals are often based on a logical, prearranged plan. "Plan-less" rehearsals can be just as pointless, but improvisational rehearsals, where the score-based dream infuses every engaging gesture and rehearsal device, are exciting, invigorating, and often mentally and physically exhausting for the conductor and singers alike. (p. 89)

—Jerry Blackstone
in "The Conductor's Dream"
from *Teaching Music through Performance in Choir, Vol. 2*

Preparation for rehearsal is a complex task. However, as conductors we must each make our own decisions regarding our path of preparation as we take our journey inward prior to rehearsal. Too often I have missed steps in the score preparation process because I was in a hurry or didn't effectively structure my study time.

A checklist is an effective method for making sure you have considered all options in your score study and rehearsal preparation process. The remainder of this chapter presents several different examples of checklists. Note, however, that all of the examples begin with some form of in-depth score analysis. Whether you choose one of these forms or develop one to meet your own specific needs, use a checklist to make sure you don't miss any steps in this very important process.

The first two types of checklist are shown in Figures 30-1 and 30-2. Both checklists provide a means by which you can plan your score preparation process, but they are slightly different in style and content. The **checklist** in **Figure 30-1** is designed to cover the major aspects of score study and rehearsal preparation included in this volume.[1] The second example in **Figure 30-2** is one that may be used from rehearsal to rehearsal as a final reminder to make sure you have fully considered all aspects of the rehearsal preparation process.

---

1 For more in-depth information concerning the points that pertain to warm-up, reference *The Choral Warm-Up* (GIA, 2005) by this author.

Figure 30-1. Checklist example #1.

Rehearsal Planning Checklist[2]

Work: _____

Composer: _____

Score Analysis

- ❑ Herford analysis
- ❑ Hillis analysis
- ❑ Haasemann analysis
- ❑ LMSA (Laban Movement Score Analysis)
- ❑ Thurmond Note Grouping
- ❑ Relating music to life experience: storying
- ❑ Text and translations
- ❑ Analysis of melodic shapes and phrasing tendencies

Score Marking

- ❑ Aural structure
- ❑ Mode of work
- ❑ Assignment of solfege
- ❑ Syllable to parts
- ❑ Breathing and phrasing
- ❑ Determining dominant ostinati for intonation teaching

Rehearsal Planning

- ❑ Phrases to maintain awareness of alignment through Body Mapping principles
- ❑ Select neutral syllable(s)
- ❑ Select appropriate tempo
- ❑ Select method(s) of rhythm entrainment: use of metronome
- ❑ Assign dominant ostinati for intonation teaching to accompanist
- ❑ Select choral warm-up exercises
- ❑ Select appropriate aural immersion exercises to prepare the mode of the work
- ❑ Create rehearsal Post-It notes and place in score regarding rehearsal techniques

Immediately Prior to Rehearsal

- ❑ How to access quiet
- ❑ Consideration of QiGong and other techniques to access center

The Rehearsal

- ❑ Create the listening atmosphere in rehearsal
- ❑ Mark the score
- ❑ Identify the harmonic structure
- ❑ Sound the piece on neutral syllable
- ❑ Focus on pitch (solfege) and rhythm (count-singing)
- ❑ Dynamics and phrasing
- ❑ Diction teaching procedures and staccato singing on text

---

2   The author of this book wishes to thank Henry Pronato for his help in developing this form.

Figure 30-2. Checklist example #2.

Reminder Checklist for Score Study and Rehearsal Planning[3]

Name of Work:—————————————————————————————————
Composer:——————————————————————————————————

Score Study

❑ Make sure you have a good edition!
❑ Research the composer and the piece, including the appropriate performance practices of the genre, time period, and style.
❑ Prepare a word-for-word translation of the piece.
❑ Complete a harmonic analysis of the score.
❑ Include a solfege analysis of all parts.
❑ Mark the score for breathing and phrasing.
❑ Use color to emphasize entrances, dynamic changes, articulation markings, tempo markings, contrasting sections, and themes.
❑ Make musical decisions based on accurate information from your research.

Rehearsal Planning

❑ Determine the vocal requirements of the piece.
❑ Select an aural immersion exercise that will introduce the choir to the mode.
❑ Make a decision concerning appropriate neutral syllables for rehearsal. Teach musical elements of a piece with neutral syllables.
❑ Consider appropriate tempo for rehearsal and performance. Rehearse the work at a slower tempo, and maintain a consistent tempo.
❑ Plan a choral warm-up. Select general and specific exercises that relate to the piece being rehearsed.

Teaching the Piece

❑ Establish the context for aware listening.
❑ Sound the harmonic structure before singing.
❑ Invent devices to teach pitch, rhythm, and text with minimal vocal effort.
❑ Use counting/singing on nonsense syllables to correct errors of pitch, rhythm, and text.
❑ Teach one layer of musical element at a time.
❑ Add dynamics and phrase shape.
❑ Impart the shape and forward movement of the work.
❑ Establish the movement of air early in the rehearsal process.
❑ Use a multi-layered diction teaching process—heightened/exaggerated/sustained speech or staccato singing on text.
❑ Use a conducting gesture that provides the correct signals to the choir.
❑ Be aware of the proper production of the vowels that will influence intonation.

---

3   The author of this book wishes to thank Margaret Palermo Foote for this checklist design.

The Howard Swan Rehearsal Planning Guide

Several decades ago, Howard Swan published a two-page rehearsal planning guide. In his book, *Conscience of a Profession* (Hinshaw Music, 1987), the form is published with no explanation in the text. From reading the text, however, one could surmise that such a form has oversight possibilities for both score study and planning the rehearsal process.

The focus of Swan's rehearsal planning guide is understanding the stylistic or historical factors that are contained within a work. His rehearsal planning guide is organized into two parts: (1) the "What" of rehearsal and (2) the "How and When" of rehearsal. This paradigm is an interesting way to organize the rehearsal process after score study has been completed.

Broad Categories Planning Guide

The example shown in **Figure 30-3** is broader in scope; it provides for a more general overview of the rehearsal process and focuses upon important aspects of the score study process. The strength of this type of checklist lies in its broad overview and clarity of content.

The example shown in **Figure 30-4** is another variation on the rehearsal preparation process. To develop this checklist, decisions were made regarding the focus of the rehearsal, which grew out of informed score study. This example has a section covering broad pedagogical reminders, with the specifics of the rehearsal being attached to the form.

Figure 30-3. Checklist example #3.

Rehearsal Preparation Checklist

SCORE ANALYSIS / STUDY
Graphs – Herford
Colorization – Hillis
Grouping phrases – Thurmond
Possible vocal technique issues – Haasemann
Solfege analysis

☐ Mode(s):

☐ Trouble spots (mm.):

CHOIR SET-UP
☐ Determine seating of voice parts that most accurately reflects the musical work.
☐ Individually hear and place voices.
☐ Give accompanist general layout of all rehearsals and specific format for the day.
☐ *(optional)* Share a copy of your score analysis for the accompanist's outside study.

REHEARSAL WARM-UP
☐ Use a warm-up template specified for the day's rehearsal.

INTRODUCTION OF PIECE
☐ Allow the choir to listen to the piece while you conduct it.
☐ Use the "Day-Tay" method to show phrasing.
☐ Employ count-singing with harmonic immersion accompaniment.
☐ Employ body movement consistent with rhythm and tempo.
☐ Sing melody on a neutral syllable.
☐ Add text.

Figure 30-4. Checklist example #4.

Rehearsal Planning Checklist

SCORE STUDY

- ❑ Composer background
- ❑ Hillis analysis
- ❑ Herford/Harmonic analysis
- ❑ Tabiteau Note Grouping phrase analysis
- ❑ LMSA (Laban Movement Score Analysis)
- ❑ Mark score for breathing and phrasing
- ❑ Determine aural structure of work
- ❑ Determine mode
- ❑ Determine solfege to use with choir
- ❑ Determine neutral syllable for first rehearsal
- ❑ Determine appropriate tempo for rehearsal and performance
- ❑ Plan choral warm-up, with both general and specific ideas for the piece to be rehearsed
- ❑ Select aural immersion exercise to introduce mode of the piece to be rehearsed

TEACHING THE PIECE
Pedagogical Reminders

- ■ Be sure to use specific vocal warm-ups for the piece being taught. Encourage singers to listen to the singers around them more than themselves, and encourage them to listen with their right ear.

- ■ Play the piece on the keyboard.

- ■ Introduce the composer and provide a background of the piece to put the piece into context of the composer's life and work.

- ■ Sing the piece using a neutral syllable without text. Provide alternating dominant in upper tessitura to hold tonality. Repeat phrases (rote singing) so singers become familiar with the harmonic structure.

- ■ Use solfege to secure pitch and rhythm.

- ■ After pitch and rhythm are secure, use a diction teaching process (e.g., heightened speech, sustained speech, staccato singing on text). Use the method you feel will be most effective for development of the ensemble.

- ■ Add dynamics and phrase shape. Encourage the singers to mark their scores carefully.

The Use of Post-It Notes

A valuable tool I have found is the use of **Post-It notes** (or other sticky notes) to remind me of finite details that may be forgotten when I become involved with rehearsal (examples shown in **Figure 30-5** and **Figure 30-6**). We often sacrifice listening in rehearsal while trying to remember what needs to be rehearsed, including minor details. These notes are also extremely valuable when you want to improve the performance between performances. You free your mind from the cognitive issues so the "listening half" of your brain can focus on the music rather than the language involved with remembering the details. This will help improve both the efficiency and the pace of a rehearsal.

Figure 30-5. Post-It notes example #1.

Figure 30-6. Post-It notes example #2.

Chapter 31

The Moments Prior to Rehearsal

Suggestions for Entering Into Rehearsal

Those who are great, need to tell us so little. We must know how to listen and we will understand. (p. 71)

False notes can be forgiven, false music cannot. Have confidence that you can do it. In life you are alive. Believe in life, it is your life. It is a question of vitality. (p. 74)

All that we know by heart enriches us and helps us find ourselves. The true personality is aided by the personality of others. That is why we must develop. (p. 75)

Your hands must be full of magnetism. Put the fingers and mind to work, and you will have music. (p. 77)

—Nadia Boulanger
from *Master Teacher*
by Don G. Campbell

The minutes prior to rehearsal are perhaps the most pivotal part of the rehearsal preparation process. Those minutes, if well spent and approached with care, can deepen the rehearsal experience for both you and your choir. You have a chance to clarify the pedagogical directions you have chosen and prepare your inner self to make a meaningful journey through the choral rehearsal process.

While I don't think any conductor would deny that quiet time before a rehearsal is beneficial, as conductors we generally don't seriously consider how to best structure that time so it can be the true capstone of our rehearsal preparation. Yet I have found that how this time is spent has everything to do with the success of the rehearsal that follows. This time can serve as a valuable entry point into the rehearsal process.

In all likelihood, there are as many ways of approaching this entry point as there are persons reading this text. I believe that this time needs to be devoted to what I call "preparation of the person"—a process of quieting yourself and making sure your internal human self is in order. What follows are suggested techniques for "preparation of the person." No matter the technique, you will find that this time quickly becomes an indispensable part of your rehearsal preparation process.

Use of the Swiss Exercise Ball

The use of a Swiss Exercise Ball can do much to prepare a conductor's body alignment for rehearsal as well as in many ways address a conductor's interior preparation issues. It can help release muscular tension and allow you to focus on breathing and creating a calm state to take into the rehearsal room. I refer to this process as **constructive rest**.

Before beginning any conducting session or rehearsal, start with a short period of constructive rest on an exercise ball as follows (see **Figure 31-1**):

- Kneel with the ball in front of you.
- Drape your body over the ball. Your abdomen should contact the ball.
- Let your arms drape in a relaxed fashion around the ball.
- Remain silent and breathe. (Listen to your breath, and use the time to quiet your body.)

Figure 31-1. Constructive rest position on a Swiss exercise ball.

By doing this, you allow your spine to lengthen and lose the tensions of the day that cause your spine to assume a position without an upward release. The more time you can spend in constructive rest, the more you will realign your body in an appropriate way to develop conducting technique.

One of the most difficult problems for both beginning and experienced conductors is being able to "let go" of their bodies and gestures in such a way that allows for freedom in the sound of an ensemble. This inability to "let go" is often the result of muscular tension and improper alignment, and the use of an exercise ball makes significant progress toward either partial or total elimination of this problem.

You can also use the exercise ball in a sitting position. To do this, you must immediately reorganize the core of your body or risk falling off of the ball. In other words, you must remain in a state of total body awareness to stay on the ball. Alignment problems often begin to unknowingly manifest themselves when we are conducting because we are not constantly monitoring our bodies. Left uncorrected, a faulty kinesthetic sense of body alignment is established, which severely compromises conducting technique. As a result, natural musical impulses are greatly reduced or stopped because they cannot travel freely and unencumbered through our neural pathways to the ensemble. Use of the Swiss exercise ball puts you in constant touch with your body, forcing you to continually self-monitor alignment. Over time, severe alignment issues disappear.

Pre-Rehearsal QiGong

Without appearing to be a fanatic of New Age practices, I believe musicians become afflicted and compromised for some very simple reasons. As human beings, we are simply incapable of giving out energy on a daily basis in practice, rehearsal, or performance without replenishing our "store" of energy at some point during the day (or week). Working in an artistic environment with such depleted energy stores produces an instability that, depending upon the circumstances, could result in potentially unpredictable reactions. Any practice that could maintain our contact with the larger world while restoring needed energy is certainly worth serious consideration.

There are also various meditative/physical studies and/or practices that allow body, mind, and spirit to maintain contact with each other. Yoga practitioners sing the praises of its constant practice and integration into one's lifestyle. Tae Kwon Do practitioners tout its benefit to overall mental and spiritual health, as well as its ability to center oneself and one's energies. Alexander Technique has gained many musician practitioners because of the body awareness it teaches. Unfortunately, many musicians happen upon the benefits of these practices only after they encounter some type of stress or tension that, in turn, impacts their music making.

Perhaps it is time for the music profession to study and embrace those practices that have the potential to "recharge" the body, spirit, and mind of musicians. Perhaps a root of the problems we face as musicians in our dealings with others is that the practice of our art leaves our spirits and bodies so depleted of energy that little remains within us to see ourselves through challenging or pressing human and/or musical situations. In response, I would like to present here a relatively new viewpoint on the use of the ancient Chinese healing practice of QiGong[1] as one way in which musicians could replenish their energy stores through acquisition of the energy of Qi.[2]

---

1   I was first introduced to this practice in Sedona, Arizona, at the MiiAmo Spa. After one class, I immediately felt the results of this relatively simple and direct approach taught by Paulette, who is on staff at that spa. I was also impressed because many of its central principles were not only easily acquired in one class but were directly in line with the principles I believe are centrally important to the art of conducting.

2   My first familiarity with the term *Qi* (pronounced *chee*) came from a school of conducting pedagogy in Japan, where a minimum number of gestures are taught. All gestures are taught as movement toward or away from the Qi, which has been referred to in the Western World as the "ictus."

What Is QiGong?

In my opinion, this phenomenon (of QiGong) can be compared with the launching and receiving principle in radio, for it is a special "field" in objective reality. If only you know how to receive *Qi* with the corresponding specific means, you can receive *Qi* to obtain its curing effect. (p. 68)

—Ou Wen Wei
in *Pan Gu Mystical QiGong*

If there is one concept that comes up in all forms of Chinese medicine it is that of Qi, or vital energy. Qi is the very backbone of the Chinese healing arts. It refers to the energy of the Universe that is channeled from nature and runs through all of us. To have Qi is to be alive, while to have none is to be dead.

QiGong also relies on the manipulation of this vital energy. This is done through "meridians," channels that pass through all the vital organs of the body. There are twelve of these meridians, which correspond to twelve organs. These meridians are interconnected, so that one runs into the other and passes through the body like an invisible river of energy. Anyone can learn simple exercises to manipulate his or her own Qi. This practice is known as *internal* QiGong. (p. xiii)

The root of the way of life, of birth and change, is Qi; the myriad things of heaven and earth all obey this law. Thus Qi in the periphery envelops heaven and earth. Qi in the interior activates them. The source wherefrom the sun, moon, and stars derive their light, the thunder, rain, wind and cloud their being, the four seasons and the myriad things their birth, growth, gathering and storing; all this is brought about by Qi. Man's possession of life is completely dependent upon this Qi. (pp. 283–284)

—Master Hong Liu
in *The Healing Art of QiGong*

Let me try to summarize both the practice of QiGong and its benefits to musicians at the risk of over-simplifying the concepts of this practice.[3] Basically stated, the mind/body exercises as advocated by the specific practice of QiGong allow the body to function in parallel as a type of radio device. Through QiGong, one learns to use the body as a "receiver" of energy (or Qi) that is constantly around us. This energy is carried in atoms and particles energized by the sun and moon that are available for our "collection." The exercises represent the collection devices that allow us as musicians to "recharge" and "refocus," with direct benefits upon our physical, mental, and spiritual health. Acquisition of Qi may be felt as vitality. At times, one can feel a certain magnetic or energy force between one's hands. Most importantly, acquiring Qi possesses both conscious action and super-conscious action.

Again, at the risk of sounding very New Age, QiGong aims at achieving within oneself a certain balance and harmony of the energy that is *around* you and *within* you. The energy within you can only be replenished from sources that are external to you. QiGong provides a way of harvesting the energy that is omnipresent in the environment around you. The key to acquisition is a mind that is calm and a spirit that is open and loving. Finally, QiGong teaches body positions that maximize this energy acquisition.

---

3 I would encourage readers who are interested in acquiring skills for this practice to not only find a practitioner in QiGong (available at www.Pangushengong.org) but to also read and study the concise book by Ou Wen Wei, *Pan Gu Mystical QiGong* (Multi-Media Books, 1999).

A parallel to this principle can be found in biology. The growth of plants (and to a certain extent, living things in another chemical context) requires the use of the energy of the sun and photosynthesis. Photosynthesis converts solar energy into life-giving energy and food for plant life. The practice of QiGong allows for the acquisition of beneficial energies of the sun and moon to repair and revitalize the soul, spirit, and body in a powerful and direct way.

Energy Flow in QiGong

One of the most valuable images necessary in the practice of QiGong is the concept of energy. This image is especially valuable for conductors and musicians. When visualizing the flow of energy throughout the body, we must visualize that the energy flows through the entire body like water. This flow is constant, and its speed is directly relational to the amount of external energy that can be brought into the body. Stated another way, we must be in a constant state of awareness of our entire body for energy to flow throughout all parts of our body in this way. Unawareness leads to severe blockages in energy which, in turn, will manifest themselves in human interaction problems and musical issues.

QiGong is another vehicle by which we as musicians can maintain a state of constant physical awareness. Physical awareness is the catalyst for spiritual awareness (to be discussed in the pages that follow). The goal is for musicians to acquire the skills by which energy acquisition becomes habitual and that feeling of liquid energy flow within the body is both a constant and a norm for our daily existence.

The one concept I have found most difficult to impart to both my choirs and other conductors is how "energy" flows through the body. Many believe the body is a vibrating mass of protoplasm—that energy somehow reaches the ensemble by sheer power of perception. That perception will, with certainty, lead to a minimal transference of energy to ensemble, instrument, or audience.

Many others believe energy is generated from a furnace-like source in the body and then is, almost literally, "hurled" or thrown out at the ensemble ("energy implosion"). Such a bombardment usually has the opposite effect. It usually creates a driven, aggressive sound in the choir. Such energy dispersion is also the product of persons who are unable to "let go" and trust themselves or their ensemble. They believe that music "is made" rather than being a reaction as a result of correct energy transference to the ensemble. These persons are perceived as being "energetic," but their energy generally has a detrimental effect upon the musicians they come in contact with. There is also another characteristic of such persons that has direct bearing on the musician's walk. I have observed that such energy flow, because of its inward and cumulative effect, often breeds frustration. Energy "held within" ourselves becomes so powerful that it turns us on ourselves, and frustration and a type of "nervousness" and impatience are the by-products because the "energy" is not being used.

An analogy might be helpful. One of the older homes I once lived in came equipped with a coal insert for the fireplace. This insert was equipped with sliding iron shutters on the front door to allow for proper ventilation of the coal fire. Once when I added coal to the fire, I neglected to open the vents. I left the room and returned about twenty minutes later, and the entire insert glowed red hot! Not until I opened the vents and allowed heat into the room did the metal cool to its normal color and state. Musicians who do not either practice or conceptualize the correct flow of energy constantly "overheat." This "overheating" needs to be eliminated from the body through some type of "cool down." Unfortunately for many of us, we get rid of this overheated and misdirected energy in many negative ways.[4]

Two Paradigms for Energy Sharing or Dispersion for Musicians

Two of the most helpful paradigms I have found to support this energy dispersion process are as follows. In QiGong, one of the paths of energy through the body is called the "fire path."[5] The path runs down the center of the body from the forehead toward the outside of the body cavity, down through the pelvis, upward along the spine, around the back of the skull, and completes its cycle over the top of the skull. This energy flow, if allowed to occur, is constant. Energy is then shared in two ways with other musicians.

First, the most powerful transference of energy occurs from the circulation of energy that travels along the external core of the body. If the arms are used correctly by the conductor, the center of the body is left "open" for that energy to be

---

4   In *The Musician's Soul*, the concept of mimetics certainly is a synonym for what is being described here. Conscious thought is similar to the vent doors in the coal furnace. Conscious thought of love and care begins to channel life energies in a positive direction to other musicians or the ensemble.

5   Yang, *The Root of Chinese QiGong*, p. 85.

both sent and perceived by the ensemble.[6] That energy is sensed like a vertical pillar or rod from the pelvis upward to the top of the head.[7] This is a powerful energy core that must be kept "open" and "free" as much as possible.

Second, other energy or Qi is transferred through the arms and out to the ensemble through the palms of the hands.[8] This is possible because the arms are connected to the body energy circulation via the sternoclavicular joint.[9] The proper perception of both of these paths of energy circulation are essential for the maintenance of a healthy "energy" and sharing of that energy (Qi) in a healthy way with the ensemble. Examine the illustration shown in **Figure 31-2** and note the direction of the arrows that detail the overall pattern of energy flow throughout the body.

Figure 31-2. Pattern of energy circulation in the body.

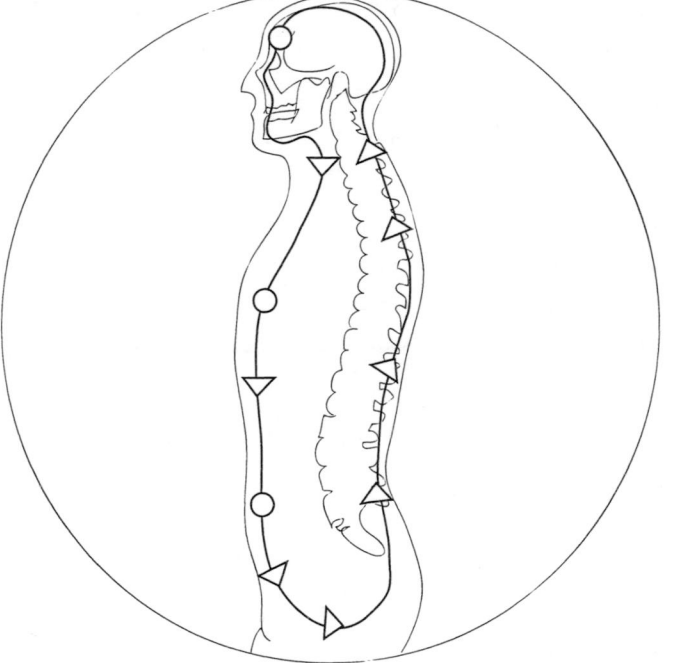

---

6   The correct use of the arms is dealt with extensively in the text, *Learn Conducting Technique with the Swiss Exercise Ball.* The reader is highly encouraged to read the section regarding the axis of both right and left arms.

7   Also remember that the eyes are immediately adjacent to this pillar of energy and play their own role in the sharing of vital energies.

8   This energy or "chi" is a synonym for *ictus.* Pre-rehearsal meditative activities, such as QiGong, not only allow for the energy pathways to be freed but also allow the mechanisms to *release* that energy into the ensemble.

9   The sternoclavicular joint is described and mapped on the DVD by Heather Buchanan and this author, *Body Mapping and Basic Conducting Patterns.* It is essential that the entire arm and its structure be understood and mapped if one desires appropriate energy flow to be shared with the ensemble.

The Danger of Energy Implosion for Musicians

One of the root problems for musicians is an inability to channel the energy they have in a healthy way. While many of us have been taught as artists to "send" energy to the ensemble and to the audience, there seems to have been little instruction on how to route that energy through the body or how to acquire more stores of energy when the supply is depleted for one reason or another.

Imploded energy sets off a chain reaction within musicians that can be self-mutilating, frustrating, and hurtful to those who surround us. How does imploded energy feel within us? It results in restlessness, unhappiness, frustration, anger in varying degrees, inordinate self-criticism, frustration with others, and a general level of impatience with all those who "get in the way" of the music. Understand that we don't mean to do this. But in our own defense, to my knowledge no one has ever discussed the healthy and desirable path of energy through the body and out of the body. Energy used and acquired through these pathways is rejuvenating and invigorating. Energy channeled incorrectly leads to depression and dark moods that, invariably, have detrimental effects on the music we make and the people we love.

The solution is simple. Perception and correct mapping of the energy flow through the body and out of the body is key. When energy flow is correct, much good musical work and human work follows in kind. For me, QiGong has provided a valuable vehicle to solve this crucial puzzle in the pre-rehearsal preparation for a conductor. If we examine any musicians who are admired, impeded energy flow is not a characteristic of their being. For some reason, either through the persons they are or the lives they have lived, energy always flows from them to others in a fluid, effortless way. I believe this is so because it channels through them in a correct way and its flow outward is not impeded in any way whatsoever.

Energy Circulation Applied to Ensembles

Recently, I have come to believe that the concept of energy flow should be taught to ensembles. While individual musicians can be helped with this paradigm, its effects can be logarithmically multiplied when applied to larger groups of musicians. The danger with any ensemble is that in the heat of performance or rehearsal, energy flow is impeded or blocked. Sound is not as vibrant as it could be, and pitch problems become the norm. One of the root problems of intonation difficulties is impeded energy flow within individual musicians. Conductors would do well to discuss energy flow with their ensembles and show them the diagram shown in Figure 31-2. If possible, have them also perform music from the QiGong starting position!

The Basic QiGong Exercise Sequence: The Twenty-Six Repetitions

In the specific practice of QiGong, the following exercises are performed sequentially.[10] Slow and constant movement is the key to ample energy acquisition. Twenty-six repetitions are required for each movement. This number is based upon spiritual numerology. A verbal recitation at the beginning and end of the exercise sequence frames the entire repetition sequence.

A prerequisite to all of these exercises is a sense of core body alignment. An approach to core alignment can be found in *Learn Conducting Technique with the Swiss Exercise Ball* (GIA, 2004). In fact, one can best arrive at the core alignment of one's body through awarenesses gathered from sitting on a Swiss exercise ball, as described in that text. Being organized like an apple around a core, where the core is one's pelvis, is central to vital energy flow through the body. Without organizing one's body around its core, it will be difficult—if not impossible—to experience the free flow of energy throughout the body. At all times during these exercises, awareness of one's alignment and body core must be maintained through constant body awareness. The alignment shown in **Figure 31-3** is necessary for this to happen during the execution of the QiGong exercises.

---

10 For readers desiring additional detail, two sources should be consulted. *Pan Gu Mystical QiGong*, by Ou Wen Wei, offers a detailed, step-by-step description of this approach to QiGong, which is recommended by this author. I would also encourage readers to visit the Web site of the Pan Gu Shengong International Research Institute: www.pangushengong.org.

Figure 31-3. Proper core body alignment.

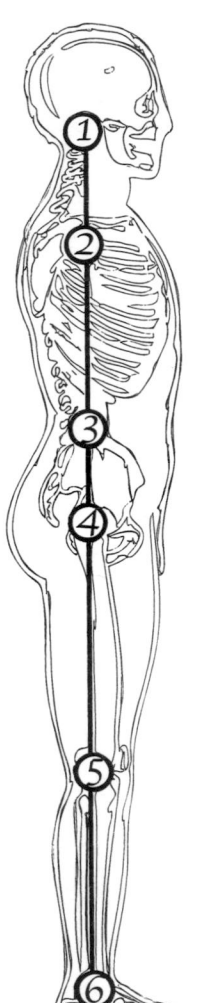

Proper images for breathing should be employed at all times. The correct process for breathing is detailed in *Evoking Sound: Body Mapping and Basic Patterns for Conductors* (GIA, 2002). Body Mapping, as demonstrated with the eight-handed breathing exercise, is central to this process. Throughout all of the exercises, it is most important to remember that the air comes into the body in a wavelike motion from top to bottom. Exhalation also occurs in a wavelike motion from top to bottom.

For those interested in gaining a deeper understanding and, consequently, benefit from QiGong, it is widely believed that a practice unique to QiGong should be studied and mastered. This breathing technique attempts to wed breath with spirit. Obviously, such a technique would be beneficial to musicians.[11]

---

11 For those interested in such an insight, the reader is referred to Chapter 5, "The Practice of Embryonic Breathing," in the book by Yang entitled *QiGong Meditation: Embryonic Breathing*.

Before we enter this practice, I must emphasize one more thing. That is the entire embryonic breathing practice occurs through inner self-observation. That means "self inner feeling." This feeling is the way your mind communicates with your physical body, Qi and Shen. This feeling can be shallow or profound, depending on how much you are able to calm your mind down and feel it. The level of feeling is unlimited, and normally follows the depth of your mind and awareness. Naturally, wrong feeling or mental perception can also lead you into fascination, illusion, and imagination. These false and unrealistic feelings can lead you to a state of emotional disturbance, and further away from the correct practice of Qi cultivation. (p. 323)

—Jwing-Ming Yang
in *QiGong Meditation*

All of the exercises must be performed in a slow tempo, between approximately quarter=42 and quarter=60. The speed of the movement in the hands must be both constant and unvarying. It is the constant slow speed of the hand movements that allows one to both feel and gather energy from the atmosphere surrounding one's hands. Control and maintenance of a consistent speed is most important in the performance of the exercise sequence. And remember, twenty-six repetitions for each exercise!

Starting Position and Recitation

Starting position is most important. The palms up position of the hands allows for energy or Qi to enter the body and, in essence, recharge it (see **Figure 31-4**). The belief is that energy enters the energy meridians of the body through the palms. Approximately two minutes should be spent in this position as one focuses one's thought on the breath, devoid of ego. To assist in getting ego out of the way and beginning the proper flow of energy, many practitioners of QiGong encourage an out-loud recitation. This recitation, no matter its form, should include elements of giving, sharing, acquiring, and love. A sample of such a recitation follows:

> Take kindness and benevolence as basis;
> Take frankness and friendliness as bosom.
> Speak with reason; Treat with courtesy;
> Move with emotion; Act with result.[12]

Figure 31-4. Starting position and recitation.

Left Side Motion

Move to the position shown in **Figure 31-5**, where the hands are parallel on the left side of the body. The hands should be no more than sixteen inches apart. Move the hands in a slow and circular clockwise motion, with the lower hand following the motion of the upper hand, but slightly behind the upper hand. This should be performed with one complete rotation every two seconds. Twenty-six complete cycles should be performed.

---

12   Ou Wen Wei from title page of *Pan Gu Mystical QiGong*.

Figure 31-5. Left side motion.

Motion Transfer from Left to Right

After the twenty-six rotations are completed, move both hands to the center of the body, parallel with the navel (see **Figure 31-6**). Transition the same position to the right side of the body. As you transition, the hand that was on the bottom is now on the top, on the right side of the body.

Figure 31-6. Motion transfer from left to right.

Right Side Motion

Perform the same circular motion with the left hand on top, and the right following it (see **Figure 31-7**). This should be performed with one complete rotation every two seconds. Twenty-six complete cycles should be performed.

Figure 31-7. Right side motion.

Middle Motion

After the motion has been completed on the right side of the body, turn the hands so they are parallel with the mid-line of the body (see **Figure 31-8**). Then rotate the hands, one following the other, for twenty-six forward rotations, with each rotation taking at least two seconds. The slower the rotations, the greater the benefit.

Figure 31-8. Middle motion.

Drawing Open Motion

After the repetitions have been completed in middle motion, still the hands. Open the arms slowly while inhalating (see **Figure 31-9**).

Figure 31-9. Drawing open motion.

Drawing Close Motion

After exhaling and moving to the drawn open position, return to the middle position while exhaling, arriving at a flower or "cupped" position of the hands (see **Figure 31-10**).

Figure 31-10. Drawing close motion.

Flower/Focusing Motion

After the drawing close motion, bring the hands into a cupped position as if they are holding a flower. This hand position should mirror the position of the chin line and be approximately two to four inches below the chin (see **Figure 31-11**). Stay in this position for approximately two minutes. If time permits, repeat the entire sequence again.

Figure 31-11. Flower motion (focusing motion).

Acquiring, Understanding, and Practicing Authentic Presence

In reading Parker Palmer's book, *A Hidden Wholeness* (Jossey-Bass, 2004), I was struck by an analogy, or rather a life situation, in the book that may hold one of the keys for us as artists. While Palmer has a viewpoint on this subject, I would like to draw a slightly different parallel for musicians and artists. I found it remarkable that before I had ever read this book, I had pondered the exact same situation and tried to reason through what these "new" feelings were. Palmer brought clarity to my visions and feelings; I encourage you to read his account, but I would like to share my perspective with you.[13]

I believe that if one can combine the mimetical state suggested in *The Musician's Soul* with the "authentic presence" described below, both of these paradigms detail

---

13   Readers of this book are strongly encouraged to read Parker Palmer's book, *A Hidden Wholeness* (Jossey-Bass, 2004). This incredible book may provide additional strategies for a musician's walk. Of particular interest are the sections that describe the Möbius strip, referred to by Palmer as his "Quaker PowerPoint." The Möbius strip analogy contains a powerful paradigm for conductors and musicians of all types. I highly encourage every reader to read and study this remarkable book.

the "door inward" to many answers needed for any rehearsal. The combination of the two constitutes a balanced state of awareness for music making. Once achieved, I believe that not only relationships with other musicians but also one's music making would ascend to inspired and profound human expression.

It might be helpful to try to describe what it "feels" like to be in that heightened and aware state. At this writing, it will be almost four years since my mother passed after a long and painful battle with cancer. I must admit I found the whole "situation" very difficult to deal with. My sister, a nurse, was a godsend in this situation. She was strong where I was weak and ineffective. My mother's companion, Charlie, was also more infinitely effective in helping my mother. Many times I felt angry because I felt conflict between the deep love I had for my mother and my total inability to deal with the realities of life that were present. Helplessness seemed to be a dominating emotion. The immediate result for me, ironically, was physical illness. The illness provided me with a convenient way to be both physically and spiritually absent.

My schedule at school, grueling as usual, was compounded by inhumane situations that I would rather not discuss. In my phone conversations with my mom, I could hear the pain in her voice and her desperation. I tried to calm her with my words. But because I did not understand this idea of authentic presence, I could be of no help to her.

I was jolted out of self-imposed isolation one day when she called me. In essence, she forced me into a type of action or state that authentic presence brings. She called to tell me how much pain she was in. The cancer in her lower spine was unbearable. She told me she could no longer lie down. She had sat at our family kitchen table for over a week, eating and sleeping there because she could no longer lie prone. I cried silently on the other end of the phone. And then she did it. She said. "Jim, I am sitting here at this table waiting to die; I cannot bear it anymore."

I called my sister immediately. By the next afternoon, hospice had been contacted and Mom had a bed in the living room. For the first time in many weeks, she could lay prone and sleep. Increased medication helped. In a few days, I was well enough to go and visit.

I will try to describe what is essentially indescribable. It is that very same feeling I now realize through the help of Parker Palmer that I have when, I believe, artistic music making occurs. I am paraphrasing Palmer's concept and calling it "authentic presence." The difference is a bit semantical, but I think it is an important distinction for musicians.

As I approached the front door of my mother's home, my stomach turned with fear. I had to force myself up what seemed the endless two steps to the porch. When

I walked into the house, Mom lay there, very calm and semi-sedated. She heard my voice and we reached for each other. I tried to speak but could not; it was like I had nothing to say. All I felt was an incredible sense of love and an abiding calm in her presence. How odd. I believed that I would bring her "support" and "calm," yet she was the calm presence in that room. My Aunt Joyce, Charlie, and I sat for what was about an hour and half and said almost nothing. While the situation would have been previously labeled as "sad" by me, I found myself in an incredibly heightened state of being—a state of *authentic awareness*. Looking back, it was a strange alchemy of love and calm acceptance, and it was truly, stunningly beautiful. It is a wordless calm combined with a humble place. Four years later, I realize that when I am at my best musical place, I have that same feeling. And now I try to go there...every rehearsal, every performance, every class. It is what I am calling *authentic presence*. It was what Martin Buber, I believe, meant in part in trying to describe "I and thou."

Mom passed about nine days later, with her family and best life friends at her side in a room that was stunningly quiet on a bright and beautiful Spring day in March. God ended her suffering and left us all a gift...the gift of authentic awareness. Ironic, isn't it? You learn what life is through one's passing.

One strange aside: I avoided even thinking or rehashing those days for many weeks. As we cleaned out my family's homestead, there was one item left on the first floor: the Victorian claw-footed kitchen table. It was the table my father died at. It was the table my mother suffered at. Since I gave it to my parents, my sister said I should take it. I had told my wife that I was going to send it to auction. I didn't want it in the house. It was too painful. She was insistent, and I gave in. That table is now in the family room in my home, and I now must publicly confess that it is my favorite spot to study scores and to just touch. Because of the experiences it represents, it allows me an express "ticket" to a strong and abiding feeling of authentic presence. Let it be known: In rehearsal, concerts, and classes, I am always imagining myself with my mom in those final days. The table is my vehicle for that now frequent, almost daily, journey. I realize that it is not enough to love others. The power in that love is to be serenely aware so musicians can hear and give of their gifts and their spirit. I learned how not to fear from being fearful—an ironic and profound twist that is one of life's great lessons.

Search your own life for your authentic awareness situation and you, too, will have arrived at a better place for your art and your rehearsals.

Time with Self

Aside from actual score study and the hidden mysteries within any composer's language, the portal that seems to allow for the best entry into the rehearsal process is something that allows us to access quiet in some form. A calm inside allows us to hear, to actively react to sound, and to "be" in front of our ensembles.

Passion vs. Ego

Estranged from the music of our own lives, we endure our ordinary days with existential anxiety. We worry about the past and anticipate the future. All the while overlooking the season of the moment. If we were to embrace the past without excessive judgment and calmly step, not leap, into the future, we might feel the vitality of the all-embracing soul.

The principle of being present to life is also complicated by the soul's odd sense of time, so different from the literal measurements of the clock and calendar. The soul exists in cycles of time, full of repetition, and it has equal portions of flowing temporality and static eternity. Responsive to the soul, we may easily drift out of literal life several times a day to revisit people and places of the past or imagine the future. These visitations are entirely different from the ego's anxious attempts to resolve the past or control the future. They are more like a summer's week on the beach, a way to get away and find a fresh perspective. (p. 7)

—Thomas Moore
in *The Original Self*

405

Spiritual emptiness is not only an open mind but also an open self. We have to get ourselves out of the way—our explanations, our goals, our habits, and our anxieties. We often try to avoid disaster and fill life with order and meaning, but just as often life unravels all of our careful preparations. (p. 10)

Psychologically, emptiness is the absence of neurosis, which is essentially an interfering with the unfolding of life and the desires of the deep soul. Various neuroses, such as jealously, inferiority, and narcissism, are nothing more than anxious attempts to prevent life from happening, and when emptied, they transform into their opposites: Jealousy empty of ego is passion. Inferiority empty of ego is humility. Narcissism empty of ego is love of one's soul. We could understand our struggles with these emotions as an invitation to emptiness. The point is not to get rid of them but to let them get rid of us. (pp. 13–14)

—Thomas Moore
in *The Soul's Religion*

For a rehearsal to be truly productive, and for singers to sing at their potential, I have found that it is important for conductors to have a clear understanding of the difference between passion and ego. Many conductors confuse passion and ego, and meld the two diverse elements into a caustic mix. Many conductors believe they are passionate about their art, but mistakenly use their ego to propel and inject their passion into the rehearsal room. This caustic interaction, in a way, contaminates and poisons the rehearsal, and negatively affects the final musical product that is the result of musical labors in rehearsal.

Simply stated, passion is passion, and ego is ego. A conductor's ego has no place in the rehearsal process or in the performance. The conductor's work prior to and during rehearsal should be to mollify ego through a sense of humbleness. I heard Julius Herford say, in his advice to graduates from a Westminster Choir College commencement address, to seek out colleagues who go about their work quietly and humbly, for it is with them that the greatest musical results will be realized. The most potent antidote for ego is, indeed, humbleness applied in copious amounts. Passion can be a powerful energizing force within any rehearsal, but when combined with ego it becomes debilitating both musically and humanly. Ego rears its ugly head in the heat of rehearsal when things aren't going well and the conductor calls upon his or her will to "move things forward." Ego combined with passion is perceived as physical aggressiveness through both gesture and word. Ego is often felt within as an undue sense of urgency and an awareness of only self, with the music occupying a vague "exterior" role.

Ego is certainly a part of all of our beings. To believe we can make it "go away" is foolish. However, we can keep it in check through some very simple means. An ability to call upon internal silence during the rehearsal process, especially when things run amuck, is perhaps the most important tool we can employ. A genuine and profound love of those who are in rehearsal has both a humbling and deeply warming effect upon our very souls that translates into better rehearsals and better music making. And simply caring more about the many others who sing for us is perhaps the best way. Without a doubt, passion makes us fully alive human beings. Passionate rehearsals devoid of ego should always be our goal as we enter into the rehearsal room and live with others through the communal experience that we call a rehearsal.

The Conductor's Presence in Rehearsal

Man sees things that surround him long before he becomes aware of his own self. Many of us are conscious of the hiddenness of things, but few of us sense the mystery of our own presence. (p. 61)

—Abraham Joshua Heschel
in *Between God and Man*

For whatever reason, it seems that few of us appreciate or even understand the power of our presence in a choral rehearsal, a presence embodied as palatable human spirit. Left to its own honest devices, the human spirit emits a powerful energy to all those it comes into contact with. But our true presence can be hidden from others through insecurity, ego, and unawarenesses. If we as conductors could just "be" in front of others, then our presence would fill the rehearsal space with invigorating energy. Thus, one of the most important aspects of any rehearsal is understanding all the elements that allow us to just "be." Yet too often, those elements are the most ignored or unexamined aspects of our personal beings.

Great conductors/teachers have one unifying characteristic. They are at all times caring and loving to everyone they teach or work with, including themselves. They have respect for others and what they do, and they learn from others by quiet observance. They have the unique ability to be able to rejoice in the achievements of others, while objectively looking at their own achievements and realizing their own gifts, too. They have an overriding passion with care and human condition of others. Music is almost an afterthought, a by-product of living. Because of these characteristics, students under their tutelage grow at alarming rates both as musicians and as people.

The challenge for all of us as conductors is relatively simple but requires both outward and inward focus. After score study is done, then our task is to enter the rehearsal room as the individuals we really are so that what we have learned through score study can speak through our very actions, words, and teaching. Rehearsal preparation, then, becomes a process by which we come to rehearsal and just "be" in front of our ensemble, church choir, or any group with whom we wish to make music.

After all the careful score study and preparation, it seems the choral rehearsal reduces itself down to one important element: How many ways can we remind ourselves how to be? For each of us, the answer is very different and is a product of the life we have lived and how we choose to live and "be" in front of others as we create with our ensembles this incredible art known as music.

One thing that sets man apart from animals is a boundless, unpredictable capacity for the development of an inner universe. There is more potentiality in his soul than in any other being known to us. Look at the infant and try to imagine the multitude of events it is going to engender. Indeed, the enigma of the human being is not in what he is but what he is able to be. (p. 39)

—Abraham Joshua Heschel
in *Who is Man?*

People say that what we're all seeking is a meaning for life. I don't think that's what we're really seeking. I think that what we are s eeking is an experience of being alive, so that our life experiences on the purely physical plane will have resonances with our innermost being and reality, so that we actually feel the rapture of being alive. That's what it's finally about. (p. 5)

—Joseph Campbell
in *The Power of Myth*

One of the most beautiful stories I know concerns a certain African tribe in which, at the time when the boy passes into manhood he must go off into the jungle by himself—there to indulge in an orgy of dancing and shouting and wailing and sobbing, He must leave the village—for his sounds would make the people in the village ill.

Kathleen Ferriers and Eileen Farrells and Toscaninis and Walters are great because they find the basic and, finally, simple human sound in what for the rest of us are mazes of complexity. (p. 346)

—Robert Shaw
in *Robert Blocker, The Robert Shaw Reader*

Chapter 32

Postscript

The Rehearsal as a Connecting Experience

Only connect! That was the whole of her sermon. Only connect the prose and the passion, and both will be exalted, and human love will be seen at its highest. Live in fragments no longer. Only connect, and the beast and the monk, robbed of the isolation that is life to either, will die. (Chapter 22)

...railway termini...are our gates to the glorious and the unknown. Through them we pass out into adventure and sunshine, to them, alas! we return. (Chapter 2)

—E. M. Forster
in *Howards End*

"Life," wrote a friend of mine, "is a public performance on the violin, in which you must learn the instrument as you go along." (p. 200)

—E. M. Forster
in *A Room with a View*

Hell is a place where nothing connects with nothing. (p. 45)

—Vartan Gregorian, citing Dante
in *Howard Gardner*,
Five Minds for the Future

B oth volumes of *Evoking Sound: The Choral Rehearsal* have focused on preparing for an event for which, in reality, there is no way to prepare. As conductors we can merely make ourselves ready for our encounter with the human spirits in rehearsal, where each spirit has a deep desire not only to be listened to and heard, but in some small way to connect with each other—and perhaps to a larger world. It is not foolishness to consider the rehearsal and all its preparations as a grand journey we take each day—the journey being a choir, laden with life and with its own desire to speak and be heard.

Creativity Misunderstood: Individual vs. Group

If we are to make any progress with our own understanding of rehearsal technique and the psychologies we use to deploy that technique to an ensemble, a paradigm shift is necessary. We must delve deeper into the rehearsal process and rehearsal psyche.

Much of the focus of music education and the training of choral musicians has been on defining and understanding the creative process in individuals. We have studied how individuals learn, and we have detailed methods that, in reality, deal with teaching individuals within a group. Group musicianship and group creativity are assumed to be the natural outgrowths of individual musicians herded together in an ensemble. However, that is not necessarily accurate. Recent excitement surrounding critical pedagogy has taken our eye off the ball. While we need to consider individuals and the experiences they bring to musicing, are not those individual "characteristics" transformed and even mutated when they are in a group setting? How does one individual's experiences translate when that person becomes part of a larger corporate experience? Is the power of the group more powerful than the individuals within it?

For better or worse, rehearsals are group sport. Truman Capote once remarked that he preferred writing novels to plays because he didn't enjoy group sports. The problem with rehearsal technique, and perhaps choral music in general, is that we have not examined how individual creativity and music learning changes when in a group setting (an ensemble). We all know it does, yet for that reason at times the right rehearsal technique eludes us. It eludes us because we tend to craft our rehearsals thinking about how to teach individuals rather than groups. Or worse yet, we craft rehearsals as if we were teaching ourselves rather than our students. In any case, groups are more difficult to teach! Howard Gardner, in his book *Five Minds for the Future* (Harvard Business School Press, 2007), makes this observation. Despite what we have discovered from the extensive research on how individuals learn, we have come to very little understanding of how creativity transforms itself in a group setting. The problems we encounter in rehearsal become obstacles because not only are we under-prepared in basic score learning processes, but we also fail to understand how groups of persons (ensembles) create and *learn* together.

Rehearsal technique, to paraphrase Capote, *is* group sport, and to *not* shape our pedagogy around the psychology of group creativity has been detrimental to the learning process. I believe we have subliminally considered this, but the psychology of the creative process of the group has not informed and directed our pedagogical focus. A good, productive rehearsal requires constant consideration and study of the powerful community of creative beings. Martin Buber understood the human potential that is unlocked when persons are in community. Group creative powers never stagnate (unless they are allowed to do so through poor rehearsal technique and inadequate score study). Hence, rehearsal technique, while made up of the same basic building blocks and method, must constantly change because the ensemble constantly changes from rehearsal to rehearsal! To further compound the issue, through rehearsal technique we must transform individual listening skills into listening skills that happen within a group.

So rehearsal preparation is vital; we must possess the keys to open any magical musical doors that present themselves in rehearsal. Aside from "learning the music," rehearsals must transform themselves into life-nourishing and life-giving experiences. The desired end result of effective rehearsal preparation and technique is that the conductor and the singers leave the rehearsal better people than when they walked in the door.

Great music can be viewed as the catalyst for such deep exploration without any further justification. Music provides us with the vehicle to explore life in all of its facets and can, if taught well, bring us to understand through sound what words alone simply cannot accomplish. Rehearsal preparation and technique is key, yet no book can ever prepare conductors for the spontaneity that is present in a rehearsal room. Even in the best of rehearsals the unexpected appears, and it is only because of preparation and experience that an answer to the musical issue at hand also miraculously appears.

Humility as Rehearsal Technique

Always the wish that you may find patience enough in yourself to endure, and simplicity enough to believe; that you may acquire more and more confidence in that which is difficult, and in your solitude among others. (p. 120)

—Rainer Maria Rilke
in Julia Cameron, *Walking in This World*

Humility can be both a curse and a blessing, and the same can be said for ego, too. Flexibility or firmness, gentle concern or ruthless determination, collaboration or competition: which is more important, which will contribute to our music making? Do we even have a choice?

Egotistical behavior can alienate, antagonize, and polarize those around you, isolate you, and even help you to lose your job; and yet every artist I have interviewed feels that a healthy ego is essential to artistry. The question remains: how do we strike a healthy balance between humility and ego? (p. 225)

When you use ego to compete against another person rather than striving within yourself, the game changes from an Inner Game of artistry to an Outer Game of "beat the competition"—and that's not a game you can ever really win, because it zaps your energy, it takes your attention away from the music. (p. 234)

—Barry Green
in *The Mastery of Music*

While conductors must enter the rehearsal room fully equipped with technical "tools," as Frauke Haasemann used to instruct her students, a rehearsal's success is deeply impacted by the amount of "awe" and "wonder" one can realize in the rehearsal event. The powerful community that is a choir can speak in a voice stronger than any single person alone as long as awe and wonder about the creative tasks at hand are always present. When I feel like I have had a good rehearsal, I feel relatively quiet and insignificant in comparison to the many individuals in the room. Conversely, my worst rehearsals are those in which I assumed a dominant role over the process which, if left alone, is remarkably organic!

The Foundations of Rehearsal Technique

Perhaps the most valuable rehearsal technique I ever learned, I learned in childhood. Rehearsal technique consists of equal parts of preparation and **recall**. Remembering what it was like to play for hours on end and marveling in the simple beauty of my life as a child, or at least how I remember it, informs my praxis (as music educators like to say). In addition to studying and analyzing all of the component parts of a score, as conductors and teachers we must infuse a healthy dose of awe and wonder in every rehearsal.

I do know what I want someone to give me for Christmas. I've known since I was forty years old. Wind-up mechanical toys that make noises and go round and round and do funny things. No batteries. Toys that need me to help them out from time to time. The old-fashioned painted tin ones I had as a child. That's what I want. Nobody believes me. It's what I want, I tell you.

Well, okay, that's close, but not quite exactly it. It's delight and simplicity that I want. Foolishness and fantasy and noise. Angels and miracles and wonder and innocence and magic. That's closer to what I want.

It's harder to talk about, but what I really, really, really want for Christmas is just this: I want to be five years old again for an hour. I want to laugh a lot and cry a lot. I want to be picked up and rocked to sleep in someone's arms, and carried up to bed just one more time. I know what I really want for Christmas: I want my childhood back.

Nobody is going to give me that. I might give at least the memory of it to myself if I try. I know it doesn't make sense, but since when is Christmas about sense, anyway? Christmas is about a child, of long ago and far away, and Christmas is about the child of now. In you and me. Waiting behind the door of our hearts for something wonderful to happen. A child who is impractical, unrealistic, simpleminded, and vulnerable to joy. A child who does not need or want to understand gifts of socks or potholders. (pp. 173–174)

—Robert Fulghum
in *All I Really Need to Know I Learned in Kindergarten*

Belief in Rehearsing

While preparation for rehearsal is important, it is also preparation for understanding life and living (or at least understanding it to the best of one's capacities) that makes the alchemy of rehearsal preparation and community come alive in sound. The rehearsal is like a carefully controlled environment that allows, over time, carefully rehearsed musical elements to coalesce into something even more powerful than the composer's voice. Believing in that process will indeed allow that miracle to happen.

What is belief in rehearsing? It is a belief that communities of people can find profound answers through sound. And conductors must understand that they have little to do with the process except to ignite musical materials that can be deeply informed through careful preparation and to be a constant catalytic and inspiring presence—a truly humble and relatively quiet role in the whole process.

A presence, a spirit, and one who desperately wants to "always connect," in the words of E. M. Forrester,[1] is perhaps the best description of a conductor in rehearsal. Remember that as conductors we learn about the instrument (our choir) as we move along! I am sure we would all agree that no ensemble is static, nor is it predictable. A child in "conductor's clothing" that wants for nothing more than the

---

1 The author of this book wishes to thank his colleague, Andrew Megill, for reminding him of the wisdom of Forster.

daily experiences of awe and wonder can greatly make a mark on this world that so desperately cries out for what music can bring through carefully prepared rehearsals and performances.

I am not sure I have explained this well. Self-knowledge is so important that I do not care how high you are raised up to the heavens. I never want you to cease cultivating it. As long as we are on this earth, there is nothing more essential than humility. Enter the room of self-knowledge first, instead of floating to other places. This is the path. Traveling along a safe and level road, who needs wings to fly? Let's make the best possible use of our feet first and learn to know ourselves. (p. 46)

Do you think that your deep humility, your self-sacrifice, your bountiful charity and commitment to being of service to all beings meaningless? (p. 294)

—St. Teresa of Avila
in *The Interior Castle*

Bibliography

Aaron, J. "A study of the effects of vocal coordination on pitch accuracy, range, pitch discrimination, and tonal memory of inaccurate singers." Ph.D. dissertation. The University of Iowa, 1990.

Abramson, Robert. *Feel It! Rhythm Games for All*. Warner Brothers Publications, 1998.

————. *Rhythm Games for Perception and Cognition*. Warner Brothers Publications, 1997.

Adler, Kurt. *Phonetics and Diction in Singing*. Minneapolis, MN: University of Minnesota Press, 1967.

Allison, Jay, and Dan Gediman, ed. *This I Believe: The Personal Philosophies of Remarkable Men and Women*. New York: Henry Holt, 2006.

Archibeque, Charlene. "Making Rehearsal Time Count." *The Choral Journal,* September 1992, pp. 18–9.

Armstrong, Kerchal, and Donald Hustad. *Choral Musicianship and Voice Training: An Introduction*. Carol Stream, IL: Somerset Press, 1986.

Azzara, Christopher, and Richard Grunow. *Developing Musicianship through Improvisation*. Chicago: GIA Publications, Inc., 2006.

Baldwin, James. "Some Techniques for Achieving Better Choral Tone Through Vowel Purity." *The Choral Journal,* September 1985, pp. 5–12.

Barlow, W. *The Alexander Technique*. New York: Alfred A. Knopf, 1973.

Barone, Tom. *Touching Eternity: The Enduring Outcomes of Teaching*. New York: Columbia Teachers College, 2001.

Beck, Joseph G. *Selected Writings of John Finley Williamson*. St. Louis, MO: Author House, 2004.

Beittel, Kenneth R. *Zen and the Art of Pottery.* New York: Weatherhill, Inc., 2000.

Bertalot, John. *5 Wheels to Successful Sight Reading.* Minneapolis, MN: Augsburg Fortress, 1993.

———. *Immediately Practical Tips for Choral Directors.* Minneapolis, MN: Augsburg Fortress, 2003.

Bertaux, B. "Teaching Children of All Ages to Use the Singing Voice, and How to Work with Out-of-Tune Singers." In Darrel Walters and Cynthia Taggart (eds.), *Readings in Music Learning Theory.* Chicago: GIA Publications, Inc., 1989. pp. 92–104.

Blocker, Robert, ed. *The Robert Shaw Reader.* New Haven, CT: Yale University Press, 2004.

Bloom, Benjamin. *Stability and Change in Human Characteristics.* New York: Wiley, 1964.

Bollew, Jospeh A. "Is falsetto false?" *The Etude,* July 1954, p. 14.

Bonhoffer, Dietrich. *Life Together.* New York; HarperCollins, 1954.

Boone, D. R. *The Voice and Voice Therapy.* Englewood Cliffs, NJ: Prentice-Hall, 1977.

Bouhuys, Arend. *The Physiology of Breathing.* London: Gruene and Stratton, 1977.

Boyd, Malcolm. "Structural Cadences in the Sixteenth Century Mass." *The Music Review.*

Bradley, M. "Prevention and correction of vocal disorders in singers." *The NATS Bulletin,* May/June 1980, p. 39.

Bravender, Paul E. "The Effect of Cheerleading on the female singing voice." *The NATS Bulletin,* 37, 1980, p. 39.

Brodnitz, Friederich. "On Change of Voice." *The NATS Bulletin,* 40, 1984, pp. 24–6.

Brown, Ralph Morse. *The Singing Voice*. New York: Macmillan Co., 1946.

Brown, William Earl. *Vocal Wisdom: Maxims of Giovanni Battista Lamperti*. Enlarged Edition. Boston, MA: Crescendo Publishers, 1973.

Buchanan, Heather, and Matthew Mehaffey, eds. *Teaching Music Through Performance in Choir,* Volume 1. Chicago: GIA Publications, Inc., 2005.

Buchanan, Heather, and Matthew Mehaffey, eds. *Teaching Music Through Performance in Choir,* Volume 2. Chicago: GIA Publications, Inc., 2007.

Bunch, Meribeth. *Dynamics of the Singing Voice*. New York: Springer-Verlag, 1982.

Burgin, John Carroll. *Teaching Singing*. Metuchen, NJ: Scarecrow Press, 1973.

Campbell, Don G. *Master Teacher: Nadia Boulanger*. Washington, DC: The Pastoral Press, 1984.

Campbell, Joseph. *The Power of Myth*. New York: Doubleday, 1988.

Christy, Van A. *Expressive Singing*. Dubuque, IA: William C. Brown and Co., 1974.

———. *Foundations in Singing*. Dubuque, IA: William C. Brown and Co., 1976.

Clippinger, David Alva. *The Head Voice and Other Problems*. Boston, MA: Oliver Ditson, 1917.

Coffin, Berton. "The Instrumental Resonance of the Singing Voice." *The NATS Bulletin,* 31, 1974, pp. 26–39.

———. "The Relationship of Breath, Phonation and Resonance in Singing." *The NATS Bulletin,* 31, 1975, pp. 18–24.

Collins, D. L. *The Cambiata Concept*. Arkansas: The Cambiata Press, 1981.

Colwell, Richard. *The Evaluation of Music Teaching Learning*. Englewood Cliffs, NJ: Prentice-Hall, 1970.

Condon, W. S. "Multiple Response to Sound in Dysfunctional Children. *Journal of Autism and Childhood Schizophrenia,* 5(1), pp. 37–56.

Cooksey, John M. "Development of a Contemporary, Eclectic Theory for the Training and Cultivation of the High School Male Changing Voice." *The Choral Journal,* October 1977.

———. "Development of a Contemporary, Eclectic Theory for the Training and Cultivation of the High School Male Changing Voice: Part II: Scientific and Empirical Findings; Some Tentative Solutions." *The Choral Journal,* October 1977, pp. 12–4.

———. "Development of a Contemporary, Eclectic Theory for the Training and Cultivation of the High School Male Changing Voice: Part III: Developing an Integrated Approach to the Care and Training of the Junior High School Male Changing Voice." *The Choral Journal,* October 1977, pp. 7–9.

———. "Development of a Contemporary, Eclectic Theory for the Training and Cultivation of the Junior High School Male Changing Voice. *The Choral Journal,* 18, October 1977 and January 1978.

Cooper, Morton. "Vocal Suicide in Singers." *The NATS Bulletin,* 16, 1970, p. 31.

Corbin, Lynn A. "Practical Applications of Vocal Pedagogy for Choral Ensembles." *The Choral Journal,* March 1986, pp. 5–10.

Corporon, Eugene. "The Quantum Conductor." In *Teaching Music Through Performance in Band.* Chicago: GIA Publications, Inc., 1997, pp. 11–26.

Coward, Henry. *Choral Technique and Interpretation.* Salem, NH: Ayer Company Publishers, 1972.

Custer, Gerald. "From Mathematics to Meaning: New Perspectives on the Microrhythm Debate." *The Choral Journal,* August 2005.

———. "Provoking Meaning: Thoughts About Choral Hermeneutics." *The Choral Journal,* December 2001.

———. "The Conducting Project Paper." *The Choral Journal,* November 2004.

Dalcroze, Emile-Jaques. *Notes Bariolles.* Geneva: J. H. Jeheber, 1948.

———. *Rhythm, Music and Education.* Great Britain: The Dalcroze Society, 1927, 1967.

Darrow, G. F. *Four Decades of Choral Training.* Metuchen, NJ: The Scarecrow Press, 1975.

Dart, Thurston. *The Interpretation of Music.* New York: Harper and Row, 1963.

Davison, Archibald T. *Choral Conducting.* Cambridge, MA: Harvard University Press, 1940.

de Angelis, Michael, CRM. Ed. Nicoli A. Montani. *The Correct Pronunciation of Latin According to Roman Usage.* Chicago: GIA Publications, Inc., 1973.

Decker, Harold A., and Julius Herford. *Choral Conducting Symposium.* Englewood Cliffs, NJ: Prentice-Hall, 1988.

Demorest, Steven. "Customizing Choral Warm-Ups." *The Choral Journal,* February 1993, pp. 25–8.

———. "Structuring a Musical Choral Rehearsal." *Music Educators Journal,* January 1996, p. 25.

Donaldson, Robert P. "The Practice and Pedagogy of Vocal Legato." *The NATS Bulletin,* 29, 1973, pp. 12–21.

Doscher, Barbara M. *The Functional Unity of the Singing Voice.* Metuchen, NJ: The Scarecrow Press, 1988.

Duarte, F. "The Principles of Alexander Technique Applied to Singing: The Significance of the Preparatory Set." *Journal of Research in Singing,* 5–1, pp. 3–21.

Ehmann, Wilhelm, and Frauke Haasemann. *Voice Building for Choirs*. Chapel Hill, NC: Hinshaw Music, Inc., 1982.

Ehmann, Wilhelm. *Choral Directing*. Minneapolis, MN: Augsburg Publishing House, 1968.

———. "Performance Practice of Bach's Motets." *American Choral Review,* VII (September 1964), pp. 4–5; (December 1964), pp. 6–7; (March 1965), p. 6; (June 1965), pp. 8–12.

Eichenberger, Rodney. *What You See Is What You Get* (video). Chapel Hill, NC: Hinshaw Music, Inc.

Ericson, Eric. *Choral Conducting*. New York: Walton Music Corporation, 1976.

Fairchild, Johnson E. *Personal Problems and Psychological Frontiers*. New York: Sheridan House, 1957.

Feder, R. J. "Vocal Health: A View from the Medical Profession." *The Choral Journal,* 30–7, pp. 23–5.

Finn, William J. *The Art of the Choral Conductor,* Volumes I and II. Evanston, IL: Summy-Birchard Company, 1960.

———. *The Conductor Raises His Baton*. New York: Harper and Brothers, 1944.

Fisher, R. E. "Choral Diction with a Phonological Foundation." *The Choral Journal,* 27–5, pp. 13–8.

Floyd, Richard, Craig Kirchhoff, Allan McMurray, and H. Robert Reynolds. *Conducting from the Inside Out: Disc Three–Kindred Spirits* (DVD). Chicago: GIA Publications, Inc., 2006.

Fowler, Charles, ed. *Conscience of a Profession: Howard Swan*. Chapel Hill, NC: Hinshaw Music, Inc., 1987.

Frisell, Anthony. *The Baritone Voice*. Boston, MA: Crescendo Publishers, 1972.

———. *The Soprano Voice.* Boston, MA: Bruce Humphries, 1966.

———. *The Tenor Voice.* Boston, MA: Bruce Humphries, 1964.

Froseth, James O., and Albert Blaser. *Rhythm: Phonetic Rhythm Syllables. MLR Verbal Association Skills Program.* Chicago: GIA Publications, Inc., 2000.

Froseth, James O., and Phyllis Weikart. *Movement to Music in Confined Spaces.* Chicago: GIA Publications, Inc., 1981.

Fuchs, Peter Paul. *The Psychology of Conducting.* New York: MCA, 1969.

Fuchs, Viktor. *The Art of Singing and Voice Technique.* New York: London House and Maxwell, 1964.

Fulghum, Robert. *All I Really Need to Know I Learned in Kindergarten.* Revised edition. New York: Ballantine Books, 2004.

Gackle, Lynn. "The Adolescent Female Voice: Characteristics of Change and Stages of Development." *The Choral Journal,* 31–8, pp. 17–25.

Gajard, Dom Joseph. *The Solesmes Method.* Collegeville, MN: The Liturgical Press, 1960.

Garcia, Manuel. *A Complete Treatise on the Art of Singing.* Donald V. Paschke (trans.). New York: Da Capo Press, 1972.

Gardner, Howard. *Five Minds for the Future.* Boston, MA: Harvard Business School Press, 2006.

Garretson, Robert L. "The Singer's Posture and the Circulatory System." *The Choral Journal,* April 1990, p. 19.

Glenn, Carole, ed. *In Quest of Answers: Interviews with American Choral Conductors.* Chapel Hill, NC: Hinshaw Music, Inc, 1991.

Goetze, Mary. "Factors Affecting Accuracy in Children's Singing." *Dissertation Abstracts International,* 46, 2955A.

Goodkin, D. *Now's the Time: Teaching Jazz to All Ages.* San Francisco, CA: Pentatonic Press, 2004.

Gordon, Edwin E. *Advanced Measures of Music Audiation.* Chicago: GIA Publications, Inc., 1989.

———. *Instrument Timbre Preference Test.* Chicago: GIA Publications, Inc., 1984.

———. *Intermediate Measures of Music Audiation.* Chicago: GIA Publications, Inc., 1982.

———. *Introduction to Research and the Psychology of Music.* Chicago: GIA Publications, Inc., 1998.

———. *Learning Sequences in Music.* Chicago: GIA Publications, Inc., 1989.

———. *Learning Sequences in Music.* Revised edition. Chicago: GIA Publications, Inc., 2007.

———. *Rating Scales and Their Uses for Measuring and Evaluating Achievement in Music Performance.* Chicago: GIA Publications, Inc., 2002.

———. "Research Studies in Audiation: 1." *Council for Research in Music Education,* 84, 1985, pp. 34–5.

———. *Rhythm: Contrasting the Implications of Audiation and Notation.* Chicago: GIA Publications, Inc., 2000.

———. *The Iowa Tests of Music Literacy.* GIA Publications, Inc., 1991.

Green, Barry. *The Mastery of Music: Ten Pathways to True Artistry.* New York: Broadway Books, 2003.

Green, Elizabeth A. H. *Practicing Successfully: A Masterclass in the Musical Art.* Chicago: GIA Publications, Inc., 2006.

———. *The Modern Conductor.* Upper Saddle River, NJ: Prentice-Hall, 1997.

Haasemann, Frauke, and Irene Willis. *Group Vocal Technique for Children's Choirs.* (unpublished manuscript).

Haasemann, Frauke, and James Jordan. *Group Vocal Technique.* Chapel Hill, NC: Hinshaw Music, 1991.

———. *Group Vocal Technique: The Vocalise Cards.* Chapel Hill, NC: Hinshaw Music, 1991.

———. *Group Vocal Technique* (video). Chapel Hill, NC: Hinshaw Music, 1991.
This video is a wonderful teaching/learning tool that documents in film the teaching of Frauke Haasemann. It is highly recommended to all students of vocal technique for choirs.

Hackney, Peggy. *Making Connections: Total Body Integration Through Bartenieff Fundamentals.* New York: Routledge, 2002.

Hisley, Philip D. "Head quality versus nasality: a review of pertinent literature." *The NATS Bulletin,* 28, 1971, pp. 4–15.

Hofbauer, Kurt. *Praxis der Chorsichen Stimmbildung.* Mainz: Schott Verlag, 1978.

Huff-Gackle, Lynne Martha. "The adolescent female voice: characteristics of change and stages of development." *The Choral Journal,* March 1991, pp. 17–25.

———. "The effect of selected vocal techniques for breath management, resonation, and vowel unification on tone production in the junior high school female voice." Ph.D. dissertation. University of Miami, 1987.

Huther, Gerald. *The Compassionate Brain: How Empathy Creates Intelligence.* Boston, MA: Trumpeter, 2006.

James, David. "Intonation problems at the level of the larynx." *The NATS Bulletin,* 39, 1983, pp. 14–6.

Jordan, James, and Marilyn Shenenberger. *Ear Training Immersion Exercises for Choirs.* Chicago: GIA Publications, Inc., 2004.

————. *The Choral Warm-Up: Accompanist Supplement with Accompaniment CD.* Chicago: GIA Publications, Inc., 2004.

Jordan, James, and Matthew Mehaffey. *Choral Ensemble Intonation.* Chicago: GIA Publications, Inc., 2001.

Jordan, James. "Audiation and Sequencing: An Approach to Score Preparation." *The Choral Journal,* XXI/8, April 1981, pp. 11–3.

————. "Choral Intonation: A Pedagogical Problem for the Choral Conductor." *The Choral Journal,* April 1987.

————. *Evoking Sound: Fundamentals of Choral Conducting and Rehearsing.* Chicago: GIA Publications, Inc., 1996.

————. "False Blend: A Vocal Pedagogy Problem for the Choral Conductor." *The Choral Journal,* XXIV/10, June 1984, pp. 25–6.

————. *Learn Conducting Technique with the Swiss Exercise Ball.* Chicago: GIA Publications, Inc., 2004.

————. *The Choral Ensemble Warm-Up.* Chicago: GIA Publications, Inc., 2005.

————. *The Musician's Soul.* Chicago: GIA Publications, Inc., 1999.

————. *The Musician's Spirit.* Chicago: GIA Publications, Inc., 2002.

————. "Toward a Flexible Sound Ideal Through Conducting: Some Reactions to Study with Wilhelm Ehmann." *The Choral Journal,* XXV/3, November 1984, pp. 5–6.

Joyner, D. R. "The Monotone Problem." *Journal of Research in Music Education,* 17–1, pp. 114–25.

Judd, Percey. *Vocal Technique.* London: Sylvan Press, 1951.

Kagen, Sergius. *On Studying Singing.* New York: Dover Publications, 1960.

Keenze, Marvin H. "Singing City Choirs." *The Journal of Church Music,* X, September 1968, pp. 8–10.

Kemp, Helen. *Of Primary Importance.* Garland, TX: The Choristers Guild, 1989.

Kirk, Theron. *Choral Tone and Technique.* Westbury, NY: Pro-Art, 1956.

Klein, Joseph J. *Singing Technique: How to Avoid Vocal Trouble.* Princeton, NJ: D. VanNostrand, 1967.

Kundera, Milan. *The Curtain: An Essay in Seven Parts.* New York: HarperCollins, 2007.

Lamperti, Francesco. *The Technics of Bel Canto.* New York: G. Schirmer, 1905.

Lamperti, Giovanni Battista. *Vocal Wisdom.* New York: Taplinger Publishing Company, 1957.

Landeau, Michael. "Voice Classification." *The NATS Bulletin,* October 1963, pp. 4–8.

Langveld, M. "The secret place in the life of the child." *Phenomenology and Pedagogy,* 1 (2), pp. 181–91.

Large, John, Edward Baird, and Timothy Jenkins. "Studies of Male Voice Mechanisms: Preliminary Report and Definition of the Term 'Register.'" *Journal of Research in Singing,* 4, 1981, pp. 1–26.

Leonard, C. *The Silent Pulse.* New York: E. P. Dutton, 1978.

Lieberman, Phillip. *Intonation, Perception and Language.* Cambridge, MA: The MIT Press, 1967.

Little, Meredith Ellis, and Natalie Jenne. *Dances and the Music of J. S. Bach.* Bloomington, IN: Indiana University Press, 2001, p. 20.

Lowinsky, Edward E. *Tonality and Atonality in Sixteenth Century Music.* Berkeley, CA: University of California Press, 1962.

Lynch, David. *Catching the Big Fish: Meditation, Consciousness and Creativity.* New York: Penguin Books, 2006.

Macfarland, Ann L. "Effects of Overt Speech Upon Accuracy and Expression of Rhythmic Movement." Ph.D. dissertation. Temple University, 2006.

Madaule, Paul. *When Listening Comes Alive: A Guide to Effective Learning and Communication.* Norval, Ontario: Moulin Publishing.

Mari, Nanda. *Canto e voce.* Milan: G Ricordi, 1970.

Marshall, Madeleine. *The Singer's Manual of English Diction.* New York: G. Schirmer, 1963.

Mason, Lowell. *Manual of the Boston Academy of Music for Instruction in the Elements of Vocal Music on the System of Pestalozzi.* Boston, MA: J. H. Wilkins and R. B. Carfter, 1839.

Matthay, Tobias. *Musical Interpretation.* London: Joseph Williams, 1914.

McKinney, James. *The Diagnosis and Correction of Vocal Faults.* Nashville, TN: Broadman Press, 1982.

Miller, Kenneth C. *Principles of Singing.* Englewood Cliffs, NJ: Prentice Hall, 1983.

Miller, Richard. *English, French, German and Italian Techniques of Singing.* Metuchen, NJ: Scarecrow Press, 1977.

———. *On the Art of Singing.* New York: Oxford, 1996.

———. "The Solo Singer in the Choral Ensemble." *The Choral Journal,* March 1995.

———. *The Structure of Singing.* New York: Schirmer Books, 1986.

———. *Training Soprano Voices.* New York: Oxford University Press, 2000.

———. *Training Tenor Voices.* New York: Schirmer Books, 1993.

Moe, Daniel. *Basic Choral Concepts*. Minneapolis, MN: Augsburg, 1968.

Moore, Carol-Lynne, and Kaoru Yamamoto. *Beyond Words: Movement Observation and Analysis*. New York: Gordon and Breach, 1988.

Moore, Thomas. *Original Self: Living with Paradox and Authenticity*. New York: HarperCollins, 2000.

———. *The Soul's Religion: Cultivating a Profoundly Spiritual Way of Life*. New York: HarperCollins, 2002.

Moriarty, John. *Diction: Italian, Latin, French and German*. Boston, MA: E. C. Schirmer, 1975.

Mussulman, Joseph A. *Dear People...Robert Shaw*. Bloomington, IN: Indiana University Press, 1979.

Noble, Weston. *Creating the Special World*. Chicago: GIA Publications, Inc., 2005.

Noddings, Nel. *Caring*. Berkeley, CA: University of California Press, 1984.
> *Concerning rehearsal technique, the author spends considerable time discussing a feminine approach to rehearsals. Nell Noddings, in her three books on schools, makes a persuasive argument concerning this paradigm. The reader is encouraged to read these books.*

———. *Educating Moral People: A Caring Alternative to Character Education*. New York: Teachers College Press, 2002.

———. *The Challenge to Care in the Schools: An Alternative Approach to Education*. Second Edition. New York: Teachers College Press, 2005.

O'Donohue, John. *Beauty*. New York: HarperCollins, 2004.

Palmer, Parker. *A Hidden Wholeness*. San Francisco, CA: Jossey-Bass, 2004.

———. *Let Your Life Speak*. San Francisco, CA: 2000.

Parker, Alice. *The Anatomy of Melody*. Chicago: GIA Publications, Inc., 2006.

Phillips, Kenneth H. "The Effects of Group Breath Control Training on Selected Vocal Measures Related to the Singing Ability of Children in Grades Two, Three and Four." Ph.D. dissertation. Kent State University, 1983.

Pikovsky, A., M. Rosenblum, and J. Kurths. *Synchronization: A Universal Concept in Nonlinear Sciences.* Cambridge, MA: Cambridge University Press, 2001.

Piston, Walter. *Counterpoint.* New York: W. W. Norton and Company, 1947.

Proctor, Donald. *Breathing, Speech and Song.* New York: Springer-Verlag, 1980.

Pysh, Gregory M. "Chorophony: The Art of Father Finn." *The Choral Journal,* November 1996, p. 37.

Rao, Doreen. *Choral Music Experience, Vol. 1: Artistry in Music Education.* New York: Boosey and Hawkes, 1987.

———. *Choral Music Experience, Vol. 2: The Young Singing Voice.* New York: Boosey and Hawkes, 1987.

Rector, Barbara K. *Learning with the Help of Horses: Adventures in Awareness.* Bloomington, IN: AuthorHouse, 2005.

Reid, Cornelius L. *The Free Voice: A Guide to Natural Singing.* New York: Joseph Patelson Music House, 1965.

———. *Voice: Psyche and Soma.* New York: Joseph Patelson Music House, 1965.

Roberts, E., and A. Davies. "The Response of 'Monotones' to a Program of Remedial Training." *Journal of Research in Music Education,* 1975, 23, 4, pp. 227–39.

Robinson, R., and A. Winold. *The Choral Experience.* New York: Harper's College Press, 1976.

Robinson, Ray. "Wilhelm Ehmann's Approach to Choral Training." *The Choral Journal,* November 1984, pp. 5–7.

Rose, Arnold. *The Singer and the Voice*. New York: St. Martin's Press. 1971.

Rouner, Leroy S., ed. *Selves, People and Persons: What Does It Mean to Be a Self?* Notre Dame, IN: Notre Dame University Press, 1992.

Rushmore, Robert. *The Singing Voice*. New York: Dodd and Mead, 1971.

Sable, Barbara Kinsey. *The Vocal Sound*. Englewood Cliffs, NJ: Prentice-Hall, Inc., 1982.

Salamunovich, Paul. *Chant and Beyond* (DVD). Houston, TX: Quaid-Schott Media Productions, 2006.

Sataloff, R. T., and J. R. Spiegel. "The Young Voice." *The NATS Journal,* 45 (3) 1989, pp. 35–7.

Sataloff, R. T. "Ten Good Ways to Abuse Your Voice: A Singer's Guide to a Short Career." *The NATS Journal,* (Part 1) 42–1, pp. 23–5.

———. "Ten Good Ways to Abuse Your Voice: A Singer's Guide to a Short Career." *The NATS Journal,* (Part 2) 43–1, pp. 22–6.

Schnebly-Black, Julia, and Stephen F. Moore. *The Rhythm Inside: Connecting Body, Mind, and Spirit Through Music*. Alfred Music, 2003.
> *This book is an excellent overview and practical application of the work of Dalcroze. Book includes CD of musical examples. A highly recommended text.*

Scott, Anthony. "Acoustic Peculiarities of Head Tone and Falsetto." *The NATS Bulletin,* 33, 1974, pp. 32–5.

Seashore, Carl E. *The Psychology of Musical Talent*. Boston, MA: Silver-Burdett, 1919.

Sellars-Young, Barbara. *Breathing Movement Exploration*. New York: Applause Books, 2001.

Shaw, Robert. "Carnegie Hall Presents Robert Shaw: Preparing a Masterpiece: A Choral Workshop on Brahms' A German Requiem: Part I." New York: Carnegie Hall, 1991 (available only through the Carnegie Hall Store: www.carnegiehall.org).

———. "Letters to a Symphony Chorus." *The Choral Journal,* April 1986, pp. 5–8.

Shrock, Dennis. "An Interview with Margaret Hillis on Score Study." *The Choral Journal,* 31, February 1991, pp. 7–12.

Shuter-Dyson, Rosamund, and Clive Gabriel. *The Psychology of Musical Ability.* London: Methuen, 1981.

Sokolove, Michael. "Follow Me." *The New York Times Magazine (Play),* February 2006.

Stransky, J., and R. B. Stone. *Joy in the Life of Your Body.* New York: Beaufort, 1981.

Sundberg, Johann. *The Science of the Singing Voice.* DeKalb, IL: Northern Illinois University Press, 1987.

Sunderman, Lloyd Frederick. *Artistic Singing: Its Tone Production and Basic Understandings.* Metuchen, NJ: Scarecrow Press, Inc., 1970.

Swan, Howard. *Conscience of a Profession.* Chapel Hill, NC: Hinshaw Music, 1987.

Swanson, Frederick J. "The Changing Voice." *The Choral Journal,* March 1976, pp. 5–14.

———. *The Male Singing Voice Ages Eight to Eighteen.* Cedar Rapids, IA: Laurence Press, 1977.

Swears, Linda. *Teaching the Elementary School Chorus.* West Nyack, NY: Parker, 1985.

Taff, Merle E. "An Acoustic Study of Vowel Modification and Register Transition in the Male Singing Voice." *The NATS Bulletin,* 22, 1965, pp. 8–35.

Taggart, Cynthia Crump. "The Measurement and Evaluation of Music Aptitudes and Achievement." In Darrel Walters and Cynthia Crump Taggart (eds.), *Readings in Music Learning Theory*. Chicago: GIA Publications, Inc., 1989, pp. 45–55.

Thakar, Markand. *Counterpoint: Fundamentals of Music Making*. New Haven, CT: Yale University Press, 1990.

Thomas, Franz. *Bel Canto*. Berlin: George Achterberg Verlag, 1968.

Thomas, Kurt. *The Choral Conductor*. New York: Associated Music Publishers, 1971.

Thurmond, James Morgan. *Note Grouping*. Camp Hill, PA: JMT Publications, 1989.

Treash, Leonard. "The Importance of Vowel Sounds and Their Modification in Producing Good Tone." *The NATS Bulletin,* 4, 1943, p. 3.

Vennard, William. *Developing Voices*. New York: Carl Fischer, Inc., 1973.

———. *Singing: The Mechanism and the Technic*. Revised Edition. New York: Carl Fischer, Inc., 1967.

Vonnegut, Kurt. *Breakfast of Champions*. New York: Bantam, 1973.

Waengler, Hans Heinrich. "Some Remarks and Observations on the Function of the Soft Palate." *The NATS Bulletin,* 25, 1968, p. 24.

Wall, Joan. *Diction for Singers*. Dallas, TX: Pst Inc, 1990.

———. *International Phonetic Alphabet for Singers*. Dallas, TX: Pst Inc., 1989.

Waring, F. *Tone Syllables*. Delaware Water Gap, PA: Shawnee Press, 1951.

Webb, Guy, ed. *Up Front!* Boston, MA: E. C. Schirmer, 1994.

Weikart, Phyllis. *Teaching Movement and Dance: A Sequential Approach to Rhythmic Movement*. Yipsalanti, MI: High Scope Press, 1989.

Williamson, John Finley. "Choral Singing" (articles individually titled). Twelve articles in *Etude,* LXVIII and LXIX (April 1950–October 1951).

Williamson, John Finley. "Training the Individual Voice Through Choral Singing." *Proceedings of the Music Teachers National Association,* XXXIII, 1938, pp. 52–9.

Wong, Eva. *Cultivating Stillness.* Boston, MA: Shambhala, 1992.

Wright, E. *Basic Choir Training.* Croydon, England: The Royal School of Church Music, 1955.

Zemlin, Willard R. *Speech and Hearing Science.* Englewood Cliffs, NJ: Prentice Hall, Inc., 1988.

About the Authors

James Jordan is considered to be one of the most influential choral conductors and educators in America. His books covering rehearsal and teaching pedagogy, conducting technique, and the spirituality of musicing have had a dramatic impact upon teaching and conducting. He has been called a "visionary" by *The Choral Journal*. His career and publications have been devoted to innovative educational changes in the choral art that have been embraced around the world. A master teacher, Dr. Jordan's pioneering writing and research concerning the use of Laban Movement Analysis for the teaching of conducting and movement to children has dramatically changed teaching in both those disciplines. Called the "Father of the Case Study," he was the first researcher to bring forward the idea of the case study as a viable and valuable form of research for the training and education of teachers.

One of the country's most prolific writers on the subjects of the philosophy of music making and choral teaching, Dr. Jordan has produced numerous major textbooks and several choral series bearing his name, as well as other books such as *Evoking Sound, The Musician's Soul,* and *The Choral Warm-Up*. His most recent project is the DVD *The Anatomy of Conducting*, produced in collaboration with Eugene Migliaro Corporon.

Dr. Jordan also serves as Executive Editor of the *Evoking Sound Choral Series*, published by GIA Publications in Chicago. This series presents choral literature at the highest levels for high school and college choirs. In addition to new compositions by America's finest composers, the series also presents new editions of standard choral repertoire, edited with singers in mind.

Dr. Jordan teaches and conducts at Westminster Choir College of Rider University in Princeton, New Jersey, one of the foremost centers for the study and performance of choral music in the world, where he is associate professor of conducting and senior conductor. From 1991–2004, he served as conductor of The Westminster Chapel Choir. In the fall of 2004, he founded one of Westminster's highly select touring choirs and performing choirs, The Westminster Williamson Voices.

The Westminster Williamson Voices is involved in educational recordings of significant educational choral literature for the next few years for GIA Publications, which will culminate in the recording of approximately one hundred essential pieces of choral literature. The first recording in that series, *Teaching Music through Performance in Choir*, Volume 1, Levels 1–3 (GIA CD-650) was released in 2006, and the second recording, *Teaching Music through Performance in Choir*, Volume 2, Levels 1–5 (GIA CD-719) was released in 2007.

During the 2004–05 academic year, Dr. Jordan was also Visiting Distinguished Professor of Music Education at West Chester State University.

Dr. Jordan has had the unique privilege of studying with several of the landmark teachers of the twentieth century. He was a student of Elaine Brown, Wilhelm Ehmann, and Frauke Haasemann. He completed his Ph.D. in Psychology of Music under Edwin Gordon. He has been the recipient of many awards for his contributions to the profession. He was named Distinguished Choral Scholar at The University of Alberta. He was made an honorary member of Phi Mu Alpha Sinfonia in 2002 at Florida State University.

Each year, Dr. Jordan presents more than thirty keynote addresses and workshops around the world. A comprehensive listing of his workshops, seminars, and publications can be found on his page of the GIA Publications Web site, www.giamusic.com/jordan, or at www.evokingsound.com

Eugene Migliaro Corporon is conductor of the Wind Symphony and Regents Professor of Music at the University of North Texas. As Director of Wind Studies, he guides all aspects of the program, including the masters and doctoral degrees in Wind Conducting. Mr. Corporon is a graduate of California State University–Long Beach and Claremont Graduate University. His performances have drawn praise from colleagues, composers, and critics alike. Mr. Corporon has held positions at the University of Cincinnati College–Conservatory of Music, Michigan State University, University of Northern Colorado, University of Wisconsin, and California State University–Fullerton. His ensembles have performed at the Midwest International Band and Orchestra Clinic, Southwestern Music Educators National Conference, Texas Music Educators Association Clinic/Convention, Texas Bandmasters Association Convention/Clinic, International Trumpet Guild Conference, International Clarinet Society Convention, North American Saxophone Alliance Conference, Percussive Arts Society International Convention, National Wind Ensemble Conference, College Band Directors National Association Conference, Japan Band Clinic, and Conference for the World Association of Symphonic Bands and Ensembles. Having recorded over six hundred works, including many premieres and commissions, his groups have released fifty recordings on the Toshiba/EMI, Klavier, Mark, CAFUA, Donemus, Soundmark, GIA, Albany, and Centaur labels. These recordings, two of which have appeared on the Grammy nomination ballot, are aired regularly on radio broadcasts throughout Asia, Europe, and North America. Mr. Corporon maintains an active guest-conducting schedule and is in demand as a conductor and teacher throughout the world. He is Past President of the College Band Directors National Association and has been honored by the American Bandmasters Association and by Phi Beta Mu with invitations to membership.

Gerald S. Custer is a multifaceted choral musician, active as conductor, composer, editor, teacher, and author. A native of Baltimore, he earned his B.Mus. in Choral Music Education at Westminster Choir College, where he studied conducting with Robert Simpson, Dennis Shrock, and Robert Carwithen, choral literature with Elaine Brown, and composition with Harold Zabrack and Malcolm Williamson. He also served as assistant conductor of Westminster's Collegium Musicum, directed student choral and operatic ensembles, and participated in conducting masterclasses with Wilhelm Ehmann and Robert Shaw. He earned his M.Mus. in Orchestral Conducting with additional work in Historical Musicology at George Washington University, where he founded and conducted the University Chamber Singers and served as assistant conductor of the Alexandria (Virginia) Symphony Orchestra. While a graduate student at GWU, Mr. Custer was appointed adjunct instructor in the university's Department of Music, teaching voice and music theory in the Columbian College of Arts and Sciences. He is presently pursuing his Doctor of Musical Arts in Choral Conducting at Michigan State University.

Mr. Custer has directed choral activities at Schoolcraft College and Oakland Community College in Michigan, has served as visiting faculty at St. John's Provincial Seminary and Madonna University, and has also served as interim music director and conductor of the 100-voice Saginaw Choral Society. For ten years, he was conductor and music director of The Arbor Consort, a semi-professional chamber choir that was the featured ensemble-in-residence at the Michigan Renaissance Festival. He has also served as both arranger and guest conductor of the Dodworth Saxhorn Band, the nation's premier nineteenth century brass band. He is active in musical theater as well.

Recognized for his innovative scholarship in the performance of Renaissance choral music, Mr. Custer has taught on the summer conducting faculty at Westminster Choir College and published articles in *The Choral Journal* of the American Choral Directors Association, *Homiletic and Pastoral Review, Bella Voce, Pastoral Renewal*, and other professional journals. He is the featured choral methods columnist for *GIA Quarterly* and serves as a choral clinician for GIA Publications. He was a contributor to Raymond Robinson's *The Choral Experience* and has authored chapters on Renaissance performance practice, choral rehearsal technique, and the philosophy of choral music for each book in this landmark two-volume work, *The Choral Rehearsal*. His most recent work includes *Metric Flexibility in the Performance of Renaissance Choral Music* and *A Performer's Guide to Metric Flexibility* (GIA). A prolific composer, his original compositions, arrangements, and scholarly performing editions of Renaissance choral music appear in the *Evoking Sound, Music from Westminster*, and *Calvin Institute for Christian Worship* choral series published by GIA Publications.

Mr. Custer is presently Director of Music at the First Presbyterian Church of Farmington in Farmington Hills, Michigan, where he leads a multiple choir program and directs an active performing arts series.

Lynn Eustis is Associate Professor of Voice at the University of North Texas. She earned her Bachelor of Music from Bucknell University, her Master of Music from the Curtis Institute of Music, and her Doctorate of Music in Opera from Florida State University. A performer herself, Dr. Eustis appears regularly as a soloist with a variety of professional organizations.

Matthew J. LaPine is an educator, conductor, and composer in central New Jersey. He received the designation Master of Music in Choral Conducting and Music Education from Westminster Choir College of Rider University, where he graduated with distinction. He also received his Bachelor of Music in Music Education from Westminster, graduating summa cum laude. As a conductor, Mr. LaPine has been the rehearsal assistant for the Westminster Jubilee Singers, and he has led rehearsals of the Westminster Symphonic Choir. His work with James Jordan includes teaching, conducting, and working as his graduate assistant with such ensembles as the Westminster Schola Cantorum and the Westminster Williamson Voices.

Mr. LaPine has been featured as a repertoire resource guide author in *Teaching Music through Performance in Choir*, Volume 2, as well as *Teaching Music through Performance in Middle School Choir* (forthcoming), both published by GIA. He contributed the chapter "Prognosticating the Choral Ensemble's Ear" to Volume 1 of *The Choral Rehearsal*. Additionally, Mr. LaPine has created an edition of Brahms's *Fest-und Gedenksprüche*, featuring a scholarly edition of the work with a complete harmonic immersion solfege™ analysis, available as part of the *Evoking Sound Choral Series* (GIA).

Mr. LaPine currently teaches at The Wardlaw-Hartridge School in Edison, New Jersey, where he teaches middle and upper school choral music, voice, keyboarding, and music theory, and also acts as music director and assistant director for the school's musical. He also teaches early childhood general music classes and elementary and middle school voice classes at the Westminster Conservatory of Music, located in Princeton, New Jersey. Mr. LaPine lives in Metuchen, New Jersey, with his new wife, Jessica.

Tony Thornton is Artistic Director of the Los Angeles Choral Artists and the Tucson Masterworks Chorale. Active as a conductor, teacher, clinician, and author, he received his Bachelor of Music from Westminster Choir College and his Master of Music in Choral Conducting from Louisiana State University. He is currently completing his Doctor of Musical Arts in Choral Conducting and Historical Musicology at The University of Arizona. He has studied conducting with Joseph Flummerfelt, Kenneth Fulton, Frauke Haasemann, Margaret Hillis, Bruce Chamberlain, Donald Neuen, and Constantina Tsolainou. For eight years, he sang in the Robert Shaw Festival Singers.

Mr. Thornton is author of *The Choral Singer's Survival Guide* (Vocal Planet, 2005), also available from GIA Publications. He is currently compiling and editing future volumes of historical and structural analyses of major choral-orchestral works.